MACROS, MENUS, AND MIRACLES FOR LOTUS® 1-2-3®

Related Titles of Interest from John Wiley & Sons

MACROS, MENUS, AND MIRACLES FOR LOTUS® 1-2-3®

Second Edition

E. Michael Lunsford

WILEY

John Wiley & Sons, Inc.

New York • Chichester • Brisbane • Toronto • Singapore

This publication is designed to provide accurate and authoritative information in regard to the subject matter covered. It is sold with the understanding that the publisher is not engaged in redeering legal, accounting, or other professional service. If legal advice or other expert assistance is required, the services of a competent professional person should be sought. FROM A DECLARATION OF PRINCIPLES JOINTLY ADOPTED BY A COMMITTEE OF THE AMERICAN BAR ASSOCIATION AND A COMMITTEE OF PUBLISHERS.

Library of Congress Cataloging-in-Publication Data

Lunsford, E. Michael.
    Macros, menus, and miracles for Lotus 1-2-3 / E. Michael Lunsford —
2nd ed.
        p.   cm.
    Includes bibliographical references.
    ISBN 0-471-52432-8
    1. Lotus 1-2-3 (Computer program)   2. Macro instructions
(Electronic computers)   3. Business—Data processing.   I. Title.
HF5548.4.L67L86   1990
650'.028'55369—dc20   89-78215
                                                                        CIP

Printed in the United States of America
90 91 10 9 8 7 6 5 4 3 2 1

To Merlyn, the love of my life

ACKNOWLEDGMENTS

This book would not have been possible without the love and support of my wife, Merlyn, my daughter, Sage, and my son, Hassin.

I also owe a debt of gratitude to my mother, Elizabeth Lunsford; to my agent from Waterside Productions, Bill Gladstone; to Bob Ballinger, of Northeastern Graphic Services, Inc.; and to the following personnel at John Wiley & Sons, Inc.: Ruth Greif, Director of Production and Manufacturing; Kate C. Bradford, Associate Managing Editor; Katherine Schowalter, Executive Editor; and Ellen Greenberg, Assistant Editor.

CONTENTS

11   COUNTERS AND THE {FOR} LOOP   198

12   USING THE {GET} COMMAND   223

16   USING PRINT CONTROL MACROS   322

17   CREATING MACRO APPLICATIONS   339

INDEX   360

INTRODUCTION

Why Use Macros?

Like so many Lotus users, I worked with 1-2-3 for over a year before discovering macros. It wasn't that I hadn't heard of macros. From time to time my co-workers would wonder at my not using this powerful feature of 1-2-3. However, in spite of comments like, "Macros are real time-savers, why aren't you using them?," I stubbornly held to the defense that I was already a fast typist and couldn't imagine that macros could really save enough time to make them worth the trouble.

I had no idea what macros were all about, of course, or how they could benefit me in my work with 1-2-3. The only macros I had seen were either extremely complex programs created by someone else for a specific spreadsheet or very simple macros that saved only five or six keystrokes. The first type seemed inapplicable to my work and the second type seemed only marginally faster than accomplishing the same tasks manually.

Then one day, as I was typing the @sum formula for the fortieth time on a single spreadsheet, it struck me that the 13 to 17 keystrokes it normally takes to type that formula should be automated. All I had to do was create a macro that would type the letters **@sum(** and paint in the range of the numbers to sum, then close the parenthesis and press Return. In no time I had written my first macro that did exactly that—it summed any vertical range of numbers automatically and all I had to do was press a few keys.

That was the beginning of an important turnaround in my use of 1-2-3. In a short time I had a collection of everyday macros that would help me in my work with all types of 1-2-3 worksheets, from balance sheets to financial analysis, from database worksheets to marketing forecasts. I realized that macros need not be complicated to save dozens of keystrokes. In fact, it seems the simplest kinds of macros get the most use.

In a short time, writing and using macros pushed me ahead in my overall knowledge of 1-2-3 and provided me with the means to do things in 1-2-3 that were not possible without macros. I could, for example, combine text and numbers with a word-processing macro that provides an automatic word-wrap. This feature is not normally a part of 1-2-3, yet it becomes available through the use of macros.

I had caught "macro mania," along with a strong desire to share what I had learned with other 1-2-3 users. And from this combination of dreaded disease and evangelistic fervor was born the software package, *101 Macros Plus for Lotus 1-2-3*. The success of the package was instantaneous, resulting in the development of similar programs for Symphony, Excel, and WordPerfect, all published now by Individual Software, Inc. Also from that base was born the idea for a strong tutorial book, to be called *Macros, Menus, and Miracles for Lotus 1-2-3*.

Who Should Read This Book?

Whether you have been exposed to macros before or have only heard about them, this book is for you. Macros presented in this book cover 1-2-3 Release 2.0, 2.01, 2.2, and 3.

Lotus 1-2-3 users do not typically explore the world of macros until working with 1-2-3 for at least three months. This is primarily due to the perception that one must master the fundamentals of the program before launching into the more advanced subject of macros. This learning period is not necessary before exposure to macros, however. As you will see in the first few chapters, there are simple one-liners that can help the novice user eliminate unnecessary typing and menu steps from his or her first day with 1-2-3.

Intermediate users who have used macros written by others or created a few of their own will find a wealth of information in this book about the syntax of macro keywords, the combined use of menu steps and macro commands, and special tips and techniques for writing custom macros. The collection of macros used here to teach the fundamentals of macro writing are the same general, generic utilities, keystroke savers, and shortcuts as found in the *101 Macros Plus for Lotus 1-2-3*; so in addition to an education, the reader will gain a solid collection of useful macros that can be applied to any spreadsheet or 1-2-3 application without modification.

Advanced macro writers will be especially interested in the many uses of string formulas, self-modifying macro lines, and the @cell and @cellpointer functions. The macros presented here are laid out and explained with a detail that makes them extremely easy to add to, change, modify, customize, and most importantly, learn from. Working examples of the use of macro keywords provide a new level of learning not found in simple descriptions in the Lotus 1-2-3 manual and the advanced macros in the last few chapters teach a level of macro writing that sets the average macro writer apart from the exceptional macro "guru."

What This Book Can Teach You

This book is divided into 17 chapters, beginning with a chapter called "What is a Macro?" Macros are defined in terms of their use in saving keystrokes and frustration, storing commands, adding new features not normally considered a part of 1-2-3, automating the spreadsheet, and adding custom menus to the spreadsheet. It is pointed out that macros are also an excellent learning tool, since a healthy by-product of writing macros is a dramatic increase in your working knowledge of 1-2-3.

Chapter 2, "How Do Macros Work?," covers the basic principles, alternatives to the Alt key, what to do if nothing happens when you invoke a macro, macros that take up more than one row, use of the apostrophe in writing macros, how to stop a macro, where to locate your macros, uppercase versus lowercase in the writing of macros, and the use of macro range names.

Chapter 3, "A Few Short Macros," offers a few short one-liners, including a macro to insert an apostrophe, macros to move your cursor to the left or right a designated number of cells, a jump macro to jump your current cell to the top of the page, a macro to move to the lower left corner of your spreadsheet, a macro to widen the column by one space, format macros, an @sum macro, a macro to verify that the vertical sum of a column matches the horizontal sum, an @date macro, a macro to copy the data from the cell above, and automatic execution macros.

Chapter 4, "Using Step, Record, and Learn Keys," presents techniques for debugging your macros using the Step key, and methods for recording your keystrokes. In Release 2.2 this is done by establishing a /Worksheet Learn Range and activating the Alt- F5 Learn Feature. The Record Buffer of Release 3, on the other hand, is a 512-byte area of computer memory in which 1-2-3 records all your keystrokes in the background as you type them.

Chapter 5, "The Macro Programming Commands," describes in detail the seven categories of advanced macro programming commands, including commands to control the screen, allow user input, control program flow, interrupt program flow, manipulate data, manipulate files, and access add-ins. The macros in this chapter include a Data Entry macro, a Save and Print macro with a simple subroutine, a File Combine macro, an Automatic Graph macro, a macro to jump to the left-most column or top-most row, a menu macro to delete a row or column during Global Protection, a looping macro to prune files, and a File Extract macro.

Chapter 6, "The Art of Range Naming," describes macros to jump around the spreadsheet, a self-modifying file retrieve macro, macro commands to turn off the screen refresh, instructions for using the @cellpointer command and {let} command, macros using subroutines with place-markers, macros to view or recalculate ranges of the spreadsheet, a macro to transpose a matrix of columns to rows, and copy command macros, including a macro to copy to alternate cells, macros to copy a relative formulas as absolute, and Copy & Stay and Move & Stay macros that leave your cell pointer at the TO cell.

Chapter 7, "Creating a Background Macro Library," explores the use of macro libraries in Release 2.2 and 3, and, although Release 2 and 2.01 do not provide a way to operate your macros from outside the current worksheet, ways to simplify the transfer of macros from worksheet files on disk to the current worksheet. In Release 2.2, you can use the MACROMGR.ADN application to hold macros in a type of hyperspace outside the current worksheet. Although Release 3 does not have a Macro Library Manager add-in as found in Release 2.2, you can have background macros in two ways: either in an extra background worksheet in the same file or in a separate active file.

Chapter 8, "Toggles and the Macro Run Key," introduces the use of toggles in your macros, including a toggle to jump to often visited areas of your spreadsheet. Also covered are use of the Alt-F3 Macro Run key in Release 2.2 and 3, a Macro Launcher for Release 2 and 2.01 to simulate the Alt-F3 Macro Run key in Release 2.2 and 3, and ways to jump your cell pointer to special areas such as a notepad area, appointment calendar area, pop-up calculator window, and a custom help screen.

Chapter 9, "Using the {If} Command," explores use of the {if} command with the @cellpointer function to facilitate data entry and modification of data in your worksheet. We will also look at two prompt commands, {getlabel} and {getnumber}. The macros covered in this chapter include a Label Format macro, a Number Format macro, a macro to Indent a Column, a macro to Add Leading Zeros, a Rounding macro, a macro to Eliminate the ERR Messages in a spreadsheet, a Data Entry macro, a macro to Modify Cell Data by a Constant, a Borders macro, a Financial Functions macro, and a Columnwidth Underline macro.

Chapter 10, "String Formulas and String @functions," reviews the science of string formulas and the use of the special string manipulation features of 1-2-3 to combine two or more elements into a single word or phrase. It defines the concept of string formulas and the individual string @functions and explores their purpose and application in cells of the spreadsheet to create variable entries and in macros that require variable or self-modifying lines. String @ functions used in combination with other @ functions of 1-2-3 in this chapter include @upper, @lower, @proper, @length, @find, @left, @right, @mid, @trim, @clean, @repeat, @Code, @Char, @exact, @replace, @value, @n, and @s.

Chapter 11, "Counters and the {for} Loop," shows ways to make your macro loop a designated number of times in one of two ways: by using {if} with the {let} command or by using the more advanced {for} command. The macros covered in this chapter include macros to change the width of any number of columns, to allow a type of slide show of your graphs, to squeeze the filled cells in a column together into one contiguous range of viable data, to change zeros in your worksheet to blank spaces, to test a matrix of numbers for a particular value and insert another value in its place, to enhance the existing /Range Search capability of Release 2.2 and 3 by adding a new feature called Previous, to change number-labels to values, to vertically display a series of dates exactly one month apart, and to add or delete a prefix in each entry in a column.

Chapter 12, "Using the {Get} Command," defines and explores uses of the {get} command in combination with macro techniques and commands of previous chapters. You will see how {get} can be used to create a *Yes/No* prompt, to quit a macro upon your press of the Escape key, to create a special "action key" for yourself, to differentiate between a press of letter/number keys and directional or function keys, and to have your macro evaluate and act on your response to special {indicate} prompts.

Chapter 13, "Manipulating Strings in your Macros," explores the use of string technology to display a variable message in the upper panel; center titles of variable length across the screen; display changing choice explanations in custom menus; use @cellpointer("address") with {let}, {contents}, and {blank} in Release 2 and 2.01; combine commands like /Range Unprotect with variable cell addresses; display an absolute cell address as a relative address; create range names that change based on the counter in a {for} loop; and calculate and display a relative cell location based on your current cell address.

Chapter 14, "Macros to Manipulate a Database," covers macros that use variable strings and the combination of several features including operators such as #not# and @functions such as @exact, @iserr, @value, and @choose to facilitate the use and manipulation of databases in 1-2-3. The examples we will look at include macros to create date headings, view duplicate entries, find a string within a string, delete blank or zero-value rows, and subtotal like items in a database.

Chapter 15, "Using File Control Macros," explores macros designed to switch your file directory instantly; automatically save a file, save a backup, and beep when finished; present a message in your upper screen indicating the size of a file in bytes; list a filename table in your worksheet; create a table of active files in Release 3; and save a Macro Library .MLB file in Release 2.2.

Chapter 16, "Using Print Control Macros," explores macros to print alternate columns, print in elite compressed style, judge the width of your print range prior to printing, print prompted quantities of a file, automatically change your print setup codes, and print prompted quantities of labels.

Chapter 17, "Creating Macro Applications," the final chapter, covers the creation of special applications including a program to automate and maintain an address database, to print form letters and address labels from that database, to create a checkbook ledger, and to automatically type out your checkbook amounts in words as they might be written on a check.

Purchasing Software from the Author

By using the coupon at the end of this book, you can purchase discount copies of *101 Macros Plus for 1-2-3* developed by the author, E. Michael Lunsford. In addition, the following software, also published by Individual Software, Inc., is available at a discount:

101 Macros Plus for Symphony
101 Macros for Excel-PC
101 Macros for Excel-MAC
101 Macros for WordPerfect
Individual Training for 1-2-3 Macros
Individual Training for WordPerfect
Individual Training for dBASE IV
Professor DOS with SmartGuide for DOS

WHAT IS A MACRO?

Definitions and Applications

In the most simple terms, a macro is a collection of saved keystrokes and/or saved commands that can be executed with a simple two-keystroke combination. In the case of Lotus 1-2-3, this means simultaneously pressing the Alt key plus a single-letter key (such as, Alt-A, Alt-B, Alt-C, and so on).

For example, you may find that you seem to be typing your company name quite often on a given spreadsheet. Let's suppose your company name is **MARVELOUS BOSS AND ASSOCIATES, INC.** That's quite a few characters to type over and over again, but it can be made much easier if you store those keystrokes in a macro that you invoke by simply pressing Alt-M. With such a macro, 1-2-3 will type your company name for you automatically—and so fast, it would not look like typing at all. The company name would just appear, instantly.

You may have noticed that it can take from 27 to 29 keystrokes to type a date in 1-2-3 using the @date format. To enter 12-Dec-90 in a format that Lotus can read as a number, you must type **@Date(90,12,12)** and press Return, select /Range Format Date 1 and press Return, then select /Worksheet Column-width Set 10 and press Return.

With a simple macro, however, this same exercise can be reduced to a two-keystroke combination (say, Alt-D, for example) which types in the **@Date(87,** then waits for you to type in the month and day, then closes the parenthesis, formats the cell to the date format, and changes the column width to 10—all together saving you a total of 22 keystrokes.

Saved Keystrokes—and Saved Frustration

As you can imagine, saving yourself all those keystrokes also has the effect of saving much of the frustration that goes along with dull, repetitive work. Consider, for example, the frustration of typing in the command: **@sum(A273..A288)**.

Not only is it difficult for even experienced typists to type shift-key characters like the @ key and the parentheses ( ), but having to take the time to determine the range of the column you want to sum can be downright error-prone.

Consider, then, the Add macro, which types for you the **@sum** and opening parenthesis, paints in the range of the column, closes the parenthesis, and presses Return. This not only saves you an impressive amount of time several times a day, it also saves you a great deal of frustration.

Speaking of frustration, what about the frustration of that annoying beep you get when you enter a number–letter combination (like **123 Main Street** or **49ers Forever**) and forget the apostrophe? No problem, just activate the Beep macro—a frustration saver that goes back and enters the apostrophe for you.

Have you ever experienced the frustration of a /Copy command that will not stay at your destination cell? There are times when you want to copy from one cell to another and *stay* at the TO cell. In this book you will learn about a Copy-&-Stay macro that offers you a choice of whether to do a Standard copy, a Reverse copy, or a Copy-&-Stay copy.

Storing Commands

By storing keystrokes and commands (like the F5 Goto key, for example), you can actually add new features to 1-2-3 which are not normally considered a part of the Lotus repertoire.

For example, how about a Goto key that remembers where you've been? Take a look at our Go-Return macro.

Imagine that your cursor is on cell R223 and you want to visit an area that's four screens down, three screens to the right, two columns to the left, and one row up. You press PgDn four times, Ctrl-RightArrow three times, LeftArrow twice, and UpArrow once, and finally you're there. You change a cell or just check its value, and now you want to return to your original location. What do you do?

Well, if you've forgotten the cell row and column location where you started (cell R223, remember), you'll probably press PgUp four times, Ctrl-LeftArrow three times, RightArrow twice, and DownArrow once.

Instead, you can use the Go-Return macro—it "remembers" where you started out. Not only that, it also remembers the last place you visited, so you can jump back and forth between the last two locations with a single two-keystroke combination.

Adding Other New Features

In addition to storing keystrokes and commands, the 1-2-3 macro structure can actually be considered a programming language. In fact, according to *Lotus Magazine*, more people are programming with macros than with any other language—even Basic!

As short but powerful programs, macros can be used to provide a host of new features.

Word-processing features are not standard with Lotus 1-2-3, but with a Word-Processing macro, it becomes possible.

How about a macro-driven pop-up Calculator with scientific functions and memory? Or a pop-up Notepad or Calendar? These features, too, are possible with macros.

Perhaps you're interested in fancy graphics or elaborate borders to dress up your spreadsheets. Explore the ASCII Menu macro as well as the macro called Zippy Borders.

You can add features like the ability to hide invisible notes in your spreadsheet with the Hidden Messages macro. Or you can add a feature that will tell you exactly how wide a print range is before you print it out.

Automating Your Spreadsheet

Perhaps most important—and certainly the most commonly used feature of the macro language—is the ability to automate your spreadsheets. There are many examples of this in our collection of macros.

Consider the Data Entry macro that, aside from solving the Num-Lock problem, actually automates your entry of data down a column or across a row.

Or there's the Automatic Tickler macro that warns you that *Today's the day* for some deadline or event.

How about a Titles Toggle to automate the turning off and turning back on of your titles? Or the macros which automate an address database, including the macros to add new names and addresses, build form letters, and print labels automatically?

You can automate the double-spacing of a spreadsheet prior to the printout or automate the recalculation, saving, and printing out of a file—including prompts for filename, print quantities required, saving a backup copy, and more.

Add Menus to Your Spreadsheet

Not only can you automate your spreadsheet, but you can do it with pauses and prompts for manual entry at desired points. This includes single-line prompts or instructions about what to do next, as well as full-blown custom-made menus which give you choices, explain the choices, and branch to the subroutine that carries out your choice.

Menus have been used throughout the macros in this book. Some excellent examples are the Copy Command macro, the Enter Phrase macro, the Go-Return macro, the Calculator macro, and the Move-Data-&-Stay macro.

You will be adding new features as well as adding prompts and menus which take you through these new features step-by-step.

Macros as a Learning Tool

Finally, macros are a great learning tool. Whether you are exploring the Lotus commands and keystrokes used in a prewritten macro, or working out the menus and command sequences required to write your own macro, a healthy by-product of the exercise will be a dramatic increase in your working knowledge of Lotus 1-2-3.

Summary

In its simplest form, a macro is a collection of saved keystrokes and/or saved commands that can be executed with a simple two- keystroke combination. However, macros can be much more, as summarized here:

- Macros can speed up your work with 1-2-3, saving you time, keystrokes, and a great deal of frustration.
- Macros can store information as well as keystrokes and commands.
- Macros can offer impressive new features, like word processing, not otherwise available in 1-2-3.
- You can use macros to completely automate your spreadsheet including automatic data entry, manipulation of data, cursor movement, and printing.
- With macros you can create custom menus designed to your own specifications.
- By learning 1-2-3 macros, you will inevitably learn a great deal more about 1-2-3.

In Chapter 2, you will be taken, step by step, through the creation of your own first macro.

2

HOW DO MACROS WORK?

Basic Principles

In the spirit of learning by doing, we'll have you write your own macro to see how it's done. The macro that is easiest to demonstrate is a macro that simply types a word in the cell occupied by your cursor. We'll use the word LOTUS.

As a first step, move to an unoccupied area of the spreadsheet—say, cell AB2. Now type the word **LOTUS** and follow it with the character that looks like this: ~ . This character, called a *tilde*, is read by 1-2-3 in its macro language as an Enter command. You should now have the following typed in cell AB2: **LOTUS~** .

Now move your cursor to the left to cell AA2 and type an apostrophe, a backslash, and an **A**, which on your command line will read: **'\A** , but which in cell AA2 will show up just as: **\A**, without the apostrophe.

Note: We are using a backslash here, not a forward slash. This is very important.

This **\A** identifies the word **LOTUS** in cell AB2 as a macro that will be invoked later by pressing Alt-A. Note, however, that initially this is for identification only. There is another step that must be taken before the macro will work.

Range Naming Your Macro

The first cell of the macro must receive a range name. (In this case, the entire macro is only one cell.) There are two ways to give a range name to that first cell:

1. Place the cursor on cell AA2 (where we have previously typed \A), call up the 1-2-3 menu, and select /Range Name Labels Right Return.
2. Place the cursor on the cell to be named and press /Range Name Create.

Note, however, the second method is not recommended and should NOT be used for the macros in this collection. Using the /Range Name Labels Right method is preferred instead, for three reasons:

1. It takes fewer keystrokes.
2. It prompts you to take care of an important practice—that is, you first identify the macro by typing \A in the cell to the left of the macro.
3. Later, when you have internal range names (like LOOP, MENU, COUNTER, and so on) in your macros, or if you have more than one macro to name, you can use the /Range Name Labels Right command, followed by PgDn or End DownArrow to name several internal range names or macro range names at once.

We now add one last step that is a convention used throughout this program. Move to cell AC1 and type:

*** AMAZING MACRO ***

We have used the \A in cell AA2 to identify how we invoke the macro. Now, by typing ***** AMAZING MACRO ***** in cell AC1, we have identified just what the macro does— amazing us, of course, by typing the word **Lotus**.

That's all there is to creating a simple macro. Your macro should look like the example in Figure 2.1.

Invoking Your Macro

Now we can invoke the macro. Move down several cells, to cell AA5, for example, and while pressing the Alt key, press the letter of the macro—in this case, the letter A. The word **Lotus** will be typed immediately into that cell.

Now move to cell AA8 and press Alt-A again. Again you should see the word **Lotus** typed into the cursor cell.

Note: Do not invoke this particular macro when the cursor is resting on any occupied cell—especially cells occupied by the macro itself. The macro's function is to type the word **Lotus**, which means it will type over any information contained in the current cell when you invoke the macro.

FIG_2-1.WK1

Figure 2.1 An Example of a Simple Lotus Macro

What to Do if Nothing Happens

If the macro does not work at all, the reason probably has to do with improper naming of the first cell of the macro. To check this, press the F5 Goto key, followed by \A. If you get a beep and an error message that says *Illegal cell or range address*, this means that the macro has not been range-named. If the cursor jumps to another location, but it is not the location just to the right of the \A, the range naming has been done incorrectly. If either of these problems occurs, go back to the instructions above and repeat the steps for giving your macro a range name.

Note: You can always check whether a range name exists by pressing the F5 Goto key, followed by the range name and Return. If the cursor jumps to the desired location, the range has been properly named.

Macros That Take up More Than One Row

Suppose you want your macro to type **Lotus 123**? You can do this one of two ways:

1. Change the first line of the macro to read:

    Lotus 123~

2. Alternately, you can delete the tilde from cell AB2, move your cell pointer to cell AB3, and enter:

'123˜

Notice that although you type an apostrophe (check the upper panel), the entry in the cell will actually look like this:

123˜

without the apostrophe. This is an important distinction. Always remember that, in a macro, each line of code is a label. To enter a line of macro code that begins with a slash (/), a number (such as **4567**), or an arithmetic operator (such as + or **@**), you must first type a label prefix (apostrophe).

Refer to the macro shown in Figure 2.2. When you use this macro; pressing Alt-A will cause 1-2-3 to play back the contents of the cell named \A, typing the word **Lotus**, then play back the contents of the next cell down, typing **123** and entering it. Unfortunately, it will look like this: **Lotus123** without a space between the word **Lotus** and the **123**. Move back to cell AB2 now, switch to the Edit mode by pressing the F2 Edit key, add a space after the word **Lotus**, and press Return. Pressing Alt-A will now cause your macro to type **Lotus 123**.

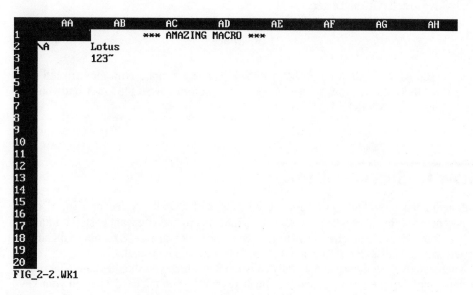

FIG_2-2.WK1

Figure 2.2 A Macro Consisting of More Than One Line

In fact, macros continue to play back the next cell below until they hit a cell that has no label (a blank cell or a cell with a value in it), or until they come to a branching command or a special {quit} command that means "quit the macro and return to READY mode."

Because macros always continue down to the next cell, two conventions have been used in this program which eliminate the possibility of having a macro continue past its intended end point. The first is to follow every macro with a blank cell. This works out nicely, because the cell just to the right of that blank cell can easily be used as a title for the next macro.

The second convention is to end every macro with the {quit} command, or one of the branching commands. This extra precaution will protect against the possibility that you may delete a row in your spreadsheet which in your macro area happens to coincide with the blank cell on which you were depending to stop a macro.

What the Macro Sees Is What You Get

Suppose instead of having your macro type **Lotus 123**, you wanted it to type **1-2-3 WORK-SHEET**? You would think that all you need to do is move to cell AB2 and enter '**1-2-3 Space** (that would appear as **1-2-3** in the cell, without the apostrophe) then move to cell AB3 and type **WORKSHEET~**.

If you do that, however, trying to run the macro will result in a beep and a shift to the Edit mode. This is because the macro is trying to type the visible contents of cell AB2 (the **1-2-3** Space without the apostrophe) and the word **WORKSHEET**. Just as manually typing the phrase **1-2-3 WORKSHEET** without starting with an apostrophe will cause a beep, so setting up the macro to type those same characters for you will cause a beep. What is the solution? Move to cell AB2 and enter:

$$\text{"1-2-3 Space}$$

which in cell AB2 will show up as '**1-2-3** with only one apostrophe. Now move to cell AB8 and press Alt-A. The macro will type an apostrophe before it types the **1-2-3**, and you will get the entry **1-2-3 WORKSHEET** in cell AB8.

How to Stop a Macro

Although a macro will always stop if it encounters a blank cell, a value, or a {quit} command, there will be times when you start the wrong macro and you want to stop it immediately before it does too much damage to your worksheet; or you may be running a macro designed with an endless loop that will continue until you stop it manually.

There are two techniques to manually stop a macro which you should know. The first is to simultaneously press the Ctrl and the Break keys. If you do not have a key on your keyboard that reads "Break," try the Pause—it should be the same thing.

Although pressing Ctrl-Break will stop your macro, you may be greeted with an Error message in the upper right panel, and the Words **Ctrl-Break** in the lower left of your screen. Simply press Esc at this point and you should be returned to the READY mode.

The second technique is actually a Macro Pause. If you decide you want to pause the macro without stopping it altogether, simultaneously press Ctrl-Num Lock. Then when you want to start up the macro again, press any key.

Where to Locate Your Macros

If you have Release 2/2.01, your macros must reside somewhere in the worksheet before they can be invoked. (In Release 2.2 and 3, you have the additional option of accessing macros from a separate Macro Library which does not reside in the current worksheet. This is discussed in more detail in Chapter 7.) If you are placing your macros in the worksheet, you will want some advice on exactly where to place the macros. Some people prefer to keep their macros in the area off to the right of the spreadsheet. The example used in the previous section, where the macro is in cells AA2 and AB1..AB3, uses such a convention. The problem with this idea, however, is that you must be very careful about doing a row insert or a row delete in your "on-screen" spreadsheet, because you can easily interrupt an "off-screen" macro with an unwanted empty space or completely destroy the macro by deleting an important line.

Some experts suggest placing the macros in the same general area off to the right, but starting their working spreadsheets below the last line of the last macro. So, for example, you may have your macros in AA1 through AC30, and your spreadsheet would start at A31. This gets away from the problem of destroying your macros with row inserts or deletes in your working spreadsheet, but it wastes all of the space above your spreadsheets and below your macros. Further, because of differences in the widths of your spreadsheets, you may find it hard to remember from spreadsheet to spreadsheet exactly where your macros are kept. Our recommendation is to keep all of the macros in a location starting at cell A1, with the working spreadsheets starting in the area immediately below the last macro.

There are two reasons why you might consider this a good idea:

1. You will always know where to go to get to your macros.
2. With your macros starting in cell A1 you can always go to your macro area simply by pressing the Home key. Also, if you have the titles of a spreadsheet locked in (so that Home takes you to the upper left corner of the spreadsheet just below the titles), you can always use the F5 Goto key followed by the Home key. Then, after "visiting" your macros, if you want to return to your spreadsheet, just press Escape. Alternately, if you want to stay in the macro area to make some change, press Return. Your titles will still be locked in, but your cursor will be in the macro area. After you've made the changes you want, you can press End Home and then Home to return to your spreadsheet area.

There is, however, one drawback to this method that must be noted. Just as putting your macros to the right of your spreadsheets can cause problems when inserting or deleting rows, so putting your macros in the area above your spreadsheet can cause problems when inserting or deleting columns. However, column insertion is much less common than row insertion, and the widest macro is only nine columns wide (including range name identifiers) so the problem is not as great using the "topside" convention. Be aware, however, that any column insertions or deletions in the first nine columns of your spreadsheet must take the macro area into account.

To summarize, then, it is suggested that you use the A column for your range identifiers, the B column for the start of your actual macros, and the C column for macro names. See Figure 2.3 for an example.

FIG_2-3.WK1

Figure 2.3   Locating Your Macros Starting at Cell A1

Uppercase Versus Lowercase

You may have noticed the use of uppercase and lowercase in the creation of macros. Using uppercase and lowercase has become a standard convention to make macros easier to read and decipher, but there is some disagreement about which case should be used for macro commands and which for worksheet range names.

   Lotus Magazine has opted for the use of uppercase for commands (using /C for the copy command instead of /c, for example) and lowercase for range names; you may want to adopt this convention if you plan to do much copying of macros from that worthy publication.

   On the other hand, most of the typing in a given macro usually consists of macro commands, which means that using the *Lotus Magazine* convention results in more use of uppercase than of lowercase. To a proficient typist, this approach seems counter-intuitive. In contrast, using lowercase for commands and uppercase for range names tends to be easier to read and a great deal less cumbersome to type. This latter convention is, therefore, the technique used and recommended here.

Macro Range Names

Macros can be named with a backslash and any letter of the alphabet (\A, \B, \C, and so on). Lotus macros should not, however, be range-named with a backslash-number combination such as \1, \2, or \3, since such macros cannot be invoked by pressing Alt and a number. The only exception to this is the \0 macro, a special Autoexecute macro which is discussed in more detail in Chapter 3.

Accordingly, there is an apparent limit of 27 macros for each of your spreadsheets. Even this limit can be broken, however, through use of the Alt-F3 Macro Run key (in Release 2.2 or 3 only), or through a special macro called a Macro Launcher that calls on other macros by mnemonic range name. So, for example, the Amazing Macro above could also be given the range name AMZ or even 123 and it could be executed by first invoking the Macro Run key or the Macro Launcher and then entering the mnemonic range name.

However, before we get to that, you will want a way to remember your standard macro range names. To the greatest extent possible, try to arrange your macros alphabetically and have the letter calling the macro correspond to the first letter of the macro name. Thus the Amazing macro is called by pressing Alt-A, the Beep macro by pressing Alt-B, and so on.

In addition to the range names used to call the macro, the range names *within* the macro (such as DLOOP or DCOUNTER) should always start with the letter of the macro. This is only a convention, and not a rule, but you will find this technique invaluable. It not only enables multiple use of a much-needed word like LOOP, but it reduces the possibility of an accidental redundancy of range names.

Summary

In this chapter you have learned how to write your first simple macro. Some of the important points covered in this chapter are:

- It is better to use /Range Name Labels Right to name your macros than /Range Name Create.
- Range names go in the first column, the macro starts in the second column over, and the title of the macro identifying what it does goes in the third column.
- If nothing happens when you press the Alt-letter combination, use the F5 Goto key to check whether your macro has been properly range-named.
- Macros always continue reading down to the next cell until they hit a blank cell, a number, a {quit}, or a branching command. Because of this feature, every macro should end with a {quit} or a branching command.
- Every line of a macro is a label and must start with an apostrophe.
- You can stop a macro by pressing Ctrl-Break and pause a macro by pressing Ctrl-Num Lock.
- Consistently locate your macros in an area where they are easy to get to. Starting your macros at cell A1 is one way to do this.
- Use lowercase for macro commands and uppercase for range names.
- Macros can be named with a backslash and one of the 26 letters, with a backslash and a zero (for an automatic executing macro), or with a mnemonic name to be invoked with the Alt-F3 Run key (Release 2.2 and 3) or a special Macro Launcher (described in Chapter 8).
- Start all of your internal macro range names with the name of the macro.

In Chapter 3 we examine a few short, but useful, macros you can enter into a 1-2-3 worksheet file and start using immediately.

3

A FEW SHORT MACROS

Getting Started

In this chapter we will start with a few simple one-liners—macros which are the easiest to grasp, quickest to write, and simplest to use immediately.

The Beep Macro

Our first macro in this chapter is a frustration-saver. Most people who have used 1-2-3 or Symphony have experienced the frustration of trying to enter a number–letter combination (like **17ea** or **123 Main St** or **23 Skidoo**), only to have the computer beep because they did not start the entry with an apostrophe.

Try it now. Starting with a blank worksheet, type **123 Main St** and press Return. You will hear the beep and the program will shift to the Edit mode. One solution at this point is to press Home, then the Apostrophe, and finally Return. This is faster than scrolling through the entry with the LeftArrow key to insert your apostrophe, but an even better solution is to automate the process with a macro.

In cell C1, type *****BEEP MACRO*****. Then in cell A2, type **'\B**. This will show up in your panel as '\B with an apostrophe, but in cell A2 it will read simply \B. In cell B2, enter:

$${home}'~{quit}$$

Now move back to cell A2 and press /Range Name Labels Right Return. This procedure has named the macro \ **B**, and it can now be invoked by pressing Alt-B.

Move your cell pointer to cell A5 to try out the macro by typing **123 Main St** and pressing Return. At the beep, *while* pressing the Alt key, press the letter B. You should see the entry **123 Main St** appear in cell A5. Check the upper panel to see that the apostrophe has been entered by the macro.

This is a very simple macro that only saves one keystroke, but it eliminates a great deal of frustration by allowing you to beep back by pressing Alt-B. Only use this macro in response to the beep, however. If you press Alt-B when you are *not* in the Edit mode, the cursor will move to A1 (the destination of the Home key) and insert a single-quotation mark. For this reason, and because there is always the possibility of hitting the Home key by mistake with or without this macro, it is always a good idea to keep cell A1 on all of your worksheets completely empty.

You will have noticed that we have typed **{home}** in braces. This is one of an entire list of special key indicators in the 1-2-3 macro language which represent keys on your keyboard. See Table 3.1 for a list of all of the special macro key indicators and their descriptions.

Editing Your Macros

Because the Beep macro involves use of the Edit mode, this is a good point to discuss ways of editing your macros. We have already pointed out that pressing Home in the Edit mode takes you to the beginning of a cell entry in the upper panel. Conversely, pressing the End key will take you to the end of a cell entry. You probably already knew that pressing the LeftArrow and RightArrow keys will move you to the left and right along the entry, but did you know that pressing Ctrl-LeftArrow and Ctrl-RightArrow will move you in five-character jumps to the left and right?

To erase characters to the left, use the Backspace key. To erase characters to the right, use the Delete key. To type over characters while in the Edit mode, switch to Overwrite by pressing the Insert key. When you're finished with your editing, press Return, the DownArrow key, or the UpArrow key. This will enter the changes in your current cell (see Table 3.2).

Left and Right Macros

One handy use of macros is the ability to move rapidly a designated number of cells to the left or right. For example, you can represent one press of the RightArrow key by storing the word {right} in a macro. To tell your macro to go to the right twice, use {right 2}. To create a macro that moves to the right eight times (thus saving six keystrokes), move to cell C3 and type *****RIGHT MACRO***** . Move to cell A4 and type '\ **R**. In cell B4, type:

{right 8}{quit}

Now move back to cell A4, select /Range Name Labels Right, and press Return. To try the macro, press Alt-R. Your cursor should move eight cells to the right.

Table 3.1　Special Macro Key Indicators for Release 2, 2.01, 2.2, and 3

Macro Keyword	Description
~	Tilde (macro version of the Return key)
{home}	Home key
{end}	End key
{down} or {d}	DownArrow key
{left} or {l}	LeftArrow key
{right} or {r}	RightArrow key
{up} or {u}	UpArrow key
{pgdn}	PgDn key
{pgup}	PgUp key
{bigleft}	Ctrl-LeftArrow (move left one screen)
{bigright}	Ctrl-RightArrow (move right one screen)
{help}	F1 Help key (Release 2.2 and 3 only)
{edit}	F2 Edit key
{name}	F3 Name key
{abs}	F4 Abs key
{goto}	F5 Abs key
{window}	F6 Window key
{query}	F7 Query key
{table}	F8 Table key
{calc}	F9 Calc key
{graph}	F10 Graph key
{menu}	/ or < (calls main command menu)
{esc} or {escape}	Escape key
{bs} or {backspace}	Backspace key
{del} or {delete}	Delete (use only in Edit mode)
{insert}	Overwrite (use only in Edit mode)
{{} and {}}	Use to have braces appear as { and }
{~}	Use to have tilde appear as ~

New Macro Keywords for Release 3 Only

{zoom}	Alt-F6 zooms window to full size
{firstcell} or {fc}	Move to Home of first worksheet
{lastcell} or {lc}	End-Home of last nonblank worksheet
{nextsheet} or {ns}	Move to next worksheet
{prevsheet} or {ps}	Move to previous worksheet
{file}	File, used with other keywords
{firstfile} or {ff} or {file}{home}	Move to first active file
{lastfile} or {lf} or {file}{end}	Move to last active file
{nextfile} or {nf} or {file}{ns}	Move to next file
{prevfile} or {pf} or {file}{ps}	Move to previous file

Table 3.2 Editing Function of Keys

Key Description	Edit Function
Home	Cursor jumps to beginning of entry
End	Cursor jumps to end of entry
LeftArrow	Cursor moves to the left
RightArrow	Cursor moves to the right
Ctrl-LeftArrow	Cursor moves in five-character jumps to the left
Ctrl-RightArrow	Cursor moves in five-character jumps to the right
Backspace	Cursor erases characters to the left
Del	Cursor erases characters to the right
Ins	Toggle between normal/overwrite
Return	Enter changes and return to Ready mode
Esc	Ignore changes, leave cell entry as is

To build a macro that moves to the left, move to cell C5 and type *****LEFT MACRO*****. In cell A6, type '\L. In cell B6, type:

{left 8}{quit}

Use the /Range Name procedure to name the macro as above. Now press Alt-R to move eight cells to the right and Alt-L to move back eight cells to the left. Notice that if you try the Alt-L macro from column A, you will hear eight beeps, just as you would if you tried pressing the LeftArrow key eight times from column A.

Both the Right macro and the Left macro can be altered to move left any desired number of cells or they can be changed to prompt you for how many cells you want to move, or even offer you a customized menu of up to eight different sizes of jumps to the right or left. We will discuss this in more detail later.

These macros are so simple that some of their applications tend to be overlooked, even by the most seasoned 1-2-3 users. One little-known feature of macros is the fact that they can be used in the middle of other standard 1-2-3 menu selections. If, for example, you want to copy from one cell to another cell eight columns to the right, press /Copy and at the prompt *Enter range to copy FROM*, press Return to select the current cell. At the prompt *Enter range to copy TO*, press Alt-R. The pointer will move to the right for you, where you can simply press Return to enter the COPY TO cell and complete the copy command. If you want to copy to a cell nine columns to the right instead of eight, select /Copy and press Return, then press Alt-R to move eight columns, RightArrow to move one more cell to the right, and finally Return. In this way you can combine the /Copy command structure, the Right macro, and manual movement of your pointer to speed up your copying.

Try using this macro in the middle of 1-2-3 print menus. After pressing /Print Printer Range, use the Alt-R macro to paint in the range to the right. If you make an eight-cell jump too far to the right, press Alt-L to back up eight cells.

You can use these macros in any 1-2-3 menu selections involving range painting or cell movement, including /Range Format, /Range Erase, /Range Value, /Data Fill, /Data Query Input, Criterion, and Output—in fact, in any situation where the program asks you to *Enter Range*. You can also use this technique with the F5 Goto key in response to the prompt *Enter address to go to*.

The advantage of this approach over the use of Ctrl-RightArrow and Ctrl-LeftArrow, which jumps the cell pointer a full screen to the right or left, is that you can jump a designated number of cells every time. With the Ctrl-RightArrow and Ctrl-LeftArrow combinations, your pointer moves a variable number of cells depending on the width of the columns in the current screen.

The Jump Macro

Here's another frustration-solver, as well as a real time-saver. Suppose you're moving down a typical worksheet, entering data or changing already existing data. You may have noticed that it can slow you down significantly to enter data at the bottom of the screen, while entering data when you're at the top of the screen is much easier—you can see what's coming up next, for one thing.

If you've ever thought it would be nice to have a macro that will jump your pointer and the cell your pointer occupies to the top of the screen, here's your solution.

In cell C7, type ***** JUMP MACRO ***** . In cell A8, type '**\J** Return, select /Range Name Labels Right, then in cell B8 enter:

{down 18}{up 18}{quit}

Now try the Jump macro. Place your cursor at or near the bottom of the screen and press Alt-J. The macro will quickly move down 18 cells, then up 18 cells. The effect will be to relocate the current cell to the top of the page. Try the macro from halfway down your screen and the effect is the same. In fact, from any point on your screen, the macro will relocate the current cell to the top of the screen.

This has become a favorite macro because it is both simple and useful in that it allows a view of the current cell and the page beneath it at once. Note that 18 {down} commands were used instead of one {PgDn} so you don't become disoriented.

Over from End Home

This is another movement macro that adds a new feature to 1-2-3. You may be familiar with the ability of 1-2-3 to jump your cell pointer to the lower right corner of the spreadsheet by pressing the End key and the Home key, but what would you think of a macro that moves you to the lower left corner?

In column C, type *****OVER FROM END OF WORKSHEET***** . Down one row, in column A, type '**\O** . (**Note:** This is the letter "O," not a zero.) Select /Range Name Labels Right and press Return. In column B, enter:

{end}{home}{down}{end}{left}{quit}

Now wherever you are in your worksheet you will be able to jump to the lower left corner by pressing Alt-O.

Widen Column by One Space

Normally, in order to widen the width of a column, you would select /Worksheet Col-umnwidth Set and then enter the number that represents your desired column width, or use your RightArrow or LeftArrow key to increase or decrease the column width. (At this point, a common oversight is to forget to press Return.)

In order to create a macro to widen the column automatically, type

*** WIDEN COLUMN BY 1 SPACE ***

in column C. Down one row, in column A, type \ **W.** Select /Range Name Labels Right and press Return. Move to column B and enter:

/wcs{right}~{quit}

Note that in order to enter this, you will need to start by typing a label prefix (apostrophe), since typing the forward slash / key without a label prefix calls up your command menu. In the Edit line, the macro will look like this:

'/wcs{right}~{quit}

Now try your macro. Move your cursor to column D and press Alt-W. The width of column D will increase by one space. Press Alt-W three more times, and the column width will in-crease by three more spaces.

Naming Your Macros All at Once

At this point, your new macro worksheet should look like Figure 3.1. You will notice that something has been added: between each macro range name there is a colon (:). These are simply cell-fillers added to facilitate the range naming. By ensuring that there is something in each cell in column A, you make it possible to name all of the range names at once.

Try it now. Place a colon in every empty cell in column A down to the last range name. Then move to cell A2 (which should read \ **B**) and select /Range Name Labels Right and press the End key, the DownArrow key, and finally Return. This method will highlight all the range names with a single stroke, and accomplish in one operation the range naming of all of your macros.

Of course, going through this process of adding colons does not save keystrokes the first time you write a macro, but it can greatly facilitate the renaming of ranges if you find you have to do a /Range Name Reset, or if you want to transfer the macro to another file using /File Combine. As you will discover, transferring macros using /File Combine works well to copy macros from file to file, but it does not transfer the range names in the process. These will all have to be renamed after the transfer is complete.

```
A1: ':                                                              READY

        A         B         C         D         E       F       G       H
1   :                     *** BEEP MACRO ***
2   \B        {home}'~{quit}
3   :                     *** LEFT MACRO ***
4   \L        {left 8}{quit}
5   :                     *** RIGHT MACRO ***
6   \R        {right 8}{quit}
7   :                     *** JUMP MACRO ***
8   \J        {down 18}{up 18}{quit}
9   :                       *** OVER FROM END OF WORKSHEET ***
10  \O        {end}{home}{down}{end}{left}{quit}
11  :                     *** WIDEN COLUMN WIDTH BY 1 SPACE ***
12  \W        /wcs{right}~{quit}
13
14
15
16
17
18
19
20
```
FIG_3-1.WK1

Figure 3.1   Six Simple Macros (Beep, Left, Right, Jump, Over, Widen)

Format Macros

The format macros shown below are more examples of macros which call up the main menu of 1-2-3 and step through the menu choices for you.

Examine Figure 3.2. You will note that all four format macros are essentially the same except for the fourth character. The purpose of the macros is to change the formats of a cell or a range with just a few keystrokes. Instead of selecting /Range Format Currency and pressing Return twice to change a cell to a dollar format, you can press Alt-D and Return. This introduces the use of a new macro keyword—the macro pause. You can get your macro to pause in mid-play by inserting a bracketed question mark, like this: {?} .

In this example, the pause allows you to decide whether to reformat a range of numbers, or to accept the single-cell range offered in the upper panel. When the macro pauses at the command *Enter range to format:*, you can paint in a range and press Return or designate just the current cell by pressing Return. In either case, pressing Return is the macro's signal to continue where it left off.

These macros can be changed, of course, to select some choice other than the two-decimal point default offered by 1-2-3. As an example, you can change the Dollar Format macro to reflect no decimals by having it read: **/rfc0~{?}~{quit}.**

The Add Macros

Probably the most commonly typed formula in 1-2-3 is the **@sum** formula. Unfortunately, this formula requires keystrokes which are difficult to type (the @ sign and parentheses), it

A1: ' :   READY

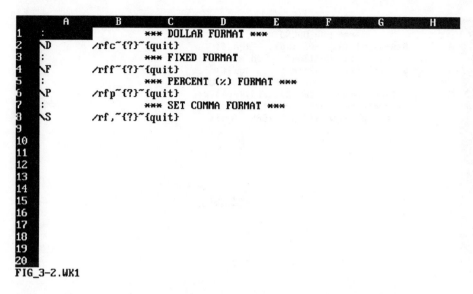

```
      A        B        C         D          E        F        G        H
1    :               *** DOLLAR FORMAT ***
2   \D     /rfc~{?}~{quit}
3    :               *** FIXED FORMAT
4   \F     /rff~{?}~{quit}
5    :               *** PERCENT (%) FORMAT ***
6   \P     /rfp~{?}~{quit}
7    :               *** SET COMMA FORMAT ***
8   \S     /rf,~{?}~{quit}
9
10
11
12
13
14
15
16
17
18
19
20
```
FIG_3-2.WK1

Figure 3.2 Four Format Macros (Dollar, Fixed, Percent, Set Comma)

involves thinking about and establishing the @sum range, and it all too often results in incorrect range cell coordinates—sometimes even leading to a circular reference (CIRC).

The Add macro facilitates the summing of a column using the @sum formula (see Figure 3.3). To invoke the macro, place your cell pointer two cells below the last number in the column you wish to sum and press Alt-A. The macro types **@sum(** and moves up one cell, anchors the cursor with the Period (.) key, moves up one more cell, then uses End UpArrow to highlight to the top of the column of numbers. The two periods that follow reverse the order in which the range coordinates will appear so that they read from top to bottom. A final close of the parenthesis and a tilde complete the formula.

It is important to note that any blank cells in the column will cause an incorrect range in the @sum formula. This can be precluded by altering the macro to move to a similar-length column which is filled, paint in the vertical range, and return to the original column. Alternately, you may wish to insert a pause in the macro so that you can verify the range before it is established. That way, if you need to increase the range you can simply highlight upwards with your arrow key and press Return to continue the macro. For this option, use the macro line:

@sum({up}.{end}{up}{?}..)~{quit}

If you prefer to have a cell with dashed lines between the column and the sum (instead of a blank cell), change the macro to:

{up}\-{down}@sum({up}.{end}{up}..)~{quit}

Or better yet, you can have your macro insert a series of dashes which number one less than the width of the column, thereby providing a blank space (a kind of gutter) between dashed lines you end up creating in a row. To do this, change the macro to:

`E15: @IF(@ROUND(@SUM(E13..E11),2)=@ROUND(@SUM(D15..B15),2),@SUM(E13..E11),@ERR)`

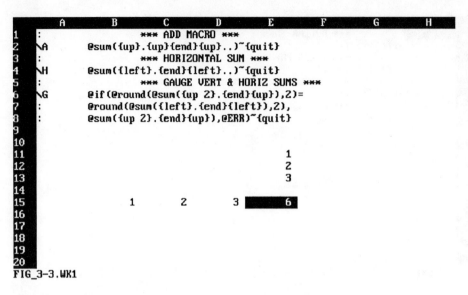

FIG_3-3.WK1

Figure 3.3 Three Add Macros (Add, Horizontal Sum, Gauge Vert...)

$$\{up\}@repeat("-",@cell(width,\{up\})-1)\{calc\}$$
$$\{down\}@sum(\{up\}.\{end\}\{up\}..)\tilde{}\{quit\}$$

The principles used in the Add macro can also be used to create a macro that types the @avg formula or the @count formula.

If you'd like to have a macro to sum the row to the left, try the Horizontal Sum macro. As with the Add macro shown above, you can include a macro pause to verify and change the sum range if necessary by modifying the macro to read:

$$@sum(\{left\}.\{end\}\{left\}\{?\}..)\tilde{}\{quit\}$$

The Add macro and Horizontal Sum macro can be combined in a macro which will allow you to compare the horizontal versus the vertical sums of a matrix, and provide an error message in the event that the two sums are not equal. Refer to the Gauge Vert & Horiz Sums macro in Figure 3.3.

@if(@round(@sum({up 2}.{end}{up}),2)=   Begins with an @if statement that will be used for the logic, *if the vertical equals the horizontal sum, insert the vertical sum, otherwise insert an Error message.* The @round formula is used to ensure that any differences in the two sums are not the result of rounding problems. Finally on this line we have the standard Add macro, followed by the number 2 for rounding to two decimal points, and an equals sign as part of the @if logic.

@round(@sum({left}.{end}{left}),2),   Types the rounded version of the Horizontal Sum macro, followed by a comma to continue the @if logic.

@sum({up 2}.{end}{up}),@ERR)~{quit}   Provides a vertical sum as the conclusion of the @if statement if the two sums are equal, or an ERR entry if the two sums are not equal, after which the macro quits.

The @Date Format Macro

Beginning users of 1-2-3 tend to type dates as labels rather than using the more complicated @Date format. This certainly works for straight data entry, but it eliminates the possibility of doing math with your dates, and it makes sorting by date error- prone. The dates 1/1/90, 3/1/90, and 11/1/90 sorted in ascending order, for example, would appear in the order 1/1/90, 11/1/90, and 3/1/90.

The solution to this question of ease-of-entry versus math and sort capability is to create a macro to handle the @Date entry for you.

As you'll see in Figure 3.4, the macro types:

@date(90,

then waits for you to enter the month, a comma, and the day; closes the parenthesis for you; formats the cell using /Range Format Date 1 Return; then changes the column width to 10— the column width required to accommodate a standard date format.

This macro is designed to type in the current year, which can be changed from year to year by editing the macro. You can also edit the year on an as-required basis. To do this, press Alt-D. At the pause, press Backspace twice, change the year, type in a comma, then type the

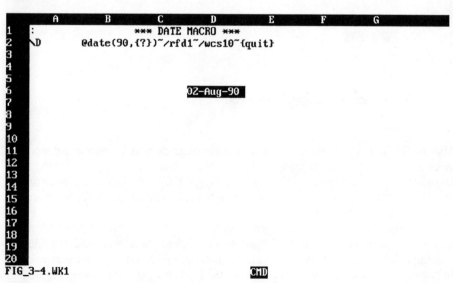

Figure 3.4 The Date Format Macro

month, a comma, and the day. You can also eliminate the year entirely from the basic macro if you want, and fill it in at each execution of the macro.

This is one of the most commonly known and used macros in the world of 1-2-3, without which your macro library would be incomplete. As you can see, this macro saves up to 22 keystrokes with each use.

Up/Copy Data

Another simple but very useful macro is shown in Figure 3.5. The Up/Copy Data macro allows you to copy into the current cell the information from the cell above.

B18: (C2)   READY

```
        A       B       C       D       E       F       G       H
1   :                *** UP/COPY DATA ***
2   \U      /c{esc}{up}~~{quit}
3   :                *** FORMAT COPIED FROM ABOVE ***
4   \F      /c{esc}{up}~~/re~{quit}
5   :                *** INSERT ROW WITH DATA ***
6   \I      /wir~{goto}.{end}{home}.{esc}~{up}
7   :       /c{down}{end}{left}{up}~{down}{end}{left}~
8   :       {down}{goto}.{home}.{esc}~
9   :       {up 8}{down 8}{quit}
10  :                *** INSERT ROW WITH FORMAT ***
11  \R      /wir~{goto}.{end}{home}.{esc}~{up}
12  :       /c{down}{end}{left}{up}~{down}{end}{left}~
13  :       {down}{goto}.{home}.{esc}~/re{end}{right}{?}~
14  :       {up 8}{down 8}{quit}
15
16
17          $1.00           1    100.00%               1.0
18
19          $1.00           1    100.00%               1.0
20
FIG_3-5.WK1
```

Figure 3.5 Four Macros to Copy Data or Format

After typing and range-naming this macro, enter some extraneous data in a blank cell. Move to the cell beneath it and press Alt-U. The macro invokes the copy command, then presses Escape to free the cursor. At this point it moves to the cell above, presses Return to establish the FROM cell, and jumping automatically back to the original cell, again presses Return to establish the TO cell.

The result is a macro that can save a great deal of data entry time. At any point where the information you are about to enter is identical to the information in the cell immediately above, simply press Alt-U and watch the information copied instantly into the current cell.

To copy just the format of the cell above, try the Up/Copy Format macro in Figure 3.5. This macro is identical to the Up/Copy Data macro, except that it erases the copied data, leaving just the format in the current cell.

These same principles can be used to copy data or just formats from the entire row above. Refer to the Insert Row With Data macro in Figure 3.5.

/wir~{goto}.{end}{home}.{esc}~{up}   First inserts a new row, then uses the F5 Goto key in an unusual way to jump the cell pointer to the right-most cell of the current row. The macro does this by pressing Goto, then pressing the Period key (.) to anchor the cell pointer. Then it presses End Home, which highlights a range to the lower right of the active area of the worksheet. Another Period rotates the free corner of this range to the lower left. Then the macro presses Escape to collapse the range to the anchor cell. It's complicated, but the effect is to jump the cell pointer to the right-most active cell of the newly inserted row. Finally, the cell pointer is moved to the cell immediately above it.

/c{down}{end}{left}{up}~{down}{end}{left}~   This line of the macro copies the row above into the newly inserted row. It starts with a /Copy command, copying the entire row by highlighting down one cell, then all the way to the left, then up one cell. For the Copy TO location, the cell pointer is moved down one cell to the new row and all the way to the left. The cell pointer automatically jumps back to the FROM area at this point.

{down}{goto}.{home}.{esc}~   Moves the cell pointer back to the new row and jumps it to the left-most cell (column A) using the same Goto technique as above.

{up 8}{down 8}{quit}   Finally, the cell pointer position is adjusted more towards the center of the screen by moving down eight cells, then up eight cells.

Even more useful than the macro that inserts a new row and copies the data from the row above, is a macro that inserts a new row and copies only standard formats into your new row.

You have probably experienced this frustration: many of the cells of your spreadsheet are formatted, but when you add a new row it is entirely unformatted. The typical solution to this is to make your entries in the new row and format the cells one-by-one. Now with the Row Insert with Format macro, this will be done automatically for you. As you will see, this macro is identical to the Row Insert with Data macro, except that it erases the copied data, leaving just the formats in the new row.

Note, however, this macro includes a bracketed question mark pause during the /Range Erase function. This is required to allow you to verify or, if required, to increase the range of data in the row to be erased.

Automatic Execution Macros

Doing a standard /File Retrieve is the kind of menu selection that 1-2-3 users go through so often that it becomes second nature, so a macro to automate that process may seem fairly unamazing. However, the File Retrieve can include an extra bonus—the ability to display all of your filenames at once. This could also be done manually, of course, but selecting /File Retrieve and pressing the F3 Name key is cumbersome compared with the \0-Auto123 File Retrieve macro shown in Figure 3.6.

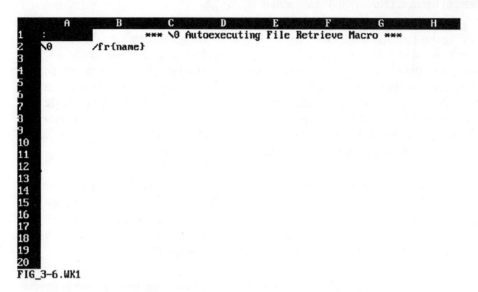

FIG_3-6.WK1

Figure 3.6   0-Auto123 File Retrieve Macro

More importantly, this particular macro is especially appropriate for automatic execution. To create a macro that will execute as soon as a file is retrieved, the macro is named \0.

Note: This is a zero, not the letter "O" and it represents the only macro name that uses a number rather than a letter.

To create a entire autoexecute file that will show on the screen automatically as soon as you boot up Lotus 1-2-3, save the file in your default directory with the name AUTO123. This way, instead of a blank screen at boot-up, you will see the AUTO123 file for a split second, then the \0 macro itself will activate and give you a choice of all of your files. Then you can simply point to the file you want to retrieve and press Return.

Although you can name a macro \0, it is designed to be activated only upon /File Retrieve of the file containing it. You will not be able to run a \0 Autoexecute macro by pressing Alt-0 manually. You can get around this limitation, however, by starting another pass-through macro in the cell just above the \0 macro.

One way to create such a pass-through macro would be to give it the command {branch \0}. This {branch} command tells the macro to continue its operation at the specified location: in this case, at the cell named \0.

Alternately, with the pass-through macro is in the cell immediately above the \0 macro you can simply use the {esc} command, which the macro will process to no effect before it continues at the \0 cell.

However, we will be using the easiest of all pass-through techniques here: the empty brackets {} that are read by Lotus as a null command. As you will see in later chapters, this pass-through command is useful for more than giving double starting names to autoexecute macros; it can be used to give both an Alt-Letter name and a mnemonic name to your macros, allowing them to be invoked directly or by way of the Alt-F3 Macro Run key (Release 2.2 and 3 only) or the Alt-Z Macro Launcher discussed in Chapter 8.

Summary

In this chapter we have introduced a collection of short macros that you can start using right away:

- A Beep macro to respond to the computer's beep when you've forgotten to start a number–letter combination with an apostrophe.
- Left and Right macros to jump your cursor a designated number of cells to the left or right.
- The Jump macro to jump your cursor and the cell your cursor occupies to the top of the page.
- A macro to move your cursor instantly to the lower left corner of your screen.
- A macro to widen your current column by one space each time you press Alt-W.
- Format macros to format a cell or a range of cells in the Fixed, Currency, or Percent format.
- An Add macro that types the @sum formula for you, automatically determining the range of the column to sum.
- A macro to gauge and verify that the vertical sum of a column matches the horizontal sum of a row.
- An @Date macro that types the beginning of the @date formula, pauses for the month and day, formats the cell for the date format, and widens the column to 10.
- Macros which copy the data or format from the cell or row above.
- An automatically executing /File Retrieve macro that you can save in an AUTO123 file.

In addition to these macros, the following concepts were presented:

- You can edit your macros using the F2 Edit key and the LeftArrow, RightArrow, Ctrl-LeftArrow, Ctrl-RightArrow, Backspace, and Delete keys.
- Name all of your ranges at once using /Range Name Labels Right End DownArrow. The inclusion of colons between range names will make this possible.
- To create an entire autoexecute file that will show on the screen automatically as soon as you boot up 1-2-3, save the file with the name AUTO123.

In Chapter 4 we will look at the use of the Step mode, the Macro Debugger (Release 2.2), the Macro Record key (Release 3), and the Macro Learn key (Release 2.2).

4

USING STEP, RECORD, AND LEARN KEYS

Debugging Your Macros

The single most common error in writing macros is the omission of an important tilde ˜ . Therefore, if your macro seems to operate incorrectly, or stops altogether, you should first check to see that all of the tildes required in your macro have, in fact, been typed in. Be careful, though. Depending on the resolution of your screen, a quotation mark can look like a tilde, and vice versa. You may think the tilde is there, only to find after much searching and frustration that it was actually a quotation mark all along.

The second most common mistake is the omission of a parenthesis or a bracket, or interchanging of parenthesis and brackets by typing a bracket where a parenthesis is required, or a parenthesis where you need a bracket.

Another frustrating error is the accidental inclusion of one or more blank spaces at the end of a line of macro text. This can be maddening, since such spaces are not visible on the screen. Pressing the F2 Edit key, however, can reveal the intruding spaces in the upper panel. Just look for the location of the blinking cursor in the Edit mode. If the cursor is immediately after the last letter, there are no extraneous spaces.

Another error that may occur frequently is reference to a range name that has not yet been named or for which the name has been deleted. Once you start writing macros with liberal use of range names, this type of problem will arise from time to time. When your macro refers to a missing range name, you will hear a beep and get an error message which states *Invalid cell or range address* or *Invalid range in BRANCH* (or *MENUBRANCH* or *MENUCALL*, and so on), followed by the cell address in the macro where the problem occurred.

To check the location or existence of a range name, press the F5 Goto key and enter the range name. If all is correct, your cell pointer should jump to the expected location in the worksheet. Alternately, select /Range Name Create and enter the range name. After determining the status of the range name, press a series of Escapes to back out of the /Range Name menu.

If the range name does not exist as called out in the macro, you must either correct the name in the macro (it may be misspelled, for example), or move to the proper location where the macro should exist and use /Range Name Labels Right or /Range Name Create to establish the missing range name.

The Step Command

If you are not able to locate a macro error by scanning through the macro itself, try the Step key. In Release 2, 2.01, and 2.2, you can shift to the Step Mode macro by pressing Alt-F2. In Release 3, press Alt-F2 and select *STEP*. You should see the word *STEP* appear at the bottom of your screen. Once you are in the Step mode, invoke your macro, then press Return several times. You can watch the macro play out a keystroke at a time at every press of the Return key, and easily discover where the macro is hanging up.

You can also hold down the Return key and watch the macro step very quickly through its keystrokes and commands. If you have quick reactions, you may even be able to use this method of holding down the Return key until you are almost at the part of the macro where a problem occurred, then press Return in succession to step more slowly through the next keystrokes. This may take some practice, but it can be a real time-saver for long, complicated macros with a problem near the end.

In Release 2.2, you will get an additional bonus when you use Step. Each line of the macro and its cell address will appear at the bottom of the screen as it is being played out. This is called the Macro Debugger, a significant macro feature that you can expect to see in all future releases of 1-2-3.

With the Macro Debugger, you can watch the macro code below your screen as the macro runs, allowing you to both read the macro and see its results at the same time. Figure 4.1 gives you an example of the Step mode Macro Debugger in action. (Although in this example the actual macro is also shown on-screen, this is done for clarity only; normally the macro would be out of sight.)

The macro in this example is the Add macro from Chapter 3, used to underline and sum a column of numbers. As you can see, the range of numbers is being highlighted automatically in response to the {up}{end}{up} commands of the macro. At the base of the macro, the current line of the macro is displayed at the bottom of the screen. As you press any key (we recommend the Return key) each macro instruction will be executed in turn and the next instruction will be highlighted.

You can turn the Step mode OFF at any time during macro execution and ON at any point where the macro is pausing for an interactive command such as a bracketed question mark

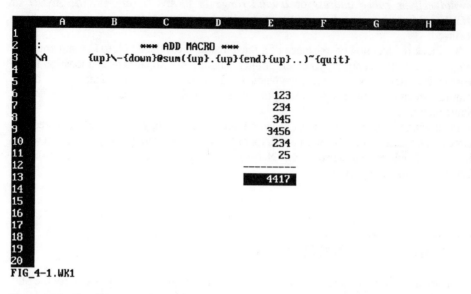

FIG_4-1.WK1

Figure 4.1   The Step Mode Macro Debugger in Release 2.2

pause. If your macro is running in Step mode, simply press Alt-F2 and the macro will return to normal speed. If you are running at normal mode and the macro has paused for your input, press Alt-F2 to switch to Step mode. If the macro produces an Error message in the Step mode, press Ctrl-Break to break out of the macro. (You may have to press Escape at this point as well.) Then use the F2 Edit key to modify the macro.

After you are finished debugging your macro, be sure to leave the Step mode by pressing Alt-F2 again.

Using the Alt-F2 Record Key in Release 3

Release 3 has added new features of its own to the Alt-F2 key, based on its new Record Buffer. The Record Buffer is a 512- byte area of computer memory in which 1-2-3 records all your keystrokes in the background as you type them, always saving your most recent keystrokes. As the buffer fills up, 1-2-3 discards keystrokes from the beginning of the buffer (your earliest keystrokes) to make room for your most recent keyboard input.

The Record Buffer is completely unobtrusive; for the most part, you will not be aware of the buffer at all until you press Alt-F2. As you can see from Figure 4.2, pressing Alt-F2 will give you the menu choices, *Playback, Copy, Erase,* and *Step.*

The Record key menu choices are described as:

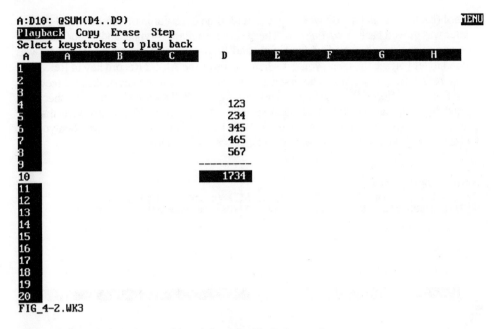

FIG_4-2.WK3

Figure 4.2 A Simple Spreadsheet Created in Release 3

Playback	Gives you access to the Record Buffer where you can view your latest keystrokes, edit the keystrokes, and highlight any portion of the keystrokes you wish to play back starting from your current cell. This allows playback of your keystrokes without having to create a macro in your worksheet.
Copy	Allows you to view your latest keystrokes in the Record Buffer, edit the keystrokes, and highlight any portion of the keystrokes you wish to copy in macro format into your spreadsheet.
Erase	Erases the entire Record Buffer so the keystrokes you type from that point on are recorded starting at the beginning of the buffer.
Step	Exactly duplicates the Step key in Releases 2 and 2.01, permitting you to step through a given macro one keystroke at a time. This option does *not* include the Macro Debugger feature found in Release 2.2.

An Example of the Alt-F2 Record Feature

The simple spreadsheet in Figure 4.2 was created in Release 3 by starting with a blank worksheet and entering the numbers **123, 234, 345, 456,** and **567** in cells D4..D8. Then the cell pointer was moved to D10. From there the cell pointer was moved up one cell, the repeating symbol (backslash) and a dash were typed to underline the column of numbers, and the cell pointer was moved back down one cell. The @sum formula was typed, and for the range the UpArrow was pressed, then End UpArrow, and finally a closing parenthesis. Alt-F2 was pressed to let you see the menu you get when you press the Alt-F2 Record key in Release 3.

The reason for going through all that was to show you how those keystrokes are recorded in the Record Buffer of Release 3. Refer now to Figure 4.3. This view of the worksheet was created by pressing the Alt-F2 key and selecting *PLAYBACK*. You will notice that the spreadsheet drops down to display the entire 512- byte buffer, just as it drops when you use the F2 Edit key on a cell entry in Release 3 that exceeds 80 characters.

```
A:D10: @SUM(D9..D4)                                                    EDIT
Press TAB to anchor cursor, then highlight keystrokes to play back:
{R 3}{D 3}123{D}234{D}345{D}456{D}567{D 2}{U}\-{D}@sum(A:D9..A:D4)~
```

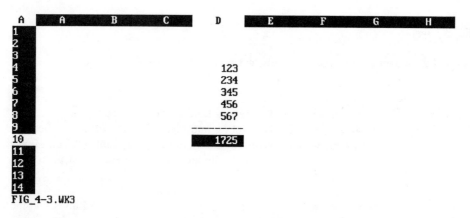

```
FIG_4-3.WK3
```

Figure 4.3   Invoking Record Playback in Release 3

As you can see, as each element of the spreadsheet was created, the keystrokes used were automatically saved in the Record Buffer. The format that the Record Buffer uses is the macro command language. Note, however, that the simpler bracketed {D} and {U} are used instead of the longer {down} and {up} commands we have used throughout this book. Either are appropriate; we have simply used the longer version in this book for clarity.

You may notice one other thing about the recorded keystrokes: the arrow keys used to highlight the @sum range were not recorded, only the result was. This is somewhat unfortunate. Although playing back these keystrokes will correctly sum the specific column originally summed, you will not be able to copy these keystrokes into the worksheet and use them as a general, generic macro that will sum a column of numbers in any location in the worksheet.

If you want to play back any portion of the recorded keystrokes, press Tab to anchor the cursor, then highlight the keystrokes to play back. In this same way, if you select *COPY*, you can press Tab to anchor the cursor, then highlight the keystrokes to copy into your worksheet. You will be prompted for the range to *Copy TO*, to which you can respond by pointing to and highlighting the cells spanning the first row where you want to macro to appear. The keystrokes will appear starting at the first cell of the Copy TO range and continuing downward from there.

At that point all you need do is range-name the first cell of the macro with a backslash-letter combination (\A, \B, and so on), move your cell pointer to the location where you want your macro to start, and press the appropriate Alt-letter combination (Alt-A, Alt-B, and so on).

In addition to recording standard keystrokes and macro keywords, the Record Buffer will also record composed characters you can create using the Compose key. It will not, however, record Alt-F1 Compose, Alt-F2 Record, Alt-F3 Run, or Alt-F4 Undo, nor will it record Ins, Scroll Lock, Caps Lock, Num Lock, Print Screen, or Ctrl-Break. When you use Ctrl-Break to leave a menu, 1-2-3 records the equivalent number of {esc} keystrokes.

As a final note on this feature, you may find the Record Buffer both intriguing and frustrating. It can be intriguing because it offers a new functionality and a new way to reenter recent data that in some way have been written over or erased. Unfortunately, you may experience some frustration at realizing that the keystrokes you want to play back have been shoved out of the Record Buffer by more recent keystrokes, or finding that some of your keystrokes cannot be recorded in the buffer at all, or having to do more editing than you might have expected after copying the keystrokes into a macro area.

Using the Alt-F5 Learn Key in Release 2.2

If you have Release 2.2, you may find the Alt-F5 Learn key more to your liking—though it has limitations of its own. Although available as a separate add-in for Release 2 and 2.01, the Alt-F5 Learn key is a welcome addition to the function keys of Release 2.2. Now, as an alternative to manually typing your own macros, you can use the Release 2.2 Learn feature to record your keystrokes as you work, so that later 1-2-3 can automatically and instantly perform those same repetitive tasks for you.

Creating the Learn Range in Release 2.2

Before the Alt-F5 Learn key can be used, you must call up the main command menu and create a Learn Range—a location in the worksheet where 1-2-3 can record your keystrokes. This is done as:

1. Move to an area where your keystrokes can be recorded without interfering with the function or appearance of your worksheet. (One convenient way to do this is by pressing End Home PgDn—an area guaranteed to be blank, and a place where inserting or deleting rows will not destroy your input.)
2. Select /Worksheet Learn Range. You will see a prompt *Enter Learn range:* in the upper control panel.
3. At the prompt, lock in your cursor with the Period (.) key and highlight a single-col-

umn range. Trying to highlight a multicolumn range will also work, but only because 1-2-3 is programmed to automatically reduce it to a single-column range in any case. See the example in Figure 4.4.

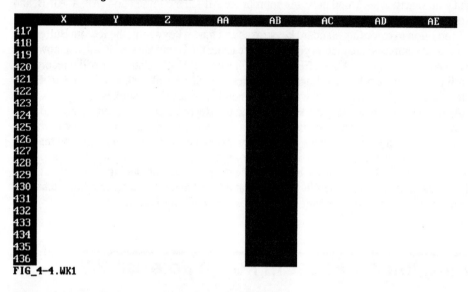

```
AB436:                                                              POINT
Enter learn range: AB418..AB436
```

FIG_4—4.WK1

Figure 4.4 Creating a Learn Range in Release 2.2

Note: It is best to highlight a range that is much larger than you think you will need, so 1-2-3 does not run out of space while recording your keystrokes. It is very common to run out of Learn range space long before you ever thought you would, so try making the range four times larger than you think you will need. If 1-2-3 does run out of space while recording your keystrokes, it will interrupt you with the error message *Learn range is full.* Instructions for what to do in that case are covered later in this section.

---

4. Move to the area of the worksheet where you want to start performing the task to be recorded. Typically, the Learn range is not visible as you perform this task.
5. Press the Alt-F5 Learn key to start the recording. You will see a *LEARN* indicator appear in the lower part of your screen.
6. Perform the task you want to automate. Don't worry if you make a mistake, you can always go back and edit the recorded keystrokes later.
7. At the end of the task, press the Alt-F5 Learn key again to turn off the recording feature. The *LEARN* indicator will disappear.
8. Move to the Learn range. If you pressed End Home PgDn to go there originally, press End Home End UpArrow now to return.
9. Review the recorded keystrokes and make any changes that seem appropriate. As you edit the recorded keystrokes, be sure not to leave any empty cells in the middle

of the macro, or 1-2-3 will interpret the blank cell as the end of the macro. If you made more mistakes than you would like to change, erase the Learn range using /Worksheet Learn Erase and start again at Step 1.

10. Once you are satisfied that the macro has no errors, type an apostrophe and a back-slash–letter combination (type '\A, for example) in the cell to the left of the first cell of the Learn range and press Enter. The apostrophe will not appear in the cell display, only in the upper panel.

11. To range-name your recorded keystrokes for invoking as a macro later, select /Range Name Labels Right and press Return at the cell where you just entered your back-slash-letter combination.

How to Handle an Error During Learn

If, while the LEARN feature is recording your keystrokes, you suddenly get an error message indicating that you have run out of space in your Learn range, do one of the following:

- Erase the Learn range by selecting /Worksheet Learn Erase, then make the Learn range larger by selecting /Worksheet Learn Range and pressing PgDn several times and Enter. At this point you can start the entire process over again at Step 1.
- Alternately, you can leave the recorded keystrokes in place and establish a second Learn range below the previous range. Do this by selecting /Worksheet Learn Range and pressing the Period key (.) twice, then End, DownArrow, PdDn several times, Period (.) twice again, DownArrow, and Enter. When you press Enter, your cell pointer will jump back to the location where you were interrupted, and you can proceed with your task where you left off.

How the Learn Feature Records Your Keystrokes

As with the Alt-F2 Record key in Release 3, the Alt-F5 Learn feature records your keystrokes in the 1-2-3 macro language. For example, when you press the F2 Edit key, the Home key, the Delete key, and Enter, the macro commands recorded by 1-2-3 will be **{edit}{home}{del}~** .

In addition to recording standard keystrokes and macro keywords, the Learn feature in Release 2.2 will record composed characters you can create using the Compose key. It will not, however, record Alt-F1 Compose, Alt-F2 Record, Alt-F3 Run, or Alt-F4 Undo, nor will it record Ins, Scroll Lock, Caps Lock, Num Lock, or Print Screen. Unlike the Alt-F2 Record key in Release 3, when you use Ctrl-Break to leave a menu, Release 2.2 records the new macro keyword {break} instead of using the equivalent number of {esc} keystrokes.

There is another, more significant difference in the way the Alt-F5 Learn feature records your keystrokes as compared with the Alt-F2 Record feature of Release 3. As we pointed out in Figure 4.3, you will not be able to create a general generic macro using the Record feature in Release 3 without some extensive editing.

Refer now to Figure 4.5, however, to see that the Learn range in Release 2.2 correctly captured exactly the keystrokes typed. Unfortunately, some of the keystrokes are isolated in

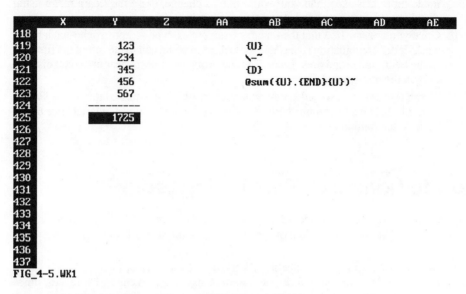

Figure 4.5   Using the Learn Range in Release 2.2

single cells, but that can be easily rectified through use of the /Range Justify command at cell AB 418. The important thing to note here is that creation of the @sum range in the macro consists of the abbreviated version of {up}.{end}{up}. This is written is such a way as to be useful for a summing macro that we can use anywhere in the spreadsheet.

Summary

In this chapter we examined techniques for debugging your macros using the Step key and methods for recording your keystrokes using the Record key in Release 3 and the Learn key in Release 2.2. The items covered were:

- The most common errors in your macros will be omission of a tilde where required, omission of a parenthesis or bracket, accidental inclusion of blank spaces, and reference to range names that do not exist as called out.
- To check the location or existence of a range name, press the F5 Goto key and enter the range name. If all is correct, your cell pointer should jump to the expected location in the worksheet.
- If you are not able to locate a macro error by scanning through the macro itself, use the Step key to run the macro a keystroke at a time at every press of the Return key.
- The Record Buffer of Release 3 is a 512-byte area of computer memory in which 1-2-3 records all your keystrokes in the background as you type them. Pressing Alt-F2 will offer the choices *Playback*, *Copy*, *Erase*, and *Step*.

■ If you want to play back any portion of the recorded keystrokes, press Tab to anchor the cursor, then highlight the keystrokes to play back. In this same way, if you select *COPY*, you can press Tab to anchor the cursor, then highlight the keystrokes to copy into your worksheet.

■ The Alt-F5 Learn feature of Release 2.2 will record your keystrokes as you work, so that later 1-2-3 can automatically and instantly perform those same repetitive tasks for you. However, before the Alt-F5 Learn key can be used, you must call up the main command menu and create a Learn range.

■ If you get an error message during Learn, erase the Learn range and start over or establish a second Learn range and continue where you left off.

■ As with the Alt-F2 Record key in Release 3, the Alt-F5 Learn feature records your keystrokes in the 1-2-3 macro language.

In Chapter 5 we will explore some of the advanced macro programming commands such as {branch}, {menubranch}, {indicate}, and {break}.

5

THE MACRO PROGRAMMING COMMANDS

Beyond Macro Keywords

In addition to the macro keywords which serve as macro equivalents for function keys, directional keys, and task keys on your keyboard, 1-2-3 has a strong collection of advanced macro programming commands which also appear in curly brackets, as shown in Table 5.1. These advanced programming commands can be broken down into seven categories. They include commands to control the screen, allow user input, control the program flow, interrupt the program flow, manipulate data, manipulate files, and access add-ins. These commands are listed by group in Table 5.2

Macro Range Names

Beginning 1-2-3 users tend not to do much naming of ranges in the worksheet until they start writing macros. Once you discover macros, however, range naming becomes second nature.

Table 5.1 Advanced Macro Programming Commands

Programming Command	Description
{ }	Null subroutine
{?}	Pause for input until Return is pressed
{app1} - {app4}	Invokes add-ins, same as Alt-F7 thru Alt-F10
{appendbelow}	Copies data to row below database (Release 3)
{appendright}	Copies data to column right of database (Release 3)
{beep}	Plays one of four tones
{blank}	Erase the cell or range designated
{bordersoff}	Turns borders off, same as {frameoff} (Release 2.2 and 3)
{borderson}	Turns borders on, same as {frameon} (Release 2.2 and 3)
{branch}	Continues the macro at another location
{break}	Back out of all menu levels (Release 2.2 and 3)
{breakoff}	Disables the use of Ctrl-Break
{breakon}	Enables the use of Ctrl-Break
{clearentry} or {ce}	Clear display such as default filename (Release 3)
{close}	Closes a file opened with {open}
{contents}	Copies a cell's displayed value to a location
{define}	Designates a cell to store subroutine parameters
{dispatch}	Branch to the address shown in the dispatch cell
{extend}	Same as Alt-F10, calls Add-in Manager
{filesize}	Return the size of the file designated
{for}	Run a macro subroutine a specific number of times
{forbreak}	End the execution of a {for} loop prematurely
{form}	Pause for input, similar to /Range Input (Release 3)
{frameoff}	Turn frame off, same as {bordersoff} (Release 2.2 and 3)
{frameon}	Turn frame on, same as {borderson} (Release 2.2 and 3)
{get}	Store the next keystroke in the designated cell
{getlabel}	Store the prompted label in the designated cell
{getnumber}	Store the prompted number in the designated cell
{getpos}	Find the current byte pointer position of a file
{graphoff}	Turn graph view off (Release 2.2 and 3)
{graphon}	Turn graph view on (Release 2.2 and 3)
{if}	Test a condition and branch accordingly
{ifkey}	Tests whether a key name is currently valid
{indicate}	Replace the Ready mode indicator with a message
{let}	Copies the value of a cell or label to a cell
{look}	Looks to see if the user has typed a keystroke
{menubranch}	Displays a designated menu of up to eight choices
{menucall}	Calls up to eight menu choices as subroutines
{onerror}	Branches to a routine if the macro sees an error
{open}	Opens a file before reading, writing, or sizing it
{paneloff}	Freezes the upper control panel
{panelon}	Unfreezes the upper control panel
{put}	Enters a value or string into a table
{quit}	Quits the macro, returns to Ready mode
{read}	Reads a portion of text or sequential data file
{readln}	Copies a line from an ASCII file to the worksheet
{recalc}	Recalculates the designated range rowwise
{recalcol}	Recalculates the designated range columnwise
{restart}	Stops subroutine from returning to the main routine
{return}	Returns control from subroutine to the main routine
{setpos}	Changes the byte pointer position in an ASCII file
{wait}	Causes the macro to pause for a designated time
{system}	Suspends 1-2-3 and runs /System command
{windowsoff}	Freezes the worksheet portion of the screen
{windowson}	Unfreezes the worksheet portion of the screen
{write}	Writes a string of characters to an ASCII file
{writeln}	Writes a complete line to an ASCII file
{(*rangename*)}	Branches to a subroutine

Table 5.2 Advanced Macro Programming Command Groups

Command Groups	Programming Commands
Screen Control	{bordersoff}, {borderson}, {clearentry} or {ce}, {frameoff}, {frameon}, {graphoff}, {graphon}, {indicate}, {paneloff}, {panelon}, {windowsoff}, {windowson}
User Input	{?}, {get}, {getlabel}, {getnumber}, {look}, {menubranch}, {menucall}
Program Flow	{ }, {(*rangename*)}, {branch}, {define}, {dispatch}, {for}, {forbreak}, {if}, {ifkey}, {onerror}, {return}, {restart}, {system}
Program Interrupt	{beep}, {break}, {breakoff}, {breakon}, {quit}, {wait}
Data Manipulation	{appendbelow}, {appendright}, {blank}, {contents}, {form}, {let}, {put}, {recalc}, {recalcol}
File Manipulation	{close}, {filesize}, {getpos}, {open}, {read}, {readln}, {setpos}, {write}, {writeln}
Add-In	{app1}, {app2}, {app3}, {app4}, {extend}

Not only are areas of the spreadsheet named more often, but individual lines of the macros are given internal macro names to allow custom menus, loops, counters, and so on.

In keeping with the convention that the range name which identifies the macro such as \A, \B, and so on, be shown in the column to the left of the macro, macro range names such as JLOOP or ZMENU are also shown to the left of the lines of the macro they refer to. As noted before, this facilitates both naming of the ranges as well as later identification of the macro range names.

From time to time your macros will refer to a cell location in the spreadsheet. In such cases it is *strongly* recommended that cell locations be called by range names rather than by cell coordinates. This convention is also recommended for the branching commands such as {branch} or {menubranch}. For example, you might write {**branch JLOOP**} rather than {**branch A32**}, or {**menubranch ZMENU**} rather than {**menubranch A59**}. There are several reasons for this:

1. Referring to range-named cells will make your macros more general and usable across more than one spreadsheet. So if you decide you want to transfer the macro to another spreadsheet, you can use it right away without having to change row and column cell references.

2. Cell references typed in a macro do not change automatically as they do in spreadsheet formulas if you delete or insert rows or columns. Macros are commands entered as labels, you'll remember, and labels do not change when you calculate the spreadsheet. So a macro's reference to cell J234 will remain unchanged when you delete row 233, which would cause your macro to use the wrong location in its operation.

3. You will want to be able to move your entire macro or macro subroutine to a different

location within the worksheet without having to worry that it may branch to an incorrect line in the macro itself. By giving range names to your branching destinations, you can move your macros with impunity.

Although range names can be either uppercase or lowercase, all range names in this book are shown in uppercase for better legibility.

Range names can also include dashes, commas, dollar signs, and so on, but use of these symbols is not encouraged. Rather, the standard conventions which you already use in creating your filenames have been adopted here in the creation of range names, including an attempt to keep to eight letters or less (not always achieved, but recommended) and the use of the underline symbol to separate words in a range name (not required since spaces are acceptable, but recommended).

The most often used range names found in the macros themselves end in the words MENU, LOOP, or COUNTER. This is because the most useful and typical kinds of programming techniques available in the 1-2-3 macro language are the calling up of a custom-made menu, the looping of a macro back to the ALOOP, BLOOP, CLOOP, and so on, or the counting of the number of times a particular loop has been run.

As stated in Chapter 2, we recommend that all range names shown to the left of a particular macro start with the letter of that macro. Since there will usually only be one A macro, one B macro, and one C macro, this convention will reduce the possibility of accidentally using a macro range name like LOOP redundantly in two separate macros.

Data Entry Down

Probably the most well-known use of the {branch} command is found in a simple Data Entry macro. Rather than enter information in a column by typing the entry, then pressing the DownArrow key, then typing the second entry and pressing the DownArrow key again, try the simple macro in Figure 5.1.

The macro starts with a pause, waiting for your entry. Once you make the entry and press Return, the macro continues by moving down one cell. The {branch} command is an instruction to continue the macro at the stated location. In this case, the location is the cell which has been range-named \D. In other words, the macro loops back to the beginning and starts over again.

It should be noted here that the {branch} command is not an instruction to the *cell pointer* to move to a range name or row/column cell location. We have the F5 Goto key for that, written in macro language as {goto}. Instead, this command is an instruction to the macro to continue at a different location, regardless of what the cell pointer is doing.

Suppose after entering a few dozen numbers in this way you realize that five cells up the entry is incorrect? You could press Ctrl- Break to leave the macro, of course, then move up five cells, correct the entry, move back down again, and finally resume the macro; but there is a better way.

The {?} pause waits for a press of the Return key before it can continue. This means that you can enter data at this point, or you can move the cell pointer. In fact, you can move the cell pointer up five cells, type the correct input, then use the DownArrow key to enter it. Since you have not pressed the Return key, the macro is still in the Pause mode. You could actually change several cells in this way: typing the entry, entering it with the DownArrow

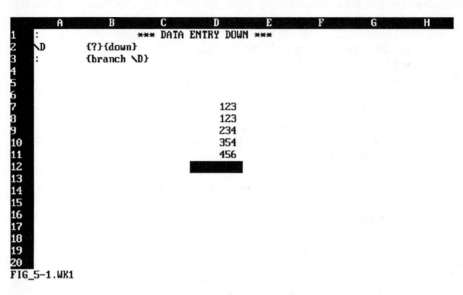

FIG_5-1.WK1

Figure 5.1　Data Entry Macro Moving Down

key instead of the Return key, typing another entry and entering it with the DownArrow key, and so on. When you're ready to resume the use of the Data Entry macro, place your cell pointer on the last entry at the bottom of the column and press Return.

If you want your entry centered as you move down the column, you could type the caret symbol [^] before each entry or you could center the entire column after the fact by selecting /Range Label-Prefix Center and painting in the column you want to center. Alternately, you could have the macro take care of all that for you. It's easy enough to make the change. Just include a caret (^) in front of the bracketed question mark. Now the macro will type the centering symbol first, pause for your entry, insert the entry, move down one cell and loop back to the beginning of the macro.

Note: To type this line of the macro, you must actually type '^{?}{**down**} with an apostrophe, even though all that will appear on the screen is ^{?}{**down**} .

This is an important distinction, because without the beginning apostrophe, 1-2-3 will take the caret to be an instruction to center the entry {?}{**down**} rather than including the caret as a visible part of the working macro.

In this same way, you can modify the Data Entry macro to right- justify each entry by first typing quotation marks, or to left-justify a number-label entry by first typing an apostrophe. Remember, though, that you must actually type '"{?}{**down**} so that it will appear as "{?}{**down**} or '"{?}{**down**} so that it will appear as '{?}{**down**} .

You may also want a Data Entry macro that will make entries moving in a row to the right rather than down. This is an easy modification: just change the word {down} to the word {right}. Given these choices of all of the possible ways you may want your Data Entry macro to operate, it might make more sense to put the choices into a menu. That way, rather than modify your macro or write several different macros to automate the all kinds of data entry, you could have one menu-driven macro that covers all possibilities. Just such a macro is presented in Chapter 9, called, the Data Entry macro.

Calling a Subroutine

A subroutine is actually another macro—a kind of sub-macro which the main macro temporarily branches to, after which it returns to the place where it left off. The command that tells your macro to branch to a subroutine and return is the range name of the subroutine enclosed in brackets.

The Save and Print macro in Figure 5.2 includes a simple example of a subroutine, called {SOUND}. The purpose of the macro is to calculate the worksheet and sound four tones to indicate the calculation is complete, save the file and sound four tones to indicate the /File Save is complete, and finally print the worksheet and sound four tones to indicate the printing is complete.

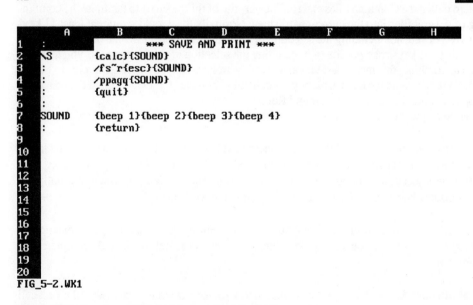

Figure 5.2 Save and Print Macro with Subroutine

To create this example, it is important that you remember to give the subroutine the range name SOUND. Actually, you can create both range names at the same time by placing your cell pointer on the \S and selecting /Range Name Labels Right and pressing PgDn and Return.

The subroutine SOUND consists of the four {beep} commands and a {return} command.

By including in the {beep} commands the numbers 1 through 4, you can create four different tones. The {return} command is an instruction that tells the macro to return to the place in the main routine where it left off. As you can see, using this subroutine saves us from having to type the four {beep} commands at the end of the first three lines of the macro. By calling it SOUND, we are able to give a short description of what the subroutine does.

You can probably interpret the third line of the macro easily by pressing the indicated keystrokes. You will see that they equate to /Print Printer Align Go Quit. However, you may have a question about the second line. It accomplishes a /File Save of the current file, and selects Replace; but you may wonder why we have included an Escape command. This is a convention that you will see often in this book. The Escape covers the possibility that you will be using the macro in a file that has not yet been saved. If the file is new, there will be no Replace choice offered, so we need a way to undo the pressing of the R key in case it isn't needed. If it is needed, of course, the Escape command has no effect.

Writing Your First Menu Macro

In the subsequent pages you can step through your own first creation of a few more utilitarian macros that depend very much on the use of custom-made menus. Let's start with a macro called the Combine Files macro. The purpose of this macro is to facilitate the combining of several files into the current worksheet. Normally this would require at least 11 keystrokes per file, not including the selection of the filename. Instead we can do the same task with just one keystroke per file (not including the selection of the filename). If you have ten files to combine, this means a savings of 100 keystrokes. To type this macro, refer to Figure 5.3. To range-name the macro, place your cell pointer on the \C, select /Range Name Labels Right, and press End DownArrow and Return.

Here's how the macro works.

{end}{home}{down}{end}{left}   The macro starts by moving the cell pointer to the lower right corner of the worksheet, then down one cell, and over to column A. This places your cell pointer just below the lower left corner of the current worksheet, which is usually the appropriate place to /File Combine a new file into the worksheet.

/fcce{?}~   The macro selects /File Combine Copy Entire, then waits for your selection or typing of the filename you want to combine. When you press Return, the tilde completes the command.

{menubranch C_MENU}   Tells the macro to look for a custom menu where the first cell of the menu is named C_MENU. It then calls up all of the items of the menu and pauses for a menu choice. The macro does not read the {quit} command at this point—in fact, this command is only included so that the macro will simply quit if you hit Escape instead of selecting one of the menu choices. This is because pressing Escape once your custom menu appears in the upper panel will always cause the macro to return to the end of the {menubranch} command and continue reading from there. If there is no {quit} command after the {menubranch}, pressing Escape will cause the macro to type whatever happens to be in the next cell down. In this case, it would cause the macro to type the word PROCEED.

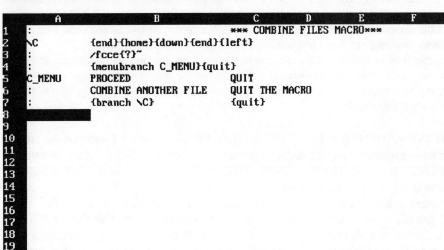

A8: [W11]   EDIT
Enter name of file to combine: C:\123\

```
              A              B                C      D      E      F
1    :                                  *** COMBINE FILES MACRO***
2    \C           {end}{home}{down}{end}{left}
3    :            /fcce{?}~
4    :            {menubranch C_MENU}{quit}
5    C_MENU       PROCEED               QUIT
6    :            COMBINE ANOTHER FILE  QUIT THE MACRO
7    :            {branch \C}           {quit}
8
9
10
11
12
13
14
15
16
17
18
19
20
```
FIG_5-3.WK1   CMD

Figure 5.3 The Combine Files Macro with Menu

It would then continue down to type the next cell, and so on until the macro reaches a tilde or some inconsistency that prevents it from continuing.

Because of this potentially dangerous feature of the {menubranch} command, every use of {menubranch} here is followed by a {quit} command, or by another menubranch command that allows the macro to continue at a different menu level. This is an important convention which also permits the ability to back out of menus level-by-level just as you can back out of standard menus already available in 1-2-3.

PROCEED   QUIT   These are the menu choices which will appear once the macro has read the command {menubranch C_MENU}. Note that the range name C_MENU in cell A4 is shown just to the left of the word PROCEED, indicating that cell B5 has been given the range name C_MENU. In other words, only the first cell of the menu choices requires a range name. Use of the {menubranch} command will cause the macro to automatically look for other menu choices to the right of this first choice—up to a total of eight choices.

A few things can go wrong even at this early stage in the creation of menus, and it seems appropriate to mention them here. First, you must use the {menubranch} command to call up menus, not the {branch} command. While this seems a simple instruction, it will surprise you how often you type {branch} by mistake.

Because the menu command looks for all menu choices to the right of the first choice, you can accidentally include data not intended as menu choices if you do not realize that there happens to be data in the cells immediately to the right of your menu choices. This can even result in the error message *Invalid use of menu macro command* if the total space taken up by the extraneous menu choices exceeds the amount of space provided for menu choices in the upper panel. For that matter, even intended menu choices can result in the error message if the choices take up too much space. In such a case, you will have to edit your menu choices to shorten them down to a total of 80 characters, including spaces.

Another typical mistake in the creation of menus is an obvious one: forgetting to give a range name to the name of the menu. If you try to run the macro without range-naming the menu, you will get an error message when you run the macro that warns you *Invalid range name in MENUBRANCH*.

COMBINE ANOTHER FILE   QUIT THE MACRO   These are the entries which provide explanation and direction pertaining to the menu choices. As with standard Lotus menus, having the cursor on the first choice will cause the explanation for that choice to appear in the upper panel. Moving the cursor to the second choice will pull up the second explanation. It is possible to have explanations exceeding 80 characters in this line of the macro (the macro will still run), but you will not be able to read more than the first 80 characters of any such explanation. The Edit key is not available to you at this point. In fact, no keys are available to you at this point except LeftArrow and RightArrow, the Return key, the first letter of each menu choice, the Escape key, and Ctrl-Break.

{branch \C}   If you select *PROCEED*, the macro will branch back to the beginning and start all over.

{quit}   Of course, if you select *QUIT*, the macro reads the {quit} command and returns to Ready mode.

A Menu Macro to Transfer Drives

Let's look at another menu macro offering a few more choices. The Transfer to Alternate Drive macro (see Figure 5.4) is designed to change your file directory and start a /File Retrieve operation, offering a full-screen view of all of the files in that directory.

{menubranch TMENU}{quit}   Tells the macro to call up the menu named TMENU. If you press Escape after the menu choices appear in the upper panel, the {quit} command is read and the macro quits. The four menu choices are *A-DRIVE*, *B-DRIVE*, *C-DRIVE*, and *QUIT*.

If you select *A-DRIVE*, the macro branches to the commands:

/fdA:~   Selects /File Directory and switches to the A drive.

/fr{name}   Selects /File Retrieve and presses the F3 Name key to display a full-screen view of all the files in the A drive.

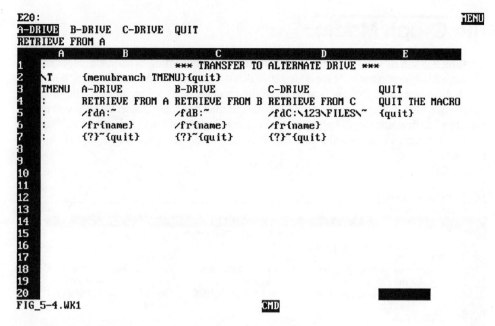

```
E20:                                                                    MENU
A-DRIVE   B-DRIVE   C-DRIVE   QUIT
RETRIEVE FROM A
        A           B               C               D               E
1   :                   *** TRANSFER TO ALTERNATE DRIVE ***
2   \T      {menubranch TMENU}{quit}
3   TMENU   A-DRIVE         B-DRIVE         C-DRIVE         QUIT
4   :       RETRIEVE FROM A RETRIEVE FROM B RETRIEVE FROM C QUIT THE MACRO
5   :       /fdA:~          /fdB:~          /fdC:\123\FILES\~  {quit}
6   :       /fr{name}       /fr{name}       /fr{name}
7   :       {?}~{quit}      {?}~{quit}      {?}~{quit}
8
9
10
11
12
13
14
15
16
17
18
19
20
FIG_5-4.WK1                              CMD
```

Figure 5.4   Menu Macro to Transfer to Alternate Drive

{?}~{quit}   Pauses for your selection of a file to retrieve. After you make your selection and press Return, the tilde completes the entry and retrieves the file.

Strictly speaking, the {quit} command is not necessary here, since retrieval of another file will cause the macro to quit as the current worksheet file is dropped. It is included, however, to start you on the habit of always ending a macro with a {quit} or branching command; to provide a visible signal as you read the macro that this is the end of the macro; and to permit use of this macro in a macro library that operates from outside of the current worksheet. (We discuss this in more detail later.)

If you select *B-DRIVE* at the menu choices, the macro operates in much the same way as the *A-DRIVE* selection. The *C-DRIVE* selection is somewhat different, however, including not only the drive, but a subdirectory path as well.

/fdC:\123\files\~   This is a line of the macro that you will want to change to your own 1-2-3 default directory. (It would be entirely coincidental if your default directory happened to be C:\123\files.)

You may want to include other menu choices for more 1-2-3 subdirectories. You can do that by moving the QUIT menubranch choice to the right, and writing another menu choice in its place. Just give the menu choice a title that corresponds to the particular subdirectory to which you want to switch (such as Sales, Cash, Inventory, and others).

The Graph Macro

Creating a graph in 1-2-3 can be a confusing and time-consuming experience, especially if it's something you do not have the occasion to do very often. Figure 5.5 shows a menu macro which automates and prompts you through the creation of line, bar, and pie graphs. This macro uses both the menu pause and the bracketed question mark pause. To help you to see exactly what this macro is doing, a /Graph Settings Sheet is included in Figure 5.6, showing the main /Graph menu and the full-screen settings you get when you select /Graph in Release 2.2.

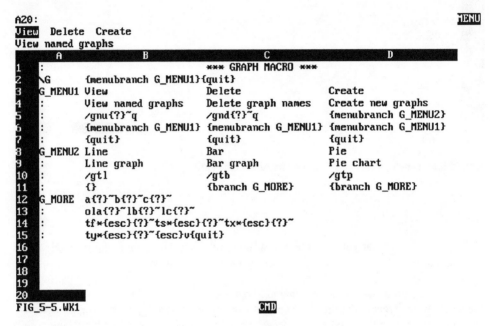

Figure 5.5   A Menu Macro to Automate Graphing

{menubranch G_MENU1}{quit}   Tells the macro to do a {menubranch} to the range name called G_MENU1. If you press Escape at the menu choices, the command {quit} is read and the macro quits. The three menu choices are *View*, *Delete*, and *Create*.

If you select *View*, the macro selects /Graph Name Use, then pauses for your selection of the graph to use. Assuming you have previously named two or more graphs using /Graph Name Create, you can now point to the graph of your choice and press Return. The graph will appear and remain on your screen until you press Return. At this point the macro selects Quit from the /Graph menu and does a {menubranch} back to the three choices: *View, Delete* and *Create*. If you press Escape after the menu appears, the macro reads the {quit} command and returns to Ready mode.

If you select *Delete*, the macro selects /Graph Name Delete, then pauses for your selection of the graph to delete. It then returns to the *View, Delete*, and *Create* menu.

If you select *Create*, the macro does a {menubranch} to the range name called

```
A2:                                                                      MENU
Type  X  A  B  C  D  E  F  Reset  View  Save  Options  Name  Group  Quit
Line  Bar  XY  Stack-Bar  Pie
                         ─── Graph Settings ───────────────────────
  Type: Line                    Titles: First
                                        Second
   X:                                   X axis
   A:                                   Y axis
   B:
   C:                                           Y scale:      X scale:
   D:                            Scaling        Automatic     Automatic
   E:                            Lower
   F:                            Upper
                                 Format        (G)           (G)
  Grid: None        Color: No    Indicator     Yes           Yes

    Legend:             Format:  Data labels:               Skip: 1
  A                     Both
  B                     Both
  C                     Both
  D                     Both
  E                     Both
  F                     Both
```

FIG_5-6.WK1

Figure 5.6 Graph Settings Sheet in Release 2.2

G_MENU2. If you press Escape at the menu choices, the command {quit} is read and the macro quits. The three menu choices are *Line*, *Bar*, and *Pie*.

Note: The command {menubranch G_MENU2} is followed by the command {menubranch G_MENU1}. Since pressing Escape at the second menu will cause the macro to continue where it left off after {menubranch G_MENU2}, having added the command {menubranch G_MENU1} at this point causes the macro to call up the first menu if you press Escape. Following this command is a {quit} command which causes the macro to quit if you press Escape a second time—effectively emulating the "backing-out" capability that you find in standard Lotus menus.

/gtl   Selects /Graph Type Line to establish Line as the graph type.

{ }   This is a pass-through macro command that the macro simply ignores to proceed to the next cell down. In this case it is not necessary, but is only provided to make the macro slightly more readable.

If you choose *Bar*, the macro Selects /Graph Type Bar to establish Bar as the graph type.

{branch G_MORE}   Rather than repeat the last four lines of the macro in this column and below the *Pie* choice, the {branch} command is provided here to branch over to the cell which has been range named G_MORE.

a{?}~b{?}~c{?}~   Selects the A-range, then pauses so you can paint in the first range of numbers you want graphed. If an A-range has already been established, you can either accept it by pressing Return or change it by pressing Backspace and highlighting a different range before pressing Return. The macro pauses for your input after making the menu selections for the B-range and C-range in this same way.

/ola{?}~lb{?}~lc{?}~   Selects Options Labels A-Range, B-Range, and C-Range in turn, pausing so you can paint in the first, second, and third ranges of legends.

tf*{esc}{?}~ts*{esc}{?}~tx*{esc}{?}~   Selects Titles First, then types an asterisk (this could have been any character) to ensure there is something in the prompt line, then presses Escape to clear the prompt line. (If there were nothing in the title to clear and a character were not typed here, the Escape command would back your macro up one level in the /Graph menu, which is not what you want.) The macro then pauses for your manual typing of the First graph title. The Second and X-range graph titles are completed in this same way.

ty*{esc}{?}~{esc}v{quit}   Selects Titles Y-Range, clears the prompt line and pauses for your entry of the Y-Range, than backs up one /Graph menu level and selects View to display the Graph. The macro will automatically pause until you press Return, at which point the macro quits.

Using {Indicate} and {Break} in a Graph Macro

Release 3 has a Quick Graph function which you can access with your cell pointer in any graphable matrix by pressing the F10 key. Later we will look at an elaborate macro you can use in Release 2.2 to simulate the Quick Graph function. In the meantime, you may be interested in a Graph macro, useable in Release 2.2 and 3 only, which gives you more choices than a Quick Graph feature can offer. This macro also introduces you to two new commands, {indicate} and {break} (Figure 5.7).

Like the Graph Macro described above, this macro begins by doing a {menubranch} to G_MENU1, offering you the choices to *View*, *Delete*, or *Create* a graph. The commands below these choices are identical to the previous version. This macro also has one new menu choice: *Quit*.

The second menu at G_MENU2 is essentially the same as the second menu described above, except that you are offered two additional choices: *XY* and *Stackbar*. The macro doesn't really begin to appear significantly different from the previous version until it reaches the branch location named G_MORE.

{indicate "Should include Left Titles (columnwise graph) or Top Titles (rowwise graph)"}   This is your first exposure to an {indicate} command. In Release 2.2 and 3, the {indicate} command can replace the *READY* indicator with a message of up to 80 characters. In this case, the message is provided to remind you that the range you are about to highlight for your graph should include titles along the left side of your graph matrix if you plan a columnwise graph, or titles along the top side if your plan a rowwise graph.

```
              A           B                 C                D              E           F
 1    :                         *** GRAPH MACRO ***
 2    \G         {menubranch G_MENU1}{quit}
 3    G_MENU1    View              Delete             Create          Quit
 4    :          View named graphs Delete graph names Create new graphs Quit the macro
 5    :          /gnu{?}~q         /gnd{?}~q          {menubranch G_MENU2} {quit}
 6    :          {menubranch G_MENU1} {menubranch G_MENU1} {menubranch G_MENU1}
 7    :          {quit}            {quit}             {quit}
 8    G_MENU2    Line              Bar                XY              Stack-Bar     Pie
 9    :          Line graph        Bar graph          XY graph        Stacked bar graph Pie chart
10    :          /gtl              /gtb               /gtx            /gts          /gtp
11    :          {}                {branch G_MORE}    {branch G_MORE} {branch G_MORE} {branch G_MORE}
12    G_MORE     {indicate "Should include Left Titles (columnwise graph) or Top Titles (rowwise graph)"}
13    :          g{?}~{menubranch G_MENU3}{indicate}{break}{quit}
14    G_MENU3    Columnwise        Rowwise            Adjust_Range
15    :          Use Cols as data rangUse Rows as data rangAdjust group range to include column or row titles
16    :          c                 r                  {esc}{?}~{menubranch G_MENU3}
17    :          {}                {branch G_MORE2}   {indicate}{break}{quit}
18    G_MORE2    {indicate "Use Top Titles (columnwise graph) or Left Titles (rowwise) or ENTER for None."}
19    :          olr{?}~ {indicate}tf*{esc}{?}~ts*{esc}{?}~tx*{esc}{?}~
20    :          ty*{esc}{?}~~{esc 2}v{quit}
21    GKEY       ~
22
```

FIG_5-7.WK1

Figure 5.7 A Graph Macro for Release 2.2 and 3

g{?}~{menubranch G_MENU3}{indicate}{break}{quit}   The macro selects Group, a new /Graph command choice available in Release 2.2 and 3, that allows you to highlight an entire range of numbers and titles to graph. After your input, the macro does a {menubranch} to G_MENU3, offering you the choices *Columnwise*, *Rowwise*, and *Adjust_Range*.

Note: If you press Escape after the menu comes up, the {indicate} command will return the indicator to *READY*, the {break} command will escape backwards through the /Graph menu until you are again at the Ready mode, and the macro will quit.

The *Columnwise* choice has an explanation line which advises you to make that selection if you plan to use columns as data ranges. If so, the macro types **c** for Columnwise. The null subroutine has no effect, and the macro continues at G_MORE2.

The *Rowwise* choice is to used if you plan to use rows as data ranges. If so, the macro types **r** for Rowwise and branches to G_MORE2.

The *Adjust_Range* choice is to allow you to adjust the group range to include column or row titles in case you neglected to do so at the first opportunity. If you select this choice, the macro escapes the current /Graph menu level to go back to the Group prompt. After you adjust the Group range and press Return, the macro again gives you the choices *Coulmnwise*, *Rowwise*, and *Adjust_Range*.

{indicate "Use Top Titles (columnwise graph) or Left Titles (rowwise) or ENTER for None."}   This {indicate} command applies to your graph legends, and prompts you to highlight the converse of the titles you included in your Group range. In other words, if you included a column of vertical titles in the Group range, you should highlight the top row of titles for your Legend. If you included a horizontal row of titles in the Group range, you will want to highlight a left column of titles for your Legend.

olr{?}~{indicate}tf*{esc}{?}~ts*{esc}{?}~tx*{esc}{?}~   Selects Options Legend Range and waits for your input, returns the Indicator to *READY* with an {indicate} command, then prompts you for your First, Second, and X Range Titles.

ty*{esc}{?}~{esc}v{quit}   This repeats the last line of the previous Graph Macro, allowing input of your Y-Range title. The macro then backs up one menu level and selects View so you can see the graph you have created. When you press Return after viewing the graph, the macro quits.

Find Left Side or Top

One feature which is not already available in 1-2-3 is the ability to jump to the left edge of the worksheet (staying in the same row) or to the top line of the worksheet (staying in the same column). Normally to jump to the left edge you must use Ctrl-LeftArrow repeatedly or End LeftArrow if all the cells in a row are either filled or entirely blank. Both of these techniques can be awkward, especially if your cell pointer is more than a few screens away from Column A.

Fortunately, you can create a macro like the one in Figure 5.8 to handle this for you. The Left Side or Top macro works by locking in your titles and pressing the Home key. If you lock in vertical titles at any location in the spreadsheet, pressing Home takes you to the top cell in your current column just to the right of the titles. With horizontal titles, pressing Home takes you to the left-most cell just below the titles in your current row. Try this manually and you'll see how the macro works.

{menubranch FMENU}{quit}   Pressing Alt-F will cause the menu choices *LEFT SIDE* and *TOP* to appear. Press L to jump to Column A or press T to jump to Row 1.

/wth{home}/wtc{quit}   When you select *LEFT SIDE*, the macro causes a /Worksheet Titles Horizontal sequence, and a press of the Home key to jump your cell pointer to the left-most cell under the newly created horizontal titles. This is followed by a /Worksheet Titles Clear and a Quit command.

/wtv{home}/wtc{quit}   If you select *TOP*, the macro causes a /Worksheet Titles Vertical sequence, and a press of the Home key to jump your cell pointer to the uppermost cell to the right of the newly created vertical titles. This is followed by a /Worksheet Titles Clear and a Quit command.

You will be impressed by how quickly this macro executes to create the titles, move the cell pointer, delete the titles, and quit. Take note, however: this macro will not work properly

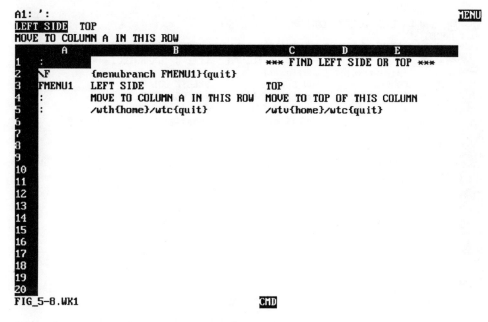

Figure 5.8 A Menu Macro to Find Left Side or Top

if you have already locked in your titles on the current worksheet. In fact, it will instantly clear away any titles you may have locked in, so use the macro judiciously.

If you tend to use titles often, you can precede this macro with another toggle macro to turn your titles off and back on automatically. See the Titles Toggle macro in Chapter 7.

Row or Column Delete with Unprotect

Sometimes the potential danger that a macro can do is so great that it becomes important to provide a safeguard against its accidental use. Menus, in addition to offering choices, can also offer safeguards; and the macro in Figure 5.9 provides an excellent example of this. The purpose of the macro is to facilitate the deletion of a column or row when the entire worksheet is protected.

{menubranch RMENU}{quit} Branches to the menu offering the choices *CANCEL*, *ROW_DELETE*, or *DELETE_COLUMN*. (We did not use *COLUMN_DELETE* because the word Cancel and the word Column both start with the letter C.)

The *CANCEL* choice simply leads to a {quit} command. It has been used as the first choice so that an accidental pressing of the Return key will not delete a row or column in error and to require that the operator make a conscious decision to press R or D before actually deleting a row or a column. You will notice that the explanation line below these two choices both say PROCEED AT RISK. Rather than using this line to explain what is about

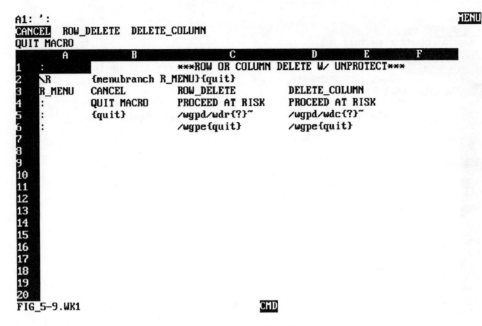

Figure 5.9   Row or Column Delete Macro with Unprotect

to happen, the line has been used to provide a warning for what is otherwise an obvious menu choice.

/wgpd/wdr{?}˜   Selects /Worksheet Global Protect Disable, then /Worksheet Delete Row, and pauses for painting in of the number of rows you want to delete.

/wgpe{quit}   Selects /Worksheet Global Protect Enable and quits, thus turning the global protection back on again. Of course, this macro would never be used in a worksheet that is not globally protected. Such use would result in a row or column delete as expected, but it would lock in global protection, resulting in the inability to make further entries until the global protection has been turned off or selected areas of the worksheet have received a /Range Unprotect.

Prune Number of Files

The macro in Figure 5.10 is an example of a menu macro which loops back on itself. This provides a handy way of getting your macro to repeat a series of keystrokes with just one manual keystroke on your part. The purpose of the macro is to eliminate unwanted worksheet, graph or print files to reduce the amount of memory they take up on your hard disk or floppies. Without a macro this exercise can take from 7 to 12 keystrokes per file. That means 70 to 120 keystrokes to eliminate ten files.

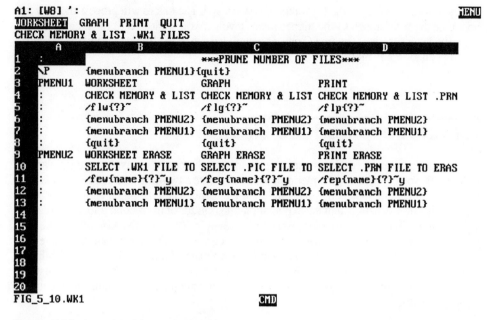

Figure 5.10 Looping Macro to Prune Number of Files

{menubranch PMENU1}{quit}   Branches to the menu choices *WORKSHEET, GRAPH, PRINT,* or *QUIT.* Under each of the first three choices is the explanation line, CHECK MEMORY AND LIST.

/flw{?}~   Types the /File List command, and selects Worksheet. This causes the screen to be replaced with a complete list of all of the worksheet files available for deletion. At this point you can scroll through the files to determine the amount of memory each file occupies. When you press Return, the screen will revert to its original view of the worksheet.

{menubranch PMENU2}   This command in cell B6 branches to the second menu choices *WORKSHEET ERASE, GRAPH ERASE, PRINT ERASE,* and *QUIT.* You are prompted to select the .WK1 file, .PIC file, or .PRN file you want to erase.

/few{name}{?}~y   Types /File Erase Worksheet, replaces the screen with a list of all of your .WK1 files, then pauses for your selection. When you press Return, the file you select will be erased.

{menubranch PMENU2}   This command in cell B12 branches again to the second menu. If you want to erase another worksheet file, you can press the letter W or Return at this point. You can repeat this looping exercise of pointing to the file to erase, pressing Return twice, then pointing to the next file to erase, pressing Return twice, and so on until all of your unwanted files are eliminated.

If you want to return to the first menu, press Escape. The macro will process the very last line, causing it to branch to the higher menu level. If you want to quit the macro instead, press the letter Q twice. The first Q causes a menubranch to the first menu and the second Q returns you to Ready mode.

Xtract File to Reduce Size

In addition to creating custom menus to provide for choices or to give safeguard warning statements, you can also use the menu structure to create a two-line instruction. This is done by having the menubranch call up a single-choice menu. Then the menu choice is used for the first line of instruction, and the explanation line is used for the second line of instruction. The macro in Figure 5.11 provides just such an example. This example also offers an excellent technique to enable your macro to leave the current worksheet file and continue processing in a separate file. Unless you have the advantage of a Macro Library capability as provided by Release 2.2 and 3, leaving the file that contains a processing macro will usually cause the processing macro to quit. Here we have a technique for continuing such a macro in a separate file.

A1: ':   `READY`

	A	B	C	D	E	F	G
1	:	***XTRACT FILE TO REDUCE SIZE***					
2	\X	/fs{?}~r{esc}					
3	:	{goto}XMENU1~{left}{up}					
4	:	'\0~/rnlr~{home}					
5	:	/fxfXTRACT~{?}~/frXTRACT~					
6	:	{menubranch XMENU1}{quit}					
7	XMENU1	PRESS RETURN					
8	:	THEN EXPLORE SPREADSHEET TO VERIFY NEW RANGE IS CORRECT.					
9	:	{?}{esc}{menubranch XMENU2}{menubranch XMENU1}					
10	XMENU2	REJECT	ACCEPT				
11	:	WRONG RANGE.	RANGE CORRECT. REPLACE FILE WITH XTRACT FILE.				
12	:	/fewXTRACT~y	/rnd\0~{goto}XMENU1~				
13	:	/fr{?}~	{left}{up}:~				
14	:	{quit}	/fs{esc}{?}~r{esc}				
15	:		/fewXTRACT~y{quit}				
16							
17							
18							
19							
20							

FIG_5_11.WK1

Figure 5.11   The Xtract File to Reduce Size Macro

The purpose of the macro is to prompt you through a /File Xtract to reduce the size of your worksheet. You may have had this situation: For no apparent reason, it seems that your file takes much longer to save or retrieve than expected or you suddenly receive a Memory Full message when you were sure that your file didn't take up that much memory. You press

End Home to jump to the lower right corner of your spreadsheet and find that an extraneous entry has been inserted in a far-away cell of your worksheet. You would imagine, of course, that simply erasing the offending data and resaving the file would fix the problem, but if the file has been saved at this size it cannot be reduced in this way. The fact that the file has been saved just once as a large file ensures that it will always be a large file, no matter how you try to reduce it by erasing cells or deleting rows or columns.

In Release 3, Lotus corrected the problem, so that erasing the extraneous entry reduces the worksheet size. This doesn't eliminate the need for /File Xtract in that Release, though, since doing a /File Xtract is still the best way to eliminate all of the unwanted data of a large file to reduce it to a new size.

Unfortunately, reducing the size of a file by extracting a portion of the file can be a dangerous undertaking that has caused many a Lotus expert to lose an important spreadsheet. The Xtract File macro not only steps you through the ticklish task of extracting a file from a worksheet, but it includes pauses and prompts to allow for double-checking to see that your extracted range is the range you intend.

/fs{?}˜r{esc}   Saves the file first, just in case the extract portion is not acceptable and you want to return to the original file. Note that we have repeated the convention of having the macro type the letter r for replace, followed by {esc} for non-replacing files.

{goto}XMENU1˜{left}{up}   This may look like an instruction to the macro to call up the menu named XMENU1, but look again. It is actually an instruction to the cell pointer to move to the cell with the range name XMENU1, then to move one cell to the left, then one cell up. In our example in Figure 5.11, this means the cell pointer will move to cell A6.

'\0˜/rnlr˜{home}   After the cursor has moved to this location, the macro types an apostrophe, a backslash, a zero (not the letter O), and presses Return. In other words, it types the backslash-zero \0 name for an autoexecuting macro. Then, at that same cell, it selects /Range Name Labels Right and presses Return, which effectively turns on the autoexecuting macro for the next time the file with this new macro starting at cell B6 is retrieved. The {home} command moves the cursor to the Home location.

/fxfXTRACT˜{?}˜/frXTRACT˜   Starts the /File Xtract of the file, giving it the temporary filename XTRACT. The question-mark pause allows you to paint in the area you want to extract. Be sure that the extract area includes this macro. This is very important. The filenamed XTRACT is then retrieved.

At this point, you would normally expect the macro to quit, but since the new XTRACT file includes the \0 autoexecuting macro just created, the macro actually picks up where it left off in the original file and continues.

{menubranch XMENU1}{quit}   Calls up a single-choice menu which reads *PRESS RETURN*, followed by the direction to *THEN EXPLORE SPREADSHEET TO VERIFY NEW*

RANGE IS CORRECT. This technique offers a long two-part instruction that can only be done in this way through the use of a single-choice menu.

{?}{esc}{menubranch XMENU2}{menubranch XMENU1}   Pauses to allow you to move around the extracted file to see that it contains everything you need. The Escape command is included to nullify any accidental typing you may do in one of the cells that might destroy an important formula or piece of data. The macro then calls up the menu choices *REJECT* and *ACCEPT*.

/fewXTRACT~y/fr{?}~{quit}   If you reject the extracted file, the macro erases that file and does a /File Retrieve, pausing for you to type in the original filename. Note the {quit} command is not really required, since the macro stops as soon as it leaves the present file to retrieve the original file.

/rnd\0~{goto}XMENU1~{left}{up}:~   If you choose *ACCEPT*, the macro will do a /Range Name Delete of the range name \0 so that the autoexec macro will not activate the next time you retrieve this file. Then the cursor moves to the cell called XMENU1, moves left one cell, and moves one cell up. At this point it replaces the \0 with a colon so it is not accidentally range named in the future.

/fs{esc}{?}r{esc}   Does a /File Save sequence, cancels out the XTRACT name offered, pauses for your entry of the original filename (or another filename if you'd like to keep the original file in tact), and presses Replace and Escape.

/fewXTRACT~y{quit}   Finally, the macro erases the temporary file named XTRACT and quits. Now if you press End Home, you should find that your file has been reduced to the new size you require.

Summary

This chapter provided an overview of the macro programming commands. You were introduced to macro commands which pause for an entry as well as custom menus which pause for a menu choice. The macros in this chapter are summarized as:

- The Data Entry macro that automates input of data moving down a column.
- The Save and Print macro that includes a simple example of a subroutine.
- A Menu macro to facilitate the combining of several files into the current worksheet.
- A Graph macro to automate the creation of line, bar, and pie graphs.
- Another Graph macro, usable in Release 2.2 and 3 only, that simulates the Quick Graph feature of Release 3, though with more choices.
- A macro to jump your cursor to the left-most column or the top-most row, regardless of where you are in your worksheet.
- A Menu macro to delete a row or column when Global Protection is on.

- A Looping macro to prune the number of files you have in order to save space on your floppy or hard disk.
- A way to reduce the size of your worksheet with an Xtract File macro.

In Chapter 6 we introduce and explore several techniques involved in the art of range naming.

6

THE ART OF RANGE NAMING

Scope

In the last chapter we introduced a few conventions and recommendations regarding the use of named ranges. In this chapter we will review ways to get more out of range naming, different kinds of macros available through the use of range names, and ways to give your current cell a temporary place-marker.

Jump to Upper Right Corner

The macro in Figure 6.1 is an example of a macro which marks your place in the worksheet, jumps to a different place in the worksheet, then prompts you to stay there or return to your original location. In this case, your cell pointer jumps to the upper right corner of the worksheet—a feature not normally found in 1-2-3.

/rncJHERE~~/rndJHERE~/rncJHERE~~   This series of commands may appear a little redundant. First the macro types /Range Name Create JHERE Return and accepts the location offered by pressing Return. So if the range name already exists, this command just re-

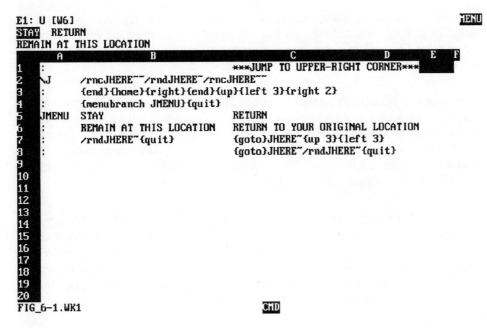

```
E1: U [W6]                                                                 MENU
STAY   RETURN
REMAIN AT THIS LOCATION
        A            B                       C                D        E    F
1       :                            ***JUMP TO UPPER-RIGHT CORNER***
2      \J           /rncJHERE~~/rndJHERE~/rncJHERE~~
3       :           {end}{home}{right}{end}{up}{left 3}{right 2}
4       :           {menubranch JMENU}{quit}
5      JMENU        STAY                     RETURN
6       :           REMAIN AT THIS LOCATION  RETURN TO YOUR ORIGINAL LOCATION
7       :           /rndJHERE~{quit}         {goto}JHERE~{up 3}{left 3}
8       :                                    {goto}JHERE~/rndJHERE~{quit}
9
10
11
12
13
14
15
16
17
18
19
20
FIG_6-1.WK1                              CMD
```

Figure 6.1   A Macro to Jump to the Upper Right Corner

names the range name at the already established location. (If the range name does not exist, the range name is then established at the current cell.) Then the macro executes a /Range Name Delete of the same JHERE range name. In the third use of /Range Name, the macro once again does a /Range Name Create of JHERE, this time definitely establishing the location of the range name at the current cell.

This may seem like a lot to go through to get the name JHERE assigned to the current cell, but it is an important convention that should be used whenever you are having your macro do any range naming.

You may wonder why we bother with the first step. After all, the second step will delete any previously established use of the range name, so why not just start with a /Range Name Delete before the final /Range Name Create? This would be a great idea, except that the range name may *not* already exist, and trying to delete a range name that does not exist will cause an error and your macro will stop. So to cover all contingencies, create (or recreate) the range name, delete the range name, and finally create the range name in the desired location.

Some 1-2-3 users have suggested that the same effect could be achieved by using /Range Name Create Backspace, followed by a description of the range location and a Return. This does work, but it can create problems in Release 2.0 and 2.01. If the range name you are trying to relocate happens to share the same cell coordinates with another range name, moving one range name in this way will inadvertently move the other range name as well. This "tag-along" move of range names can wreak havoc with your worksheet, so it is not recommended.

Incidentally, when typing the **/rnc~~ /rnd~ /rnc~~** sequence, notice that the creation of a range name requires two tildes, whereas the deletion requires only one. As mentioned in an earlier chapter, the most common error in writing macros is the tendency to leave out required tildes. This tendency seems to come up often in the range naming sequence, so expect that this may be the problem if your macro stops at this point.

{end}{home}{right}{end}{up}{left 3}{right 2}　　Since pressing End Home always jumps the cell pointer to the lower right corner of the worksheet, all we have to do to program the macro to jump farther, to the upper right corner, is to move one cell to the right—which is guaranteed to be in an empty column—press End UpArrow to go to the top of the worksheet, then move left one cell. The final {left 3} and {right 2} commands are included to position the cell pointer more towards the center of the screen.

{menubranch JMENU}{quit}　　Calls up the menu choices *STAY* and *RETURN*. If you select *STAY*, the macro deletes the temporary place-marker named JHERE and quits. If you select *RETURN*, the macro processes a {goto} command to go back to your original location JHERE, moves up three cells and left three cells to adjust the cell pointer more towards the center of the screen, then uses {goto}JHERE~ to return again to your original place-marker. Finally, the macro deletes the range name JHERE and quits.

Using {Windowsoff} and {Paneloff}

This is a good place to explore the {windowsoff} and {paneloff} commands. The {windowsoff} command is used to suppress refreshing of the worksheet during operation of a macro, and the {paneloff} command is used turn off the display of instructions in the upper panel. Both of these commands can be thought of as instructions to freeze an area of the screen in its current state.

Refer now to a modified version of the Jump to Upper Right Corner macro in Figure 6.2. The {windowsoff} and {paneloff} commands have been added to the first line of the macro and to the first line under the RETURN choice of the menu. The {panelon} and {windowson} commands have been added to the fourth line of the macro. Here's why:

{windowsoff}{paneloff}　　These commands accomplish three things: the annoying flicker of a typical macro can be completely eliminated, the macro will operate faster, and you will be less likely to become disoriented because the screen stays unchanged while it is processing commands.

{panelon}{windowson}　　Although turning on the windows and panels can be done in any order you like, typing {panelon} before {windowson} is recommended to suppress one last flicker of the window which would occur if the command read {windowson}{panelon} instead. The upper panel is turned back on just before the {menubranch} command so you can see the menu choices *STAY* and *RETURN*. The windows are turned back on at this point so you can see the upper left corner of the worksheet where the previous line of the macro sent your cell pointer.

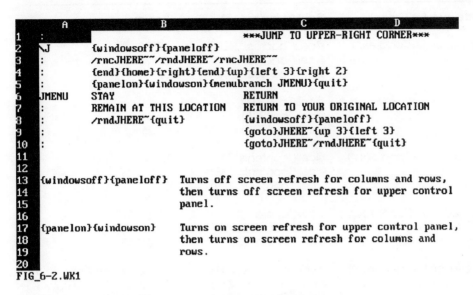

```
A1: ':                                                              READY

         A              B                    C              D
1    :                              ***JUMP TO UPPER-RIGHT CORNER***
2    \J      {windowsoff}{paneloff}
3    :       /rncJHERE~~/rndJHERE~/rncJHERE~~
4    :       {end}{home}{right}{end}{up}{left 3}{right 2}
5    :       {panelon}{windowson}{menubranch JMENU}{quit}
6    JMENU   STAY                         RETURN
7    :       REMAIN AT THIS LOCATION      RETURN TO YOUR ORIGINAL LOCATION
8    :       /rndJHERE~{quit}             {windowsoff}{paneloff}
9    :                                    {goto}JHERE~{up 3}{left 3}
10   :                                    {goto}JHERE~/rndJHERE~{quit}
11
12
13   {windowsoff}{paneloff}   Turns off screen refresh for columns and rows,
14                            then turns off screen refresh for upper control
15                            panel.
16
17   {panelon}{windowson}     Turns on screen refresh for upper control panel,
18                            then turns on screen refresh for columns and
19                            rows.
20
FIG_6-2.WK1
```

Figure 6.2 Modified Macro to Jump to Upper Right Corner

{windowsoff}{paneloff}   Refer to cell C8. If you select *RETURN*, the first command once again turns off changes to the main screen, and paneloff turns off changes to the upper panel. You may wonder, then, how you are able to watch your cell pointer jump instantly back to the original cell—especially since if you glance farther down the macro, you will notice that the macro ends without a corresponding {windowson}{panelon}. This is because ending a macro automatically returns the windows and panel to an "on" condition; and {windowson}, whether spelled out or automatic, will always cause the screen to display the end result of any instructions given to the cell pointer while the windows were off.

Using the @Cellpointer Command

Two of the most important @function commands you will be using in macros are @cell and @cellpointer. Both @functions return information about the cell based on one of several attributes. The difference between the two is that the @cell function returns information about a designated cell, while @cellpointer returns information about the current cell location.

Table 6.1 provides three examples each for all of the attributes using the @cellpointer and @cell functions. The first example refers to protected cell Z37 (width 12) which is also named HERE, and has the centered label ^Total in it. The second example refers to unprotected cell Z38, is formatted with the currency format, and contains an @sum formula that totals $1230.67. The third example refers to cell Z39, which is also the first empty cell of an entirely blank column Z39..Z42 named EMPTY.

Table 6.1   Use of the @cell and @cellpointer Functions

@cellpointer (String)	@cell(string,range)	Returns
@cellpointer("address")	@cell("address",HERE) @cell("address",Z38) @cell("address",EMPTY)	$Z$37 $Z$38 $Z$39
@cellpointer("col")	@cell("col",Z37) @cell("col",Z38) @cell("col",Z39)	26 26 26
@cellpointer("contents")	@cell("contents",Z37) @cell("contents",Z38) @cell("contents",Z39)	Total $1,230.67 0
@cellpointer("coord") (Release 3 only)	@cell("coord",Z37) @cell("coord",Z38) @cell("coord",Z39)	$A:$Z$37 $A:$Z$38 $A:$Z$39
@cellpointer("filename") (Release 2.2 and 3 only)	@cell("filename",Z37) @cell("filename",Z38) @cell("filename",Z39)	C:\123\FILES\COST.WK3 C:\123\FILES\COST.WK3 C:\123\FILES\COST.WK3
@cellpointer("format") (Returns "A" in Release 3 if format is automatic)	@cell("format",Z37) @cell("format",Z38) @cell("format",Z39)	G (default) C2 ($, 2 dec) (blank)
@cellpointer("protect")	@cell("protect",Z37) @cell("protect",Z38) @cell("protect",Z39)	1 (protected) 0 (unprotctd) 1 (protected)
@cellpointer("prefix")	@cell("prefix",Z37) @cell("prefix",Z38) @cell("prefix",Z39)	^ (blank) (blank)
@cellpointer("row")	@cell("row",Z37) @cell("row",Z38) @cell("row",Z39)	37 38 39
@cellpointer("sheet") (Release 3 only)	@cell("sheet",Z37) @cell("sheet",Z38) @cell("sheet",Z39)	1 1 1
@cellpointer("type")	@cell("type",Z37) @cell("type",Z38) @cell("type",Z39)	v (for value) l (for label) b (for blank)
@cellpointer("width")	@cell("width",Z37) @cell("width",Z38) @cell("width",Z39)	12 12 12

Cell Z37:	**Total**	<----- ^Total
Cell Z38:	**$1,230.67**	<----- @sum(Z30..Z36)
Cell Z39:		<----- (blank cell)

Once the @cell formula is entered in one of the forms shown above, 1-2-3 will convert the range to a beginning-ending form, like this: Z38..Z38.

Using the {Let} Command

The @cell and @cellpointer functions are most useful in macros when combined with the {let} function. The {let} command is like saying "Let this cell *become like* this cell." Some examples of the {let} command are as:

{let J27,Z39}	J27 will show the contents of Z39
{let J27,999}	J27 will show the number 999
{let J27,"Sales"}	J27 will show the word Sales
{let J27,"Sales"&"man"}	J27 will show the word Salesman
{let J27,@cell("width",Z39)}	J27 will show the width of Z39
{let J27,27+1}	Value in J27 increases by 1

As you can see, the first example **{let J27,Z39}** can be used to accomplish the same thing as the /Copy command, except that with a copy command you specify the FROM cell first, followed by the TO cell, like this: **/cZ39~J27~**. On the other hand, using the {let} command, you specify the destination cell first, followed by what you want to go into the destination cell. The {let} command is also visibly faster than the copy command. Unfortunately, the {let} command only returns a label or a value to the TO cell. If your macro requires that either the formula or the cell format of the FROM cell be copied, it is best to revert back to the standard Copy command.

A Self-Modifying File Retrieve Macro

You can do quite a bit more with the {let} command than you can with the copy command, however, especially when used with @cell or @cellpointer. The /File Retrieve macro in Figure 6.3 shows how the @cellpointer formula works in conjunction with the {let} command. The purpose of the macro is to allow you to accomplish a /File Retrieve of a file by pointing to a cell containing the filename. This is also our first example that uses the principle of the *self-modifying macro*.

A self-modifying macro rewrites its later lines before it runs them. In this case the first line of the macro rewrites its third line based on the location of the cell pointer when you press Alt-F. The macro then selects /File Retrieve, types the contents of the modified line, then enters it with the tilde in the last line.

Figure 6.3 includes a simple table of filenames in the current directory. Of course, as you

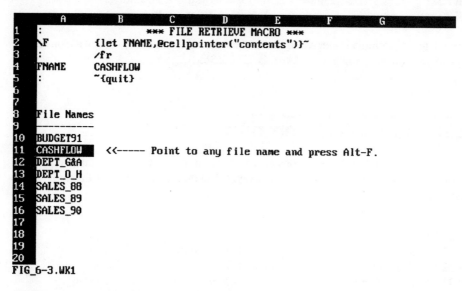

FIG_6-3.WK1

Figure 6.3   A File Retrieve Macro Using @cellpointer

recreate this macro, you will want to change the table to reflect files from your own current directory.

This macro is most effective in an AUTO123 file that retrieves automatically when you first start your 1-2-3 session. The idea here is to list only the files you visit most often, thereby facilitating your /File Retrieve of specific worksheets at start-up.

{let FNAME,@cellpointer("contents")}~   Causes the cell named FNAME to display the contents of the current cell. If, for example, you point to the cell containing the filename CASHFLOW before pressing Alt-F, this command will cause the word CASHFLOW to be entered into the cell of the macro itself named FNAME.

/fr   Selects /File Retrieve. If you want to have this macro designate a specific directory path, you can modify it by adding an asterisk and {escape} command, followed by the file directory. For example, you may change the line to read: **/fr*{esc}c:\123\files** .

CASHFLOW   Although we have entered a filename in this cell named FNAME, the macro will work just as well if FNAME is blank, since the macro fills it in with the first {let} command.

~{quit}   The tilde completes the command, whereupon the new file is retrieved. Unless you are working with a Macro Library macro that operates from outside the current worksheet file, the macro will quit at this point without the {quit} command. We have included it here as a convention as to cover the use of this macro in a Macro Library as discussed in Chapter 7.

Using @cellpointer to Create a Place-marker

The @cellpointer formula can also be used in conjunction with {let} to create a place-marker. Rather than use the /Range Name Create method to give a range name to the current cell as described above, you can use @cellpointer("address") to store the absolute address of the current cell in another named cell, then use the {goto} command to return to the stored location.

If, for example, you are on cell AB237, having your macro run the command {let UHERE,@cellpointer("address")} will cause the cell named UHERE to display the absolute address of the current cell like this: $AB$237. Once that information is stored in UHERE, your macro can move you around the spreadsheet and return to your original location by executing a {goto} command, then doing a subroutine branch to UHERE to read the cell address $AB$237, and finally continuing after the subroutine call by typing a tilde to complete the {goto} sequence.

Figure 6.4 shows two simple examples using place-markers. In the first example, the current cell is range named AHERE using /Range Name Create, /Range Name Delete, and /Range Name Create again. After a macro pause that allows you to move anywhere in the worksheet, the macro executes a {goto} command to go to AHERE, the originally range-named location. In the second example, the current cell is not range-named. Rather, the cell which was prenamed UHERE is made to display the current cell pointer address. After a macro pause, the macro executes a {goto} command, followed by a *subroutine* call to UHERE, where the macro reads the original cell address before it returns to enter a tilde, jumping you to your starting point.

```
A1: [W8] ':                                                          READY

         A        B        C        D        E        F        G
1    :                    *** FIRST EXAMPLE OF PLACE-MARKER ***
2    \F        /rncFHERE~~/rndFHERE~/rncFHERE~~
3    :         {?}
4    :         {goto}FHERE~
5    :         {quit}
6    :
7    :                    *** USING LET TO CREATE PLACE-MARKER ***
8    \U        {let UHERE,@cellpointer("address")}
9    :         {?}
10   :         {goto}{UHERE}~
11   :         {quit}
12   :
13   UHERE     $B$18                <--- UHERE is used as a subroutine.
14   :         {return}
15
16
17
18
19
20
FIG_6-4.WK1
```

Figure 6.4 Two Examples Using Place-markers

Note: In the first example, the final {goto} command is followed by the range name AHERE, while in the second example, the {goto} command is followed by a bracketed subroutine call to the range name UHERE. The important difference is that the second example requires that UHERE be surrounded by brackets. If you neglect to do this, the macro will not return to your original location, but instead will jump to B9, the cell which was pre-named UHERE.

A Place-marker Macro to List and Print Range Name Table

The macro in Figure 6.5 provides a good example of the use of the {let} command with @cellpointer("address") to create a place-marker. The purpose of the macro is to store the current cell address, create a table of all your range names beyond the End Home position, print the table, and return to your original cell location.

```
A1: ':                                                                    READY
```

```
              A        B        C         D         E        F
1     :                   *** LIST & PRINT RANGE NAME TABLE ***
2     \L        {windowsoff}{paneloff}
3     :         {let LHERE,@cellpointer("address")}
4     :         {end}{home}{right}{end}{up}/rnt~
5     :         /wcs12~{right}/wcs12~{left}
6     :         /ppr{bs}.{end}{down}{panelon}{windowson}{right}{?}~
7     :         {windowsoff}{paneloff}
8     :         agpq/re{end}{down}{right}~
9     :         {goto}{LHERE}~
10    :         {left @min(@cellpointer("col")-1,3)}
11    :         {up @min(@cellpointer("row")-1,5)}
12    :         {goto}{LHERE}~{quit}
13    LHERE     $B$8
14    :         {return}
15
16
17
18
19
20
FIG_6-5.WK1
```

Figure 6.5 Macro to List and Print Range Name Table

{windowsoff}{paneloff}   Turns off changes to the main worksheet area and the upper panel, thus suppressing flicker and speeding up the macro.

{let LHERE,@cellpointer("address")}   Causes the cell named LHERE at B14 to display the address of the current cell pointer location.

{end}{home}{right}{end}{up}/rnt~   Moves to the End Home location and to the right one column, then jumps to the top-most cell (row 1) of that column where the macro executes a /Range Name Table command.

/wcs12~{right}/wcs12~{left}   Selects /Worksheet Columnwidth Set 12 in the current column and the column to the right, then moves back to the left again.

/ppr{bs}.{end}{down}{panelon}{windowson}{right}{?}~   Selects /Print Printer Range, presses Backspace to free the cell pointer, presses the Period (.) key to lock in the pointer, highlights the range-name table, turns on the panel and windows, and pauses so you can view the table before printing. If you decide to keep the table in place without printing, you can press Ctrl-Break at this point.

{windowsoff}{paneloff}   Turns off the windows and panel to complete the macro without screen flicker.

agpq/re{end}{down}{right}~   Selects /Align Go Page Quit, then /Range Erases the range-name table.

{goto}{LHERE}~   Presses the F5 Goto key, then does a subroutine branch to read the address in LHERE, and enters that address with the tilde.

{left @min(@cellpointer("col")-1,3)}   This is an interesting command designed to reposition your current cell more towards the center of the screen. In addition to the ability to add values to the directional commands as in {left 19} or {up 7}, you can also add @functions which equate to values. Using the @min function in combination with @cellpointer("col"), you can cause your cell pointer to be moved either to the left one cell less than the number of the current column, or to the left three cells. In other words, if you are in the second column (Column B), this command will move you 2 minus 1 = 1 cell to the left. If you are in the third column (Column C), you will be moved 3 minus 1 = 2 cells to the left. In any column greater than C, you will be moved three cells to the left.

{up @min(@cellpointer("row")-1,5)}   Moves your cell pointer either up one cell less than the number of the current row, or up five cells. In other words, if you are in Row 4, this command will move you 4 minus 1 = 3 cells up. In any row greater than five, you will be moved five cells up.

{goto}{LHERE}~{quit}   Returns you to your original cell again. Since moving your cell pointer to the left and up several cells had the effect of moving your original cell to the right and down several cells, your original cell was positioned more towards the center of the screen. This line of the macro returns you to the original cell and the macro quits.

$B$8   This cell, range-named LHERE, is used as a subroutine in the line above. It can be blank before your run the macro, since the macro writes to it with the {let} command in the second line.

{return}   The {return} command is usually added at the end of a subroutine. It tells the macro to return to the place where it left off before it ran the subroutine, which in this case happens to be at the tilde before the final {quit} command.

We will be using the @min(@cellpointer) technique often in place-marker macros throughout this book. You will find that this technique keeps you from being relocated to the upper left corner of your screen when you return to your original cell.

Viewing a Named Range

A place-marker is not always required to leave your present location and return with a single keystroke. In some cases, the built-in features of 1-2-3 will allow a kind of View-and-Return operation. For example, you can visit cell A1 by pressing the F5 Goto key, then the Home key. When you want to return, press Escape. You can visit the End Home location in the same way by pressing the F5 Goto key, then End Home, and finally Escape.

Here's a little trick to view a named range and Return. Press /Range Name Create, press the F3 Name key twice to get a full-screen view of all your range names, select or type in an existing range name, and press Return. The cell pointer will jump to the range name and highlight it. You can then view all four corners of the range by pressing the Period [.] key. When you want to return to your original location, press Return. This will complete the /Range Name Create sequence, recreating the range name in its previously established location, whereupon your cell pointer will automatically jump back to the original cell.

Explore Four Corners of the Worksheet

The macro in Figure 6.6 allows you to view all four corners of your entire worksheet, then returns to your original cell when you press Return. In the process, it makes clever use of the /Range Name Create sequence to highlight a range (from Home to End Home) while providing you with an instructional prompt.

We have covered another way of creating an instructional prompt by doing a {menubranch} to a single-choice menu. For example, your macro may have the instruction **{menubranch CMENU}**, where CMENU looks like this:

CMENU   **PRESS RETURN.**
                   THEN PAINT IN THE RANGE.

The drawback of this type of instructional prompt, however, is that it requires you to press Return before you can proceed with any other activity in the macro.

The Xplore 4 Corners macro in Figure 6.6 provides allows you to press the Period key, the pointer keys, or the Return key in response to what looks like an instructional prompt, though it is actually a range name being created.

{paneloff}   Suppresses screen flicker and the *Enter name* prompt that would otherwise appear at the next macro instruction.

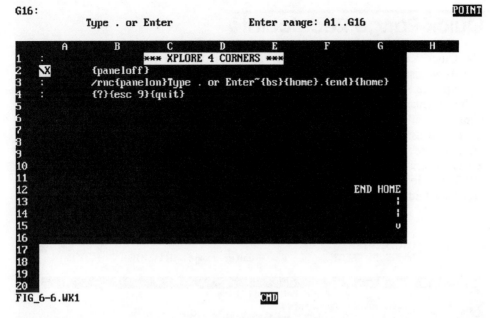

Figure 6.6   Macro to Explore 4 Corners of the Worksheet

/rnc{panelon}Type . or Enter~{bs}{home}.{end}{home}   Selects /Range Name Create without displaying the *Enter name* prompt, then turns on the upper panel to type the range name *TYPE . OR ENTER.*

If you have a worksheet with an End Home position of G147 for example, the upper panel will look something like this in Release 2, 2.01, and 2.2:

> **Type . or Enter   Enter Range: A1..G147**

Unfortunately, in Release 3, the {panelon} command restores the /Range Name Create prompt, so the upper panel will look like this:

> **Enter name to create: Type . or Enter   Enter Range: A:A1..A:G147**

This is a unique use of a 15-character range name (the maximum length), which even in Release 3 will not look like a range name at all, but rather like an instruction.

   For the range, the macro presses Backspace to free the pointer, Home to jump to cell A1, the Period (.) key to lock in the pointer, and End Home to highlight to the lower right corner of the worksheet.

{?}{esc 9}{quit}   The macro pauses so the user can either type the Period (.) key to explore the four corners of the worksheet, or press Enter to end the macro. If the user presses Enter, the macro escapes from the /Range Name Create menu without input, and returns to Ready.

Quick Range Recalculate

The Quick Range Recalc macro in Figure 6.7 is another example of a macro that imbeds an instruction directly into the name of the range during a /Range Name Create sequence.

If you'd like to calculate a single cell in your spreadsheet, try pressing F2 Edit Return. Assuming the cell does not depend on serial calculation of several other cells, you'll see the cell recalculate instantly. This little trick is much faster than pressing F9 Calc to calculate the entire spreadsheet when all you're interested in for the moment is how one cell calculates. It works because pressing F2 Edit Return creates the same effect as entering the formula in the cell for the first time. Since typing a formula for the first time returns current information, pressing F2 Edit effectively updates, or recalculates, the current cell.

```
H16: (F2) @SUM(H9..H15)                                              POINT
           RANGE TO CALC?              Enter range: H11..H16

        A       B        C        D        E        F        G        H
1    :              *** QUICK RANGE RECALC ***
2    \Q     {windowsoff}{paneloff}
3    :      /rncRANGE TO CALC?~~/rndRANGE TO CALC?~
4    :      /rnc{panelon}RANGE TO CALC?~{windowson}{?}~
5    :      {paneloff}{windowsoff}{recalc RANGE TO CALC?}
6    :      /rndRANGE TO CALC?~{quit}
7
8
9              JAN      FEB      MAR      APR      MAY      JUN     TOTAL
10          -------- -------- -------- -------- -------- -------- =========
11   EAST    1285.00  1372.00  1459.00  1546.00  1633.00  1720.00  9015.00
12   WEST    1092.25  1166.20  1240.15  1314.10  1388.05  1462.00  7662.75
13   NORTH   1413.50  1509.20  1604.90  1700.60  1796.30  1892.00  9916.50
14   SOUTH   1484.18  1584.66  1685.15  1785.63  1886.12  1966.60  9592.33
15          -------- -------- -------- -------- -------- -------- =========
16   TOTAL   5274.93  5632.06  5989.20  6346.33  5903.47  7040.60 36186.58
17
18
19
20
FIG_6-7.WK1                              CMD
```

Figure 6.7 The Quick Range Recalc Macro

In that same way, copying a range to itself creates the effect of entering the formulas in that range as if for the first time. Therefore, copying a range to itself will update, or recalculate, that range. Unfortunately, there is no easy way to copy a range to itself from the bottom of the range—which is usually where your pointer is located when you decide you want it recalculated. From that position you will have to move to the top of the range, execute the /Copy command, paint in the range to copy from the top down, then move back to your original location at the bottom of the range.

Instead of copying a range to itself, you may want to use the macro {recalc} command as presented in the Quick Range Recalc macro in Figure 6.7.

{windowsoff}{paneloff}   Suppresses screen flicker and the *Enter name* prompt that would otherwise appear at the /Range Name Create sequence.

/rncRANGE TO CALC?~~/rndRANGE TO CALC?~   Creates a range name called *RANGE TO CALC?*, then deletes that same range name.

/rnc{panelon}RANGE TO CALC?~{windowson}{?}~   Starts by doing a /Range Name Create, then turns on the panel in midcommand to type *RANGE TO CALC?*. The main screen is then turned on, and the macro pauses so you can paint in the range you want calculated. In Release 2, 2.01, and 2.2, the upper panel will look like this:

RANGE TO CALC?   **Enter Range:**

In Release 3, the {panelon} command restores the /Range Name Create prompt, so the upper panel will look like this:

Enter name to create: RANGE TO CALC?   **Enter Range:**

It looks as if you are being prompted to enter the range you want to calculate, when in fact you are being prompted to enter the range of the area to be named *RANGE TO CALC?*. The main advantage here is that you can paint in the range from the bottom up if that is more convenient.

{paneloff}{windowsoff}{recalc RANGE TO CALC?}   Turns off the upper panel and main screen, then recalculates the range named *RANGE TO CALC?*.

/rndRANGE TO CALC?~{quit}   The macro ends by deleting the range name and processing a {quit} command. This is done primarily so your worksheet is not cluttered with unnecessary range names.

You will probably be surprised at how quickly this macro runs, considering all that it has to do. Immediately after you press Alt-Q, you will be prompted for the range to calculate and the recalculation seems instantaneous.

You can also add conditions and number of iterations to the {recalc} command if you like. You could, for example, instruct your macro to recalculate a range until the first cell of the range is greater than 100, or until 20 iterations have been performed—whichever comes sooner. That command might look like this:

{recalc RANGE TO CALC?,@cellpointer("contents")>100,20}

Although this kind of additional magic is fairly advanced and the average 1-2-3 user will not have occasion to use it, it gives you some idea of the kind of power you can have using the {recalc} command. In the meantime, you can start using the Quick Range Recalc macro right away.

There is one *very important* caveat, however, which must be taken into consideration in your use of this macro. It is critical that you keep in mind that this macro assumes there are no serial calculations outside of the range which must be recalculated before the formulas in the range will calculate properly. If you are not sure about this, or if the calculation involves something more that just a quick look at a range, you should revert to the F9 Calc key to calculate the entire file instead. In any case, it is always a good idea to do a final F9 Calc of your worksheet before you either save it or print it out for others.

Improving on the /Range Transpose Command

The /Range Name Create method of establishing an instructional prompt, using /Range Name Create as seen in the Xplore 4 Corners macro and Quick Range Recalc macro can also be used in a macro designed to improve on the /Range Transpose command.

The /Range Transpose command is used to copy columns to rows, or rows to columns. This can be especially handy if you decide after creating a matrix of headings and data that you want to transpose the entire matrix. An example of this is seen in Figure 6.8.

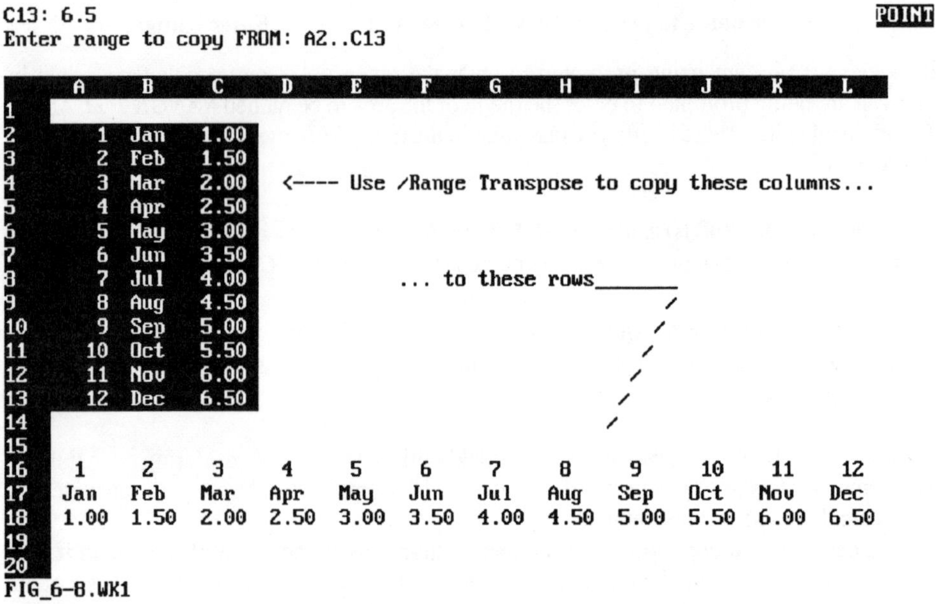

```
C13: 6.5                                                                POINT
Enter range to copy FROM: A2..C13

     A     B     C     D     E     F     G     H     I     J     K     L
1
2      1   Jan   1.00
3      2   Feb   1.50
4      3   Mar   2.00      <---- Use /Range Transpose to copy these columns...
5      4   Apr   2.50
6      5   May   3.00
7      6   Jun   3.50
8      7   Jul   4.00             ... to these rows_____
9      8   Aug   4.50                                  /
10    9   Sep   5.00                                  /
11   10   Oct   5.50                                 /
12   11   Nov   6.00                                /
13   12   Dec   6.50                               /
14                                                /
15
16     1     2     3     4     5     6     7     8     9    10    11    12
17   Jan   Feb   Mar   Apr   May   Jun   Jul   Aug   Sep   Oct   Nov   Dec
18   1.00  1.50  2.00  2.50  3.00  3.50  4.00  4.50  5.00  5.50  6.00  6.50
19
20
FIG_6-8.WK1
```

Figure 6.8 Transposing a Matrix of Columns to Rows

Unfortunately, this operation returns you to your original location and leaves the original matrix in tact. You may prefer to use a macro that accomplishes the /Range Transpose, erases the original matrix, and leaves the cell pointer at your new matrix. Such a macro is shown in Figure 6.9.

Here's how the macro works.

{windowsoff}{paneloff} Suppresses screen flicker and the *Enter name* prompt that would otherwise appear at the /Range Name Create sequence.

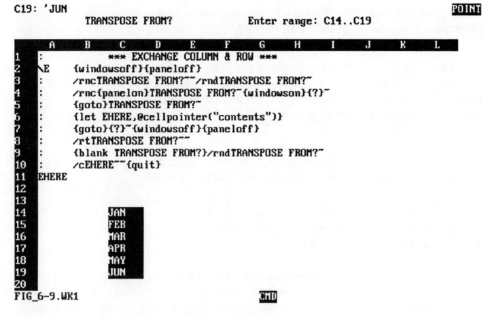

FIG_6-9.WK1

Figure 6.9 A Macro to Exchange Row and Column

/rncTRANSPOSE FROM?~~/rndTRANSPOSE FROM?~ Creates a range name called *TRANSPOSE FROM?*, then deletes that same range name.

/rnc{panelon}TRANSPOSE FROM?~{windowson}{?}~ Starts by doing a /Range Name Create, then turns on the panel in midcommand to type **TRANSPOSE FROM?**. The main screen is then turned on, and the macro pauses for the range you want to transpose.

{let EHERE,@cellpointer("contents")} Although this may seem like a use of the {let} command with @cellpointer as a place-marker to store the current address in EHERE, it is actually a way of storing the value of the current cell in EHERE for later use. It is exactly the same as selecting /Range Value and pressing Return for the *FROM* prompt and entering EHERE for the *TO* prompt (/rv~EHERE~).

{goto}{?}~{windowsoff}{paneloff} Prompts you for the location to transpose the range to, moves to that location, and turns off the windows and panel to suppress screen flicker.

/rtTRANSPOSE FROM?~~ Selects Range Transpose, then uses the range name *TRANSPOSE FROM?* as the range to transpose. The second tilde tells 1-2-3 to transpose to the current location to which you have just moved.

{blank TRANSPOSE FROM?}/rndTRANSPOSE FROM?~ This is the first example using the {blank} command. It is the exact macro equivalent to /Range Erase, and will accept a single cell address, a range, or a range name. In this case, we are blanking (erasing) the range named *TRANSPOSE FROM?*. The macro then selects /Range Name Delete to eliminate the range name *TRANSPOSE FROM?*.

/cEHERE˜˜{quit}   Copies the value stored in EHERE to the current cell. This is necessary in case the starting cell of the range you are transposing FROM is the same as the starting cell of the range you are transposing TO. If they are the same and the {blank} command erased that cell, copying the value stored in EHERE will restore it. The macro quits at this point.

The last cell of the macro has been range named EHERE, and it is used as the place to store the value of the starting cell of the range to transpose FROM.

The Copy Macros

You may have experienced this frustration. You want to copy data from cell B2 to cells B4, B6, B8, and B10. In other words, you want to copy to every other cell. So you select /Copy and press Return, then move down two cells to A6 and again press Return. So far so good. But the cursor has jumped back up to cell B2, so you press DownArrow twice again, then select /Copy and press Return, press two more DownArrows to cell B6, and again press Return. That works, but now the cursor jumps back up to cell B4. So you press DownArrow twice again, and wonder why Lotus didn't include a Copy-and-Stay-Put capability.

In this section we will discuss four solutions, two manual and two macro-driven, to this problem of the cell pointer that does not stay at the destination cell after a copy command.

The first solution does not involve a macro at all, but a strange twist of the standard copy command. By now you are used to the typical method of copying from one cell to an entire column by pressing Return at the *COPY FROM* command, and painting in the column at the *COPY TO* command. This fills every cell in the column with the data in the COPY FROM cell. Try this instead. Rather than copying from a single cell to a painted-in column, try copying from a painted-in column (blank except for the first cell) to a single cell.

This may seem counterintuitive at first, but it works. For example, if you want to copy the number **123** from cell B2 to every other cell through B10 as shown in Figure 6.10, select /Copy and at the prompt *Enter range to copy FROM,* point in the range B2..B8, and press Return. Note that most of the range you are copying from at this point is actually blank.

At the *Enter range to copy TO* prompt, move the pointer down two cells to B4 and press Return. That's all there is to it. The results are shown in Figure 6.11. The information in B4 is instantly copied into alternate cells B4, B6, B8, and B10, using only 12 keystrokes (including the highlighting keystrokes). This method has an additional benefit: the pointer returns to the original FROM cell at the completion of the copying.

If you want two different entries to be duplicated in alternate cells down a column, use the same technique. For example, if you have the word **Lotus** in cell B2 and the number **123** in cell B3, going through the same steps will result in dual entries copied to alternate cells as shown in Figure 6.12. Unfortunately, this method only works when you're copying from one or more cells in an otherwise empty column or row, to that same empty column or row. So if you're trying to copy to every other cell (B4, B6, B8, and so on) where the alternate cells in the column (B4, B6, B8, and so on) already have data, this method will not work.

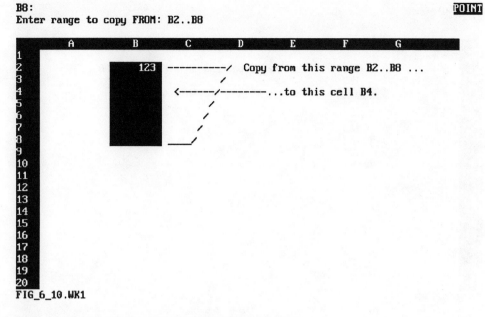

FIG_6_10.WK1

Figure 6.10 A Technique to Copy to Alternate Cells

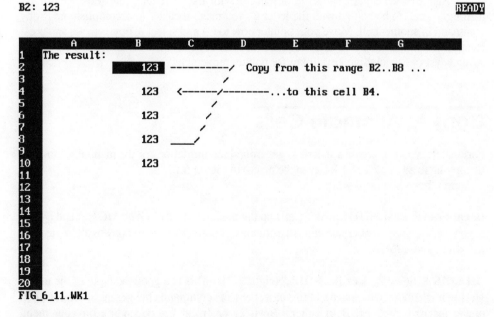

FIG_6_11.WK1

Figure 6.11 Result of Copying to Alternate Cells

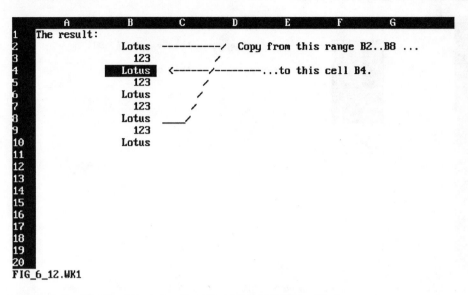

FIG_6_12.WK1

Figure 6.12   Result of Copying Dual Entries to Alternate Cells

Here's another manual method you may want to try. Place your cell pointer on cell B2, select /Range Name Create, name the current cell with just the letter C, and press Return. By naming the cell to be copied with the letter C, you make it easier to accomplish the /Copy command in another cell. Move your pointer now to C4 and select /Copy, type C, and press Return twice. Go through the same sequence at cells C6, C8, and C10. Each copy only takes seven keystrokes including keystrokes for pointer movement.

Copy to Alternate Cells

Fortunately, you can create a macro to get around the limitations of the manual techniques of copying to alternate cells. Refer to the macro in Figure 6.13.

Here's how the macro works.

{menubranch EMENU1}{quit}   Calls up the menu choices *DOWN*, *RIGHT*, and *QUIT*. If you want to copy to alternate cells in a column, choose *DOWN*. To copy to alternate cells in a row, choose *RIGHT*.

{let EDIR,"{down 2}"} or **{let EDIR,"{right 2}"}**   This is a good example of the use of {let} in a self-modifying macro. In this case, the {let} command changes the subroutine cell of the macro named EDIR to either {down 2} or {right 2}, depending on your menu selection.

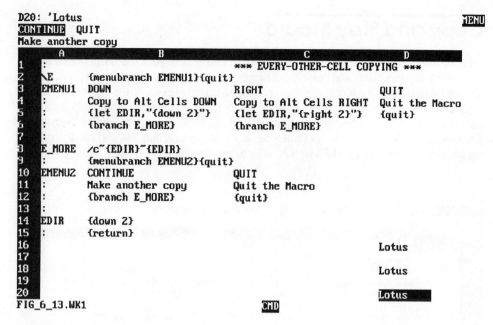

```
D20:  'Lotus                                                           MENU
CONTINUE  QUIT
Make another copy
        A              B                      C                  D
1   :                                  *** EVERY-OTHER-CELL COPYING ***
2   \E        {menubranch EMENU1}{quit}
3   EMENU1    DOWN                     RIGHT                  QUIT
4   :         Copy to Alt Cells DOWN   Copy to Alt Cells RIGHT  Quit the Macro
5   :         {let EDIR,"{down 2}"}    {let EDIR,"{right 2}"}  {quit}
6   :         {branch E_MORE}          {branch E_MORE}
7   :
8   E_MORE    /c~{EDIR}~{EDIR}
9   :         {menubranch EMENU2}{quit}
10  EMENU2    CONTINUE                 QUIT
11  :         Make another copy        Quit the Macro
12  :         {branch E_MORE}          {quit}
13  :
14  EDIR      {down 2}
15  :         {return}
16                                                        Lotus
17
18                                                        Lotus
19
20                                                        Lotus
FIG_6_13.WK1                          CMD
```

Figure 6.13 Macro to Copy to Alternate Cells

{branch E_MORE}   Branches to the looping cell of the macro named E_MORE.

/c~{EDIR}~{EDIR}   This line copies from the current cell, then branches to the subroutine at EDIR for the TO location. If you selected DOWN at the first menu, EDIR reads {down 2}. If you selected RIGHT, EDIR reads {right 2}. After the copying, the cell pointer jumps back to the current cell. A second subroutine call to EDIR moves the cell pointer back to the destination cell.

{menubranch EMENU2}{quit}   Calls up the menu choices *CONTINUE* or *QUIT*.

{branch E_MORE}   If you select *CONTINUE*, this command will cause the macro to loop back to the copy command at E_MORE. At each press of the CONTINUE selection, the macro will make another copy in the next alternate cell of the column, then move the cell pointer to that location.

The last two lines of the macro consist of the subroutine at EDIR. Notice the {return} command that instructs the macro to continue at the point where it left the main macro.

Although it takes a while to step through how the macro works, the actual performance of the macro is surprisingly quick. Almost as fast as you can press Return to select the word *CONTINUE*, the macro will copy to one more alternate cell.

We have mentioned that there are three solutions to the problem of a copy command that is not designed to stay at the destination cell. The third solution is more general, offering more features than just the copying of data to alternate cells.

Copy and Stay Macro

Imagine a situation where you want to copy from one area in your spreadsheet to a remote location. You press /Copy and paint in the range you want to copy FROM, then press Return. You move to the remote location, which requires a dozen presses of the PgDn key, several RightArrows, and a few UpArrows. You're finally there, so you press Return. But now the cursor jumps back to the FROM location, so you have to go through the same keystrokes to get back to the TO location to continue your work. It seems redundant and frustrating, and the type of problem that can best be solved by a macro (see Figure 6.14).

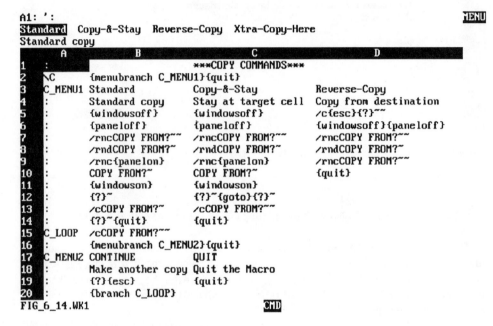

Figure 6.14 The Copy-and-Stay Macro

Here's how the macro works.

{menubranch C_MENU}{quit}   Calls up the menu choices *Standard, Copy-&-Stay, Reverse-Copy*, and *Xtra-Copy-Here*. The *Standard* copy choice is included so you can replace a manual selection of the /Copy command with a press of Alt-C and Return. So by adding only one keystroke to achieve a standard copy, you gain the advantage of three more ways to copy data. The *Standard* choice also "remembers" the cell or range copied, which comes in handy when you want to make extra copies.

{windowsoff}{paneloff}   If you select the *Standard* choice, the macro begins by turning off the windows and panel to suppress screen flicker during the /Range Name Create and Delete commands to come.

/rncCOPY FROM?~~/rndCOPY FROM?~   Using the same technique we demon-strated in the Quick Range Recalc macro, these commands create the range name *COPY FROM?*, then delete it again.

/rnc{panelon}COPY FROM?~{windowson}{?}~   Recreates the range name *COPY FROM?*, pausing for you to enter the range. Since the upper panel is off until the macro starts to type the words *COPY FROM?*, it will look like this:

COPY FROM?   **Enter range:**

In Release 3, the upper panel will look like this:

Enter name to create: COPY FROM?   **Enter range:**

   In either case, you are being prompted to paint in the range you want to copy from. The advantage of the first example, of course, is that it looks more like a real Lotus command. You may also notice that the {windowson} command is issued just prior to the question-mark pause. This is required because without this command you would not be able to see your cell pointer move to paint in the range you want to copy.

/cCOPY FROM?~{?}~{quit}   Starts the /Copy command to copy the range named *COPY FROM?* to another location. The macro pauses at the prompt *Range to copy TO:* so you can point to the cell where you want your copy to appear. When you press Return, the macro quits. Notice that we did not delete the range name *COPY FROM?* before the macro quits. The reason for this becomes clear with the *Xtra-Copy-Here* choice.

   If you press Alt-C and select *Copy-&-Stay* instead of *Standard*, the macro goes through almost the same steps, with two exceptions:

/rnc{panelon}COPY FROM?~{windowson}{?}~{goto}{?}~   As in the *Standard* choice, the macro recreates the range name *COPY FROM?*, pausing for you to enter the range. But in the *Copy-&-Stay* choice, this line also causes the *Enter address to go TO:* message to be shown in the upper panel. We could, of course, have entered just the question-mark pause at this point, but then the operator would not know what to do next. That is to say, we are not using the {goto} command to direct the cell pointer to go to a cell location, but more accu-rately we are using it to instruct the user to manually move his cell pointer there. This is the fourth method we have explored to prompt the user, the other three being:

1. A statement, followed by {?}{esc};
2. A menu choice, where the explanation line directs the user; and
3. The user of /Range Name Create where the range name is also an instructional prompt.

/cCOPY FROM?~~{quit}   As in the *Standard* choice, the macro starts the /Copy com-mand to copy the range named COPY FROM?, but in this case the copy is made at the cell where you've just moved your cell pointer. And since you moved your cell pointer to the new location *before* starting the copy command and simply made the copy at the current cell, the cell pointer stays at the destination cell.

   The *Reverse-Copy* option uses the same concept, starting the copy command from the destination cell. You can do this manually by pressing /Copy Escape, which frees your cursor to move to the FROM area. After designating the cell or range you want to copy, press Return. The cell pointer will jump back to your original location, which presumably is where you want the copied data to go, so at this point you press Return once again. Your copying is complete and your cell pointer remains at the destination cell. Without counting moving to the area to copy from and painting in the range, this is all done manually in five keystrokes and automatically by the *Reverse-Copy* option in three keystrokes.

The purpose of the *Xtra-Copy-Here* choice is to allow you to make additional copies of a cell or range already copied once using the Alt-C macro. To make an additional copy, move to a new location and press Alt-C and the letter X for *Xtra-Copy-Here*.

{branch C_LOOP}   Branching to C_LOOP is only done to allow the rest of the macro code to reside in the left-most column of the macro, simplifying placement and later range-naming of the macro's internal range names.

/cCOPY FROM?~~   Assuming you have already moved to the location where you want the extra copy to appear, the macro starts the /Copy command and responds to the prompt *Enter range to copy FROM:* by entering the range name COPY FROM?. At the prompt *Enter range to copy TO:*, the macro simply presses Enter, selecting the current cell.

{menubranch C_MENU2}{quit}   Branches to the menu choices *Continue* and *Quit*. If you select *Continue*, there is a macro pause as you point to the location where you want the new copy to appear. The {esc} command just after the bracketed question mark is included to ensure you don't type an erroneous entry at your new location before the copy is complete. When you press Return, the macro branches back to the cell named C_LOOP and executes another copy of the range name COPY FROM? at the current cell.

Copy Relative Formula as Absolute

When you move a formula from one cell to another, all of the cell references in the formula stay unchanged. On the other hand, when you use the Copy command instead of the Move command, the cell references change. This "relative copy" aspect of 1-2-3 is an important feature of the spreadsheet environment, since 90 percent of the time you want exactly that—a relative copy of the original formula.

Occasionally, however, you want an exact duplicate of a formula to appear in another cell. The way you handled this initially was probably to copy the formula from one cell to the other, move your cursor to the new copy, press F2 Edit, and change the cell references so that they exactly match the cell references in the original.

At some point you may have learned another trick: before making the copy, you change the formula to a label by pressing F2 Edit, then Home to move the blinking cursor to the beginning of the word, then apostrophe, and finally Return. Once the original is a label, you can copy it to another cell as an exact duplicate. Then all you have to do is eliminate the apostrophes from both the original and the copy, and presto!—you have two versions of the same formula.

It's handy and as a single exercise it can save you a great deal of time—especially for a long, complicated formula. If you find yourself having to do this kind of absolute (as opposed to relative) copying often, however, you may want to have the macro shown in Figure 6.15 handle it for you.

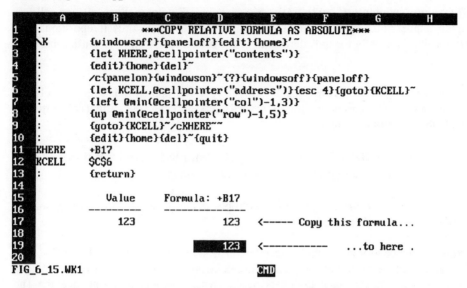

```
D19: +B17                                                        POINT
Enter range to copy TO: D19
          A         B         C         D         E        F        G        H
 1  :                     ***COPY RELATIVE FORMULA AS ABSOLUTE***
 2  \K        {windowsoff}{paneloff}{edit}{home}'~
 3  :         {let KHERE,@cellpointer("contents")}
 4  :         {edit}{home}{del}~
 5  :         /c{panelon}{windowson}~{?}{windowsoff}{paneloff}
 6  :         {let KCELL,@cellpointer("address")}{esc 4}{goto}{KCELL}~
 7  :         {left @min(@cellpointer("col")-1,3)}
 8  :         {up @min(@cellpointer("row")-1,5)}
 9  :         {goto}{KCELL}~/cKHERE~~
10  :         {edit}{home}{del}~{quit}
11  KHERE     +B17
12  KCELL     $C$6
13  :         {return}
14
15            Value      Formula: +B17
16            ---------  ---------------
17              123              123      <----- Copy this formula...
18
19                               123      <-----------    ...to here .
20
FIG_6_15.WK1                            CMD
```

Figure 6.15 Macro to Copy Relative Formula as Absolute

{windowsoff}{paneloff}{edit}{home}'~   Suppresses screen and panel flicker and avoids unnecessary update to the screen as 1-2-3 shifts to the Edit mode, presses Home to move to the beginning of the formula, enters an apostrophe to turn the formula into a label, and presses Return.

{let KHERE,@cellpointer("contents")}   Copies the label form of the current cell's formula to the cell named KHERE. This use of the {let} command achieves the same result you would get using the /Copy command, but it does it slightly faster.

{edit}{home}{del}~   Deletes the apostrophe from the original cell to change it back to a formula.

/c~{panelon}{windowson}~{?}{windowsoff}{paneloff}   Begins the copy command, copying the current cell; but at the prompt *Enter range to copy TO:*, the macro pauses so you can move to the location where you want to copy the formula. The screen and panel are turned off again before the command is completed.

Although this looks like the beginning of the copying you might expect in a macro designed to copy a relative formula as absolute, it is actually only included so you will see the prompt *Enter range to copy TO:*.

{let KCELL,@cellpointer("address")}{esc 4}{goto}{KCELL}~   While you are still in the middle of the /Copy command, the macro records your destination cell, storing the cell address in the cell named KCELL, then escapes from the /Copy command without completing it. The cell pointer is then sent to the cell address stored in KCELL—in other words, to the cell you pointed to in response to the prompt from the last line.

{left @min(@cellpointer("col")-1,3)}   Moves your cell pointer either left one cell less than the number of the current column or left three cells. In other words, it repositions your current cell horizontally towards the center of the screen as shown in an earlier macro in Figure 6.5.

{up @min(@cellpointer("row")-1,5)}   Moves your cell pointer either up one cell less than the number of the current row, or up five cells, repositioning your current cell vertically towards the center of the screen

{goto}{KCELL}~/cKHERE~~   Returns the cell pointer to the target cell, then copies the label form of the original formula from KHERE to the current cell.

{edit}{home}{del}~{quit}   Deletes the apostrophe to return the label to a formula matching the original formula, and quits.

You will notice as you use this macro that, instead of moving back to the FROM cell, this example leaves the cell pointer at the TO cell, assuming that location is your probable destination when doing absolute copies of this type. You will also find that the {up @min} and {left @min} commands, added to move the TO cell more to the center of the screen, only become necessary when the destination cell is not in the same screen as the original cell.

Absolute Value Macro

There is one drawback to the macro just reviewed: if you want to copy the original formula as an absolute formula to several different cells, it can be tiresome to run the macro over and over again to achieve that result. You could, of course, edit the original formula so that dollar signs ($) precede all the cell addresses, thus changing all the cell addresses to absolute rather than relative references; but that can be more tedious than repeatedly running our macro and you may not want to leave the original formula with absolute references—which means having to delete the dollar signs after your copying is done.

Here is another technique. Move your cursor to the first cell you want to copy TO and press the Plus key (+); then move to the cell you want to copy FROM and press the F4 Abs key. This will cause the destination cell to contain a plus sign and the absolute cell address of the original cell, something like this: $C$14. Not only will the results of that formula give you the same results as the original formula, but you can then copy the absolute-cell formula to other cells, and all of your copy cells will give the same result.

There's more. At the point where you press the F4 Abs key, try pressing it twice. The formula will show a relative column and an absolute row, something like this: +C$14. Try pressing it three times, and you'll get absolute column and relative row, like this: +$C14. Four presses of the F4 Abs key will return the formula to a straight, relative cell reference like this: +C14.

Of course, we have a macro that will copy an entire range in absolute terms without pressing the F4 key. Refer to the macro in Figure 6.16 called Xtract to Absolute-Copy a Range.

```
B19: [W13] +A19                                                    POINT
          ABS COPY FROM?                      Enter range: B15..B19

        A         B          C         D        E        F        G
1   :                       *** XTRACT TO ABSOLUTE-COPY A RANGE ***
2   \X        {windowsoff}{paneloff}
3   :         /rncABS COPY FROM?~~/rndABS COPY FROM?~
4   :         /rnc{panelon}ABS COPY FROM?~{windowson}{?}~
5   :         {windowsoff}{paneloff}/fxf0TEMP~ABS COPY FROM?~r{esc}
6   :         /mABS COPY FROM?{panelon}{windowson}~{?}~
7   :         {windowsoff}{paneloff}/fcce0TEMP~
8   :         /few0TEMP~y/rndABS COPY FROM?~{quit}
9
10                           _____ Copy this range of relative formulas...
11                          /
12            Formulas    /      ... to here___
13   Values   such as +A15 /                  \
14   --------  --------  /                      \
15      123       123  /                         \    123
16      234       234                             \   234
17      345       345                                 345
18      465       465                                 465
19      576       576                                 576
20
FIG_6_16.WK1                              CMD
```

Figure 6.16 Using /File Xtract to Absolute-Copy a Range

This macro uses two facts about 1-2-3 with which you are no doubt familiar:

■ 1-2-3 has the ability to extract a range to file with formulas intact.
■ Moving (as opposed to copying) a range of formulas makes no relative changes to the formulas.

The macro works by naming the range of formulas you want to copy, extracting a copy to another file, moving the range itself to a new location, and finally /File Combining the extracted copy of the range to the original location.

The first three lines of the macro are by now familiar, turning off the windows and panels, creating a range name called ABS COPY FROM?, turning the windows and panels back on, and pausing for you to highlight the range you want to copy.

{windowsoff}{paneloff}/fxf0TEMP~ABS COPY FROM?~r{esc} Turns off the windows and panel, selects /File Xtract Formulas, and designates the Xtract File name to be

0TEMP. Note the Xtract File name starts with a zero, not the letter O, so that the file will be among the first to be listed during later /File Retrieve operations in the unlikely event that the macro is interrupted and the filename remains in your current directory in error. The range that the macro extracts is the range named ABS COPY FROM?. The macro selects Replace, then presses Escape to cover two possibilities that the file exists (and requires a Replace to continue with the /File Xtract) or does not exists (and requires an Escape to eliminate the pressing of the letter R for Replace).

/mABS COPY FROM?{panelon}{windowson}~{?}~   Selects /Move to move the range named ABS COPY FROM?, then turns on the windows and panel to allow you to designate where you want the range moved.

{windowsoff}{paneloff}/fcce0TEMP~   After a /Move, the cell pointer jumps back to the original location. At this point, the macro turns off the windows and panel, selects /File Combine Copy Entire, and enters the filename 0TEMP that contains the original range to copy.

/few0TEMP~y/rndABS COPY FROM?~{quit}   Finally, the macro selects /File Erase Worksheet, erases 0TEMP, types **Y** for *Yes* at the warning prompt, deletes the range named ABS COPY FROM?, and quits.

The result will be two ranges with identical formulas: the original range moved to a new location, and a copy of the original range extracted then /File Combined back to the original location.

The Move Data & Stay Macro

The Move Data & Stay macro in Figure 6.17 is similar in concept to the Copy-&-Stay macro in Figure 6.14, offering the same kind of choice between a *Standard Move*, a *Move and Stay* command, and a *Reverse_Move*. (Of course, there is no Xtra-Move-Here command.) Like the Copy-&-Stay macro, this macro will take a little getting used to, but it will save much of the frustration connected with doing a standard move in 1-2-3.

If you select the *Standard Move* choice, the macro simply steps you through the selection of the /Move command, pausing after the /Move prompts for your entry.

If you select *Move and Stay*, the macro creates the range name MOVE FROM?, pauses for your designation of the range, prompts you for the location to go to, and moves the range from that location, leaving you at the destination cell at the completion of the /Move sequence.

If you select *Reverse_Move*, the macro simply prompts you for the range you want to move (assuming you are already at the destination range) and moves that range to your destination location.

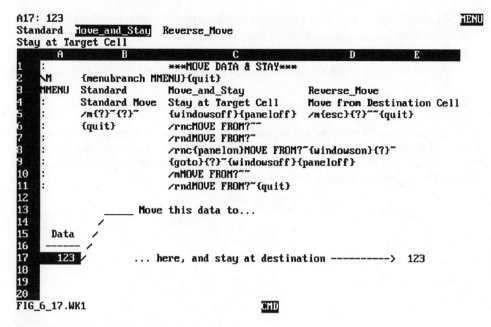

```
A17: 123                                                                   MENU
Standard  Move_and_Stay  Reverse_Move
Stay at Target Cell
        A            B                C                    D            E
 1      :                      ***MOVE DATA & STAY***
 2      \M          {menubranch MMENU}{quit}
 3      MMENU       Standard         Move_and_Stay           Reverse_Move
 4      :           Standard Move    Stay at Target Cell     Move from Destination Cell
 5      :           /m{?}~{?}~        {windowsoff}{paneloff}  /m{esc}{?}~~{quit}
 6      :           {quit}           /rncMOVE FROM?~~
 7      :                            /rndMOVE FROM?~
 8      :                            /rnc{panelon}MOVE FROM?~{windowson}{?}~
 9      :                            {goto}{?}~{windowsoff}{paneloff}
10      :                            /mMOVE FROM?~~
11      :                            /rndMOVE FROM?~{quit}
12
13                     _____ Move this data to...
14                      /
15      Data           /
16      ------         /
17       123  /           ... here, and stay at destination ----------->  123
18
19
20
FIG_6_17.WK1                                CMD
```

Figure 6.17 The Move Data & Stay Macro

Summary

In this chapter you were introduced to new concepts:

- Two ways of creating a place-marker: Using /Range Name Create-Delete-Create and using the {let} command with @cellpointer("address").
- Use of the {windowsoff} and {paneloff} commands.
- Use of the @cell and @cellpointer functions
- The concept of self-modifying macros.
- Some techniques for moving quickly and easily around your spreadsheet.
- Ways to reposition your current cell to the center of the screen.
- A new macro technique to create a range prompter by using a /Range Name Create command.
- Tips on how to copy to alternate cells or copy formulas in an absolute rather than relative way, without the use of macros.

Macros covered in this chapter which use these techniques are summarized:

- A macro to jump the cursor to the upper right corner of your worksheet and back again.
- A self-modifying File Retrieve macro.
- A macro to explore four corners of the worksheet.

- A Quick Range Recalc macro to calculate just a range of your spreadsheet.
- A macro to transpose a matrix of columns to rows.
- A macro to copy to alternate cells
- Macros to copy a relative formula as absolute, or a range of formulas as if they were absolute.
- Copy-&-Stay and Move-&-Stay macros that leave your cursor at the TO cell.

In Chapter 7 we will examine ways to create a macro library in Release 2.2 and Release 3. Chapter 7 includes techniques for running macros from within the current worksheet, though they actually reside in a location other than the current worksheet, through use of either the Alt-letter combination or the Alt-F3 Macro Run key.

CREATING A BACKGROUND MACRO LIBRARY

For Those with Release 2.0 or 2.01

If you have Release 2.0 or 2.01, you will not have the option of running your macros from a location outside the current worksheet. That feature was not introduced until the advent of Release 2.2 and 3. You can, however, keep your macros in a separate .WK1 file, named in such a way as to greatly speed up the importing of individual macros into your current worksheet. The techniques in this section can also be used in Release 2.2 and 3 to quickly transfer macros from one worksheet file to another.

Transferring Macros Between Worksheet Files

Let's assume you have a worksheet file with a dozen or so of your favorite macros. For argument's sake, we'll call this file of macros FAVORITE.WK1. In that worksheet, move your cell pointer to the upper left corner of the first macro. Typically, that would be cell A1.

Now give a two-letter range name to the macro. To make it simple and easy to remember, make the first letter M for Macro, and the second letter the same as the Alt-letter you use to invoke the macro. Thus, if your first macro is the Add macro that you invoke by pressing Alt-A, you will be giving that macro the range name MA. If your second macro is the Beep macro that you invoke by pressing Alt-B, you will be giving that macro the range name MB.

Name each separate macro in this way, by selecting /Range Name Create, and at the prompt *Enter name:*, typing **MA, MB,** and so on, and pressing Return. At the prompt *Range:*, highlight the entire macro, including the title at the top and the range names on the left side (a minimum of three columns and two rows, if you have followed our recommended macro structure). The example in Figure 7.1 shows a /Range Name Create sequence for the first macro in a typical collection of favorites.

Once you have named each of your macros with two-letter names such as MA, MB, and so on, be sure to save the file. *The following instructions will not work unless you remember to save the file after the macros have been range-named in this way.*

Now start a blank worksheet or /File Retrieve an existing worksheet and move to a blank area where you want one of your favorite macros to appear. At this point you can either select /File Combine Copy Entire and at the prompt *Name of File to Combine*, select the entire file containing your favorite macros; or you can select /File Combine Copy Named-range and at the prompt *Enter range name or address:*, type the two-letter combination you used to name one of your macros. In the example in Figure 7.2, the MA macro was already /File Combined into the worksheet in this way, and the cell pointer was moved to C3 where the MB macro is about to be /File Combined.

Creating an on-disk library of your favorite macros and /Range Naming them so you can easily import specific macros from that library may seem like a lot to go through; but you will find after the initial setting up and naming of the macros that the keystrokes to /File

C3:   **POINT**
Enter name: MA   Enter range: A1..C3

```
        A         B            C              D         E
1   :                  *** ADD MACRO ***
2   \A        {up}\-{down}
3   :         @sum({up}.{up}{end}{up}..)~{quit}
4   :                 *** BEEP MACRO ***
5   \B        {home}'~{quit}
6   :                 *** DATE MACRO ***
7   \D        @date(90,{?})~/rfd1~/wcs10~{quit}
8   :                 *** JUMP MACRO ***
9   \J        {down 18}{up 18}{quit}
10  :                *** HORIZONTAL SUM ***
11  \H        @sum({left}.{end}{left}..)~{quit}
12  :               *** GAUGE VERT & HORIZ SUMS ***
13  \G        @if(@round(@sum({up 2}.{end}{up}),2)=
14  :         @round(@sum({left}.{end}{left}),2),
15  :         @sum({up 2}.{end}{up}),@ERR)~{quit}
16  :               *** INSERT ROW WITH FORMAT ***
17  \R        /wir~{goto}.{end}{home}.{esc}~{up}
18  :         /c{down}{end}{left}{up}~{down}{end}{left}~
19  :         {down}{goto}.{home}.{esc}~/re{end}{right}{?}~
20  :         {up 8}{down 8}{quit}
```
FIG_7-1.WK1

Figure 7.1 Giving Range Names to Each Macro in a Collection

```
A4:                                                                      EDIT
Enter range name or address: MB

        A        B        C        D        E        F        G        H
1   :                 *** ADD MACRO ***
2   \A          {up}\-{down}
3   :           @sum({up}.{up}{end}{up}..)~{quit}
4
5
6
7
8
9
10
11
12
13
14
15
16
17
18
19
20
```

FIG_7-2.WK1

Figure 7.2 Importing Individual Macros from Disk

Combine the macros into your current worksheet become second nature after a while. As you will see, it will only take seven keystrokes (**/fccnMA**, for example) to identify the macro, and a few more pointer strokes and presses of the Return key to get the macro into your current worksheet.

There is only one other thing you must do before the macro will work in your current worksheet—and this is very important. Whenever you /File Combine a range or entire file, the incoming cells do *not* bring their range names with them. This means that not only will a given macro not bring its two-letter name such as MA, MB, and so on; it will also leave behind its Alt-letter range name and any internal range names it needs to run. You must therefore /Range Name all your macros again by selecting /Range Name Labels Right and at the prompt for a range, pressing PgDn enough times to highlight the internal range names of the macros.

Alternately, you can select /Range Name Labels Right and if you have filled all the cells between range names with colons as you have seen in the examples shown thus far, you will be able to press End DownArrow to highlight all the range names. This will be a faster and more accurate way of /Range Naming your macros—especially if you transfer them often from worksheet file to worksheet file.

For Those with Release 2.2 or 3

If you do not have Release 2.2 or 3, or if you are anxious to get started using some of the more advanced macros in this book, you may want to skip the rest of this chapter and go straight to Chapter 8. On the other hand, if you have either Release 2.2 or 3, you may be interested in the Macro Library capabilities of these releases.

The Macro Library Manager in Release 2.2 is an add-in called MACROMGR.ADN. With this add-in, you can keep your commonly used macros in the background (also called Hyperspace), rather than in your current worksheet. The Macro Library Manager does this by storing your macros in separate background files with an .MLB extension.

Creating a macro library to work in the background in Release 3 is quite different. Since you can have several files open and active in a 1-2-3 session using Release 3, there is no need for a special add-in like the MACROMGR.ADN of Release 2.2. If you have Release 3, you may want to skip ahead to the section on Release 3 Macro Libraries whereby background macros are kept in separate active .WK3 files.

Installing the Macro Library Manager in Release 2.2

As an add-in, the Macro Library Manager of Release 2.2 takes up extra RAM, whether or not you have created and saved macros to the Macro Library. If memory is not a consideration, you may choose to have 1-2-3 attach this add-in automatically each time you start a 1-2-3 session. This is done by selecting /Worksheet Global Default Other Add-in Set as shown in Figure 7.3. You will be given a menu prompt to assign a number (1 to 8) to the add-in, after which all add-ins and subdirectories in your main 1-2-3 directory will appear.

The Macro Library Manager is in a file called MACROMGR.ADN on the Install Disk

```
A1: '\a                                                                    MENU
Set Cancel Quit
Specify an add-in to be attached automatically, and attach it
┌──────────────────────── Default Settings ────────────────────────┐
│ Printer:                              Directory: C:\22\UPGD        │
│   Interface       Parallel 1                                      │
│   Auto linefeed   No                  Autoexecute macros: Yes      │
│   Margins                                                         │
│     Left 0    Right 240 Top 0  Bottom 0  International:           │
│   Page length     66                    Punctuation       A       │
│   Wait            No                       Decimal        Period   │
│   Setup string                             Argument       Comma    │
│   Name            Toshiba P351 series      Thousands      Comma    │
│                                            Currency       Prefix: $ │
│ Add-In:                                 Date format (D4)  A (MM/DD/YY) │
│   1                                     Time format (D8)  A (HH:MM:SS) │
│   2                                        Negative       Parentheses  │
│   3                                                                │
│   4                                     Help access method: Removable │
│   5                                     Clock display:     File name  │
│   6                                     Undo:              Disabled   │
│   7                                     Beep:              Yes        │
│   8                                                                │
└──────────────────────────────────────────────────────────────────┘
```

FIG_7-3.WK1

Figure 7.3 Setting an Add-in to Automatically Attach

that comes with your Release 2.2 package. If you have a hard disk system, the file should already be in the directory that contains your 1-2-3 System files, and MACROMGR.ADN should appear as one of the choices of add-ins you can select at this point, as shown in Figure 7.4.

```
B2:                                                                    FILES
Enter name of add-in: C:\22\*.ADN
CELLWKS.ADN    MACROMGR.ADN    FILES\         MMM\           UPGD\
┌──────────────────────── Default Settings ────────────────────────┐
│ Printer:                            Directory: C:\22\UPGD         │
│   Interface      Parallel 1                                       │
│   Auto linefeed  No                 Autoexecute macros: Yes       │
│   Margins                                                         │
│     Left 0   Right 240 Top 0  Bottom 0  International:            │
│   Page length    66                   Punctuation      A         │
│   Wait           No                     Decimal        Period    │
│   Setup string                          Argument       Comma     │
│   Name           Toshiba P351 series    Thousands      Comma     │
│                                         Currency       Prefix: $  │
│ Add-In:                               Date format (D4) A (MM/DD/YY)│
│   1                                   Time format (D8) A (HH:MM:SS)│
│   2                                   Negative         Parentheses│
│   3                                                               │
│   4                                 Help access method: Removable │
│   5                                 Clock display:      File name │
│   6                                 Undo:               Disabled  │
│   7                                 Beep:               Yes       │
│   8                                                               │
└──────────────────────────────────────────────────────────────────┘
FIG_7-4.WK1                                                      NUM
```

Figure 7.4 Selecting MACROMGR.ADN to Automatically Attach

You will be prompted to assign Alt-7, Alt-8, Alt-9, or Alt-10 to the add-in to make it easier to invoke later. Alternately, you can select *No-key* at this point.

In addition to automatically attaching the add-in, you have the option of having 1-2-3 automatically "invoke" the add-in when you start your 1-2-3 session. At the *Invoke* prompt, select *Yes* or *No*. The Release 2.2 settings sheet shown in Figure 7.5 demonstrates the results.

If you select *Yes*, you must understand that 1-2-3 will look for your individual macro libraries in the same directory as the MACROMGR.ADN—in other words, in your main 1-2-3 directory—regardless of the default directory you have established. This differs from manually invoking MACROMGR.ADN, which will cause 1-2-3 to search the default (or current) directory for your individual macro libraries.

Select *Quit*, then select *Update* to change the configuration of your 1-2-3, and finally select *Quit* to leave the Global Default Menu. Now, whenever you start up a 1-2-3 session, the Macro Library Manager add-in will be attached automatically.

If you do not want to change your 1-2-3 configuration, you can always elect to attach the MACROMGR.ADN manually by selecting /Add-in from the command menu or pressing the Alt-F10 Add-in key (if it has not been assigned to another add-in application). You will see the menu choices *Attach, Detach, Invoke, Clear*, and *Quit*. Since you cannot invoke an add-in before you attach it, the first selection you must make for the Macro Library Manager add-in is *Attach*. Then Highlight the MACROMGR.ADN choice and press Enter. As with

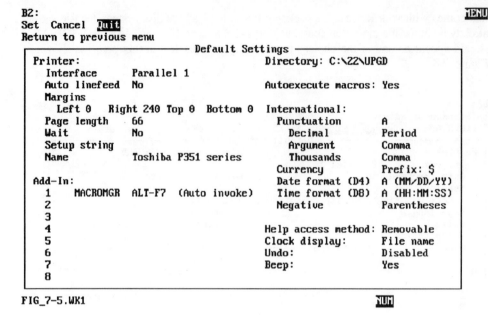

```
B2:                                                                    MENU
Set  Cancel  Quit
Return to previous menu
┌───────────────────────── Default Settings ─────────────────────────┐
│ Printer:                              Directory: C:\22\UPGD          │
│   Interface      Parallel 1                                         │
│   Auto linefeed  No                   Autoexecute macros: Yes        │
│   Margins                                                           │
│     Left 0   Right 240 Top 0  Bottom 0 International:                │
│   Page length     66                    Punctuation      A          │
│   Wait            No                       Decimal        Period     │
│   Setup string                             Argument       Comma      │
│   Name            Toshiba P351 series      Thousands      Comma      │
│                                            Currency       Prefix: $  │
│ Add-In:                                 Date format (D4)  A (MM/DD/YY)│
│   1    MACROMGR   ALT-F7  (Auto invoke) Time format (D8)  A (HH:MM:SS)│
│   2                                     Negative          Parentheses│
│   3                                                                 │
│   4                                   Help access method: Removable  │
│   5                                   Clock display:      File name  │
│   6                                   Undo:               Disabled   │
│   7                                   Beep:               Yes        │
│   8                                                                 │
└─────────────────────────────────────────────────────────────────────┘
FIG_7-5.WK1                                                     NUM
```

Figure 7.5 Setting the MACROMGR.ADN to Automatically Invoke

automatic global attachment, you will be prompted for an Alt-Function key combination to assign to the add-in, though you may select *No-key*.

Using the Release 2.2 Macro Library Manager

Once the MACROMGR.ADN is attached as described in the last section, you can invoke the add-in by pressing the appropriate Alt-Function key combination (if you assigned one), or by selecting /Add-in Invoke. If you use /Add-in Invoke, you will be given a choice of the names of all add-in applications you may have attached. Select MACROMGR and press Enter.

The following menu choices will appear: *Load, Save, Edit, Remove, Name-List,* and *Quit*. Do not select *Load, Remove,* or *Name-List* unless you have already have .MLB files on disk ready to be loaded, removed, or listed. As you might guess, you cannot Edit an .MLB macro library file unless it has first been saved or loaded.

Creating a New .MLB File in Release 2.2

If you have no .MLB macro library file, you can create one from macros in the current worksheet (assuming you have macros in the current worksheet) by selecting *Save*. You will be prompted for the macro library filename under which you want to save the macros. You might use the filename MACRO_1, for example. The file extension .MLB will automatically be added to the macro library file by 1-2-3.

If you want your .MLB file to be loaded into memory automatically whenever the Macro Library Manager is attached, save it with the filename AUTOLOAD.MLB. No macros in the library will execute automatically, not even \0 autoexecute macros, but they will be ready for you to use manually.

After you establish the macro library filename, you will be prompted to *Enter Macro Library Range.* You can respond by typing in the coordinates for a range which includes your macro titles, range names, and macro code, but it is usually better to highlight the range with your cell pointer so you can be sure you covered the entire macro area. An example is shown in Figure 7.6.

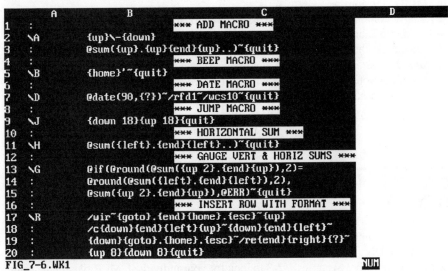

Figure 7.6 Saving Macros to a Macro Library File

You will then be prompted for whether or not you want to use a password to lock the library file. If you do decide to lock the file, you must be sure to remember the exact combination of uppercase or lowercase letters you typed for the password. When you save data in a library with a password, you can only edit the library if you enter the password again exactly as it was first entered.

As the macros are saved in their own macro library file, they are simultaneously erased from the current worksheet. Do not let this bother you; they are not lost, only moved to another file. To place a copy of the saved macros back in the worksheet as before, press the Alt-Function key combination for your Macro Library Manager (if any) or select /Add-in Invoke MACROMGR and press Enter. From the menu choices *Load, Save, Edit, Remove, Name-List,* and *Quit,* select *Edit.*

Editing an .MLB File in Release 2.2

If you select *Edit* from the /Add-in Invoke menu, you will be prompted for the macro library file to edit and a location in your worksheet to place the macros in the library file. The macros can be placed in any unprotected area of the worksheet, but you should be sure that the area is blank or contains unimportant data, because the Macro Library Manager writes over existing data when it copies the .MLB file into the worksheet.

When you bring macros saved into a macro library file back into a worksheet by selecting Edit, any range names in its macros that match range names in your worksheet set up a potential conflict. You will be prompted for whether you want to ignore or write over existing range names in the worksheet. For this reason, you should try to make all range names in any macro you write unique to that macro.

After editing .MLB macros, you can save any changes that you make by selecting /Add-in Invoke MACROMGR Save. This saves the macros back into their same macro library file with its .MLB extension.

The *Remove* command allows you to erase a macro library file from RAM memory, although the Macro Library Manager leaves a copy of the library file on disk. To use the library file again, use the /Add-in Invoke MACROMGR Load command.

The *Name-List* command will place in your worksheet a list of all the range names in any macro library files you have loaded. As with Edit, however, make sure that the area is blank or contains unimportant data, because the Name-List writes over existing data.

Loading Release 2.2 .MLB Macros with AUTO123

It is important to note here that having 1-2-3 automatically attach and invoke your MACROMGR.ADN program (via the /Worksheet Global Default Other Add-in Set sequence as described above) causes 1-2-3 to look for your individual .MLB files in the same directory as the MACROMGR.ADN file—in other words, in your main 1-2-3 directory— regardless of the default directory you have established.

There is another technique, however, that allows you to keep all your .MLB files in a separate macro subdirectory. (You may have decided to create a subdirectory for your macro files such as C:\123\MACROS, for example.)

When you call up 1-2-3, it searches the default directory and retrieves any file named AUTO123.WK1; and if the AUTO123.WK1 file includes an autoexecuting macro (a macro that begins with a backslash-zero \0), that macro runs automatically as soon as the AUTO123.WK1 file is retrieved.

Imagine, then, an AUTO123.WK1 file with an autoexecute macro that attaches and invokes your MACROMGR.ADN, loads your favorite .MLB Macro Library file, and finally does a /Worksheet Erase Yes to clear the screen. The advantage is that you can have the macro in this file load your .MLB files from any subdirectory where you've chosen to store them.

Such an AUTO123.WK1 file is shown in Figure 7.7. Be aware, however, that you must

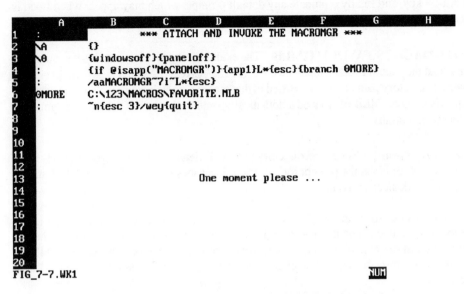

FIG_7-7.WK1

Figure 7.7   AUTO123 File to Attach and Invoke the MACROMGR.ADN

save this AUTO123.WK1 file to the 1-2-3 default directory before it will be automatically retrieved by 1-2-3 when you begin your 1-2-3 session.

{ }   The macro begins with a null pass-through command. This is done to allow the macro to have two starting names: the \A name, included for testing purposes only, and the autoexecuting \0 name, that will start the macro automatically as soon as the AUTO123.WK1 file is loaded by 1-2-3 at start-up.

{windowsoff}{paneloff}   Suppresses screen flicker and speeds the macro.

{if @isapp("MACROMGR")}{app1}L*{esc}{branch 0MORE}   This line introduces a new concept that will be covered in more detail later: the macro {if} command. For now, suffice it to say that if the statement included in the argument is true, the macro continues reading the rest of the line. If it is false, the macro skips down to the next line. In this case, the macro uses the {if} command with the @isapp function to test for whether the MACROMGR.ADN file has been attached. If so, the macro continues on this same line, running the {app1} command which invokes the MACROMGR application. (**Note:** This assumes that the MACROMGR add-in, if attached, was assigned the Alt-F7 combination for invoking.) The L denotes Load and the asterisk and Escape are included to eliminate any default prompts which may appear when Load is selected. Finally, the macro branches to the line of the macro specifying your file of favorite macros.

/aaMACROMGR~7i~L*{esc}   If the @isapp function comes up false when checking for whether the MACROMGR add-in has been attached, the macro skips the rest of the last line and continues at this one. Its purpose is to select /Add-in Attach, enter MACROMGR, assign the Alt-F7 key, and finally eliminate any default prompts which may appear when Load is selected.

C:\123\MACROS\FAVORITE.MLB   The example we are using here is set to automatically load the Macro Library file named C:\123\MACROS\FAVORITE.MLB. To change either the directory path or filename listed in that macro to match your own directory path or to specify another .MLB file to load automatically, modify this line of the macro as you type in the macro initially.

~n{esc 3}/wey{quit}   Enters the directory path and filename of your favorite .MLB macros, selects N for No at the prompt for a password, escapes from the /Add-in Attach menu, erases the worksheet, and quits.

To use this macro in an AUTO123.WK1 file, start with a blank worksheet, type in the macro lines, /Range Name the macro, and save the file. It is very important to type the file before you test the macro to ensure that it works properly, since the /Wey command in the last line will erase the current worksheet to start your 1-2-3 session off with a blank worksheet.

Rules for Using the Macro Library in Release 2.2

Twelve rules and conventions should be taken into account when using the Macro Library Manager:

1. A macro library file is brought into active RAM when you select either the Load or the Save command from the Macro Library Manager menu. You can have up to 10 libraries in memory at the same time, each library containing up to 16,376 cells or the equivalent of two columns wide by 8,188 rows long.
2. When you specify a range of macros you want to save into a Macro Library file, a cell will be allocated in conventional memory in the library file for each cell in the range, even if it is empty. To save memory, make your macros as compact as possible.
3. A Macro Library has no cell coordinates, so you cannot refer to cells or ranges in a library with cell or range coordinates, though you can refer to either by using range names.
4. You will not be able to use the /Copy or /Move commands to manipulate cell coordinate, range coordinates, or even range names in a Macro Library file (unless, of course, you count those instances where you bring the file into the current worksheet for editing with the /Add-in Invoke MACROMGR Edit command).
5. You can, however, use advanced macro commands such as the {let} command to move data between libraries, or between the worksheet and a library. For example, you can use the macro line {let MACRO_CELL,+A4}, where **MACRO_CELL** is

a named range in a Macro Library file. The macro keywords which can be used for this type of manipulation of named ranges in a Macro Library file are:

{blank}	{get}	{if}	{put}	{recalccol}
{contents}	{getlabel}	{let}	{read}	{setpos}
{define}	{getnumber}	{look}	{readln}	{wait}
{filesize}	{getpos}	{open}	{recalc}	{writeln}

6. As with worksheet files, you cannot save more than one Macro Library file with the same name. If you try, you will be prompted for whether or not you want to write over the previous library file.

7. You will not be able to save a range of macros in a Macro Library file if the range includes a link to another file. Trying this will cause an error message.

8. When you save a formula into a Macro Library, any ranges or cells that the formula references must also be saved into the same Macro Library, or the formula will not display the correct results. Even though there are no cell addresses in a Macro Library, you can have cell references within a formula. The Macro Library version simply maintains the relative position of the referenced cell to the formula.

9. When you save a range in your worksheet to a Macro Library file, any formulas still remaining in your worksheet that refer to cells within that range will continue to refer to the same cells, even though they will be empty after the /Add-in Invoke MACROMGR Save command.

10. When you edit a Macro Library file, any range names in its macros that match range names in your worksheet set up a potential conflict. You will be prompted for whether you want to ignore or write over existing range names in the worksheet. For this reason, you should try to make all range names in any macro you write unique to that macro.

11. When you specify a range name to start a macro or as an argument in a macro command, 1-2-3 searches for the range name in this order: (i) the current worksheet; (ii) the first Macro Library placed in active RAM by the Save or Load command; (iii) the second library placed in active RAM by the Save or Load command, and so on. This is another strong reason for being sure that the range names in each macro are unique to that macro.

12. A library macro can do a /File Retrieve of any file and continue to operate, with one exception. If the retrieved file contains an autoexecute macro, the autoexecute macro will run instead of the library macro.

Using the Macro Library in Release 2.2

With the background capability of a Macro Library, you can run all types of macros. What's more, you can create a macro that works across worksheet files. For example, you can have a macro that will take you from your current file by erasing the worksheet or retrieving another file, then return to the original file and cell pointer position to continue where you left off.

The macro in Figure 7.8 shows an example of just such a Macro Library macro. This is a

Figure 7.8 Place-marker Macro to Return to the Previous File

type of place-marker macro that stores the current filename, erases the worksheet, then does a /File Retrieve to return to the original worksheet file.

Be aware, however, that this macro will not work if you run it as a worksheet macro instead of as a Macro Library macro. It is important to have this macro run in the background. Otherwise, as soon as the macro comes to the second line erasing the worksheet, the disappearing worksheet will also mean a disappearing macro, and the macro will stop. So long as you save this macro into a Macro Library, however, and provided it does not also exist in the current worksheet, pressing Alt-P will cause the effect described.

Here's how the macro works.

{let PREVFILE,@cellpointer("filename")}   Causes the filename of the current worksheet to be stored in the cell named PREVFILE.

Note: The attribute "filename" was introduced with Release 2.2 and 3, and is not available in earlier releases of 1-2-3.

/weyy{esc}   Selects /Worksheet Erase Yes. In Release 2.2, if any changes have been made to the worksheet you will see an additional prompt asking whether you really want to erase the worksheet. If this is the case, the Y for Yes completes the command sequence and the {escape} command has no effect. If there have been no changes, the prompt will not appear, and the Y that the macro types will be eliminated by the {escape} command.

/fr{esc 2}{PREVFILE}~   Selects /File Retrieve, then presses Escape twice to eliminate the file directory path. The macro then does a subroutine branch to *PREVFILE*, where the filename that was stored there by the {let} command is typed for you (including the directory path). The {return} command returns the flow of the macro to the tilde at the end of the third line where the /File Retrieve sequence is completed. In the last line, the macro quits.

By itself, this macro is completely useless, since it records your current filename, erases the file, then /File Retrieves that file again, putting you back where you started. It is not intended as a stand-alone macro, however, but as an example of how to leave a file and return using a Macro Library macro. You can use the {let} command in the first line of the macro in other macros, then use the /File Retrieve that continues at a subroutine like the PREVFILE subroutine shown to jump you back to the file where you started.

Summarizing the Use of the Release 2.2 Macro Library

In the preceding few pages we have covered quite a scope of information, which may seem like a lot to be concerned with at this time. Fortunately, you do not have to bother with any of this to explore the world of macros. You may prefer to simply work with the macros in your current worksheets for the time being; then when you are ready for macro library information, you will find that these pages provide you with everything you need to know.

Using a Background Macro Library in Release 3

Although Release 3 does not have a Macro Library Manager add- in as found in Release 2.2, you can have background macros in two ways: either in an extra background worksheet in the same file or in a separate active file.

Let's review the Background Worksheet method first. Assume, for example, that you have retrieved a worksheet file and you would like some background macros to operate within that file, though not in the same worksheet. Simply create a separate worksheet by selecting /Worksheet Insert Sheet After, and then /File Combine the required macros into that separate worksheet. After range-naming the macros as described earlier, move back to the previous worksheet and access the macros from there.

If you want your macros to work across files, however, you may find a second method more appealing. Just select /File Open After and designate another .WK3 file that contains macros. So long as those macros do not contain references to range names which are specific to the macro file, the macros will work just as if they were in the current worksheet.

Fortunately, there is even a way to get these macros to work across files when they DO contain references to range names in the macro file. The technique is to provide a filename identifier before each such range name, enclosed in double angled brackets. Thus, a macro in the 3PRINT.WK3 file that refers to an internal loop range named XLOOP would be changed to refer instead to: <<3PRINT>>XLOOP.

However, this becomes something you would have to change if you /File Combine that macro into another file, so Lotus provides an alternative: the wild-card filename. The wild-card filename is a set of angled brackets surrounding a question mark. In our example using XLOOP, <<?>>XLOOP can be substituted.

So as to make the Release 3 macros we will be exploring as generic and portable as possible, many of the remaining macros in this book are shown in two ways: in the standard Release 2/2.01/2.2 form, and in a Release 3 modified form which includes this wild-card filename <<?>> preface where necessary. With rare exception, these macros will work across files perfectly well from the background, from separate active files, and whether brought in using /File Retrieve, /File Open, or /File Combine.

Note, however, that the one disadvantage of using a wild-card filename is the possibility of an error message if you mistakenly duplicate macro range names in two separate active files. For example, suppose you create another macro which branches to MTOGGLE in order to toggle a menu, and that macro also uses the <<?>> wild card. In such a case, the first macro will halt and you will see the following message at the bottom of your screen:

Invalid range: {branch} MTOGGLE

Actually, the importance of keeping your macro range names unique has always been an issue for single worksheets; but now you should extend to all of your files the care you give to making range names unique in a single file.

Starting Your Release 3 Macro Library with AUTO123

Instead of retrieving the worksheet you want to work on, then selecting /File Open After to open a separate worksheet file of your favorite background macros, you may want to do the reverse. In other words, you start by retrieving your favorite macro file, then do a /File Open Before or /File New Before to get to the worksheet you want to work on.

Just this approach is accomplished for you automatically with the Autoexecute \0 macro in Figure 7.9. This Autoexecute macro is designed for use in an AUTO123.WK3 file filled with your favorite macros. As an AUTO123 file, it will be loaded automatically when you start your 1-2-3 session, provided the file is kept in your default directory. And with its Autoexecuting macro (a macro that begins with a backslash-zero \0) the macro runs automatically as soon as the AUTO123.WK1 file is retrieved.

{ }   The macro begins with a null pass-through command. This is done to allow the macro to have alternate starting names: the \A name for use in starting the macro manually (usually for testing purposes), and the \0 name to start the macro automatically.

{menubranch AMENU}{quit}   Calls up the menu choices *Yes* and *No*, prompting you for whether you want to include this Macro Library in this session.

If you select *No* at the first menu, the macro will branch to AMENU3 and offer the choices *File_Retrieve*, *Blank_Worksheet*, and *Quit*. The *File_Retrieve* choice will do a /File Retrieve and press the F3 Name key, displaying all the files of the current directory. If you

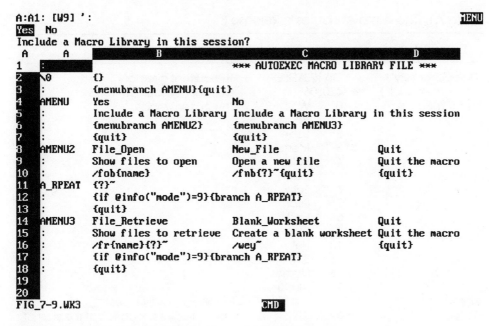

Figure 7.9 Autoexecuting Macro Library in AUTO123

select *Blank_Worksheet*, the macro will do a /Worksheet Erase Yes to provide you with a new, blank worksheet. Either way, the AUTO123 file will be replaced and you will be operating without this macro library file.

If you select *Yes*, the macro branches to AMENU2 and offers the choices *File_Open*, *New_File*, and *Quit*.

/fob{name}{?}~   The *File_Open* choice does a /File Open Before, presses F3 Name to show a list of all available files to open, and pauses for your choice.

{if @info("mode")=9}{branch A_REPEAT}   The {if} command is similar to the @if function, except that the truth or falseness of the {if} condition affects macro flow rather than returning a 1 or 0 as with the @if function. If the condition is true, the macro continues to read along the same line. If the condition is false, the macro skips to the next line down. In this case, the macro is testing for whether you are still in the "file" mode.

@info is an @function that was introduced with Release 3. It does not exist in Release 2, 2.01, or 2.2. Its attributes are as shown in Table 7.1.

By checking for whether the @info("mode") equals 9, your macro is testing for whether you have pressed Return (ending the bracketed question mark pause) because you selected a file, or because you selected another directory. If you selected another directory, the macro branches back to the bracketed question mark pause to await your selection of a file. Once you select a file, you are returned to Ready mode from the File mode, and @info("mode") no longer equals 9. The file you selected is retrieved and the macro quits.

Table 7.1 The @Info Attributes in Release 3

ExampleDescription

@info("directory")	C:\123\FILES\	The current directory
@info("memavail")	420306	Current available memory
@info("mode")	0	Wait	The current mode
	1	Ready	
	2	Label	
	3	Menu	
	4	Value	
	5	Point	
	6	Edit	
	7	Error	
	8	Find	
	9	Files	
	10	Help	
	11	Stat	
	13	Names	
	99	All Other	
@info("numfile")	1	Number of Active Files
@info("origin")	$A:$A$1	First cell pointer location at the start of the 1-2-3 session
@info("osreturncode")	0	Value returned by most recent /System command
@info("osversion")	DOS Version 3.10	Operating System version
@info("recalc")	Automatic	Current Recalc Mode
@info("release")	3.00.00	1-2-3 Release number
@info("system")	pcdos	Operating System
@info("totmem")	432898	Total available memory

/fnb(?)~{quit}   The *New_File* choice causes the selection /File New Before and pauses for your selection of a new filename.

Whether you select *File_Open* or *New_File*, the result will feel the same as having retrieved a file or having started with a blank worksheet, except that you now have your AUTO123 file containing your favorite macros in the background, and you can access those macros from the current file, or from any worksheet file you open during the current 1-2-3 session.

None of this will make any sense, however, unless you add your favorite macros to the AUTO123.WK3 file. Only after you have added the macros does the AUTO123.WK3 file becomes an effective and automatically loading Macro Library file.

Placing AUTO123.WK3 in the Default Directory

AUTO123 files will not load automatically unless they reside in your default directory. This means that you will want to either use /Worksheet Default Directory (don't forget to select

Update) to change your default directory to the directory where you keep your other macro files; or save or copy your AUTO123 file to your default directory. That way, the next time you boot up 1-2-3, the program will automatically retrieve the AUTO123 file and run its autoexec \0 macro.

Summary

In this chapter we explored the use of macro libraries. Release 2 and 2.01 do not provide a way to operate your macros from outside the current worksheet. However, you can simplify the transfer of macros from worksheet files on disk to the current worksheet by giving the macros range names such as MA, MB, and so on, /File Combining the named macros into the current worksheet, and assigning the required operating range names by selecting /Range Name Labels Right and PgDn or End DownArrow.

In Release 2.2, you can use the MACROMGR.ADN application to hold macros in a type of hyperspace outside the current worksheet. The following information applies to Release 2.2 Macro Library macros:

- To have 1-2-3 attach this add-in automatically each time you start a 1-2-3 session, select /Worksheet Global Default Other Add-in Set, assign a number (1 to 8) to the add-in, select MACROMGR.ADN, and assign Alt-7, Alt-8, Alt-9, Alt-10, or "No-key."

- In addition to automatically attaching the add-in, you have the option of having 1-2-3 automatically invoke, or run, the add-in when you start your 1-2-3 session. At the Invoke prompt, select Yes or No. Select Quit, then select Update to change the configuration of your 1-2-3, and finally select Quit to leave the Global Default Menu. Then, whenever you start up a 1-2-3 session, the Macro Library Manager add-in will be attached automatically.

- If you do not want to change your 1-2-3 configuration, you can always elect to attach the MACROMGR.ADN manually by selecting /Add-in from the command menu or pressing the Alt-F10 Add-in key.

- You can invoke the add-in by pressing the appropriate Alt-Function key combination or by selecting /Add-in Invoke.

- If you have no .MLB macro library files, you can create one from macros in the current worksheet by selecting Save.

- If you want your .MLB file automatically loaded into memory whenever the Macro Library Manager is attached, save it with the name AUTOLOAD.MLB. No macros in the library will execute automatically, not even \0 autoexecute macros, but they will be ready for you to use manually.

- If you select Edit from the /Add-in Invoke menu, you will be prompted for the macro library file to edit, and a location in your worksheet to place the macros in the library file. After editing .MLB macros, you can save any changes that you make by selecting /Add-in Invoke MACROMGR Save.

- You can create an AUTO123.WK1 file with an autoexecute macro that attaches and invokes your MACROMGR.ADN, loads your favorite .MLB Macro Library file, and finally does a /Worksheet Erase Yes to clear the screen. The advantage is that you can have the macro in this file load your .MLB files from any subdirectory where you choose to store them.

■ With the background capability of a Macro Library, you can also create a place-marker macro that will take you from your current file by erasing the worksheet or retrieving another file, then return to the original file and cell pointer position to continue where you left off.

Although Release 3 does not have a Macro Library Manager Add-in as found in Release 2.2, you can have background macros in two ways: either in an extra background worksheet in the same file or in a separate active file. The following information applies to Release 3 Macro Library macros:

■ To allow background macros to operate within a file, though not in the same worksheet, simply create a separate worksheet by selecting /Worksheet Insert Sheet After, and then /File Combine the required macros into that separate worksheet. After range naming the macros as described earlier, move back to the previous worksheet and access the macros from there.

■ If you want your macros to work across files, select /File Open After and designate another .WK3 file that contains macros. So long as those macros do not contain references to range names which are specific to the macro file, the macros will work just as if they were in the current worksheet.

■ If your macros contain references to range names in the macro file, provide a filename identifier or wild-card filename before each such range name, enclosed in double angled brackets.

■ The one disadvantage of using a wild-card filename is the possibility of an error message if you mistakenly duplicate macro range names in two separate active files. For this reason, you should make range names unique to a single file.

■ You can open a file of your favorite macros automatically with the \0 autoexec macro in an AUTO123.WK3 file as shown in Figure 7.8. If you save or copy your AUTO123 file to your default directory, the program will automatically retrieve the AUTO123 file and run its autoexec \0 macro when you start your 1-2-3 session, and your background macros will run from the current file, or from any worksheet file you open during the session.

In Chapter 8 we will explore the concept of toggle-switch macros, including macros to toggle between alternate locations, to toggle your titles on and off, to toggle Recalculation between automatic and manual, to toggle between file directories, and so on. We will also look at pop-up utilities including a pop-up notepad, pop-up calendar, and pop-up calculator.

8

TOGGLES AND THE
MACRO RUN KEY

Scope

In this chapter we will introduce the use of toggles in your macros, including a toggle to jump to often-visited areas of your spreadsheet. Also covered are use of the Alt-F3 Macro Run key in Release 2.2 and 3, a simulation of the Alt-F3 Macro Run key in Release 2 and 2.01, and ways to jump your cell pointer to special areas such as a notepad area, appointment calendar area, pop-up calculator window, and a custom help screen.

The Order of Range Names

Since we are reviewing ways of moving quickly and easily around the worksheet, this is a good place to introduce a little trick involving the use of range names to jump to often-visited areas of your spreadsheet. As already mentioned, pressing the F5 Goto key and the F3 Name key will cause all of your range names to be presented in the upper panel as possible Goto locations. This means that pressing F5 Goto, then F3 Name, then Return, will cause your cell pointer to jump to the first range name in the list.

Here's the trick. Since the range names are listed alphabetically, you can create a special range name that will always appear first in the upper panel. So if there's some prime area in your spreadsheet you think you might want to visit often, all you have to do is to name the upper left corner of that area with the special name. Then when you press F5 Goto, F3 Name, Return, your cell pointer will jump there instantly.

You might think that using the range name AAA would work for this, but it turns out that numbers are listed ahead of letters. Then how about 000? That would be a good idea, except that certain symbols come ahead of numbers. All things considered, the best choice seems to be the number sign (#). Actually, this is especially handy because you can establish several range names all over your spreadsheet that you think you might want to visit often, and give them names like #1, #2, #3, and so on. Then when you want to visit the first area you press F5 F3 Return, for the second area press F5 F3 RightArrow Return, for the third area press F5 F3 RightArrow RightArrow Return, and so on.

Using the Alt-F3 Macro Run Key in Release 2.2 and 3

There is another reason for paying attention to the order in which range names are displayed after you press F5, then F3. It has to do with another function key, the Alt-F3 Macro Run key.

Both Release 2.2 and Release 3.0 have included a new feature, the Alt-F3 Macro Run key. This is not a new idea with Lotus, since the Symphony program has had the equivalent (the F7 User key) for years. But whether or not you are familiar with Symphony, you will come to appreciate the inclusion of the Alt-F3 Run key in 1-2-3.

The purpose of the Alt-F3 Run key is to provide another way to run macros beyond the Alt-letter method we have used so far. Now, by pressing Alt-F3, you will be able to access macros by:

1. Pointing in a single-line or full-screen listing of range names to one of the back-slash–letter macro names (such as \A, \B, \C, and so on);

2. Pointing in a range name listing to any of the non-backslash range names that iden-tifies the first cell of a macro;

3. Entering any of the non-backslash range names that identifies the first cell of a macro;

4. Entering the cell address of the first cell of any macro;

5. Pointing in your spreadsheet to the first cell of any macro.

You must, of course, have macros already written and in place to use the Alt-F3 Run key. As-suming this is the case, you can simply press Alt-F3. You will see the prompt *Select the macro to run* and a single-line listing of range names. If you then follow a press of Alt-F3 with a press of the F3 Name key, the screen will be replaced with a full-screen listing of range names from which you can choose your macro range names. A Release 2.2 example of such a listing is shown in Figure 8.1.

```
A1: '*CALC                                                      NAMES
Select the macro to run:
     *CALC                B82
*CALC            *KALCULTR        *QUIKCALC        *TOGLCALC        :
  :                :                :                :                :
C                K                KCALC            KCALC2           KEY1
KEY2             KEY3             KHERE1           KMEM             KMENU1
KMENU2           KMENU3           KMENU4           KNUM             KQUIT
K_SET            Q                T                TMANUAL          \C
\K               \Q               \T               *ADD             *CALC
*CASE            *DIR             *EDITNAME        *INDICT          *JUMP
*KALCULTR        *PHONE           *RETRV           *WINDOFF         :
  :                :                :                :                :
C                C_MENU           DFILE            DNAME            DPREV
D:MENU           EFORM            FCOUNT           FCTR             FLOOP
FLOOP2           FMENU            KCALC            RDIR             RKEY
RLOOP            RNAME            RNAME2           W_MENU           \A
\C               \D               \E               \F               \I
\J               \K               \P               \R               \W
\Z
```

FIG_8-1.WK1

Figure 8.1   Using the Alt-F3 Run Key in Release 2.2

Using an Asterisk-Name as a Macro Launcher

You will notice at the top of the screen four names that start with asterisks. These are macro range names that can be used to invoke (run) specific macros through use of the Alt-F3 Run key. Throughout the rest of this book we have given every macro two starting names: the backslash-letter name you are familiar with and a macro-launcher name that can be invoked through the use of the Alt-F3 Macro Run key.

These macro-launcher names have been created starting with asterisks so they will appear among the first choices (after any number-sign range names such as #1, #2, or #3) when you press the Alt-F3 Run key. (Just as number-sign range names #1, #2, and #3 will appear before asterisk-names, so are asterisk-names listed before numbers and most other symbols.)

Following these four range names is a row of colons. In fact, the colons are range names as well, deliberately created for no other reason than to display a sparse area separating the macro range names from the rest of the range names in the worksheet. Although they appear to be identical, five of these colons are actually followed by one, two, three, four, or five spaces; they only *look* identical. (This part of the process is passed along as a tip for convenience, and is only a suggestion that you can either adopt or ignore.)

Just as the asterisk-names are easy to spot and identify, so are the backslash-range names such as \A, \B, \C, and so on. You will notice that they always follow the standard range names.

Following the backslash-range names in Figure 8.1 is another set of asterisk-names—

something you will only see in Release 2.2. The fact that more range names follow the first set of backslash-letter names means these are range names found in a loaded Macro Library .MLB file (as discussed in Chapter 7). Again, the asterisk preceding the first few range names represents a convention used to identify the macro-launcher names more easily.

If, after pressing the Alt-F3 Run key and F3 Name key, you point to any range name in this listing that represents a range residing in your worksheet (but before you press Return), the upper panel of the range name screen will show the cell or range address of the selected range name. However, if you point to a range name that resides in the Macro Library, the upper panel will show the name of the particular Macro Library .MLB file from which the range name comes.

To run a specific macro, you can point to its backslash-letter macro name at this point, or to its macro-launcher range name that represents the first cell of the macro. Under *no* conditions should you point to a non-macro range name in this screen and press Enter.

Other Uses of the Alt-F3 Macro Run Key

Other options for activating your macros come to bear if you press Escape after pressing the Alt-F3 Run key and the F3 Name key. Doing so will cause the full-screen listing to disappear and be replaced with your original spreadsheet view, except that in the top panel you will still see the prompt *Select the macro to run:*. You are now free to point to the first cell of the macro you want to run. An example, where the option has been invoked and the cell pointer rests on the first cell of a macro called TODAY'S DATE IN WORDS, is shown in Figure 8.2.

You could also type one of your asterisk range names at this point, or the cell address that corresponds to the first cell of the desired macro.

If you do decide to point to the first cell of the macro you want to run, however, you get the extra advantage of seeing what the macro looks like before you run it. This contrasts with a disadvantage: that you will no longer have the cell in view where the macro will actually be run. If you aren't careful, you may end up running the macro in an area that writes over data you would rather have saved.

One fairly significant by-product of all this convenience in the ways you can invoke your macros is the breaking of the 26-letter limit. Now, instead of having a maximum of 26 macros that you invoke by pressing the Alt key and the letters A to Z, you can name the first cells of your macros with an almost unlimited number of asterisk range names that will be accessed through the Alt-F3 Run key.

You may have noticed that the asterisk range names shown in cells A5 and A14 in Figure 8.2 actually represent the second lines of the macros shown. The first lines of these macros have backslash-letter range names, and consist of nothing but the pass-through null command { }. This is another suggested technique we have alluded to in earlier chapters, which permits dual naming of a macro. The macros shown can be invoked by pressing Alt-T and Alt-U, or by pointing to the range names *TODAY and *UPDATE in the Alt-F3 Run key range name screen.

```
B3: '{}                                                           POINT
Select the macro to run: B3
```

```
        A          B        C        D        E
 1
 2   :                   *** TODAY'S DATE IN WORDS ***
 3  \T           {}
 4  *TODAY       @choose(@mod(@int(@now),7),"Saturday","Sunday","Monday","Tuesda
 5   :           "Wednesday","Thursday","Friday")&", "{edit}{calc}
 6   :           {home}+"{end}"&
 7   :           @choose(@month(@now)-1,"January","February","March","April",
 8   :           "May","June","July","August","September","October","November",
 9   :           "December")&" "&@string(@day(@now),0)&","&@string(@year(@now)
10   :           +1900,0){edit}{calc}~{quit}
11   :                      *** UPDATE WORKSHEET DATE ***
12  \U           {}
13  *UPDATE      {windowsoff}{paneloff}
14   :           {let WHERE,@cellpointer("address")}
15   :           {goto}UPDATE~@now~{edit}{calc}~
16   :           {goto}{WHERE}~{up 3}{left 3}{goto}{WHERE}~
17   :           {quit}
18  WHERE        $D$297
19   :           {return}
20   :
```

FIG_8-2.WK1

Figure 8.2   Alt-F3 Run Used with Escape in Release 2.2

Using the Alt-F3 Run Key in Release 3

So far we have shown two Alt-F3 screens from Release 2.2. The same types of screens and accessibility are available in Release 3, with a few minor differences. The screen you will see when you press the Alt-F3 Run key followed by the F3 Name key in Release 3 is shown in Figure 8.3. In Release 3, the screen shows range names only four across, though it shows the name of any other open files in angled brackets at the end of the list. In this case, the cell pointer is pointing to another open file, and the filename below the prompt *Select the macro to run* refers to that file. If you press Enter on the filename in angled brackets, you will see another set of range names, as shown in Figure 8.4.

Simulating the Alt-F3 Run Key in Release 2.0 and 2.01

In case those of you with the earlier Release 2.0 and 2.01 of 1-2-3 are feeling left out, you'll be glad to know you can simulate the Alt-F3 Run key with a simple macro as shown in Figure 8.5.

You will need to /File Combine or create this macro in the current worksheet before you use it. Don't forget to select /Range Name Labels Right to range name the macro before using it.

To invoke this macro, press Alt-Z. (We chose Alt-Z because the letter Z is seldom used

```
A:B2: [W14]                                                                    NAMES
Select the macro to run:
C:\22\MMM\FIG_8-4.WK3
*COORD          *EDITNAME       *LISTNAM        *SHOWSUM
*UNNAME         *VERIFY         :               :
C_COPY          EGET            EMOVE           ESTART
E_KEY           MC              ME              ML
MS              MU              MV              SFORM
U_MENU          VERIFY          VKEY            VLOC
VNAME           VNONE           \0              \C
\E              \L              \S              \U
\V              <<FIG_8-4.WK3>>
```

FIG_8-3.WK3

Figure 8.3   Using the Alt-F3 Run Key in Release 3

```
A:A1: [W10] '\C                                                               NAMES
Select the macro to run:
A:B4..A:B4
*COPYSTAY       *EVRYOTHR       *INSROWDATA     *KOPYABS
*UPCOPY         *XTRAABS        :               :
C_LOOP          C_MENU1         EDIR            EKEY
EMENU1          E_MORE          KCELL           KHERE
MC              ME              MI              MK
MU              MX              \C              \E
\I              \K              \U              \X
<<FIG_8-3.WK3>>
```

FIG_8-4.WK3

Figure 8.4   Using the Alt-F3 Run Key to Point to Another File

A1: [W11]   READY

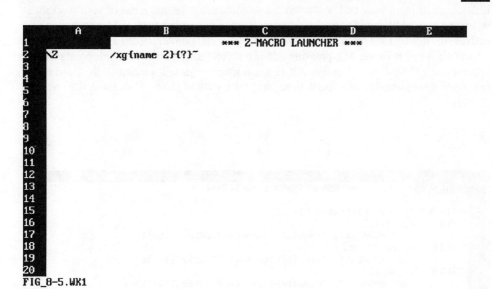

FIG_8-5.WK1

Figure 8.5 Alt-Z Macro to Simulate the Alt-F3 Macro Run Key

and it is immediately to the right of your Alt key on most computer keyboards.) You will not
see a prompt, but you will see a list of your range names—an indication that you should now
point to one of the asterisk-letter names and press Return to invoke the macro. Alternately,
you can press Escape, point to the first cell of the macro you want to run, and press Return.
The macro will run just as if you had invoked it through the Alt-letter combination.

Caution: Using the Alt-F3 Run key and Alt-Z Macro Launcher can be useful, but
only if they are handled correctly. In addition to using the extra techniques and tips included here, it is strongly suggested that you pay particular attention to the location
where your macro will run.

More importantly, you must be careful while using the spreadsheet-pointing method that
you actually point to the first cell of the macro. The tendency will be to point to the range
name identifier to the left of the actual range name; and if you do that you will get unex-
pected, and sometimes catastrophic, results.

The Home Alternate Toggle

Now that we have discussed alternate ways to start a macro using range names, let's look at
another use of range names. By including instructions in your macro to modify the information in one of its named cells, you can create a macro toggle-switch.

The Home Alternate Toggle in Figure 8.6 includes just such a toggle-switch. This macro is designed to jump your cell pointer to one of three often-visited areas of your worksheet when you press Alt-H; and as a toggle macro, it actually changes what it does each time you activate the macro. One press of Alt-H will jump your cell pointer to the first pre-established range (we'll call it Home #1); pressing Alt-H a second time jumps your cell pointer to the second range (Home #2); pressing Alt-H again jumps your cell pointer to the third range (Home #3); pressing Alt- H a fourth time jumps you back to Home #1 again, and so on.

```
A1: ':                                                            READY

         A         B        C        D        E       F       G       H
 1    :                    ***HOME-ALTERNATE TOGGLE***
 2   \H        {}
 3  *HOMEALT   {paneloff}{branch HTOGL1}
 4  HTOGL1     {goto}#1~
 5    :        {let *HOMEALT,"{paneloff}{branch HTOGL2}"}{quit}
 6  HTOGL2     {goto}#2~
 7    :        {let *HOMEALT,"{paneloff}{branch HTOGL3}"}{quit}
 8  HTOGL3     {goto}#3~
 9    :        {let *HOMEALT,"{paneloff}{branch HTOGL1}"}{quit}
10
11
12
13
14
15
16
17
18
19
20
FIG_8-6.WK1
```

Figure 8.6   First Example of a Toggle Macro

Before starting the macro, it is necessary to find three areas in your worksheet that you think you might be visiting often, and using /Range Name Create, name the upper left corner of the first area using the range name #1, the second area using the range name #2, and the third area using the range name #3.

{ }   The macro begins with a null pass-through command that allows the macro to have alternate starting names: the \H starting name you can invoke by pressing Alt-H and the *HOMEALT starting name you can invoke with the Alt-F3 Run key in Release 2.2 and 3 or with the Alt-Z Macro Launcher shown in Figure 8.5.

{paneloff}{branch HTOGL1}   The panel is turned off to suppress panel flicker, and the macro branches to the first toggle subroutine, named HTOGL1.

{goto}#1~   Presses the F5 Goto key, sending your cell pointer to the upper left corner of the first area you have range named #1.

{let *HOMEALT,"{paneloff}{branch HTOGL2}"){quit} Copies the commands {paneloff}{branch HTOGL2} to the beginning of the macro, so the next time you use the macro, it will begin by branching to the second subroutine that starts at HTOGL2 rather than HTOGL1.

The macro quits at this point, self-modified and prepared to process the direction to go to location #2. In this same way, pressing Alt-H again will cause it to self-modify to process the direction to go to location #3, and pressing Alt-H again will cause it to return again to location #1.

Note: Although we turned the panel off at the beginning of the macro, issuing a {panelon} command is not required since quitting the macro causes any {paneloff} or {windowsoff} commands to be canceled.

Using the Home Alternate Toggle in Release 3

The Release 3 version of this macro is shown in Figure 8.7. As you can see, this macro is almost identical to the .WK1 version in Figure 8.6, except that a <<?>> wild-card filename (double angle brackets surrounding question marks) has been added to the front of references to the range name *HOMEALT. Of course, the .WK1 version of the Home-Alternate Toggle without the wild-card filename <<?>> will work perfectly well in Release 3. However, if you want to modify the macro to work in the background in a separate active file, the

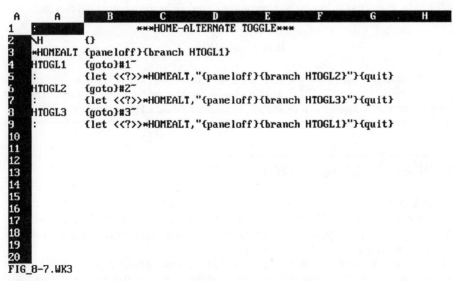

FIG_8-7.WK3

Figure 8.7 A Release 3 Macro Library Version of a Toggle

macro needs some way of finding the *HOMEALT range name referred to in the {let} commands in the fourth, sixth, and eighth lines. By supplying a wild-card filename, you let the macro know to check all other active files if the *HOMEALT filename is not found in the current worksheet file.

You may be wondering why the wild-card filename <<?>> is not required preceding the HTOGL1, HTOGL2, and HTOGL3 range names shown in the {branch} commands of the macro. The reason relates to a distinction between macro flow and range-name location.

When a macro starts in a separate file, any flow commands such as {branch}, {menubranch}, {menucall}, or the subroutine calling command {*rangename*} automatically assume that the macro flow continues in the same file as the main macro itself. On the other hand, commands with range names which affect data or cell pointer location are assumed to be in the current worksheet file unless the range names are preceded with a specific filename or the wild-card filename <<?>>.

For example, suppose you have a Release 3 macro that refers to range name LHERE that changes the contents of LHERE or moves the cell pointer to LHERE with a {goto} command. You will see the wild-card filename <<?>> in the following types of commands:

{let <<?>>LHERE,+53}
{goto}<<?>>LHERE~
{blank <<?>>LHERE}
{if <<?>>LHERE=999}{quit}

Note: The wild-card filename <<?>> is *not* required when the macro flow switches to a subroutine named LHERE. Thus, you might see a return to a place-marker like this:

{goto}{LHERE}~

where the macro flow is interrupted, runs at LHERE, then continues where it left off (at the tilde, in this case). Yet in the same macro, you might see a command that looks like this:

{goto}<<?>>LHERE~

where the macro is not running a subroutine at LHERE, but simply moving the cell pointer to the cell named LHERE. In that case, the wild-card filename <<?>> are required so the macro knows to look outside the current file if LHERE is not found.

The Titles Toggle Macro

Another fine example of a toggle macro, as well as a very useful utility, is the Titles Toggle macro shown in Figure 8.8. The purpose of this macro is to solve a typical frustration of 1-2-3: the cumbersome cell pointer movement you have to go through to reset your titles if for some reason you have to clear them temporarily.

Before we get into the macro itself, you should know about a couple of handy tricks for moving past locked-in titles without having to clear the titles first. The first trick involves use of the F5 Goto key. If, for example, you have two spreadsheets in a single file where the

`A1: [W11] ':`   `READY`

```
         A         B       C       D       E       F       G
 1  :                     ***TITLES TOGGLE***
 2  \T          {}
 3  *TITLETOG   {paneloff}{windowsoff}
 4  :           {let T_HERE,@cellpointer("address")}
 5  TOGGLE      {esc}
 6  :           {goto}IV8192~{goto}TSTART~{goto}TCORNER~
 7  :           /wtb{goto}{T_HERE}~
 8  :           {left @min(@cellpointer("col")-2,4)}
 9  :           {up @min(@cellpointer("row")-1,2)}
10  :           {goto}{T_HERE}~
11  :           {let TOGGLE,"{branch TCLEAR}"}{quit}
12  TCLEAR      /wtc
13  :           {let TOGGLE,"{esc}"}{quit}
14  T_HERE      $E$54
15  :           {return}
16
17
18
19
20
```
`FIG_8-8.WK1`

Figure 8.8 Titles Toggle Macro

second spreadsheet is below the first, you may have discovered the /Worksheet Titles Horizontal command as a way to restrict yourself to the second spreadsheet. Unfortunately, you find that when you want to visit the first spreadsheet the titles keep you out.

Try the F5 Goto key—it will allow you to move the cell pointer right past your titles. So to visit the first spreadsheet, press F5 Goto, move your cell pointer there, and press Escape when you want to return. If you want to stay at the first spreadsheet to make changes or enter data, press Return instead of Escape. Then when you want to jump back to the second spreadsheet, press End Home to go to the lower right corner of the worksheet and Home to jump to the cell in the upper left corner under the locked-in titles of the second spreadsheet.

Our second trick involving locked-in titles is a handy way to change a cell of your titles. Suppose, for example, that you notice that the heading TOTAL in cell J14 of your titles should have read SUBTOTAL. You could clear your titles to change it, you could use the F5 Goto technique to move there and make the change, or you could try this technique: Move your cell pointer to a blank cell near your current cell and type SUBTOTAL. Then select /Move, press Return, and at the message *Enter range to move to:*, type **J14**, and press Return. The title cell is changed instantly, and you hardly had to move your cell pointer at all.

This brings us to the Titles Toggle macro in Figure 8.8. Like the Home Alternate Toggle, this macro requires a little advance setup. Move to the first cell beneath your horizontal titles and the first cell to the right of your vertical titles, and range-name that cell TCORNER. Then move to the upper left cell of the titles themselves and give that cell the range name TSTART. Now you can move to any area below the rows you will be locking in as titles and press Alt-T. If you've done your range-naming properly, the titles you prepared for should appear, be locked in, and be ready to use. If you want the titles to clear, just press Alt-T again—the macro has already toggled to the Titles-off position, so it will clear the titles instantly. Press Alt-T again and the titles will lock in again.

{ } The macro begins with a null pass-through command, which allows the macro to have alternate starting names: the \T starting name you can invoke by pressing Alt-T, and the *TITLETOG starting name you can invoke with the Alt-F3 Run key in Release 2.2 and 3 or with the Alt-Z Macro Launcher shown in Figure 8.5.

{paneloff}{windowsoff}   Suppresses screen flicker.

{let T_HERE,@cellpointer("address")}   This is a place-marker command that stores the current cell address in the cell named T_HERE.

{esc}   This cell has been range-named TOGGLE because it provides the pivotal direction of the flow of the macro. With the {esc} command in this cell (we could have used the { } null command), the macro simply passes through to the next cell down. However, in the tenth line of the macro, the macro self-modifies. The cell named TOGGLE will be changed to the command {branch TCLEAR}, which will cause the macro to operate quite differently the next time you press Alt-T.

{goto}IV8192~{goto}TSTART~{goto}TCORNER~   Sends the cell pointer to the lower right corner of your worksheet, then to the range name TSTART, which brings the title rows into full view. The cell pointer then jumps to TCORNER, where you would ordinarily place your cell pointer to lock in these particular titles.

/wtb{goto}{T_HERE}~   Selects /Worksheet Titles Both, which accomplishes the title lock. The {goto} command continues at the part of the macro named T_HERE, which contains the absolute address of the original cell. The {return} command below that cell tells the macro to continue at the tilde after the {T_HERE} subroutine branch.

{left @min(@cellpointer("col")-2,4)}   Moves the cell pointer left either two cells less than the current column, or four cells, whichever is less. This is done to reorient the original cell location more towards the center of the screen.

{up @min(@cellpointer("row")-1,2)}   For the same reason, this line of the macro moves the cell pointer up either one cell less than the current row, or two cells, whichever is less.

{goto}{T_HERE}~   Jumps the cell pointer back to the original location.

{let TOGGLE,"{branch TCLEAR}"}{quit}   Changes the instruction in TOGGLE so the macro will branch to TCLEAR the next time you press Alt-T. The macro quits at this point.

/wtc   The next time you press Alt-T, the macro branches to this command to do a /Worksheet Titles Clear.

{let TOGGLE,"{esc}"}{quit}   The macro changes the instruction in TOGGLE back to {esc} so the macro will continue its normal flow without branching the next time you press Alt-T.

Using the Titles Toggle Macro in Release 3

As noted above, Release 3 can, with rare exception, run all .WK1 versions of macro without change, so long as you are running the macro from within the current worksheet file. However, to run the macro from a background Macro Library in Release 3, you must insert the wild-card filename <<?>> before certain range names in the macro.

Refer now to Figure 8.9. You will see that lines 4, 11, and 13 have been modified to include the wild-card filename <<?>>. This is because all three of these range name references are contained in {let} commands which make some change to the data in the referenced cells.

```
A:A1: [W11] ':                                                          READY

    A        A         B       C       D       E       F       G
 1  :                        ***TITLES TOGGLE***
 2  \T        {}
 3  *TITLETOG {paneloff}{windowsoff}
 4  :         {let <<?>>T_HERE,@cellpointer("coord")}
 5  TOGGLE    {esc}
 6  :         {goto}IV8192~{goto}TSTART~{goto}TCORNER~
 7  :         /wtb{goto}{T_HERE}~
 8  :         {left @min(@cellpointer("col")-2,4)}
 9  :         {up @min(@cellpointer("row")-1,2)}
10  :         {goto}{T_HERE}~
11  :         {let <<?>>TOGGLE,"{branch TCLEAR}"}{quit}
12  TCLEAR    /wtc
13  :         {let <<?>>TOGGLE,"{esc}"}{quit}
14  T_HERE    $A:$E$27
15  :         {return}
16
17
18
19
20
FIG_8-9.WK3
```

Figure 8.9 Using the Titles Toggle Macro in Release 3

All other references to range names, however, are contained in branches or subroutine calls, so the wild-card filename <<?>> is not required. Understanding this difference will save you a great deal of typing as you become more proficient with the macro language.

Switching Spreadsheet Areas with Titles

The use of titles in your worksheets can make your view of a given spreadsheet area clearer and more understandable, but it is not at all easy to switch between spreadsheet areas, each with its own set of titles. Manually, doing this would mean clearing your current titles, moving to a location to bring an alternate set of titles into view, and then setting those titles before you move to the location in this spreadsheet area where you want to work. Fortunately, you can accomplish this with a simple menu macro, as shown in Figure 8.10.

Before you start the macro, you should find three areas with titles in your worksheet that you think you might be visiting often and, using /Range Name Create, name the upper left corner of the first set of titles using the range name #1, the second set of titles using the range name #2, and the third set of titles using the range name #3. Name the cell below and to the right of your vertical titles YLOCK1, YLOCK2, and YLOCK3.

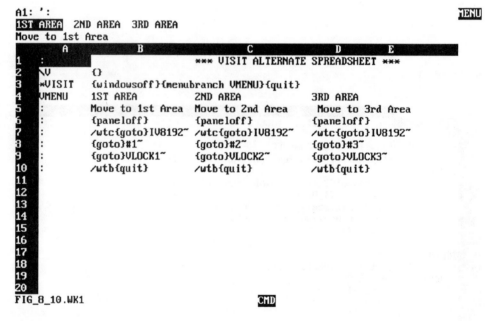

Figure 8.10 Macro to Visit Alternate Spreadsheet Areas

Here's how the macro works.

{windowsoff}{menubranch VMENU}{quit}   Begins by turning off the windows to suppress screen flicker, and calls up the menu choices *1ST AREA*, *2ND AREA*, and *3RD AREA*.

{paneloff}/wtc{goto}IV8192~   The upper panel could not be turned off until this point, or the custom menu would not have been visible. The macro turns off the upper panel to suppress screen flicker, selects /Worksheet Titles Clear, and moves the cell pointer clear of the cell (to IV8192) to ensure your titles end up in the upper right corner of the screen.

{goto}#1~{goto}VLOCK~ Jumps the cell pointer to the upper left corner of the first set of titles you have previously given the range name #1, then moves to the cell below and to the right of your vertical titles, to the cell you have named YLOCK1.

/wtb{quit} With the new spreadsheet area in place, the macro selects /Worksheet Titles Both, and quits.

Note: This macro can be used without modification as a background macro in a Release 3 Macro Library, even though it references six location range names and one macro range name. The reason relates to the range names themselves. The six location range names represent locations in the current file, and so do not need to be preceded with a wild-card filename <<?>>. As for the macro range name, it is found in a {branch} command that never requires a wild-card filename.

Toggle for Automatic/Manual Recalc

The macro in Figure 8.11 shows a different way to create a toggle. In this case, the macro is a simple five-line macro that instantly toggles between automatic and manual recalculation by setting a switch, then testing for the on/off condition of the switch.

Figure 8.11 Toggle for Automatic/Manual Recalculation

{ }   Begins with a null pass-through command, allowing alternate starting names: the \T starting name you can invoke by pressing Alt-T, and the *TOGLCALC starting name you can invoke with the Alt-F3 Run key in Release 2.2 and 3, or with the Alt-Z Macro Launcher shown in Figure 8.5.

{windowsoff}{paneloff}   Suppresses screen flicker.

{if TMANUAL=1}/wgra{blank TMANUAL}~{quit}   This is another use of the {if} command. In this case, it tests for whether the value in TMANUAL is equal to 1. Essentially, this is equivalent to testing whether your special toggle switch is set to the ON position. If so, the macro selects /Worksheet Global Recalculation Automatic, then blanks the value in TMANUAL (turning the toggle switch to OFF), and quits.

/wgrm{let TMANUAL,1}{quit}   If TMANUAL is *not* equal to 1, or in other words, if your toggle switch is not set to the ON position, the macro continues at this line, selecting /Worksheet Global Recalculation Manual, then changes the value in TMANUAL to 1 (turning the toggle switch to ON), and quits.

The Release 3 Macro Library version of this macro is almost identical, except that every reference to TMANUAL should be changed to <<?>>TMANUAL as shown in Figure 8.12 so the macro can run in the background in a separate active file.

This toggle-switch technique can be used in other macros where you need to toggle between alternating results each time a macro or subroutine is activated. Don't overlook the fact, however, that you can always achieve the same result as a toggle by using a custom

Figure 8.12 Release 3 Toggle for Auto/Manual Recalculation

menu. In the example of a switch between Automatic and Manual Recalculation, the menu choices would look like this:

AUTO   **MANUAL**
AUTOMATIC RECALC   **MANUAL RECALC**
/wgra   **/wgrm**
{quit}   **{quit}**

On the one hand, this is a simpler macro to write. On the other hand, it takes one more keystroke to activate, and you have to think about your choices when the menu comes up. You may want to experiment with both methods and decide which method makes more sense for your own specific applications.

The File Directory Toggle

Releases 2, 2.01, and 2.2 have an unfortunate drawback in the /File Directory menu selection: you do not have the option of editing the directory you are offered when you select /File Directory. To make a change at that menu level, you must completely retype the drive letter and directory path. Of course, if you make a typing mistake, your only option is to start over and type the drive letter and directory path again.

Release 3 does give you editing capabilities at this level, but even editing can take quite a few keystrokes. Consider, then, a toggle macro that will automatically toggle between three separate file directories whenever you press Alt-F. Such a macro is shown in Figure 8.13.

A1: [W11] ' :   `READY`

```
            A         B         C         D         E         F         G
1    :                      *** FILE DIRECTORY TOGGLE ***
2    \F           {}
3    *FILEDIR     {paneloff}{branch FTOGL_1}
4    FTOGL_1      /fdC:\22\upgd~
5    :            {let *FILEDIR,"{paneloff}{branch FTOGL_2}"}
6    :            {panelon}/fd{quit}
7    FTOGL_2      /fdC:\22\mmm~
8    :            {let *FILEDIR,"{paneloff}{branch FTOGL_3}"}
9    :            {panelon}/fd{quit}
10   FTOGL_3      /fdC:\22\files~
11   :            {let *FILEDIR,"{paneloff}{branch FTOGL_1}"}
12   :            {panelon}/fd{quit}
13
14
15
16
17
18
19
20
```

FIG_8_13.WK1

Figure 8.13   A File Directory Toggle Using Preset Directories

This macro requires a slight modification before it will work on your computer. The particular drives and directory paths shown at the beginning of each routine FTOGL_1, FTOGL_2, and FTOGL_3 are examples only. For your version of the macro, you must enter the drive letters and directory paths that are appropriate for your own 1-2-3 sub-directories.

{paneloff}{branch FTOGL_1}　　Turns off the upper panel and branches to the first routine, FTOGL_1. (Since FTOGL_1 begins at the next line of the macro, the {branch} command is not strictly required, but it helps to make the macro more easily understood.)

/fdC:\22\upgd~　　Selects /File Directory, then enters the drive letter and directory path.

{let *FILEDIR,"{paneloff}{branch FTOGL_2}"}　　As in the Home Alternate Toggle, this is a self-modifying macro that copies the commands {paneloff}{branch FTOGL_2} to its own beginning cell so the next time you use the macro it starts by branching to the second subroutine at FTOGL_2 rather than FTOGL_1.

{panelon}/fd{quit}　　Turns on the upper panel and selects /File Directory so you can see the directory entered for you. The macro quits, leaving you at the /File Directory menu level. If you like what you see, you can simply press Return. If you want to enter another selection, you can do so by manually typing a different selection at this point.

Alternately, press Return and Alt-F to have the macro automatically enter another pre-established directory for you. The macro has already modified its start, so pressing Alt-F this time will change the directory to the directory shown at FTOGL_2. In this same way, pressing Alt-F a third time will change the directory to the directory shown at FTOGL_3.

Switching Directories to Match Retrieved Files

If you select files from different directories often, you may be interested in a macro that selects /File Retrieve, offers you a full-screen view of subdirectories, waits for your selection of subdirectory and specific file, then changes the /File Directory for you automatically to correspond to the subdirectory of the file selected.

For example, suppose you have three subdirectories under your main 1-2-3 directory named C:\123\SALES, C:\123\BUDGET, and C:\123\TRENDS. You have been working in the SALES subdirectory, but now you want to retrieve a file from the BUDGET directory, and have your /File Directory changed to C:\123\BUDGET at the same time. Refer to the macro in Figure 8.14. This macro will not work in Release 2 or 2.01, because it is designed to continue working after it leaves the current file to retrieve another file. In fact, it will only work in a Release 2.2 .MLB Macro Library file, or in a separate active file in Release 3.

{let RNAME,@cellpointer("filename")}　　This uses the @cellpointer function in a {let} command as a type of place-marker command similar to the command, {let RNAME,@cellpointer("address")}. However, instead of storing the current cell address in RNAME, the macro is storing the current drive, directory path and filename. The

A1: ':   READY

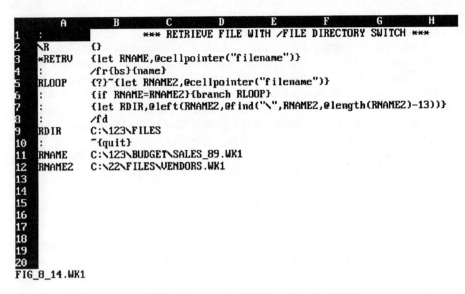

FIG_8_14.WK1

Figure 8.14 Macro to Retrieve File with /File Directory Switch

"filename" attribute of @cellpointer is unique to Release 2.2 and 3, and will not work in Release 2 or 2.01.

/fr{bs}{name}   Selects /File Retrieve, backs up from the current subdirectory to the main 1-2-3 directory, then presses F3 Name to show a full-screen view of all your subdirectories under the 1-2-3 directory.

{?}~{let RNAME2,@cellpointer("filename")}   Pauses for your selection of a subdirectory, then stores the name of the current file in RNAME2. At this point, that name should correspond to the name stored in RNAME.

{if RNAME=RNAME2}{branch RLOOP}   Since you have not selected a different file yet, this {if} statement is found to be true, and the macro branches back to RLOOP, where it pauses again—this time for your selection of a file to retrieve. As soon as that file is retrieved, the {let} command at RLOOP changes RNAME2 to the new drive, directory path and filename selected, and the macro continues again at this {if} statement. This time, RNAME will not be equal to RNAME2, and the macro skips the rest of the line to continue at the next line.

{let RDIR,@left(RNAME2,@find("\",RNAME2,@length(RNAME2)-13))}   This   {let} command introduces use of three @functions not yet discussed in this book: @left, @find, and @length. The purpose of this line is to truncate the information in RNAME2, eliminating the filename and placing just the drive letter and directory path in the cell named RDIR.

The @left function has the syntax, @left(*location or string,number of characters*), and is used to return a number of left-most characters in an entry. Thus, @left(J57,3) will return SAL if the entry in J57 is "SALES," and @left("BUDGET",3) will return BUD.

However, instead of a value (like 3, for example), you can use another set of @functions (@find and @length) to establish the *number of characters* required for an @left function.

The @find function has the syntax, @find(*item to search for, string or location to search, start-point*). Thus, the @find function in this case returns a value for the *number of characters* required by @left by searching for the last backslash character in RNAME2 that comes after the subdirectory and before the filename. It starts its search at a point 13 characters from the right of the entry in RNAME2 (using @length(RNAME2)-13) because the maximum length of a filename in 1-2-3 is 12 including the .WK1 file extension.

We will be seeing more examples of the use of string-manipulating @functions in macros later in the book, including @left, @right, @mid, @find, @length, and @string.

/fd   Selects /File Directory in advance of the self-modified cell shown just below at RDIR.

C:\123\FILES   This is just an example of the type of entry you might see in RDIR after using the macro once. Actually, to type this macro into your own worksheet, you would leave this cell blank initially. It will be completed for you by the {let} command two lines above.

˜{quit}   The /File Directory command has been completed, a tilde is typed to enter the directory, and the macro quits. The remaining two cells of the macro are storage cells only.

A variation of this macro is shown in Figure 8.15 to provide its use as a Macro Library macro in a separate active file in Release 3. Notice that the wild-card filename <<?>> has been added to the beginning of every range name reference in the macro *except* in the {branch} command in the fifth line, where it is not required. Some of the range names have also been shortened, but this is only to allow more of the macro line to fit on a single screen as you type it in.

The Pop-up Notepad and Appointment Calendar

Other interesting uses of the toggle method which also take advantage of the place-marker techniques of this chapter are found in macro-driven pop-up utilities like the Notepad macro and the Appointment Calendar macro. The Notepad macro is shown in Figure 8.16.

{windowsoff}{paneloff}{let NHERE,@cellpointer("address")}   Turns off windows and panel and creates a place-marker so you can return to the current cell after using the notepad.

{goto}IV8192˜{goto}NOTEPAD˜{end}{down}   Moves the cell pointer far from the cell which has been range-named NOTEPAD, then jumps to NOTEPAD to bring it into view.

```
A:A1: [W7] ':                                                              READY
```

```
  A      A         B       C         D         E        F        G       H
1     :               *** RETRIEVE FILE WITH /FILE DIRECTORY SWITCH ***
2     \R        {}
3     *RETRV    {let <<?>>RNAME,@cellpointer("filename")}
4     :         /fr{bs}{name}
5     RLOOP     {?}
6     :         ~
7     :         {let <<?>>RN,@cellpointer("filename")}
8     :         {if <<?>>RNAME=<<?>>RN}{branch RLOOP}
9     :         {let <<?>>RD,@left(<<?>>RN,@find("\",<<?>>RN,@length(<<?>>RN)-13)
10    :         /fd
11    RD        C:\123\FILES
12    :         ~{quit}
13    RNAME     C:\123\BUDGET\SALES_89.WK3
14    RN        C:\22\FILES\VENDORS.WK3
15
16
17
18
19
20
FIG_8_15.WK3
```

Figure 8.15   Retrieve File with Directory Switch for Release 3

```
A1: ':                                                                     READY
```

```
           A        B        C         D        E        F        G       H
1      :               ***NOTEPAD MACRO***
2      \N       {}
3      *NOTEPAD {esc}
4      :        {windowsoff}{paneloff}{let NHERE,@cellpointer("address")}
5      :        {goto}IV8192~{goto}NOTEPAD~{end}{down}
6      :        {let *NOTEPAD,"{branch NRETURN}"}{quit}
7      NRETURN  {windowsoff}{paneloff}{goto}{NHERE}~
8      :        {up @min(@cellpointer("row")-1,3)}
9      :        {left @min(@cellpointer("col")-1,3)}
10     :        {goto}{NHERE}~{let *NOTEPAD,"{esc}"}{quit}
11     NHERE    $A$1
12     :        {return}
13     NOTEPAD  *********************** MACRO NOTEPAD ***************************
14     :        Remember to get the milk.
15     :
16     :
17     :
18     :
19     :                  PRESS <ALT><N> TO RETURN TO SPREADSHEET
20     :        ***************************************************************
FIG_8_16.WK1
```

Figure 8.16   The Pop-up Notepad Macro

The End Down commands move the cell pointer to the first blank area below the last note entered.

{let *NOTEPAD,"{BRANCH NRETURN}"}{quit}   Copies a new branching command to the first active line of the macro, so the next time the macro is activated, it toggles to NRETURN. The macro quits at this point, so you are free to explore the items in the notepad, change them or add new items. When you want to return to the area where you started out, press Alt-N again. The macro will run the routine at NRETURN.

{windowsoff}{paneloff}{goto}{NHERE}~   Turns off windows and panel and jumps the cell pointer back to the original location.

{up @min(@cellpointer("row")-1,3)}   Moves the cell pointer up either one cell less than the current row, or three cells, whichever is less, to reorient the original cell location more towards the center of the screen.

{left @min(@cellpointer("col")-1,3)}   For the same reason, this line moves the cell pointer left either one cell less than the current column, or three cells, whichever is less.

{goto}{NHERE}~{let *NOTEPAD,"{esc}"}{quit}   Jumps the cell pointer back to the original location, then changes the instruction in the first active line of the macro so the macro will not branch to NRETURN the next time you press Alt- T. The macro quits at this point.

The end result of all this is that you can press Alt-N to move to a different location, and the macro quits so you can move around, enter data, or make changes without the constraints of being in a macro. Then by pressing Alt-N again, you can return to where you started in your spreadsheet.

If you will compare the Notepad in Figure 8.16 with the Appointment Calendar in Figure 8.17, you will see that the individual lines of both macros are almost identical. The difference is in the area marked off for notes, whether to be entered in a notepad form or entered in a columnar layout. These areas, incidentally, can be placed anywhere in the worksheet—they do not have to remain attached to the macros themselves as demonstrated here.

You could also combine the two macros into one with a menu choice of the area you want to visit, still using the same toggle feature to return to your original cell location in the worksheet.

THE AUTOMATIC TICKLER

The macro shown in Figure 8.18 does not have a toggle feature in the same sense as the other toggle macros covered in this chapter, but it will give different results depending on the current date.

The purpose of the macro is to alert you about an important date, meeting, appointment,

A1: ':   `READY`

```
         A          B          C          D          E          F
1    :                   *** APPOINTMENT CALENDAR NOTEPAD ***
2    \A         {}
3    *APPT      {esc}
4    APPT_ON    {let A_HERE,@cellpointer("address")}
5    :          {goto}IV8192~{goto}APPTS~{end}{down}
6    :          {let *APPT,+"{branch APPT_OFF}"}
7    APPT_OFF   {windowsoff}{paneloff}{goto}{A_HERE}~
8    :          {left @min(@cellpointer("col")-1,3)}
9    :          {up @min(@cellpointer("row")-1,3)}
10   :          {goto}{A_HERE}~{let *APPT,"{esc}"}{quit}
11   A_HERE     $A$57
12   :          {return}
13   APPTS      *                      APPOINTMENT CALENDAR
14   :          ************************************************************
15   :            DATE        TIME        NAME        COMPANY     REMARKS
16   :          25-Dec-90  12:00 p.m.  Santa Claus  Toy Workshop Expect Gifts!
17   :
18   :
19   :                         PRESS <ALT><A> TO RETURN
20   :          ************************************************************
```
FIG_8_17.WK1

Figure 8.17   The Pop-up Appointment Calendar

A1: ':   `READY`

```
         A          B          C          D          E          F          G
1    :                   *** AUTOMATIC TICKLER MACRO ***
2    \0         {if DATE_1=@int(@now)}{NOTE_1}
3    :          {if DATE_2=@int(@now)}{NOTE_2}
4    :          {if DATE_3=@int(@now)}{NOTE_3}
5    :          {quit}
6    DATE_1     22-Oct-89
7    NOTE_1     !!!    APPT WITH DR. WIDMAN AT 5:00 TUESDAY, 22 OCT !!!
8    :          {?}{esc}{return}
9    DATE_2     25-Nov-89
10   NOTE_2     !!!    DON'T FORGET APPT AT 3:00, WEDNESDAY, 25 NOV !!!
11   :          {?}{esc}{return}
12   DATE_3     03-Dec-89
13   NOTE_3     !!!    DENTIST APPT AT 5:00 TODAY !!!
14   :          {?}{esc}{return}
15
16
17
18
19
20
```
FIG_8_18.WK1

Figure 8.18   Automatic Tickler Macro Using {if}

or occasion without your having to invoke it. As you might guess, this is designed to be an automatic executing macro that starts running as soon as you retrieve the file.

This macro requires some setting up before it will operate correctly. To do this, change the input at the DATE_1, DATE_2, and DATE_3 locations by typing in three appointment dates using the @date format. Then change the notes at NOTE_1, NOTE_2, and NOTE_3. You can use any appropriate reminders or messages you like.

Here's how the macro works.

{if DATE_1=@int(@now)}{NOTE_1}   This is another example using the {if} command as discussed in other macros in this chapter. If the statement is true, the macro continues on the same line. If it is false, the macro skips to the next line down. In this case, if the date entered in DATE_1 is the same as the integer of today's date, the macro skips to the subroutine at NOTE_1. In the example in Figure 8.18, this subroutine causes the macro to type the message

!!! APPT WITH DR. WIDMAN AT 5:00 TUESDAY, 22 OCT !!!

in the upper panel.

{if DATE_2=@int(@now)}{NOTE_2}   Whether or not the macro runs the subroutine at NOTE_1, it continues at the second line, where it tests for whether the date stored in DATE_2 is the same as the integer of today's date. If so, the macro skips to the subroutine at NOTE_2, where in this case it types the message

!!! DON'T FORGET APPT AT 3:00, WEDNESDAY, 25 NOV !!!

in the upper panel.

{if DATE_3=@int(@now)}{NOTE_3}   Again, whether or not the macro runs the subroutines at NOTE_1 or NOTE_2, it continues at the third line, where it tests for whether the date stored in DATE_3 is the same as the integer of today's date. If so, the macro skips to the subroutine at NOTE_3, where in this case it types the message

!!! DENTIST APPT AT 5:00 TODAY !!!

{?}{esc}{return}   After each subroutine at NOTE_1, NOTE_2, and NOTE_3, are the commands to pause so you can see the message in the upper panel. When you press Return, the {esc} command eliminates the typed message so it is not entered in a cell, then the flow of the macro returns to the place where it left off. After all three dates have been checked in this manner, the macro quits (see the fourth line of the macro).

If you have a very important message and there is no particular spreadsheet that you are certain you will be retrieving every day, you may want to create an AUTO123 file that contains this Automatic Tickler macro. As you'll recall from earlier chapters, naming a file AUTO123 will cause 1-2-3 to retrieve the file as soon as it boots up; and having a \0 autoexec macro in that file will cause 1-2-3 to run the macro as soon as the AUTO123 file appears.

Note: You can also combine several \0 autoexec macros into one. You may, for example, want to create an AUTO123 file which starts with the Automatic Tickler macro, but instead of a {quit} statement in the fourth line, the macro might branch to another macro that automatically attaches and invokes your MACROMGR.ADN file (in Release 2.2 only), then loads your favorite Macro Library macros.

Summary

In this chapter you were introduced to the following new concepts:

- You can use the F5 Goto key with the F3 Name key to instantly jump to named ranges in your worksheet. Naming your most often-visited ranges #1, #2, #3, and so on, will cause those ranges to appear as the first choices when you press Alt-F3 Run F3 Name.

- Both Release 2.2 and Release 3.0 have included a new feature, the Alt-F3 Macro Run key. By giving your macros range names that start with an asterisk, they will appear among the first names you see when you decide to run your macros with the Alt-F3 Run key. Now, instead of a maximum of 26 macros that you invoke by pressing the Alt key and the letters A to Z, you can name the first cells of your macros with an almost unlimited number of asterisk range names that will be accessed through the Alt-F3 Run key.

- You can also press the F3 Name key after the Alt-F3 Run key to get a full-screen view of your macro range names. If any range names follow the first set of backslash-letter names in Release 2.2, these represent range names found in a loaded Macro Library .MLB file.

- In Release 3, pressing Alt-F3 Run and F3 Name causes the screen to show your range names and bracketed filenames for any other active files. If you point to a bracketed filename in this screen and press Enter, you will see another set of range names pertaining to that active file.

- Those with Release 2.0 or 2.01 can simulate the Alt-F3 Run key with the Alt-Z Macro Launcher as shown in Figure 8.5.

- You can use toggles to achieve multiple functions from a single Alt-letter macro.

Macros covered in this chapter which use these techniques include:

- A Macro Launcher to simulate pressing the Alt-F3 Run key and F3 Name key.
- A Home Alternate Toggle for instantly jumping the cell pointer to prime locations on your worksheet.
- A Titles Toggle to automatically turn your titles off and on.
- A macro to Visit Alternate Spreadsheet Areas, each with its own set of titles.
- A Recalc Toggle to turn manual recalculation off and on.
- A /File Directory Toggle using preset file directory paths.
- A /File Retrieve macro with File Directory Switch.
- Pop-up macros including a Pop-up Notepad and Appointment Calendar.

■ An Automatic Tickler macro designed to alert you about an important date, meeting, appointment, or occasion.

In Chapter 9 we will examine data entry and data modification macros using the {if} command with @cellpointer("type"). We will also introduce another type of prompt for the user: the {getlabel} and {getnumber} commands that pause for your entry of a string or a value.

9

DATA ENTRY AND MODIFICATION

Scope

In this chapter we will explore macros that make use of the {if} command in connection with the @cellpointer function to facilitate data entry and modification of data in your worksheet.

We will also explore two prompt commands, {getlabel} and {getnumber}, that pause for your entry of a string or value, then place that entry in a designated cell. This feature is especially useful for self-modifying macros that prompt you for information, then use that information to accomplish different tasks.

Using the {if} Command

So far we have made limited use of the {if} command. You have seen how testing for whether one entry is equal to another causes the macro to continue on the same line or skip to the next line and continue there. In this chapter we will take the concept further to explore other uses of the {if} command.

You are no doubt familiar with use of the @if formula in a standard 1-2-3 worksheet. In fact, the If-Then-Else concept is common to most programming languages. Basically the

137

idea is to compare two elements or states. **If** the statement of comparison is true, **Then** one thing happens, or something **Else** happens.

The @if formula in a standard worksheet is structured as:

$$@if(A23+B23,999,@na)$$

which would be read, *If the contents of cell A23 equal the contents of B23, display the number 999 in the current cell; else display NA.* In addition to values or the results of @functions, you can have an @if statement that returns a label, as in the example:

$$@if(A23+B23,"YES","NO").$$

The {if} command is the macro equivalent to an @if function, except that the example

{if A23=B23}999~{quit}
@na~

would be read *If the contents of cell A23 equal the contents of B23, continue at the same line (enter **999** and quit); otherwise skip to the next line down and enter NA in the current cell.*

Note: Another difference is that there is always a space between the word **if** and the statement (in this case A23=B23) in an {if} command.

You can compare the contents of a cell against the contents of another cell or you can compare cell contents against a string as long as you put the string in quotation marks. If you want to test whether cell A23 contains the word CONFIRMED, for example, your macro {if} statement would be:

{if A23="CONFIRMED"}999~{quit}
@na~

There are several differences, then, between the @if formula and the {if} macro command. In our example, the @if formula is typed into a cell in the spreadsheet and stays there, displaying either **999** or **NA** depending on whether the statement is true or false. If the contents of A23 or B23 change, the results displayed in the @if formula cell will change.

The {if} command, on the other hand, is typed into a macro. You can run the macro at any cell, but it *inserts* the answer rather than *displaying* the answer; and if you want the A23=B23 statement tested again—after the content of either cell has changed, for example—you must run the macro again.

There is another, more important difference between the @if formula and the {if} macro command. The macro command will allow more than simple typing of a number or a string; you can also cause your macro to accomplish a whole series of tasks depending on whether the {if} statement is true or false.

The Label and Number Format Macros

One of the most useful types of macros is a column or row modifier that moves through a range of data entries, modifying the entries until the last entry is reached. For example, you may be interested in a Label Format macro that changes all the numbers in a column to labels. Using an {if} command, this macro quits automatically if the cell pointer comes to the blank cell at the end of the column.

Actually, the {if} command can used with @cellpointer("type") to check whether the current cell contains a label, contains a value, or is completely blank, as:

{if @cellpointer("type")="l"} is true if current cell is a label.
{if @cellpointer("type")="v"} is true if current cell is a value.
{if @cellpointer("type")="b"} is true if current cell is blank.

You may have had this problem. You enter a column of part numbers, only to find after an hour of number entries that the numbers should have been entered as labels. You may find, for example, that there are some dash-number suffixes, or some part numbers with the letter A or B after it. Whatever the reason, you now have to go back to the top of the column and put an apostrophe in front of each number. This is a perfect job for a looping macro with an {if} statement. The Label Format macro in Figure 9.1 is just such a macro, designed to change the numbers or formulas in a column to their label equivalents.

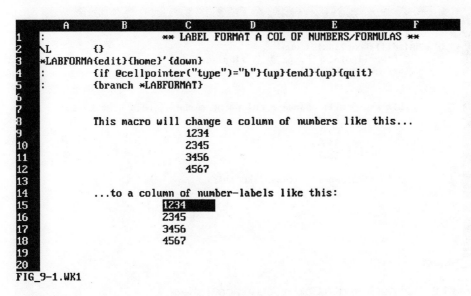

Figure 9.1 Label Format a Column of Numbers or Formulas

Before you start the macro, place your cell pointer at the first cell of the column you want changed. Here's how the macro works.

{edit}{home}'{down} The macro switches to the Edit mode, presses Home to move to the beginning of the number or formula, types an apostrophe, then moves down one cell. This changes the entry from a number to a label and positions the cell pointer to check for an empty cell.

{if @cellpointer("type")="b"}{up}{end}{up}{quit}   If the statement is true—if the cell is blank—the cell pointer is moved up one cell, then {end}{up} to the top of the column where you started.

{branch *LABFORMAT}   If the cell pointer "type" is *not* equal to "b," the macro loops back to the beginning and changes the next number to a label, moves down to test the next cell and so forth, until it reaches a blank cell or until you press Ctrl-Break to make it quit.

As you might imagine, a macro to delete the apostrophe from the beginning of each entry in a column is only a slightly modified version of the Label Format macro. Refer to Figure 9.2.

C15: 1234   READY

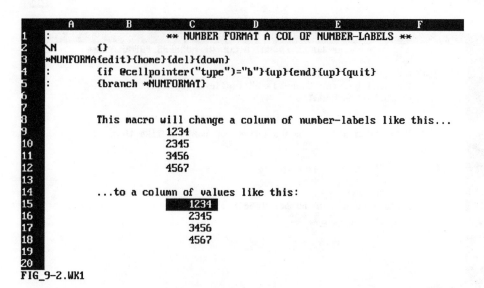

FIG_9-2.WK1

Figure 9.2 Number Format a Column of Number-Labels

{edit}{home}{del}{down}   This is the one line of the Number Format macro that differs from the Label Format macro. Instead of inserting an apostrophe each time the macro loops, this macro deletes the apostrophe, changing your number-labels to straight numbers.

The use of {if @cellpointer("type")="b"} to test for a blank cell can be used in a variety of applications, as the next few macros show.

Indent Five Spaces

The macro in Figure 9.3 is used to move down a column and indent every entry five spaces. Of course, since values are already right justified, this macro is designed to operate only on a column of labels. If you were to use it on a column that contains values, the macro would attempt to insert five spaces between the first digit and the rest of the digits of that value; and since values do not start with an apostrophe, this attempt would cause an error that makes the macro quit. As with the Number Format and Label Format macros, this macro uses {if @cellpointer("type")="b"} to test for a blank cell.

C15: [W10] '   Chair   READY

```
           A        B          C          D          E
1    :                   ***INDENT 5 SPACES***
2    \I       {}
3    *INDENT  {edit}{home}{right}     {down}
4    :        {if @cellpointer("type")="b"}{up}{end}{up}{quit}
5    :        {BRANCH *INDENT}
6
7
8             This macro will indent a column of labels like this...
9                       Chair
10                      Table
11                      Lamp
12                      Sofa
13
14            ...to look like this:
15                      Chair
16                      Table
17                      Lamp
18                      Sofa
19
20
```
FIG_9-3.WK1

Figure 9.3 Indent All Entries in a Column Five Spaces

{edit}{home}{right}   {down}   The macro starts with the switch to the Edit mode and insertion of five spaces before the label, followed by a {down} that enters the change and moves down one cell.

{if @cellpointer("type")="b"}{up}{end}{up}{quit}   If the cell is blank, the cell pointer moves to the top of the column and the macro quits.

{branch *INDENT}   Otherwise, the macro loops back to the beginning and adds five spaces to the front of the next label. The macro continues until it reaches a blank space or until you press Ctrl-Break to quit.

The Leading Zeros Macro

The macro in Figure 9.4 is similar to the Label Format macro, except that in addition to changing a number to a label, it provides leading zeros in front of the entry. This type of exercise would be handy if, for example, you entered an entire column of zip codes as numbers, only to realize that the only way to get a zip code to show leading zeros is to enter it as a label. This macro will correct the problem after the fact.

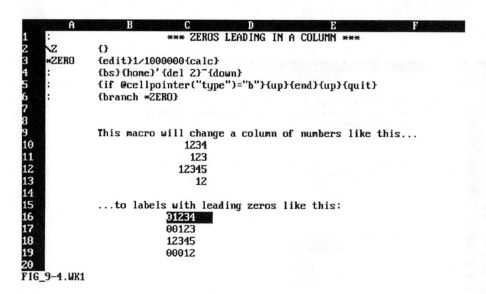

Figure 9.4 Macro to Leading Zeros in a Column of Numbers

{edit}1/1000000{calc}   Switches to the Edit mode, tacks the number 1 to the end of the number, then divides the number by 1,000,000 and calculates the cell—which turns it into a calculated value rather than a division formula. If the number is 777, for example, it becomes 7771/1000000, then 0.007771.

{bs}{home}'{del 2}~{down}   Since you are still in the Edit mode, the Backspace command erases the number 1 at the end, pressing Home moves the cursor to the beginning of the entry, the apostrophe turns it into a label, and {del 2} eliminates the zero preceding the decimal point, as well as the decimal point itself.

The rest of the macro is a repeat of the looping macros shown above, using **{if @cellpointer("type")="b"}** to test for blank cells so that the macro will know when to stop.

The @Round Macro

From time to time you may find it necessary to add the @round formula to the front of all of the entries in a column. You may find, for example, that the vertical sum in your spreadsheet does not equal the horizontal sum due to differences in rounding. Since adding @round to each entry manually requires 14 keystrokes per cell, this is the type of chore that should be handled by a looping macro. See the @Round macro in Figure 9.5.

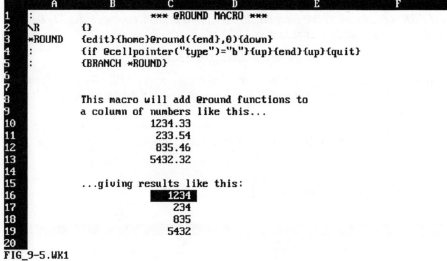

```
C16: [W8] @ROUND(1234.33,0)                                          EDIT
@ROUND(1234.33,0)

          A         B           C           D           E           F
1    :                  *** @ROUND MACRO ***
2    \R        {}
3    *ROUND    {edit}{home}@round({end},0){down}
4    :         {if @cellpointer("type")="b"}{up}{end}{up}{quit}
5    :         {BRANCH *ROUND}
6
7
8              This macro will add @round functions to
9              a column of numbers like this...
10                            1234.33
11                             233.54
12                             835.46
13                            5432.32
14
15             ...giving results like this:
16                             1234
17                              234
18                              835
19                             5432
20
FIG_9-5.WK1
```

Figure 9.5 @Round Added to Each Entry in a Column

{edit}{home}@round({end},0){down}   The macro switches to the Edit mode, moves to the front of the entry, types **@round** and an opening parenthesis, moves to the end of the entry, types a comma and a zero, and closes the parenthesis. The macro then loops back to the beginning and works on the next cell down, continuing in this way until it reaches a blank cell or you press Ctrl-Break to stop it.

Incidentally, another way to get your macro to stop is to place a number like **999** at the end of the column and use the formula **{if @cellpointer("contents")=999}** as the condition to tell the macro to stop. In fact, you can combine both techniques to have the macro pause when it reaches a blank cell (where you can decide whether to have the macro continue or quit), and end when it reaches the number 999.

A Macro to Eliminate the @ERR Message

The are several types of formulas that can cause an error message (*ERR*) to appear in one of the cells of your spreadsheet, but perhaps the most common involves formulas which try to divide by zero—a mathematical no-no. For example, if you copy a formula down an entire column that divides the number 333 by the cell to the left and some of the cells to the left of the column are not filled in yet, the formulas in those cases will return *ERR*. This can make a spreadsheet look unprofessional, error-prone, and highly suspicious if you have to distribute it to others.

One solution, of course, is to erase the offending cells until such time as the cells to the left are filled in, but having to go through the exercise of erasing and then replacing the formulas seems wasted energy and could easily result in a true error if you forget to replace one of the cell formulas later.

The better solution is to surround the formula with an @if statement which essentially states, *If ERR is displayed by this formula, display a zero instead, otherwise display the true results of the formula.* Such a formula in cell C27 might be:

$$\text{@if(@iserr(333/B27),0,333/B27)}$$

If B27 is zero, then the formula 333/B27 would normally return *ERR*. With this formula, however, 333/B27 would return zero if B27 is zero, or it would return the actual value of 333/B27 if B27 is a number.

The macro in Figure 9.6 is designed to move down a column where some of the cells return (or might return) ERR, and surround each formula of the column with

```
E17: [W14] @IF(@ISERR(+A17/0),0,+A17/0)                              EDIT
@IF(@ISERR(+A17/0),0,+A17/0)
```

```
            A          B           C           D           E
1    :                      *** ELIMINATE @ERR MESSAGE ***
2    \E          {}
3    *ELIMERR    {edit}{home}'~
4    :           {let ENTRY,@cellpointer("contents")}
5    :           {edit}{home}{del}
6    :           @if(@iserr({end}),0,
7    ENTRY       +A19/0
8    :           )~{down}
9    :           {if @cellpointer("type")="b"}{up}{end}{up}{quit}
10   :           {branch *ELIMERR}
11
12   This macro surrounds each entry in a column with an @if function
13   that changes each instance of ERR to 0.
14
15                          Value in Col A              Results after
16   Straight Value         Divided by Zero             Using the macro:
17        123                    ERR                                 0
18        234                    ERR                                 0
19        354                    ERR                                 0
20
FIG_9-6.WK1
```

Figure 9.6   Macro to Eliminate ERR Messages in a Column

@if(@iserr(...)). This is a good example of a looping macro that stops when it comes to a blank cell. It is also another demonstration of a self-modifying macro and an excellent example of a macro that combines the {if} command with the standard spreadsheet @if function.

{edit}{home}'~   Changes the formula in the current cell to a label by switching to the Edit mode, moving the cursor to the beginning of the entry, then adding an apostrophe.

{let ENTRY,@cellpointer("contents")}   This formula could be read *Let the cell called ENTRY become like the cell pointer contents*. This is the same as copying the formula that has been turned into a label from the current cell to the cell of the macro named Entry.

{edit}{home}{del}   Switches to the edit mode, moves the cell pointer to the beginning of the label, and deletes the apostrophe, returning the formula in the current cell to its original state.

@if(@iserr({end}),0,   Still in the Edit mode and still at the beginning of the formula, this line starts typing the **@if** statement which replaces the formula in the current cell. After typing **@if(@iserr** and a parenthesis, the cell pointer moves to the end of the formula, closes the parenthesis, and types a comma, a zero, and another comma.

   The next line of the macro will contain the original formula, inserted there as a label by the third line of the macro. It is "read" by the macro at this point, and thus inserted into the new @if formula.

)~{down}   Closes the parenthesis and moves the cell pointer down to the next cell in the column.

{if @cellpointer("type")="b"}{up}{end}{up}{quit}   Tests for a blank cell. If the macro finds a blank cell, it moves the cell pointer up to the top of the column and quits.

{branch *ELIMERR}   If the macro does not find a blank cell, it loops back to the beginning and starts over. It will continue in this way until it reaches a blank cell, or until you press Ctrl-Break.

   If you want to include this macro in Release 3 as a Macro Library item that will operate across active files, you must include a wild-card filename <<?>> in front of the range name ENTRY in the {let} command in the third line of the macro, as:

$$\text{\{let <<?>>ENTRY,@cellpointer("contents")\}}$$

This is required so 1-2-3 will know to look beyond the current file for the location of the cell named ENTRY you want to change.

The Data Entry Macro

In Chapter 5 we introduced a simple Data Entry macro that moves down the spreadsheet one cell at a time, pausing for your entry of data. The macro in Figure 9.7 has that feature, plus additional choices to cover the possible ways you may want to enter your data. As in the macros above, it uses the {if} command with @cellpointer("type")="b"; but in this case the purpose is to allow you to stop the macro manually at any point by moving to a blank cell and pressing Return.

```
A1:  (L/P)  :                                                              READY

        A              B                 C                D            E
 1:                             ***DATA ENTRY MACRO***
 2 \D           {}
 3 \DATAENTR  {menubranch DMENU1}{quit}
 4 DMENU1      Down               Right
 5:            Entries Going Down  Entries Going Right
 6:            {let DIR,"{DOWN}"}  {let DIR,"{RIGHT}"}
 7:            {menubranch DMENU2} {menubranch DMENU2}
 8:            {menubranch DMENU1} {menubranch DMENU1}
 9 DMENU2      Standard           Left               Right            Center
10:            Standard Entry     Entry Left Aligned Entry Right Aligned  Entry Centered
11:            {let DLOOP,"{?}~"} {let DLOOP,"'{?}~"} {let DLOOP,"""{?}~"} {let DLOOP,"^{?}~"}
12 DLOOP       {?}~               {branch DLOOP}     {branch DLOOP}    {branch DLOOP}
13:            {if @cellpointer("type")="b"}{quit}
14 DIR         {DOWN}
15:            {branch DLOOP}
16
17
18
19
20
FIG_9-7.WK1
```

Figure 9.7 A Data Entry Macro with Range Label Types

{menubranch DMENU1}{quit}   Calls up the menu choices *Down*, for entries going down a column, and *Right*, for entries moving to the right in a row.

{let DIR,"{down}"}   If you look farther down the macro, you will see the cell named DIR (for *direction*). The {let} command tells the macro to *Let the cell named DIR become like the word {down}*. As a result, the macro modifies itself so it will move *down* rather than *across* the spreadsheet during the data entry process.

{menubranch DMENU2}{menubranch DMENU1}   Calls up the second menu, with choices *Standard*, *Left*, *Right*, and *Center*.

The *Standard* choice causes the macro to pause for standard entry of a number or a label.

This means that values entered with this choice will be right justified, and labels will be left justified.

The *Left* choice begins every entry with an apostrophe, which means your data will be entered left justified as a label. This is especially handy when you are entering number–label combinations that must start with an apostrophe. In the same way, the *Right* choice begins every entry with full quotation marks so the entries will be right justified. The *Center* choice begins every entry with a centering caret (^).

{let DLOOP,"{?}~"}   Selecting the choice *Standard* causes the macro to *Let DLOOP become {?}~*, copying {?}~ into the cell named DLOOP. This is the second running modification of the macro based on your menu selection. As you will see, you are able to put any symbols between quotation marks in a {let} command, and they will be read as string entries rather than as macro commands.

{?}~   This is where the macro pauses for your entry. Had you selected *Left*, this cell would have been modified to '{?}~. Selecting *Right* would have modified it to "{?}~, and *Center* would have changed it to ^{?}~. After each of these changes the macro loops back to this cell, as a result of the {branch DLOOP} command.

{DOWN}   This line will always read either {DOWN} or {RIGHT}, depending on the choice you made at the first menu level. It causes the cell pointer to move one cell down or to the right after your entry.

{branch DLOOP}   Branches back to the cell named DLOOP, where once again the macro pauses for your entry.

{if @cellpointer("type")="b"}{quit}   When you are finished entering data and you want the macro to quit, press Ctrl-Break, or move to any blank cell and press Return. This {if} command will cause the macro to quit.

Take a look now at the commands under the menu choice *Right*. You will see that the **{letDLOOP,"""{?}~"** command seems to have one too many quotation marks. Since the symbols which you want to appear in the cell named DLOOP after selecting RIGHT are "{?}~, you might expect that **{let DLOOP,""{?}~"}** with two quotation marks preceding the bracketed pause would do the trick. As it happens, however, the first quotation mark identifies the string, and the second quotation mark would close the string if there were not a third quotation mark.

However, if that's the case, you may wonder why there isn't a fourth quotation mark to start the string that consists of the bracketed pause. The answer is that the closing quotation mark for the first string (consisting of ") can also be used as the opening quotation mark for the second string (consisting of {?}~).

This is all very complicated and fortunately it does not come up often. However, if you find in writing your own macros using strings and quotation marks that things just do not seem to work as you expected, try varying the number of quotation marks. This is all covered in more detail in Chapter 10.

This Data Entry macro is an all-purpose entry macro that moves down your spreadsheet or to the right, entering data in the standard way, with an apostrophe, with full quotation marks, or with a centering caret depending on your menu selection. It also provides another example of a way to get your macro to modify itself.

Release 3 users may want to use this as a background macro in a separate active Macro Library file. To do so, the only change you need to make is the addition of a wild-card filename <<?>> in front of the range names DIR and DLOOP in the fifth and tenth lines of the macro. (Do not forget to make this change in all four columns of these rows as required.)

Non-standard Entries Corrected

This next macro uses the {if} command with @exact as well as with the @cellpointer("type")="b" function we have already covered. Shown in Figure 9.8, this macro is designed to help you identify items in a large database that may be out-of-place, misspelled, plural when they should be singular, singular when they should be plural, or typed using an uppercase, lowercase, or proper case inconsistently.

	A	B	C	D	E
1	:	*** NON-STANDARD ENTRIES CORRECTED ***			
2	\N	{}			
3	*NCORR	{let NTEST,@cellpointer("contents")}			
4	NLOOP	{down}{if @cellpointer("type")="b"}{quit}			
5	:	{if @exact(NTEST,@cellpointer("contents"))}{branch NLOOP}			
6	:	{menubranch NMENU}{quit}			
7	NMENU	NO_CHANGE	AS_ABOVE	EDIT	QUIT
8	:	Accept the difference	Copy the cell above	Edit this entry	Quit the macro
9	:	{branch *NCORR}	/c{esc}{up}~~	{edit}{?}~	{quit}
10	NTEST	Chair	{branch NLOOP}	{branch *NCORR}	
11					
12					
13	This macro will identify misspellings, entries out of place, etc.				
14					
15		Chair			
16		Chair			
17		Chairs			
18		Chair			

FIG_9-8.WK1

Figure 9.8 Macro to Correct Non-standard Entries in a Database

Imagine a sorted database of part numbers, for example, where a given part number appears 21 times. If the twenty-first occurrence of the part number is entered incorrectly, it will not match the item immediately above it. This macro identifies any item that does not match the item above it, then pauses for your correction of an invalid item, or acceptance of the item as valid.

To start the macro, place your cell pointer on the first item in the list you want checked for correctness, and press Alt-N.

{let NTEST,@cellpointer("contents")}   Copies the displayed contents of the current cell to the cell in the macro named NTEST. This is done to store an item for comparison with the items below it.

{down}{if @cellpointer("type")="b"}{quit}   Moves down to the next cell. This is a looping point to which the macro will return after checking each item in turn. When the cell pointer comes to a blank cell, which presumably represents the end of the list, the macro quits.

{if @exact(NTEST,@cellpointer("contents"))}{branch NLOOP}   This line introduces the @exact function, used to compare strings or cell contents. If the comparison is exact, the {if} statement is evaluated as false, the macro skips to the next line. In this case, the entry in NTEST where the macro has stored a copy of the first cell of the database is compared with the current cell contents. If the comparison is exact, the macro branches back to NLOOP, moves down and checks for a blank cell, then returns to this line to test the next item.

{menubranch NMENU}{quit}   If the item stored in NTEST does not exactly match the current cell contents, the difference may be due to misspelling, wrong case, and so on. You will be offered the menu choices *NO_CHANGE*, *AS_ABOVE*, *EDIT*, and *QUIT*.

{branch *NCORR}   If the item does not match the item above it simply because it correctly represents a different item, selecting *NO_CHANGE* will cause the macro to loop back to the beginning where it stores the new item in NTEST as the item to compare against.

/c{esc}{up}~~{branch NLOOP}   If the item should match the item immediately above it, you can select *AS_ABOVE* to make an instant change. The macro selects /Copy, presses Escape, moves up to the item above for the *COPY FROM* cell, and (jumping back) presses Return at the *COPY TO* prompt. The macro then continues as before at NLOOP.

{edit}{?}~{branch *NCORR}   If the item is incorrect, but should not match the item above, selecting *EDIT* will cause the macro to switch to Edit mode and pause for your manual correction of the item. The macro then branches back to the beginning where it stores the new item in NTEST.

{quit}   Of course, you will always have the option to quit the macro by choosing the *QUIT* menu choice.

This macro performs useful housekeeping on a large database. Be aware, however, it should only be used on sorted databases that typically have several entries of most items. This macro would be of little use in a database where each item is different from the item above it.

To use this as a background macro in a separate active Macro Library file in Release 3, add a wild-card filename <<?>> in front of the range name NTEST in the second and fourth lines of the macro.

Creating Subtotals and a Grand Total

If you have ever had to take a large database and create subtotals for like items, you know what a long and tedious task that can be. Let's suppose, for example, that you have a furniture warehouse and you want a subtotal of the cost of all your chairs, all your tables, and all your lamps. Assuming that like items are grouped together (your database has been sorted), you move to the row just below the last chair entry and select /Worksheet Insert Row, press DownArrow twice, and press Return. This provides three blank rows in your spreadsheet for the subtotal. Then you move over to the amount column and type the @sum formula to get the total amount for all the chairs. Next you move down to the row just below the last table entry, select /Worksheet Insert Row, press DownArrow twice, and Return, and move over to the amount column to type the @sum formula for the table amounts. This process is repeated until you have subtotaled all your furniture items. If you have 50 furniture items, this means going through that same process 50 times. Instead, use the Total macro in Figure 9.9.

```
A1: ':                                                                    READY

        A          B         C         D         E         F         G         H
1    :                    *** TOTAL MACRO ***
2    \T         {}
3    *TOTAL     {end}{down}{down 4}GRAND TOTAL:~{right 2}
4    :          @sum({left 2}{up 4}{end}{up}{right 2}.
5    :          {left 2}{end}{down}{down 2}{right 2})~/rf,2~~
6    :          {left 2}{up 4}{end}{up}
7    TLOOP1     {let TEST,@cellpointer("contents")}
8    TLOOP2     {down}{if @cellpointer("type")="b"}{up 2}{branch TQUIT}
9    :          {if TEST=@cellpointer("contents")}{branch TLOOP2}
10   :          /wir{down 2}~{up 2}
11   :          {if @cellpointer("type")="b"}{TSINGLE}{branch TLOOP1}
12   :          {TSUM}{branch TLOOP1}
13   TSUM       {down 3}SUBTOTAL:{right 2}
14   :          @sum({left 2}{up 2}{end}{up}.{end}{down}{down})~
15   :          /rf,2~~{down 2}{left 2}{return}
16   TSINGLE    {down 3}SUBTOTAL:{right 2}@sum({left}{up 2}.{down})~
17   :          /rf,2~~{down 2}{left 2}{return}
18   TQUIT      {if @cellpointer("type")="b"}{TSINGLE}{right 2}{edit}~{quit}
19   :          {TSUM}{right 2}{edit}~{quit}
20   TEST       dfgh
FIG_9-9.WK1
```

Figure 9.9 A Macro to Subtotal and Total All Like Items

Note: There are three conditions which must be met before the macro will work:

1. The column of like items must be just to the left of the column to be subtotaled and totaled. If this is not the case with your database, you should either move the two columns together, or change every line in the macro where the words {right} or {left} are used. If, for example, column of like items is in column A and the column to be subtotaled is in column C, all {right} commands should be changed to {right 2}, and all {left} commands to {left 2}.

2. The column just to the right of the amount column must be empty, or used for label entries only (which equate to zero). If this is not the case, the grand total will inappropriately add any values in the column to the sum of all of the subtotals,

giving an incorrect answer. Be sure the amount column is followed by a blank or label column, or add a /Worksheet Insert Column command to the macro to automatically create a blank column for the subtotals and grand total.

3. There must be no blank spaces between the first entry and the last entry in your column of like items, or the first line of the macro will not work correctly.

A glance at Figure 9.10 will show you an example of a simple database to which this macro might apply and Figure 9.11 shows the results you will get by running the macro.

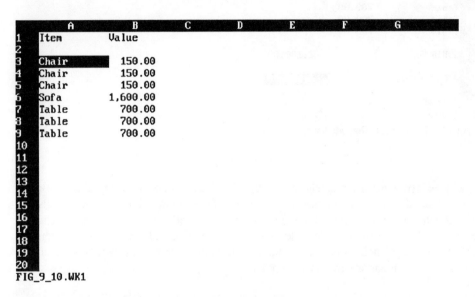

A3: [W12] 'Chair   READY

```
         A          B          C      D      E      F      G
1  Item        Value
2
3  Chair          150.00
4  Chair          150.00
5  Chair          150.00
6  Sofa         1,600.00
7  Table          700.00
8  Table          700.00
9  Table          700.00
10
11
12
13
14
15
16
17
18
19
20
```
FIG_9_10.WK1

Figure 9.10 Sample Database for the Total Macro

{end}{down}{down 4}GRAND TOTAL:~{right 2}   With your cell pointer on the first cell of the item column of the database, pressing Alt-T will cause it to move to the last item of your database, then down four more cells where it enters the words **GRAND TOTAL:** and moves to the right two cells.

@sum({left 2}{up 4}{end}{up}{right 2}.   This is the beginning of the grand total @sum formula. Since this macro is based on the assumption there are no blank spaces between the first and last entries in the column of like items, the {end}{up} command moves the cell pointer to the top of the amount column. The cell pointer is moved to the left two cells (in our example, that means to column A), then up four cells to the last item of the database, then End UpArrow to the top of the database and two RightArrows to the column to the right of the amount column (column C in our example). Pressing the Period key (.) locks in the cell pointer.

C19: (,2) [W12] @SUM(C3..C17)   READY

```
        A          B           C        D       E       F          G
1   Item       Value
2
3   Chair         150.00
4   Chair         150.00
5   Chair         150.00
6
7   SUBTOTAL:                 450.00
8
9   Sofa        1,600.00
10
11  SUBTOTAL:               1,600.00
12
13  Table         700.00
14  Table         700.00
15  Table         700.00
16
17  SUBTOTAL:               2,100.00
18
19  GRAND TOTAL:            4,150.00
20
```
FIG_9_11.WK1

Figure 9.11 Sample Results for the Total Macro

{left 2}{end}{down}{down 2}{right 2})˜/rf,2˜˜   The macro paints in the area back to the item column, then End DownArrow to the bottom of the column, down two more cells and (unhighlighting the first two columns) to the right two cells. In our example, this means painting in the range from C3 down to two cells above the grand total. The tilde enters the formula and the cell pointer jumps automatically back to the grand total cell. This cell is then formatted for commas and two decimal points.

{left 2}{up 4}{end}{up}   Moving back to the last item in the item column, the cell pointer is moved to the top of the column with the {end}{up} command.

{let TEST,@cellpointer("contents")}   Your cell pointer started on the first of the like items. This line, also named TLOOP1, stores a copy of that item in the cell named TEST to test for whether the next item down is a match.

{down}{if @cellpointer("type")="b"}{up 2}{branch TQUIT}   This line of the macro is also the first cell of a loop named TLOOP2. It moves the cell pointer down one cell and tests for whether that cell is blank. Since at this point your cell pointer is only on the second cell of the database, that cell should not be blank and the macro will continue on to the next line. If the cell is blank, the cell pointer is moved up two cells and the macro branches to the routine at TQUIT.

{if TEST=@cellpointer("contents")}{branch TLOOP2}   Compares TEST with the current cell contents. If they match, the macro branches back to TLOOP2 where it moves the cell pointer down one cell to test whether that cell is blank. If not, the macro again compares TEST with the new current cell contents. If they do not match, this means the cell pointer has come to an item that is different from the item just above it. The macro skips to the next line.

/wir{down 2}˜{up 2}   Selects /Worksheet Insert Row, presses DownArrow twice, and Return, inserting three blank rows in your database. The cell pointer then moves up two rows to check for whether the cell there is blank.

{if @cellpointer("type")="b"}{TSINGLE}{branch TLOOP1}   If the cell is blank, it means the last item was a single item. The macro therefore calls the subroutine called TSINGLE where it subtotals a single item, then branches back to TLOOP1 to address the next item.

{TSUM}{branch TLOOP1}   Otherwise, the macro calls the subroutine TSUM designed to sum the amounts for the latest identified group of like items, then it branches back to TLOOP1 to address the next item.

{down 3}SUBTOTAL:{right 2}   In the subroutine named TSUM, the macro begins by moving back down to the middle of the three newly inserted rows, types the word SUBTOTAL:, and moves two cells to the right where the subtotal amount is to appear.

@sum({left}{up 2}{end}{up}.{end}{down}{down})˜   You may recognize this as a modification of the Add macro from Chapter 3. In this case it is designed to sum a group of numbers one column to the left.

/rf,2˜˜{down 2}{left 2}{return}   After the subtotal is entered, the cell is formatted for comma and two decimals. The cell pointer moves down two cells and left two cells to the next new item (*Table* in our example) and the macro branches back to the point where it left off at {branch TLOOP1}. That branching command takes the macro back to TLOOP1 to store the name of the next item in the cell TEST in place of the original item.

{down 3}SUBTOTAL:{right 2}@sum({left}{up 2}.{down})˜   At the subroutine TSINGLE, the cell pointer is moved down to the middle of the newly inserted rows, the word **SUBTOTAL:** is typed, the cell pointer is moved two cells to the right where the subtotal amount is to appear, and the @sum formula is entered.

/rf,2˜˜{down 2}{left 2}{return}   As with the TSUM subroutine, the cell is formatted, the cell pointer moves to the next new item, and the macro branches back to the point where it left off.

{if @cellpointer("type")="b"}{TSINGLE}{right 2}{edit}˜{quit}   The macro only comes to this line (a separate routine named TQUIT) when the cell pointer reaches a blank cell that means it has come to the end of the database. Before branching to TQUIT (see the seventh line of the macro), the cell pointer was moved up two cells. If the cell is blank, it means the last item was a single item. The macro therefore calls the subroutine TSINGLE where it subtotals a single item, then returns to this line to move two cells to the right, updates the Grand Total cell with {edit}~, and quits.

{TSUM}{right 2}{edit}~{quit}   Otherwise, the macro runs the subroutine TSUM, summing the amounts for the latest identified group of like items, then returns to this line to move two cells to the right, updates the Grand Total cell with {edit}~, and quits.

To use this as a background macro in a separate active Macro Library file in Release 3, add a wild-card filename <<?>> in front of the range name TTEST in the sixth and eighth lines of the macro.

You may be impressed at how quickly this macro will run. It is so impressive, in fact, that the {windowsoff}{paneloff} commands have been deliberately omitted so you can watch the macro run through its paces. You can, of course, add these commands at the beginning of the macro. If you do, you may also want to add a command like {indicate MACRO} or {indicate SBTOT} as a reminder in the upper right panel that a macro is running. Do not forget, though, that another {indicate} command (with no argument so as to return the indicator to READY) must appear just before the {quit} command at the end of the second line of the macro.

Adjust Cell Data

Consider another tedious task. You want to change a column of numbers by multiplying every cell by some constant. So you place your cell pointer on the formula of the first cell, make the change, move down one cell, make the change, move down one cell, and so on, until you've changed the entire column.

Instead, try using the Modify Cell Data macro in Figure 9.12. This macro introduces the first of two prompting commands, {getlabel} and {getnumber}. The {getlabel} command is designed to prompt the user for a label—or for a number to be entered as a label. The {getnumber} command prompts the user for a value only. The syntax is the same for both commands:

{getlabel "*Prompt to the user*",*Location*}
{getnumber "*Prompt to the user*",*Location*}

The macro will put the user's response in any single-cell location, whether designated by cell coordinates or cell range name.

The Modify Cell Data macro uses {getlabel} to prompt for an arithmetic operator and value to be applied to every cell in a column of values. We have used {getlabel} instead of {getnumber} because of the need for an arithmetic operator, and because the response is being entered as a line of the macro, and all macro lines must be labels (must begin with an apostrophe).

{getlabel "ENTER ADJUSTMENT (EX: +7,*10,-3, ETC):",MODVAL}~   Prompts you to enter a plus (+), minus (-), multiplication (*), or division (/) sign, followed by the constant you want added to, subtracted from, multiplied by, or divided into each cell in the

```
C17: [W8] 12340                                                    READY
```

```
          A         B            C           D          E          F
1    :                       *** MODIFY CELL DATA***
2    \M         {}
3    *MODCOL    {getlabel "ENTER ADJUSTMENT (EX: +7,*10,-3, ETC):",MODVAL}~
4    MLOOP      {edit}{home}({end})
5    MODVAL     *10
6    :          {calc}~{down}
7    :          {if @cellpointer("type")="b"}{up}{end}{up}{quit}
8    :          {branch MLOOP}
9
10   This macro will apply a constant to a column of numbers like this...
11                              1234
12                               123
13                             12345
14                                12
15
16   ...with results as shown here, where each number is multiplied by 10:
17                             12340
18                              1230
19                            123450
20                               120
```
FIG_9_12.WK1

Figure 9.12 Macro to Modify Data in a Column

column. Whatever you type at this point will be entered into the self-modifying cell in the macro named MODVAL.

{edit}{home}({end})   The macro requires that you start with your cell pointer at the first value in a column of values. This line of the macro encloses the first value in parentheses by switching to the Edit mode, pressing Home to move the cursor to the beginning of the value, typing an opening parenthesis, pressing End to move to the end of the value, and typing a closing parenthesis.

The next line is the self-modified cell of the macro range named MODVAL. As a result of the {getlabel} command in the beginning of the macro, it contains the factor by which you want to adjust the cell. Although the example in Figure 9.12 shows ***10**, this cell can be left blank when you first enter the macro in your own worksheet.

{calc}~{down}   Since you are still in the Edit mode, pressing Calc changes the modified cell from a formula to a value. The cell pointer is then moved down to the next cell. If you prefer that the original formula and the new factor remain in the cell rather than the resulting value, you can always eliminate the command {calc} from the macro.

{if @cellpointer("type")="b"}{up}{end}{up}{quit}   Tests for a blank cell. If the macro finds a blank cell, it moves the cell pointer up to the top of the column and quits.

{branch MLOOP}   Otherwise, the macro branches back to the third line and applies the constant to the next cell. It continues in this way until it hits a blank cell or you press Ctrl-Break.

To use this as a background macro in a separate active Macro Library file in Release 3, add a wild-card filename <<?>> in front of the range name MODVAL in the second line of the macro.

The Borders Macro

The macro in Figure 9.13 also uses the {getlabel} command, and is designed to automate the creation of borders moving either across a row or down a column.

{menubranch BMENU}{quit}   Calls up the menu choices *ROW* and *COLUMN*. If you select *ROW*, the macro proceeds with a {getlabel} command that places your response in B_RIGHT. If you select *COLUMN*, the macro proceeds with a {getlabel} command that places your response in B_DOWN, then branches to B_DN.

{getlabel "ENTER BORDER TYPE [* - + = | x Etc: ",B_RIGHT}   Assuming   you have selected *ROW*, this line prompts for entry of the type of border you would like. If you want asterisks going across the page, type * and press Return. If you want double dashed lines, type = and press Return. Whatever you type will appear in the cell of the macro named B_RIGHT.

\   This line of the macro consists of the repeating character: the backslash. The macro types this character, then moves to the next cell named B_RIGHT to type the character you have inserted in response to the prompt line. The result is that the current cell is filled with repeats of your inserted character.

~/c~{right}.{?}~{quit}   The tilde is required to complete the entering of the inserted character in the current cell. The macro then copies the contents FROM the current cell TO a range starting with the cell to its right. The period locks in the cell pointer, and the pause waits for you to paint in the range you want to fill with the selected border character.

Selecting *COLUMN* results in the same kind of prompted entry and use of the copy command to fill in a range with the selected border—except that the entry starts with an apostrophe for a single-character entry instead of a backslash for a fill-entry, and the cell pointer moves down instead of to the right to start the copy range.

To use this as a background macro in a separate active Macro Library file in Release 3, add a wild-card filename <<?>> preceding the range names B_RIGHT and B_DOWN in cells B6 and C6 of the macro.

```
       A          B                                              C                                              D
1   :
2   \B        {}
3   *BORDER   {menubranch BMENU}{quit}
4   BMENU     ROW                                            COLUMN
5   :         ADD A HORIZONTAL BORDER                        ADD A VERTICAL BORDER
6   :         {getlabel "ENTER BORDER TYPE [* - + = ! x Etc: ",B_RIGHT}   {getlabel "BORDER TYPE * - + = ! \* \- Etc: ",B_DOWN}
7   :         \                                                            {branch B_DN}
8   B_RIGHT   *
9   :         "/c~{right}.{?}~{quit}
10  B_DN      ,
11  B_DOWN    *
12  :         "/c~{down}.{?}~{quit}
13
14
15  You can create borders in a row like this...
16  *********************************************************************************************
17
18  ...or in a column like this:
19            *
20            *
21            *
22            *
```

BORDERS MACRO

FIG_9-13.WK1

Figure 9.13 A Macro to Create Borders in the Worksheet

The Financial Functions

Financial functions in 1-2-3 such as Net Present Value (@npv), Future Value (@fv), and Internal Rate of Return (@irr) can be cumbersome to type and difficult to remember. The Financial Functions macro in Figure 9.14 simplifies the process by prompting you through creation of these formulas. This macro makes liberal use of {getlabel} prompts and self-modifying techniques.

{menubranch F_MENU}{quit}   Calls up the menu choices *PV* for Present Value, *FV* for Future Value, *NPV* for Net Present Value, *MORTGAGE-PAYMENT*, and *INTERNAL-RATE-OF-RETURN*.

{let FTYPE,"@PV("}   Using the {let} command, the purpose of this line is to change the contents of FTYPE to @PV(. This is the beginning of the Present Value formula, so it requires an opening parenthesis.

{getlabel "ENTER PAYMENT AMT/PERIOD: ",F_PRIN}~   Prompts for the first element of the Present Value formula, to be inserted into the cell named F_PRIN.

{getlabel "ENTER INTEREST AMOUNT/PERIOD: ",F_I}   Prompts for the second element of the Present Value formula, to be inserted into the cell named F_I.

{getlabel "ENTER NO. OF PERIODS: ",F_PER}   Prompts for the third element of the Present Value formula, to be inserted into the cell named F_PER.

   The next cells constitute the initial self-modification section of the macro. First the macro reads the beginning of the formula in FTYPE inserted by way of the {getlabel} command. Then the formula is filled in by branching to subroutines. The entries {F_PRIN}, {F_I}, and {F_PER} actually consists of three subroutine calls, returning to the commas which must be typed into the formula between the Payment, Interest, and Number of Periods.

)~/rff2~~{quit}   Types the closing parenthesis, formats the cell for a fixed format with two decimal points, and quits.

   The Future Value formula works in exactly the same way, with the only difference being the use of an F in the @FV prefix instead of a P as in the @PV prefix. Accordingly, selecting the FV menu choice causes the prefix @FV(to be inserted into the cell FTYPE. The macro then proceeds just as described above, finally inserting the @FV formula in the current cell.
   The Net Present Value choice causes an immediate branch to the F_NPV portion of the macro. Since this formula requires both the interest amount per period and the range of cells containing the future cash flows, there are two types of prompts in this subroutine.

{getlabel "ENTER INTEREST AMT PER PERIOD: ",F_I}   Prompts for the first element of the Present Value formula, to be inserted into the cell named F_I (2.0 version).

```
              A              B                  C                 D              E                   F
 1  :                            ***FINANCIAL FUNCTIONS***
 2  \F             {}
 3  #FIN           {menubranch F_MENU}{quit}
 4  F_MENU         PV                 NPV               FV             MORTGAGE-PAYMENT    INTERNAL-RATE-OF-RETURN
 5  :              Present value of annuity Net present value of future Future value of annuity Mortgage payment Approx. IRR for series
 6  :              {let FTYPE,"@PV("}  {branch F_NPV}    {let FTYPE,"@FV("}  {branch F_PMT}   {branch F_IRR}
 7  FV             {getlabel "ENTER PAYMENT AMT/PERIOD: ",F_PRIN}  {branch FV}
 8  :              {getlabel "ENTER INTEREST AMOUNT/PERIOD: ",F_I}
 9  :              {getlabel "ENTER NO. OF PERIODS: ",F_PER}
10  FTYPE          @PMT(
11  :              {F_PRIN},{F_I},{F_PER}
12  :              )~/rff2~~{quit}
13  F_NPV          {getlabel "ENTER INTEREST AMT PER PERIOD: ",F_I}
14  :              {paneloff}{windowsoff}/rncFUTR CASH FLOW~~
15  :              /rndFUTR CASH FLOW~
16  :              /rnc{panelon}{windowson}FUTR CASH FLOW~{bs}{?}~
17  :              {windowsoff}{paneloff}@NPV((F_I},
18  :              FUTR CASH FLOW
19  :              )~/rndFUTR CASH FLOW~/rff2~~{quit}
20  F_PMT          {let FTYPE,"@PMT("}
21  :              {getlabel "ENTER AMOUNT OF THE PRINCIPAL: ",F_PRIN}
22  :              {getlabel "ENTER ANNUAL INTEREST RATE AND PERCENT SYMBOL (ex. 8.5%): ",F_I}
23  :              {let F_I,@string(@value(F_I)/12,10)}
24  :              {getlabel "ENTER NUMBER OF YEARS:",F_PER}
25  :              {let F_PER,@string(@value(F_PER)*12,0)}
26  :              {branch FTYPE}
27  F_IRR          {getlabel "GUESS AT THE INT RATE OF RETURN: ",F_I}
28  :              {paneloff}{windowsoff}{menu}rncRANGE OF PAYMTS~~
29  :              /rndRANGE OF PAYMTS~{panelon}{windowson}
30  :              /rncRANGE OF PAYMTS~{bs}{?}~
31  :              {paneloff}{windowsoff}@IRR((F_I},
32  :              RANGE OF PAYMTS
33  :              )~/rndRANGE OF PAYMTS~/rff2~~{quit}
34  F_PRIN         200000
35  :              {return}
36  F_I            0.0097916667
37  :              {return}
38  F_PER          360
39  :              {return}
40
41  Cell B5:  Present value of an annuity:  @pv(payment,interest,n periods)
42  Cell C5:  Net present value of future cash flows:  @npv(interest,range)
43  Cell D5:  Future value of an annuity:  @fv(payment,interest,n periods)
44  Cell E5:  Mortgage payment for given principal:  @pmt(prncpl,int,n periods)
45  Cell F5:  Approx. IRR for series of cash payments:  @irr(guess,range)
```

FIG_9-14.WK1

Figure 9.14   Macro to Facilitate Entry of Financial Functions

{paneloff}{windowsoff}/rncFUTR CASH FLOW~~   The panel and windows are turned off to suppress screen flicker and the macro creates a prompting name for the range you will be painting in to encompass the future cash flow amounts.

/rndFUTR CASHFLOW~/rnc{panelon}{windowson}FUTR CASHFLOW~{bs}{?}~
Deletes, then recreates the range name FUTR CASH FLOW. The panel and windows are turned on just before the range name FUTR CASH FLOW appears. To the right of these words in the upper panel will be the words *Enter range:*. The {bs} command is included to free the cell pointer for movement to the beginning of the range of future cash flow amounts. The pause is added so you can paint in the range.

The next cells complete the Net Present Value formula by typing **@NPV(** . The macro then branches to the subroutine named F_I to pick up the interest amount. The second part of the formula is simply typed in as FUTR CASH FLOW, since that's the range you painted in to represent the future cash flow amounts. At this point the range name FUTR CASH FLOW is deleted, which leaves the formula with a range of cell addresses as you might have entered manually. The cell is given a fixed format with two decimals, and the macro quits.

Selecting *MORTGAGE-PAYMENT* from the menu choice causes the macro to branch to F_PMT, where it operates in essentially the same way as it did for Present Value and Future Value. Selecting *INTERNAL-RATE-OF-RETURN* causes the macro to branch to F_IRR, where it operates much as it did for Net Present Value, prompting you for a range to paint in.

To use this as a background macro in a separate active Macro Library file in Release 3, you must add a wild-card filename <<?>> in front of almost every range name in the macro as shown in Figure 9.15.

```
              A              B                           C                    D                  E                      F
 1   :                                ***FINANCIAL FUNCTIONS***
 2  \F            ()
 3  #FIN          {menubranch F_MENU}{quit}
 4  F_MENU        PV                          NPV                  FV                 MORTGAGE-PAYMENT       INTERNAL-RATE-OF-RETURN
 5   :            Present value of annuity Net present value of future cash  Future value of annuity  Mortgage payment    Approx. IRR for series
 6   :            {let <<?>>FTYPE,"@PV(*)  {branch F_NPV)        {let <<?>>FTYPE,"@FV(*)  {branch F_PMT)    {branch F_IRR)
 7  FV            {getlabel "ENTER PAYMENT AMOUNT PER PERIOD:",<<?>>F_PRIN)*  {branch FV)
 8   :            {getlabel "ENTER INTEREST AMOUNT/PERIOD:",<<?>>F_I)
 9   :            {getlabel "ENTER NO. OF PERIODS:",<<?>>F_PER)
10  FTYPE         @PMT(
11   :            {F_PRIN),(F_I),(F_PER)
12   :            )*/rff2**(quit)
13  F_NPV         {getlabel "ENTER INTEREST AMT PER PERIOD:",<<?>>F_I)
14   :            {paneloff}{windowsoff)
15   :            {if @isrange(FUTR CASH FLOWS))/rndFUTR CASH FLOWS*
16   :            /rnc{panelon}{windowson)FUTR CASH FLOWS*(bs)(?)*
17   :            {windowsoff}{paneloff}@NPV((F_I),
18   :            FUTR CASH FLOWS
19   :            )*/rndFUTR CASH FLOWS*/rff2**(quit)
20  F_PMT         {let <<?>>FTYPE,"@PMT(*)
21   :            {getlabel "ENTER AMOUNT OF THE PRINCIPAL:",<<?>>F_PRIN)
22   :            {getlabel "ENTER ANNUAL INTEREST RATE AND PERCENT SYMBOL (ex. 8.5%): ",<<?>>F_I)
23   :            {let <<?>>F_I,@string(@value(<<?>>F_I)/12,10))
24   :            {getlabel "ENTER NUMBER OF YEARS:",<<?>>F_PER)
25   :            {let <<?>>F_PER,@string(@value(<<?>>F_PER)*12,0))
26   :            {branch FTYPE)
27  F_IRR         {getlabel "GUESS AT THE INT RATE OF RETURN:",<<?>>F_I)
28   :            {paneloff}{windowsoff)
29   :            {if @isrange(RANGE OF PAYMTS))/rndRANGE OF PAYMTS*
30   :            /rncRANGE OF PAYMTS*(bs)(?)*
31   :            {paneloff}{windowsoff}@IRR((F_I),
32   :            RANGE OF PAYMTS
33   :            )*/rndRANGE OF PAYMTS*/rff2**(quit)
34  F_PRIN        328000
35   :            {return}
36  F_I           0.0083333333
37   :            {return}
38  F_PER         360
39   :            {return}
40
41  Cell B5: Present value of an annuity:  @pv(payment,interest,n periods)
42  Cell C5: Net present value of future cash flows:  @npv(interest,range)
43  Cell D5: Future value of an annuity:  @fv(payment,interest,n periods)
44  Cell E5: Mortgage payment for given principal:  @pmt(prncpl,int,n periods)
45  Cell F5: Approx. IRR for series of cash payments:  @irr(guess,range)
46
```

FIG_9_15.WK1

Figure 9.15 Release 3 Version of Financial Functions Macro

Using @Repeat to Underline a Cell

This section explores another the use of {getlabel} and our first use so far of @cellpointer("width") to provide the elements required for an @repeat function.

The @repeat syntax is:

@repeat(*character(s) to repeat, number of times to repeat*)

Thus, to show the letter X repeated ten times in a cell, you would use the function:

@repeat("X",10)

If the letter X is stored in another cell, say cell J22, you can use the function in this way

@repeat(J22,10)

to create the same effect. To fill the entire cell with the letter X, you could enter the function

@repeat(J22,@cellpointer("width"))

Of course, you can accomplish the same thing by typing the backslash repeating sign (\) and the letter X, but suppose you want to fill all but one space of the current cell with X? You can do this with the formula:

@repeat(J22,@cellpointer("width")-1)

This is useful information you can use to create a macro that fills all but one space of a cell with an underlining symbol (the dash or equal sign, for example). This allows you to underline several cells in a row, leaving a one-character-wide space between each underline to better separate the items being underlined. Such a macro is shown in Figure 9.16.

{getlabel "ENTER SYMBOL FOR UNDERLINE: ",COLUNDER}   Prompts you to enter an underlining symbol, such as a dash or equal sign, and places your response in the cell named COLUNDER.

@repeat(COLUNDER,@cellpointer(width")-1)   Types the @repeat function in the current cell to repeat the symbol stored in COLUNDER the number of times equal to one less than the column width.

{calc}{home}^~{quit}   Before pressing Enter to return to Ready mode, the macro uses Calc to change the @function to its displayed value, presses Home to move the cursor to the beginning of the entry, types an apostrophe to turn it into a label, enters the label, and then quits.

To use this as a background macro in a separate active Macro Library file in Release 3, add a wild-card filename <<?>> preceding the range name COLUNDER in the second and third lines of the macro.

Now that you know how to underline a cell with a width one less than the width of the current column, you can use that information to create a summing macro that underlines the column to be summed in the same way. Refer to Figure 9.17.

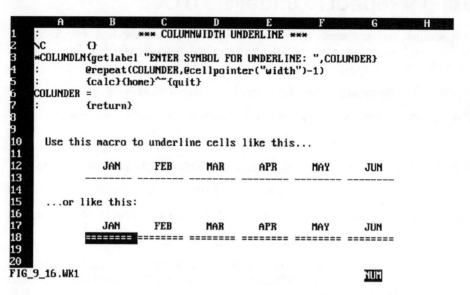

Figure 9.16 Macro to Underline a Label or Value in a Cell

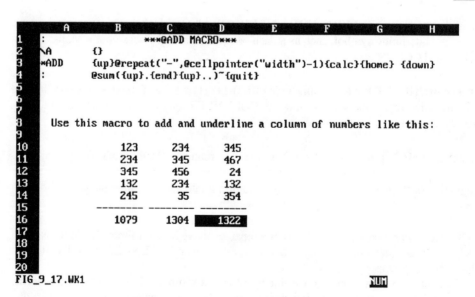

Figure 9.17 Add Macro with Special Underlining Technique

{up}@repeat("-",@cellpointer("width")-1){calc}{home} {down} Assuming your cell pointer is two cells below the last number in the vertical range of numbers you want to sum, the macro moves up one cell, types the **@repeat** function, presses {calc} to change the @function to its displayed value (for example, ——————), and moves the cursor to the beginning of the underline. There the macro enters a space (which places the gutter at the front of the underline rather than at the end) and moves down one cell, completing the entry.

Note: If you elect to eliminate the space, you will want to include an apostrophe in its place, or the entry will not be accepted and the computer will beep.

@sum({up}.{end}{up}..)~{quit} Types the @sum formula, paints in the range, adjusts the cell coordinates with two presses of the period key (..), completes the entry with a tilde, and quits.

This macro, althrough short, is one of the most useful you will find in this book, and should become a standard part of any Macro Library you create in Release 2.2 or 3. It can be used as a Macro Library macro in both releases without modification.

Summary

In this chapter we discussed the If-Then-Else concept in both the @if function and the {if} command. The {if} command can used with @cellpointer("type") to check whether the current cell contains a label, contains a value, or is completely blank. Through use of conditional branching using the {if} command with @cellpointer, you can create macros that will loop until some criteria is met, such as the determination that a cell is blank.

You were also introduced to two prompt commands, {getlabel} and {getnumber}, designed to pause for your entry of a string or value, then place that entry in a designated cell. This feature is especially useful for self-modifying macros that prompt you for information, then use that information to accomplish different tasks.

A string function, @repeat, was also used in two macros with @cellpointer("width")-1 to create underlining symbols that span a space one less than the width of the current column.

The macros covered in this chapter are:

- A Label Format macro that will move down a column of numbers, changing each number to a label.
- A Number Format macro that will move down a column of labels, changing each label to a number.
- A macro to indent each entry in a column by five spaces.
- A macro to add leading zeros to all of the numbers in a column.
- A Rounding macro to add the @round formula to each number or formula in a column.
- A macro to eliminate the ERR messages in a spreadsheet.

- A Data Entry macro to facilitate Standard, Left Justified, Right Justified, or Centered entries in a column or row.
- A macro to identify and allow correction of non-standard entries in a database.
- A Modify Cell Data macro that will apply a constant to every cell in a column.
- A Borders macro to enter borders in a column or row using any of several characters.
- A macro to facilitate entry of financial functions such as Present Value, Net Present Value, Future Value, Mortgage, and Internal Rate of Return.
- A Columnwidth Underline macro to create an underline equal to one space less than the width of the current column.
- A modification of the Add macro to include a shortened underline symbol.

In Chapter 10 we will explore the use in macros of several string and special @functions such as @left, @right, @mid, @length, @replace, @find, @upper, @lower, @proper, @trim, @repeat, and @choose.

10

STRING FORMULAS AND STRING @FUNCTIONS

Scope

In this chapter we will explore the underlying concepts and techniques of string manipulation in 1-2-3. As you will see, both string @functions and string formulas can be used to create self-modifying and variable lines in your macros. This can be accomplished by combining string @functions and string formulas with each other, as well as with cell addresses, range names, labels, string forms of values, and other @functions. We will explore the purpose and application of string techniques both in cells of the spreadsheet and in macros.

Comparing String @Functions with String Formulas

String @functions are those which allow the 1-2-3 user to manipulate strings, concatenate strings, extract portions of strings, change the case of strings, convert values to strings, and so on. A list of string @functions is shown in Table 10.1.

A string formula, on the other hand, uses the special string manipulation features of 1-2-3

Table 10.1 List and Definitions of String @Functions

String Function	Syntax	Returns
@Char	(number)	Character for an ASCII Code
@Clean	(string)	String without ASCII 0 to 31
@Code	(character)	ASCII Code for a character
@Exact	(1st item,2nd item)	1 or 0 Comparing two Items
@Find	(string,from string,start)	Offset number of found string
@Length	(string)	Length of the string
@Lower	(string)	The string in lowercase
@Left	(string,n characters)	Left-most n characters
@Mid	(string,start,n characters)	Middle n characters from start
@N	(range)	Value in upper left corner
@Proper	(string)	The string in proper case
@Repeat	(string,n times)	String repeated n times
@Replace	(string,start,n chars,input)	String with replacement input
@Right	(string,n characters)	Right-most n characters
@S	(range)	String in upper left corner
@String	(value,decimals)	Value of number-label
@Trim	(string)	String without extra spaces
@Upper	(string)	The string in uppercase
@Value	(number-label)	Value of a number-label

to combine two or more elements into a single word or phrase. To join the words "IN," "TELL," "I," and "GENT," for example, you can type

"IN"&"TELL"&"I"&"GENT"

in any cell. Just as entering an @sum formula into a cell returns the sum in that cell, so entering the string formula +"IN"&"TELL"&"I"&"GENT" into a cell returns INTELLIGENT.

String formulas must always begin with a plus sign (+) or a string @function. In this case we have started with a plus sign and the word IN in quotation marks, followed by an ampersand (&). The ampersand is the only operator for string formulas and is used to attach or concatenate the individual strings. This is followed by the word TELL in quotation marks, another ampersand, an I in quotation marks, another ampersand, and finally the word GENT in quotation marks. Try combining ALBERT and EINSTEIN by typing

+"ALBERT"&" "&"EINSTEIN"

in any cell. Again the string begins with a plus sign, followed by the word ALBERT in quotation marks, followed by an ampersand. In order to separate the first and second words, a single space in quotation marks is included: " ". The formula ends with another ampersand and the word EINSTEIN in quotation marks, returning the result: ALBERT EINSTEIN.

By itself, this unique way of entering a word or phrase in a cell seems rather useless and overly complicated. Combined with string @functions or references to other cells, however, the string formulas can provide powerful new techniques to create variable titles or headings, to manipulate and change entries in a database automatically, to make some of your macro writing more efficient, and to speed up the execution of certain types of macros.

The example in Figure 10.1 shows how you can use strings to create a variable heading. The entry in cell D13 displays the word **OVERRUN**, so the formula in cell A1 that was entered as:

> +"We are running an overhead budget "&D13&" this month."

and displays as:

> We are running an overhead budget DEFICIT this month.

```
B1: [W11] +"We are running an overhead budget "&D13&" this month."        EDIT
+"We are running an overhead budget "&D13&" this month."
```

```
              A              B          C           D          E
1                     We are running an overhead budget DEFICIT this month.
2
3     O/H Item      O/H Budget  O/H Costs
4     ------------  ----------  ----------
5     Rent               3400       3400
6     Utilities          1200       1350
7     Telephone          1500       1635
8     Office Supply       800        725
9     Janitorial         1150       1150
10    Tools               900       1300
11    Training            650        350
12                 ----------  ------------
13                      9600       9910      DEFICIT
14
15
16
17
18
19
20
F_10-1.WK1                                                        NUM
```

Figure 10.1 Using String Formulas to Create a Variable Heading

On the other hand, a display of the word **SURPLUS** in cell D13 would cause the string formula in cell A1 to display:

> We are running an overhead budget SURPLUS this month.

As you might imagine, you can easily create a series of strings that give you status on the individual budgets for rent, utilities, phone, supplies, and so on, all visible at the top of your spreadsheet and all variable depending on the cells to which the strings refer.

Using @String in String Formulas

Although you can use string formulas to refer to cells displaying labels, the identical use of string formulas referring to cells with values will return an error. As shown in Figure 10.2, the formula

```
B1: [W11] +"The overhead costs came to "&C13&" this month."          EDIT
+"The overhead costs came to "&C13&" this month."
```

```
           A              B           C          D           E
1                         ERR
2
3      O/H Item      O/H Budget   O/H Costs
4      -----------   ----------   ----------
5      Rent            3,400.00    3,400.00
6      Utilities       1,200.00    1,350.00
7      Telephone       1,500.00    1,635.00
8      Office Supply     800.00      725.00
9      Janitorial      1,150.00    1,150.00
10     Tools             900.00    1,300.00
11     Training          650.00      350.00
12                     ----------   ----------
13                    $9,600.00   $9,910.00     DEFICIT
14
15
16
17
18
19
20
F_10-2.WK1                                                    NUM
```

Figure 10.2 ERR Results from Inserting a Value Cell in a String

> +"The overhead costs came to "&C13&" this month."

which one might expect to return a string indicating that the overhead costs are $9,910.00, actually returns ERR.

Fortunately, Lotus has considered this problem and provided a solution. Instead of referring to cell C13, you can refer to the formula @string(C13,0). The @string function converts numeric values to strings and allows you to specify the number of decimal places to be used for a string (see Figure 10.3). Thus the string formula that returns the desired statement would read:

> +"The overhead costs came to "&@STRING(C13,0)&" this month."

There are two points regarding this string formula that bear mentioning.

1. At first glance, it may appear that the characters **&@STRING(C13,0)&** are enclosed in quotation marks. This is not the case. In fact, what may appear to be opening quotation marks preceding the **&@STRING(C13,0)&** are actually closing quotation marks following the first part of the string. Conversely, what may appear to be closing quotation marks following the **&@STRING(B13,0)&** are actually opening quotation marks for the last part of the string.

2. You may also have noticed that although cell B13 displays a value formatted for currency with two decimal points, the string formula shows only the number 9910 with no formatting. This is because there is no currency format for the @string function, although you can designate two decimal points by typing

B1: [W11] +"The overhead costs came to "&@STRING(C13,0)&" this month."   `EDIT`
+"The overhead costs came to "&@STRING(C13,0)&" this month."

```
             A              B              C            D            E
 1                 The overhead costs came to 9910 this month.
 2
 3    O/H Item       O/H Budget   O/H Costs
 4    ----------     ----------   ----------
 5    Rent             3,400.00     3,400.00
 6    Utilities        1,200.00     1,350.00
 7    Telephone        1,500.00     1,635.00
 8    Office Supply      800.00       725.00
 9    Janitorial       1,150.00     1,150.00
10    Tools              900.00     1,300.00
11    Training           650.00       350.00
12                    ----------   ------------
13                    $9,600.00    $9,910.00     DEFICIT
14
15
16
17
18
19
20
```
F_10-3.WK1   `NUM`

Figure 10.3   Using @String with a Value Cell in a String Formula

> **@STRING(C13,2)**
>
> You can also add a dollar sign by typing a dollar sign ($) at the end of the preceding string within its quotation marks:
>
> **+"The overhead costs came to $ "&&@STRING(C13,2)&" this month."**

Using the @string function will always display a number as a label, but it displays a label as a label-zero in Release 2.01 and up. (In Release 2, using @string with a label will return ERR—a problem that was corrected with Release 2.01.)

@Functions to Change Case

There are three string @functions designed to change the case of a string: @lower, @proper, and @upper.

Whether a string or a cell containing a string begins in uppercase, lowercase, proper case, or a mixture of any of these, its case can be changed using these @functions. The formula @lower("*APPLES*"), for example, will return the string *apples* in lowercase. If the string *APPLES* is contained in cell B3, the formula @lower(B3) will also return the string *apples*. However, referring to the cell address of a cell containing the number *123* will return ERR. This is similar to the response displayed when you attempt to combine strings with numbers in a string formula. Just as the correction for that kind of string formula error is the inclusion of an @string function, so typing @upper(@string(123,0)) is the correction here. There is no such thing as a lowercase, uppercase, or proper case for numbers, of course, but at least the formula @lower(@string(123,0)) will return the number 123. Accordingly, the formula @lower(@string(B3,0)), where B3 contains the number 123, will also return the number 123.

Referring to an actual string rather than the cell address containing a string has predictable results. @upper("sales") returns the word SALES, and @proper("12345")—since "12345" in quotation marks is a string—returns the label-number 12345. Using the formula @lower(NEXTCELL) where the range name NEXTCELL, refers to the word *APPLES*, returns *apples*, the lowercase version of that cell's label contents.

Here is a simple way to convert a column of lowercase labels to uppercase. First be sure that the column just to the right of the column of labels is blank. If not, select /Worksheet Insert Column to create a blank column at that spot. Place your cell pointer in the blank column just to the right of the first label in your original column. Type **@upper**, an opening parenthesis, a plus sign, and point to the first label in your original column by pressing LeftArrow. Close the parenthesis to complete the formula and press Enter.

You should now see an uppercase version of the first item. Copy that formula down the exact length of the original column by selecting /Copy and pressing Return, then at the *Range to Copy TO:* prompt, press the Period (.), LeftArrow, End, DownArrow, RightArrow, and Return. Then copy the displayed values of these @upper formulas to the original column by selecting /Range Value, highlighting the new column. An example of this stage of the operation is shown in Figure 10.4.

After pressing Return, you should see a prompt for *Range to Copy TO:*. Press LeftArrow to point to the original column and Return. The original column will be instantly converted all to uppercase. Now erase the new column you created by using /Range Erase or—if you inserted a new column to go through this exercise, by using /Worksheet Delete Column.

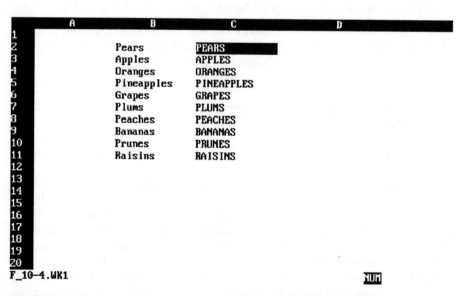

Figure 10.4 Manually Changing a Column of Labels to Uppercase

This can all be done in a macro, of course. Figure 10.5 shows a macro designed to convert a column of labels entirely to lowercase, proper case, or uppercase, based on your selection.

Before the macro starts, the pointer must be placed on the first cell of the column you want to convert. Since the macro begins by inserting a column to the right of this cell, it is important that the macro not be located in any area to the right of the column to be inserted. If so, the macro will be shifted out from under itself and attempt to continue at the next line down, but one cell to the left; and since it cannot continue in that location, it will stop or try to run whatever entry it encounters—with predictably disastrous results.

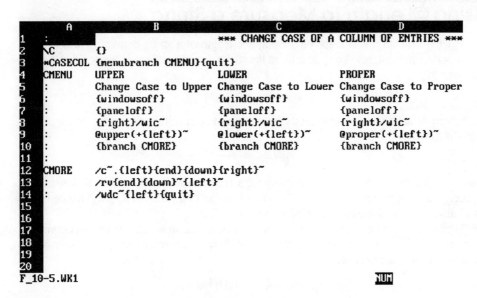

Figure 10.5 A Macro to Change the Case of a Column of Entries

{menubranch CMENU}{quit}   Offers the menu choices, *UPPER*, *LOWER*, and *PROPER*.

{windowsoff}{paneloff}{right}/wic~   Regardless of which menu choice you select, the windows and panel are turned off, the cell pointer is moved to the right one cell, and the macro selects /Worksheet Insert Column.

@upper(+{left}~ or **@lower(+{left})~** or **@proper(+{left})~**   Types the appropriate case @function and an opening parenthesis, moves left to the first cell of the original column, closes the parenthesis, and enters the function.

{branch CMORE}   Branches to the rest of the commands held in common by all three menu choices.

/c~.{left}{end}{down}{right}~   Selects /Copy and presses Return, then at the *Range to Copy TO:* prompt, presses the Period (.), LeftArrow, End, DownArrow, RightArrow, and Return.

/rv{end}{down}~{left}~   Copies the displayed values of these @functions to the original column by selecting /Range Value, highlighting the new column, and pressing Return twice.

/wdc~{left}{quit}   Deletes the temporary column inserted at the beginning of the macro, moves left to the original column, and quits.

Using @Length to Measure a String

The @length function is designed to display the length of a string consisting of a word, a phrase, or a number-label. You can refer to the string directly, as in the function that returns the value 5:

$$@length("Sales")$$

or you can indicate the string indirectly by referring to a specific cell containing the string, as in the function

$$@length(J23)$$

This example returns 5 if J23 has a string with five characters. Be aware, however, this @length function will return ERR if J23 is blank, displays a value, or displays a date based on a value or @date formula in a cell formatted for Date.

There is a way to determine the number of characters in a value when you combine @length with @string, as in this example, providing the length of the string equivalent of the value in B14 with no decimals:

$$@length(@string(B14,0))$$

You can also use a single-cell range name with @length as:

$$@length(CUSTOMER)$$

Note: Although CUSTOMER has eight letters, this @length function will return 14 if the string contained in the cell named CUSTOMER is General Electric.

You can use the @length function with @cellpointer("contents") to return the length of the contents of any cell you highlight with your cell pointer. This is useful for creation of a macro that will instantly adjust the width of the current column as shown in Figure 10.6.

This macro allows you to increase or reduce the width of a column to one space more than the number of characters in the cell you highlight. In the sample column shown, for instance, you can move your pointer to the longest phrase (**Office Supply** in B13) and press Alt-W. The column width will instantly convert to a width of 14 (13 + 1). If you later decide to change **Office Supply** to just **Supplies**, pressing Alt-W on B13 will change the column width to 9 (8 + 1).

This macro is short, so it appears deceptively simple. The second line introduces a new command, {recalc}. Its purpose is to recalculate the cell or range referred to in its argument.

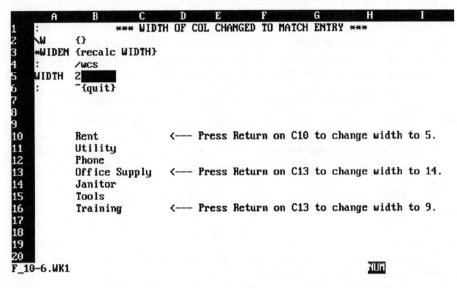

Figure 10.6 Adjust Columnwidth Based on Current Cell Contents

In this case, it is an instruction to recalculate the cell named WIDTH, cell B6. The third line begins the command to change the column width by selecting /Worksheet Columnwidth Set. The fourth line, though it displays a left-justified number here, is actually the formula

$$@string(@length(@cellpointer("contents")+1),0)$$

as shown in the upper panel.

This formula will return ERR when you first enter it as shown. Do not let this worry you, however. If you point to any cell containing a string and press the F9 Calc key, the ERR will change to a number-label (with no decimals) representing one more than the number of characters in that string.

Working from the center of this formula to the outer characters, we can analyze the string starting with the @cellpointer formula.

@cellpointer("contents")   Returns the contents of the cell the pointer happens to rest on when Alt-W is pressed.

@length(@cellpointer("contents"))+1   Returns a value equal to the length of the contents of the current cell, plus 1.

@string(@length(@cellpointer("contents"))+1,0)   The value of the current cell's length is converted to its string equivalent so it can be used in this string formula. The ending zero and closing parenthesis display the label-number with no decimals.

As noted, this macro will not work on cells displaying values.

Using @Find to Search a String

The @find function uses search criteria to search a string for one or more characters starting at a designated position in the string. This function returns ERR if a match with the search criteria is not found. If a match is found, the function displays a number representing the location of its first occurrence in the string. The format of the @find function is:

@find*(search criteria, entire string or cell, starting point)*

The starting point and the location number which the @find function returns are both based on the use of position numbers. The first character in a string is the 0 position, the second character is the 1 position, the third character is the 2 position, and so on. (This is similar to the offset principles used in the @dsum, @dcount, @choose, @vlookup, and @hlookup functions.)

Thus a search for position of the first occurrence of the letter **e** in the string **Albert Einstein** would be typed:

@find("e","Albert Einstein",0)

and would return the number **3**. The formula returns **3** rather than **4** because the letter "e" is the third letter over from the zero position.

Using @find to search for the string "Albert" returns a zero because the name Albert starts at the zero position. On the other hand, searching for the uppercase version "ALBERT" returns ERR because the @find function is case sensitive; it requires that an exact match be found for the search criteria in the searched string or cell, including a match of uppercase and lowercase.

Although a search for the letter **e** will return **3** when the starting position of the @find formula is zero, the formula

@find("e","Albert Einstein",7)

with a starting at position of 7, will return the value **12** (the position of the first lowercase "e" after the seventh letter in **Albert Einstein**). Similarly, a search for "e" starting at position 13 returns an ERR message because there is no letter "e" past position 13.

Numbers entered as labels such as the telephone number 301-555-1212 can be searched with @find, but an attempt to use @find on a number entered as a value will return ERR. The solution in that case, as with the @length function, is to add the @string function that turns the number into a label. The other possibility, though usually not practical, is to refer to the number directly, typed in quotation marks.

To locate the second occurrence of a character or string when you do not know the location of the first occurrence, try using a nested @find formula. In other words, instead of using the 0 position as your starting point for the search, substitute another @find function to locate the first occurrence, add the number 1, and provide this information as the new starting point for the second occurrence. For example, a search for the second occurrence of the letter "e" in "Albert Einstein" would be done as:

@find("e","Albert Einstein",@find("e","Albert Einstein",0)+1)

returning the value 12.

You may wonder about the usefulness of all these explanations about the @find function. After all, knowing that the second letter "e" is the twelfth character over from the beginning of a string does not really provide you with astonishing information. In conjunction with other string formulas, however, this function provides a powerful and much needed element with which many sophisticated manipulations of strings are possible.

Using @Left to Extract a String

The @left function uses the syntax

@left(*string or cell*, *number of characters*)

and returns a portion of a string consisting of a designated number of characters from the left side of the string. Thus, **@left("tangent",4)** will return the first four letters by displaying the string *tang*. Similarly, the formula **@left("entertainment",5)** will return the first five letters by displaying the string *enter*.

Note: The @left function does not work on the offset principle. In other words, the **@left("entertainment",5)** example does not count up to position 5 (the sixth character), but rather displays the five left-most characters in the string.

If you enter a number equal to or greater than the number of characters in the string, the @left function will simply display the entire string.

As with the @upper, @lower, and @proper string functions, the @left function works with a string, a cell address, or a range name referring to a single cell containing a string. An ERR message is returned if the referenced cell or range name contains a value rather than a label.

The @left function can also be used in conjunction with the @find function to extract and display a variable length string.

Figure 10.7 shows a list of first and last names in column B, where the names are of various lengths. Using a combination of @left and @find as in the example

@left(b6,@find(" ",b6,0))

you can create a formula that extracts just the first name by finding the first occasion of a blank space, then using that information to establish how many letters should be extracted from the left side of the string.

The space in the string **William Faulkner** in cell B6, for example, is determined with the function

@find(" ",b6,0)

where " " refers to the search criteria, **b6** refers to the cell being searched, and **0** refers to the search starting point in the cell. This function returns a position number 7, that is used by the @left function to extract 6 characters—the word William.

One of the more sophisticated uses of the @left function is in the creation of variable lines of a macro, especially used in conjunction with the other string-extracting @functions, @right, and @mid.

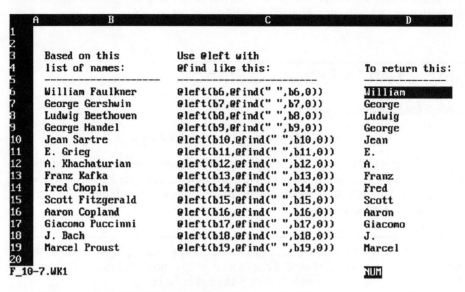

```
D6: @LEFT(B6,@FIND(" ",B6,0))                                        READY
```

```
      A          B                    C                        D
  1
  2
  3       Based on this        Use @left with
  4       list of names:       @find like this:            To return this:
  5       ------------------    ------------------          ---------------
  6       William Faulkner     @left(b6,@find(" ",b6,0))    William
  7       George Gershwin      @left(b7,@find(" ",b7,0))    George
  8       Ludwig Beethoven     @left(b8,@find(" ",b8,0))    Ludwig
  9       George Handel        @left(b9,@find(" ",b9,0))    George
 10       Jean Sartre          @left(b10,@find(" ",b10,0))  Jean
 11       E. Grieg             @left(b11,@find(" ",b11,0))  E.
 12       A. Khachaturian      @left(b12,@find(" ",b12,0))  A.
 13       Franz Kafka          @left(b13,@find(" ",b13,0))  Franz
 14       Fred Chopin          @left(b14,@find(" ",b14,0))  Fred
 15       Scott Fitzgerald     @left(b15,@find(" ",b15,0))  Scott
 16       Aaron Copland        @left(b16,@find(" ",b16,0))  Aaron
 17       Giacomo Puccinni     @left(b17,@find(" ",b17,0))  Giacomo
 18       J. Bach              @left(b18,@find(" ",b18,0))  J.
 19       Marcel Proust        @left(b19,@find(" ",b19,0))  Marcel
 20
```

```
F_10-7.WK1                                                          NUM
```

Figure 10.7   Extracting a First Name with @Left and @Find

Using @Right to Extract a String

Similar to the @left function, the @right function uses the syntax

@right(*string or cell*, *number of characters*)

and returns a portion of a string consisting of a designated number of characters from the right side of the string. Thus, **@right("alienation",5)** will return the last five letters by displaying the string *nation*. Similarly, the formula **@right("incidental",6)** will return the last six letters by displaying the string *dental*.

As with the @left function, @right does not work on the offset principle by counting up to position 5 (the sixth character), but rather displays the number of characters entered in the @right function. The @right function will work with a string, a cell address, or a range name for a single cell containing a string. Also, if you enter a number that is equal to or greater than the number of characters in the string, the @right function will simply display the entire string.

Where we were able to extract a variable length string like the first name from a list of first and last names using @left, extracting the last name is a little more difficult using @right. It can be done, however, when the @right function is used in conjunction with the @length and @find functions as in the example:

@right(b6,@length(b6)-@find(" ",b6,0)-1)

Figure 10.8 shows a list of first and last names in column B where the names are of various lengths. The formula shown in column C finds the position number of the blank space between first and last name, subtracts that number from the length of the entire name, then re-

D6: @RIGHT(B6,@LENGTH(B6)-@FIND(" ",B6,0)-1)   READY

```
     A        B                     C                          D
 1
 2
 3   Based on this    Use @left with
 4   list of names:   @find like this:                    To return:
 5   ------------     ------------------------------       ----------
 6   William Faulkner @right(b6,@length(b6)-@find(" ",b6,0)-1)  Faulkner
 7   George Gershwin  @right(b6,@length(b6)-@find(" ",b6,0)-1)  Gershwin
 8   Ludwig Beethoven @right(b6,@length(b6)-@find(" ",b6,0)-1)  Beethoven
 9   George Handel    @right(b6,@length(b6)-@find(" ",b6,0)-1)  Handel
10   Jean Sartre      @right(b6,@length(b6)-@find(" ",b6,0)-1)  Sartre
11   E. Grieg         @right(b6,@length(b6)-@find(" ",b6,0)-1)  Grieg
12   A. Khachaturian  @right(b6,@length(b6)-@find(" ",b6,0)-1)  Khachaturi
13   Franz Kafka      @right(b6,@length(b6)-@find(" ",b6,0)-1)  Kafka
14   Fred Chopin      @right(b6,@length(b6)-@find(" ",b6,0)-1)  Chopin
15   Scott Fitzgerald @right(b6,@length(b6)-@find(" ",b6,0)-1)  Fitzgerald
16   Aaron Copland    @right(b6,@length(b6)-@find(" ",b6,0)-1)  Copland
17   Giacomo Puccinni @right(b6,@length(b6)-@find(" ",b6,0)-1)  Puccinni
18   J. Bach          @right(b6,@length(b6)-@find(" ",b6,0)-1)  Bach
19   Marcel Proust    @right(b6,@length(b6)-@find(" ",b6,0)-1)  Proust
20
```
F_10-8.WK1   NUM

Figure 10.8 Extracting Last Name with @Right, @Length, and @Find

duces that number by 1 to establish the number of characters to be extracted from the right side of the string.

The space in the string **William Faulkner** in cell B6, for example, is determined with the function

$$@find(" ",b6,0)$$

where " " refers to the search criteria, **b6** refers to the cell being searched, and 0 refers to the search starting point in the cell. This function returns a position number 8, which is then subtracted from the 16 characters in B6 as determined by the formula @length(b6) to return 8. Subtracting the number 1 from this result provides the number 8—the total number of characters in the last name Faulkner.

Since we have presented in Figure 10.7 a method for extracting the first name from a full name string, and in Figure 10.8 a method for extracting the last name, these two formulas can be combined into one formula to change the order of first and last name. The list of names in column B of Figure 10.9 are presented in last name-first name order. The formula in column C is constructed to leave out the comma between names and reverse the order of names from last-first to first-last.

The formula in cell C5 is broken down as:

@right(B5,@length(B5)-@find(" ",B5,0)-1)
&""
&@left(B5,@find("",B5,0)-1)

The first or last name extractions shown in Figures 10.7 and 10.8 are useful for lists where there are no middle initials, but lists of names are rarely so accommodating. The macro in Figure 10.10 takes this into account, however, and will extract the first name, first name and middle initial, or last name from a number of combinations of initials and names.

```
C5: @RIGHT(B5,@LENGTH(B5)-@FIND(" ",B5,0)-1)&" "&@LEFT(B5,@FIND(" ",B5,0)-1
@RIGHT(B5,@LENGTH(B5)-@FIND(" ",B5,0)-1)&" "&@LEFT(B5,@FIND(" ",B5,0)-1)
```

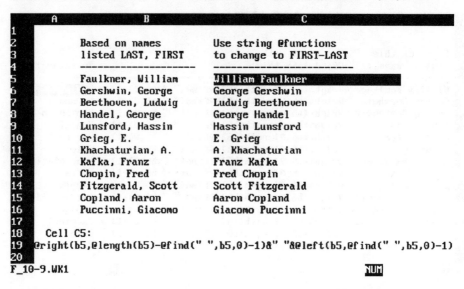

	A	B	C
1			
2		Based on names	Use string @functions
3		listed LAST, FIRST	to change to FIRST-LAST
4		-------------------	-------------------
5		Faulkner, William	William Faulkner
6		Gershwin, George	George Gershwin
7		Beethoven, Ludwig	Ludwig Beethoven
8		Handel, George	George Handel
9		Lunsford, Hassin	Hassin Lunsford
10		Grieg, E.	E. Grieg
11		Khachaturian, A.	A. Khachaturian
12		Kafka, Franz	Franz Kafka
13		Chopin, Fred	Fred Chopin
14		Fitzgerald, Scott	Scott Fitzgerald
15		Copland, Aaron	Aaron Copland
16		Puccinni, Giacomo	Giacomo Puccinni
17			
18	Cell C5:		
19	@right(b5,@length(b5)-@find(" ",b5,0)-1)&" "&@left(b5,@find(" ",b5,0)-1)		
20			

F_10-9.WK1   NUM

Figure 10.9 Reverse the Order of Names with String @Functions

A1: [W10] ':   READY

	A	B	C	D	E
1	:		*** EXTRACT NAME ***		
2	\X	{}			
3	*XTCTNAME	{windowsoff}{menubranch X_MENU}{quit}			
4	X_MENU	1ST NAME	FIRST NAME & M.I.	LAST NAME	
5	:	Extract 1st name	1st Name, Middle Initial	Extract last name	
6	:	{paneloff}	{paneloff}	{paneloff}	
7	:	{}	{branch XFMI}	{branch XLAST}	
8	XFIRST	@left({left},@find(" ",{left},0))~			
9	:	{branch XQUIT}			
10	XFMI	@if(@iserr(@find(" ",{left},@find(" ",{left},0)+1)),			
11	:	@left({left},@find(" ",{left},0)),			
12	:	@left({left},@find(" ",{left},@find(" ",{left},0)+1)))~			
13	:	{branch XQUIT}			
14	XLAST	@if(@iserr(@find(" ",{left},@find(" ",{left},0)+1)),			
15	:	@right({left},@length({left})-@find(" ",{left},0)-1),			
16	:	@right({left},@length({left})-			
17	:	@find(" ",{left},@find(" ",{left},0)+1)-1))~			
18	XQUIT	/c~.{left}{end}{down}{right}~			
19	:	/rv{left}{end}{down}{right}~~{quit}			
20					

F_10_10.WK1   NUM

Figure 10.10 Extract First Name, Last Name, or Middle Initial

C6: [W13] 'William F.   █MENU█
█1ST NAME█   FIRST NAME & M.I.   LAST NAME
Extract 1st name

```
      A            B                 C            D        E         F
1
2
3         Starting with        Place your cell pointer
4         this list of names:  here and press Alt-X.
5         -------------------  ------------------------
6         William F. Faulkner  █William F.      █  <------------
7         George Gershwin      George
8         Ludwig van Beethoven Ludwig van
9         George F. Handel     George F.
10        Jean Paul Sartre     Jean Paul
11        E. Hagerup Grieg     E. Hagerup
12        Aram Khachaturian    Aram
13        Franz Kafka          Franz
14        Fred F. Chopin       Fred F.
15        F. Scott Fitzgerald  F. Scott
16        Aaron Copland        Aaron
17        Giacomo Puccinni     Giacomo
18        J. S. Bach           J. S.
19        Marcel Proust        Marcel
20
```
F_10_11.WK1   █CMD█   █NUM█

Figure 10.11   An Example of a Database of Names

An example of a database of names is shown in Figure 10.11 above. Applying the macro in Figure 10.10 to this database, place your pointer in column B to the right of the first full name and press Alt-X. The menu selections *1ST NAME*, *FIRST & M.I.*, and *LAST NAME* will appear. Selecting *1ST NAME* will cause the macro to type the @left formula:

@left({left},@find(" ",{left},0))~   Types **@left** and an opening parenthesis and moves the pointer to the left to the first name in the database to establish the string to extract from. The macro then accomplishes an @find function, searching for the first occasion of a space from that cell starting with the first character (position 0). The result is an extraction of the first name or initial in the string before the first space.

{branch XQUIT}   Branches to a closing routine to copy the @left formula down in a column, change the @left formulas to their corresponding values, and quit.

If you select *FIRST NAME & M.I.* from the menu choices, the formula to extract the first name and middle initial is quite a bit more complicated. This is due to the necessity for verifying whether a middle initial is included in the full name being tested.

@if(@iserr(@find(" ",{left},@find(" ",{left},0)+1)),   Begins typing an @if statement that checks for an error condition in the search for two spaces in the string. The nested @find function accomplishes this search, looking for a second space in the string starting one space past the position of the first space.

@left({left},@find(" ",{left},0)),   If the error condition exists, the formula extracts just the first portion of the string up to the first (and only) space in the string.

@left({left},@find(" ",{left},@find(" ",{left},0)+1)))~   If the error condition does not exist, the formula extracts the characters from the left-most character up to the space found starting at the location after the first space in the string.

If you select *LAST NAME* from the menu choices, the extraction of the last name follows the same basic principles including a search for a second space and a determination of whether that search results in an error condition. The only real difference is the formula required to extract the last name. That formula consists of an @right function which pulls out the last name by calculating the position number of the latter space and subtracting that number from the length of the string.

/c~.{left}{end}{down}{right}~   The final routine named XQUIT copies the @left formula from the current cell. The TO cell is established by anchoring the pointer, moving to the contiguous column of full names to the left, moving End DownArrow to the bottom of that column, then moving back to Column B.

/rv{left}{end}{down}{right}~~{quit}   Changes the @left formulas to their corresponding values using the /Range Value command, paints in the column with the End DownArrow command, and quits.

Using @Mid to Extract a String

The @mid function uses the syntax

> **@mid**(string or cell, starting position, number of characters)

and returns a portion of a string consisting of characters from the middle of the entire string. It does this by extracting, from a starting position in the entire string, a specified number of characters. This definition of a starting position adds an element not required in the @left and @right formulas, as shown in the comparison below:

> **@left**(string or cell, number of characters)
> **@right**(string or cell, number of characters)
> **@mid**(string or cell, starting position, number of characters)

Since the 0 position is the position of the left-most character in the string, using 0 as the starting position in the @mid function exactly duplicates the effect you can achieve using the @left function. Thus the formula **@mid("hopeful",0,4)** starts counting at the first character (position 0) and counts four characters, returning the string *hope*. The formula **@mid("exclamation",2,4)**, on the other hand, starts counting at the third character (position 2) and counts four characters to return the string *clam*.

As with the @left and @right functions, the @mid function will work with a string, a cell address, or a range name for a single cell containing a string. If you enter a number that is equal to or greater than the number of characters in the string, the @right function will simply display the entire string.

Some typical uses of the @mid function include extracting the month or day of the month from a date typed as a label. From a typed label date **03/27/90** in cell H37, for example, you can extract the day of the month with the formula

$$\text{@mid(H37,@find("/",H37,0),2)}$$

where H37 holds the original string, the formula **@find("/",H37,0)** establishes the starting point to extract from, and the number 2 establishes the number of characters to extract.

For a more complicated use of @mid with @find, you may be interested in a macro the change entire label-dates to dates entered in the @date format—and then change them back again. Refer to the macro called Change Label-Date to @Date Formula shown in Figure 10.12.

```
B13: @STRING(@MONTH(CHG),0)&"/"&@STRING(@DAY(CHG),0)&"/"&@STRING(@YEAR(CHG)
@STRING(@MONTH(B16),0)&"/"&@STRING(@DAY(B16),0)&"/"&@STRING(@YEAR(B16),0)
```

	A	B	C
1	:	*** CHANGE LABEL-DATE TO @DATE FORMULA ***	
2	\C	{}	
3	*CHGDATE	{menubranch CMENU}{quit}	
4	CMENU	LABEL-DATE CONVERTED	CONVERT @DATE
5	:	Change label-date to @date formula	Change @date to label-dt
6	CLOOP	{let CHG,@cellpointer("contents")}	{branch CLOOP2}
7	:	{recalc CALC1}{recalc CALC2}@date(	
8	CALC1	88,1,	<--- String entry
9	CALC2	1)	<--- String entry
10	:	{down}{if @cellpointer("type")<>"b"}{branch CLOOP}	
11	:	{up}/rfd~{end}{up}~/wcs10~{end}{up}{quit}	
12	CLOOP2	{let CHG,@cellpointer("contents")}{recalc CALC3}'	
13	CALC3	ERR	<--- String entry
14	:	{down}{if @cellpointer("type")<>"b"}{branch CLOOP2}	
15	:	{up}/rfr{end}{up}~{end}{up}{quit}	
16	CHG	1/1/88	
17		Cell B8:	
18	@RIGHT(B16,2)&","&@LEFT(B16,@FIND("/",B16,0))&","		
19		Cell B9:	
20	@MID(B16,@FIND("/",B16,0)+1,@FIND("/",B16,3)-@FIND("/",B16,0)-1)&")"		

F_10_12.WK1   NUM

Figure 10.12 Macro to Change Label-Date to @Date Formula

To operate this macro, place your cell pointer at the first entry in a column of label-dates or dates entered in the @date format and press Alt-C.

{menubranch CMENU}{quit} Calls up the menu choices *LABEL-DATE CONVERTED* and *CONVERT @DATE*.

{let CHG,@cellpointer("contents")} This is the first active line of the *LABEL-DATE CONVERTED* choice. It copies the contents of the first cell in the column to the cell in the macro named CHG. In the example in Figure 10.12, CHG has had the label-date 1/1/88 copied into it. (When you first create this macro, of course, you can leave this cell empty.)

{recalc CALC1}{recalc CALC2}@date(Updates the next two cells in CALC1 and CALC2 to reflect information based on the entry stored in CHG. This is required for self-modifying lines of a macro that consist of string functions or combinations of string functions. The macro then types **@date** and an opening parenthesis and continues at the next line.

88,1,   Although in Figure 10.12 this line named CALC1 shows as the year and month of the date stored in CHG, it is actually the result of the underlying formula:

@right(B16,2)&","&@left(B16,@find("/",B16,0))&","

where B16 is the cell address for the cell in the macro named CHG. You can also see this formula redisplayed for clarity at the bottom of the Figure in cell A18. (As you type this in yourself, use the cell address that corresponds to CHG in your own worksheet.)

1)   In the same way, this line at CALC2 in Figure 10.12 displays the day of the date stored in CHG and a closing parenthesis, while it is actually the result of the underlying formula:

@mid(B16,@find("/",B16,0)+1,@find("/",B16,3)-@find("/",B16,0)-1)&")"

The purpose of this formula is to extract from the middle of a date such as 1/1/88 the day of the month (in this case the number 1). The formula does this by using the @mid(string,start,number) formula, where the start is identified by finding the first forward slash (/), and the number of characters in the day of the month is identified by subtracting the found position of the second slash from the found position of the first slash.

{down}{if @cellpointer("type")<>"b"}{branch CLOOP}   Moves the cell pointer down, at the same time entering the @date formula created with the last three lines of the macro. If the cell pointer has not reached the end of the columns of date, the macro loops back to CLOOP to construct the @date formula for the next label-date it encounters.

{up}/rfd~{end}{up}~/wcs10~{end}{up}{quit}   When the cell pointer does reach a blank cell representing the end of the column, it moves up to the last entry, formats the entire column for date format, changes the column width to 10 to accommodate the date format, moves to the top of the column, and quits.

{let CHG,@cellpointer("contents")}{recalc CALC3}'   If you selected *CONVERT @DATE* at the beginning of this macro because the column you want to convert is a column of @date format values, the macro begins by storing a copy of the contents of the first cell to CHG, then recalculates (updates) the next cell at the range name CALC3 and types a label-prefix apostrophe in preparation for entry of the displayed contents of CALC3.

ERR   Although this cell displays ERR at this point, its underlying formula is:

@string(@month(B16),0)&"/"&@string(@day(B16),0)&"/"&
@string(@year(B16),0)

When placed on an @date format value, this formula concatenates the string value of the month (no decimals), a forward slash (/), the string value of the day (no decimals), a forward slash (/), and the string value of the year (no decimals). The remainder of this routine named CLOOP2 is the same as the closing line of CLOOP at B11, except that the column width is not changed and the format is reset.

Setting up this macro may seem like a lot to go through to change some dates from one format to another, but if the change is being made to a large database, the trouble of creating the macro is more than offset by the savings in keystrokes and time.

@Trim and the {Contents} Command

The purpose of the @trim function is to trim away extraneous spaces in a string. This is especially useful when importing files over from other programs such as database files that include spaces between the fields.

This function does not trim away all spaces, only leading spaces, trailing spaces, or spaces combined with other spaces. For example, the phrase *General   &   Administrative* with several spaces between the words would condense to *General & Administrative*. Similarly, the label-number *4 7 3 2* (necessarily entered as a label because it is not possible to place spaces between characters in a value) is displayed with the @trim formula as *4 7 3 2*.

The formula @trim(B13) returns an ERR message when B13 consists of the value 12345. The formula @trim(@string(B14,0)), on the other hand, properly returns the label-number 12345.

The @trim function is especially useful in modifying the results of the {contents} command. The function of the {contents} command is similar to the {let} command in that it causes 1-2-3 to store the contents of one cell at a destination cell. However, there are three major differences between {let} and {contents}, as:

1. The {contents} command can only store information from a specified cell, while the {let} command can store a specified value or string as well as the contents of a specified cell.
2. Whereas the {let} command stores both values and labels, the {contents} command stores only a label version of a value or label.
3. When storing a value as a label, the {contents} command also stores the displayed format of that value unless otherwise specified.

The syntax of the {contents} command is:

{**contents** *destination,source-cell,[width],[cell-format]*}

where *[width]* and *[cell-format]* are optional attributes allowing you to specify these attributes that would otherwise default to the width and cell format of the source cell. The *[cell-format]* attribute, if specified, must follow the code numbers as shown in Figure 10.13.

Let's look at an example of the {contents} command that does not include optional attributes. Assuming a spreadsheet where cell F7 has a column width of 11 and contains the value 123 formatted for currency, the command

{**contents D14,F7**}

stores a label with three leading spaces and one trailing space in cell D14 as:

A1: [W2]   READY

```
     A     B          C          D          E              F              G
1
2          Codes for             0..15      Fixed, 0-15 decimals
3          [Cell-Format]         16..31     Scientific, 0-15 decimals
4          Attributes of         32..47     Currency, 0-15 decimals
5          the {Contents}        48..63     Percent, 0-15 decimals
6          Command               64..79     Comma, 0-15 decimals
7                                 112        +/-
8                                 113        General
9                                 114        D1 (DD-MMM-YY)
10                                115        D2 (DD-MMM)
11                                116        D3 (MMM-YY)
12                                117        Text
13                                118        Hidden
14                                119        D6 (HH:MM:SS AM/PM)
15                                120        D7 (HH:MM AM/PM)
16                                121        D4 (Long Intn'l Date)
17                                122        D5 (Short Intn'l Date)
18                                123        D8 (Long Intn'l Time)
19                                124        D9 (Short Intn'l Time)
20                                127        Worksheet's Global Cell Format
F_10_13.WK1                                                               NUM
```

Figure 10.13 Codes for (*Cell-Format*) Attribute in {Contents}

' *$123.00*

This is when the @trim function comes in handy. By trimming the leading and trailing spaces, it allows a change of the result of the {contents} command to a label as:

'$123.00

This can be seen in the sample use of the {contents} command and @trim function in Figure 10.14.

To operate the macro, place your cell pointer on cell D7 and press Alt-A. The macro works as:

{contents AHERE,@cellpointer("address")}~   Copies a label version of the current cell location in cell AHERE. In the upper panel you can see the leading and trailing spaces shown in cell B13.

{let BHERE,@trim(AHERE)}~   Copies to BHERE a version of the contents in AHERE with leading and trailing spaces eliminated.

Using @Trim to Change a Column Width

In Figure 10.6, we showed how you can use the @length function in a self-modifying macro to change the width of a column to match the label in the current cell. Unfortunately, that macro will not work on values. In this section we will show how you can use the @trim func-

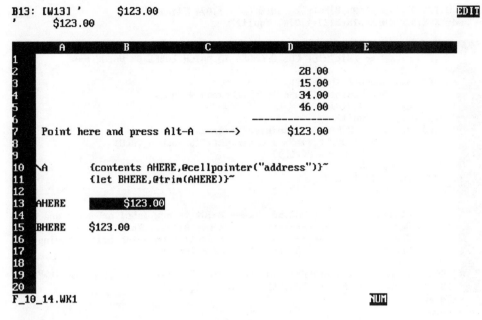

Figure 10.14 Sample Use of the {contents} Command and @Trim

tion and the {contents} command to improve the macro so it works on values as well as labels (refer to Figure 10.15).

Here's how the macro works.

{windowsoff}{paneloff}   Turns off the windows and panel to suppress screen flicker.

{if @cellpointer("type")="v"}{branch W_VALU}   Checks for whether the current cell contains a label or a value. If it contains a value, the macro branches to W_VALU.

{recalc WIDTH}   Otherwise, the macro recalculates the self-modifying formula in the next cell down, at WIDTH.

/wcs13~{quit}   This is the displayed value of the underlying formula in B6 (also shown at the bottom of Figure 10.15). This formula can be broken down as:

+"/wcs"
&@string(@length(@cellpointer("contents"))+1,0)
&"~{quit}"

The formula calculates a number one greater than the length of the cell pointer contents, turns it into a string showing no decimals, precedes the result with the /Worksheet Columnwidth Set sequence, and follows it with a tilde and {quit} command.

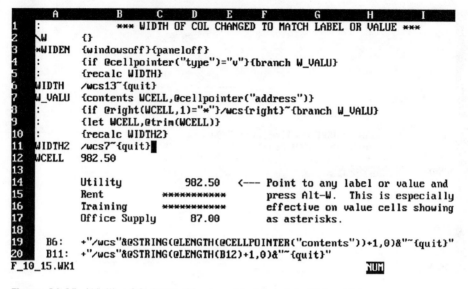

Figure 10.15 Width of Column Changed to Match Label or Value

Note: When you first enter the formula, it will return ERR. However, do not let that worry you; simply move to any cell containing a label and press the F9 Calc key to see a display such as shown in cell B6.

{contents WCELL,@cellpointer("address")} This is the beginning of the routine when the macro branches if the cell pointer starts on a cell containing a value. It copies a label version of the value to WCELL, including the characteristics of the cell's width and format.

{if @right(WCELL,1)="*"}/wcs{right}~{branch W_VALU} If the current cell shows a series of asterisks because it is too narrow to show its value, the macro selects /Worksheet Columnwidth Set, increases the width by one with the {right} command, and branches back to the previous line named W_VALU to once again copy a label version of the current cell's displayed value to WCELL.

{let WCELL,@trim(WCELL)} Otherwise, the macro uses the {let} command to trim the leading and trailing zeros from the label version of the current cell stored in WCELL. Later, the macro will use this stored label to calculate a revised width.

{recalc WIDTH2} Recalculates the self-modifying formula in the next cell down, at WIDTH2.

/wcs7~{quit}   This is the displayed value of the underlying formula in B11 (also shown at the bottom of Figure 10.15). This formula can be broken down as:

+"/wcs"
&@string(@length(B12)+1,0)
&"~{quit}"

where B12 is the cell address for the cell in the macro named WCELL. (As you type this in yourself, use the cell address that corresponds to WCELL in your own worksheet.)

The formula calculates a number one greater than the length of the contents of B12, turns it into a string showing no decimals, precedes the result with the /Worksheet Columnwidth Set sequence, and follows it with a tilde and {quit} command.

Note: To use this macro in a Release 3 Macro Library using separate active files, precede every reference to WCELL or cell B12 with the wild-card filename <<?>>.

Using {Contents} with Optional Attributes

You may be wondering about the conditions under which you might make use of the optional attributes of the {contents} command. The macro in Figure 10.16 provides one example. The purpose of the macro is to allow you to edit a formula's range names without having to retype the entire names. In Release 2, 2.01, and 2.2, pressing the F2 Edit key on a formula causes the formula to display in the Edit Control Panel showing cell coordinates in place of any range names the formula may reference.

```
E19: [W13] +APPLES*APPLE_QTY+PEARS*PEAR_QTY+ORANGES*ORANGE_QTY            EDIT
+APPLES*APPLE_QTY+PEARS*PEAR_QTY+ORANGES*ORANGE_QTY
```

	A	B	C	D	E	F
1	:	*** EDIT A FORMULA WITH RANGE NAMES ***				
2	\E	{}				
3	*EDITNAME	{windowsoff}{paneloff}/rncEHERE~~/rndEHERE~/rncEHERE~~				
4	:	{contents EFORM,EHERE,240,117}				
5	:	/rndEHERE~{let EFORM,@trim(EFORM)}				
6	:	{EFORM}{panelon}{windowson}{edit}{quit}				
7	EFORM	+APPLES*APPLE_QTY+PEARS*PEAR_QTY+ORANGES*ORANGE_QTY				
8	:	{return}				
9						
10				Apples	$0.27	
11				Apple_Qty	237	
12						
13				Pears	$0.23	
14				Pear_Qty	438	
15						
16				Oranges	$0.32	
17				Orange_Qty	184	
18						
19	Total Cost of Fruit (Apples, Pears, Oranges):				223.61	
20						

```
F_10_16.WK1                                        CALC    NUM
```

Figure 10.16 Macro to Edit a Formula with Range Names

For example, suppose you have a formula with the range names SALES88 and SALES89 that you would like to edit to reference the range names SALES90 and SALES91. It would be handy to be able to simply press F2 Edit, move the cursor to the numbers 88 and 89 in the range names, and change them to 90 and 91; but when you press F2 Edit, the range names are displayed as cell coordinates, and to make a change you will have to eliminate the cell coordinates and type in the entire revised range names.

There is a way to do this more easily using the F4 Abs key. Press F2 Edit, move to the cell coordinate representing the range name you want to modify, and press F4 Abs. The coordinates will be replaced with an absolute form of the corresponding range name, preceded by the dollar sign ($) absolute indicator. Delete the dollar sign, and you have a relative form of the range name you can easily change. Unfortunately, if the macro is long and complicated, you may go through quite a number of keystrokes to use this process.

The macro in Figure 10.16 does all of this for you. Here's how the macro works.

{windowsoff}{paneloff}/rncEHERE˜˜/rndEHERE˜/rncEHERE˜˜   Turns off the windows and panel to suppress screen flicker and speed up the macro, then creates, deletes and recreates the range named EHERE at the current cell.

{contents EFORM,EHERE,240,117}   Copies the contents of the current cell named EHERE into EFORM. A width of up to 240 characters is specified to override the default: the column width of the current cell. Code 117 specifies Text format (see Figure 10.13) to override the default of current cell format.

/rndEHERE˜{let EFORM,@trim(EFORM)}   The macro deletes EHERE, then—in case the length of the contents of the current cell is less than the width, causing extraneous spaces in EFORM—it trims any leading or trailing zeros from the copy in EFORM.

{EFORM}{panelon}{windowson}{edit}{quit}   Runs the subroutine at EFORM, typing the contents of EFORM in the upper panel, then turns the windows and panel back on, switches to Edit mode, and quits.

To see an example of the macro running, set up your worksheet like Figure 10.16, select /Range Name Labels Right and highlight D10 through D17, enter the formula shown in the upper panel in E19, and (still at cell E19) press the F2 Edit key. You will see the formula in the Edit Control Panel showing cell coordinates instead of range names. Press Escape, then Alt-E. You will see the formula in the Edit Control Panel showing range names as in Figure 10.16, which you can then edit.

Using @Clean to Eliminate ASCII Characters

Just as the @trim function eliminates extraneous spaces from an imported file, so does the @clean function eliminate extraneous characters represented by ASCII codes 0 to 32 that may be imported in the process of pulling in another file. These codes may be special formatting characters or indentations or print attributes such as those used to print italic type.

The @clean formula will work on any string up to 240 characters in Release 2, 2.01, or

2.2, or 516 characters in Release 3. As with the other string functions, referencing the string directly requires that the string be enclosed in full quotation marks. A more likely scenario, however, is that the @trim function will refer to a cell address or range name representing a single cell. The @trim function will not work on a range of more than one cell, since the function only works with one string at a time.

Since ASCII characters 0 to 32 are not visible within 1-2-3, the string being "cleaned" and the @clean version of the string will look identical. For this reason, it is a good idea to use the @clean function on every string or line being imported where the string is suspected to have one or more of the 0 to 32 ASCII codes.

The @Repeat Function

Chapter 9 shows two examples of the @repeat function in the Columnwidth Underline macro and Add & Underline a Column macro as shown in Figures 9.11 and 9.12. Here we will examine more of the characteristics of @repeat.

Just as you can fill a cell with a double underline by pressing \=, you can also fill a cell 12 spaces wide by typing **@repeat("=",12)**. The difference, however, is that the @repeat function can be used to extend past the width of one cell to any width required up to 240 characters.

You can also use this handy feature to play with different combinations to see how repeating two symbols across the width of your screen will look. Thus, the formula **@repeat("=",65)** in Column A of your worksheet will display a line as:

=- =-=-=

The @repeat function can also be used in a macro to create boxes in your worksheet, as shown in Figure 10.17.

To operate the macro, move your cell pointer to any blank area of your worksheet and press Alt-M.

{getnumber "TOP BORDER IS HOW MANY SPACES WIDE? ",MWIDTH}~
Prompts you to enter a number representing the desired width of the box you want to create, storing that number in MWIDTH.

{windowsoff}{paneloff}   Turns off the windows and panel to suppress screen flicker and speed up the macro.

+"'+"&@repeat("-",MWIDTH)&"+"{edit}{calc}~{down}   This line of the macro enters a string formula in the current cell that starts and ends with a plus sign (+) and includes the dash symbol (-) repeated the number of times you specified in response to the {getnumber} prompt at the beginning. The macro then processes the {edit}{calc} commands, turning the formula into its displayed value

'+ - - - - - - - - - -+

then moves down one cell. You can see the results of this line in the upper panel of Figure 10.17.

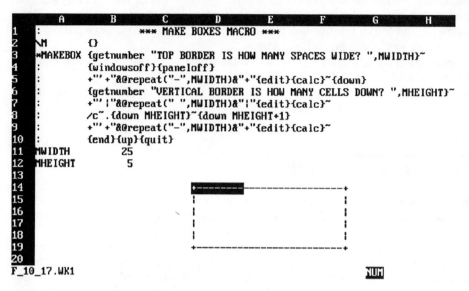

Figure 10.17 The Make Boxes Macro Using @Repeat

{getnumber "VERTICAL BORDER IS HOW MANY CELLS DOWN? ",MHEIGHT}~
Prompts you to enter a number representing the desired height of the box you want to create, storing that number in MHEIGHT.

+"'|"&@repeat(" ",MWIDTH)&"|"{edit}{calc}~   Enters a string formula that starts and ends with a vertical line symbol (|) and includes a space repeated the number of times you specified in response to the {getnumber} prompt for width. The {edit}{calc} commands turn the formula into its displayed value

'| |

/c~.{down MHEIGHT}~{down MHEIGHT+1}   Copies the preceding entry down the worksheet the number of times you specified in response to the {getnumber} prompt for height, then moves the cell pointer down one cell more than that number.

+"'+"&@repeat("-",MWIDTH)&"+"{edit}{calc}~   This is a repeat of the fourth line of the macro, creating the bottom of your graphic

'+ — — — — — — — — — — +

{end}{up}{quit}   The macro ends by moving to the top of the box and quitting.

We have used plus and dash signs for the box that this macro creates, since in Release 2, 2.01, and 2.2 you do not have access to appropriate ASCII characters for creating fancy boxes unless you rerun Install, choose Advance Options, select Modify

Current Driver Set, choose Text Display, press PgDn, and select *Universal Text Display-ASCII-No LICS*.

In Release 3, however, you can create more impressive boxes using the Lotus Mutibyte Character Set (LMBCS) and substituting @code and @char functions in your macro.

The @Code and @Char Functions

The @code and @char functions are mirror images of each other and are used to replicate and manipulate the ASCII characters for ASCII codes 33 through 255.

The @code function uses the syntax:

@code(*character*)

and the @char function uses the syntax:

@char(*code*)

For example, **@char(33)** will return the character corresponding to the ASCII code 33: the exclamation point (!). Conversely, typing **@code("!")** will return the number 33.

To explore the ASCII characters that cannot be invoked in 1-2-3 by pressing a single key on your keyboard, follow these steps:

1. Move to an area of your worksheet that has at least two blank columns and select /Data Fill, highlight a vertical range covering 255 cells, and select a Start of 0, a Step of 1, and a stop of 8192.

2. Move to the blank column to the right and type **@char** and an opening parenthesis, type a plus (+) symbol, point to the cell to the left, close the parenthesis, and press Return.

3. Copy the formula down 255 cells by selecting /Copy and at the *Range to Copy FROM:* prompt, highlight to the left one cell, press End Down, unhighlight back to the right, and press Return twice.

That's all there is to it. Now you can explore the symbols and make a note of the symbols you might like to use to dress up your spreadsheet—perhaps by surrounding the @char function with the @repeat function to create an entire line of a specific symbol.

If you have Release 3 or in Release 2, 2.01, or 2.2, and you decide to select NO LICS at the Install level as described above, you will be especially interested in symbols that can be used to make a fancy box. These are shown in Figure 10.18.

You should be aware, however, that your printer may not print out many of these symbols, or may print something different on your paper than you see on the screen. To test which symbols your printer can accommodate, simply print out the range of @char functions you created following the steps just outlined here.

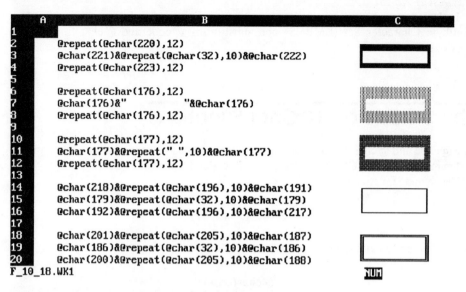

Figure 10.18 Using ASCII-No LICS or LMBCS to Create Boxes

The @Exact Function

The @exact function was covered in the last chapter. To review, this function is used to compare two strings for an exact match, including a match of uppercase versus lowercase. The syntax of this function is:

$$\text{@exact}(\textit{first string, second string})$$

If the first string is exactly the same as the second string, this function returns the number 1 indicating the condition is true. If the two strings do not match, a 0 is returned indicating that the condition is false.

The Non-Standard Entries Corrected macro shown in Figure 9.8 is one example of the use of @exact. That macro is designed to move down a sorted database cleaning up slight variations in the way the data was entered.

The @Replace Function

The @replace function is used to replace a portion of a string with specified characters, or to add or delete specified characters in a predefined location of a string. The format is as:

$$\text{@replace}(\textit{string or cell,starting location,\# characters,new string})$$

The @replace function applied to the word "Application" to return the word "Indication," for example, would be typed:

$$@replace(\textit{"Application"}0,4,\textit{"Ind"})$$

Accordingly, you can use @replace and the string ANTELOPE HILL in cell B7 to return the word ANTHILL by typing:

$$\textbf{@replace(B7,3,6,"")}$$

To eliminate the middle initial from a name such Edvard H. Grieg in cell C8 to display Edvard Grieg, you can type:

$$\textbf{@replace(\textit{C8},@find(" ",C8,0),3,"")}$$

The View @Sum macro in Figure 10.19 provides an interesting example of a self-modifying macro that uses @replace in combination with @left and @length to create a variable line.

Figure 10.19 Macro to View the Range of an @Sum Formula

The purpose of the macro is to automatically highlight the range in an @sum macro, providing you with a view of the range without your having to manually verify the cell coordinates and visit the range with your cell pointer.

To operate the macro, place your cell pointer on any cell with an @sum formula and press Alt-V. The message *SUM RANGE IS:* will appear in the left of the top panel, and the range coordinates will appear in the right. More importantly, the range will be highlighted, whereupon you can verify whether the range is what you want. If not, you can manually adjust the range with your pointer keys. Any adjustment you make will automatically update the @sum formula at the same time.

Here's how the macro works.

{windowsoff}{paneloff}{edit}{home}'~   Turns off the windows and panel to suppress screen flicker and speed up the macro, then converts the @sum formula to a label.

{let VFORM,@cellpointer("contents")}~   Copies the label form of the @sum formula to VFORM.

{edit}{home}{del}~{recalc VRANGE}   Changes the @sum label back to a formula by deleting the apostrophe, then recalculates the self-modifying cell of the macro named VRANGE.

/rncSUM RANGE IS:~~/rndSUM RANGE IS:~/rncSUM RANGE IS:~   Begins the creation of a new range named SUM RANGE IS: in preparation for a later use of this range name as a prompt to the user.

F11..F15   This line establishes the range coordinates for the range name SUM RANGE IS:. Although in our example this cell displays **F11..F15**, it is actually the result of running the macro on the @sum formula (that in this case sums the range F11..F15). Underlying this display is the formula:

$$\text{@left(@replace(B11,0,5,""),@length(@replace(B11,0,5,""))-1)}$$

where B11 is the cell address for the cell of the macro named VFORM. (As you type this in yourself, use the cell address that corresponds to VFORM in your own worksheet.)

The @replace portion of this formula is used to eliminate the five left-most characters of the @sum formula in B11 by replacing them with the null string "" . By itself the formula @replace(B11,0,5,"") would display **F11..F13)**, with a closing parenthesis. The @left portion of the formula is used to eliminate the parenthesis on the right by extracting the number of characters equal to one less than the length of the results of the @replace formula, leaving us with **F11..F13**.

~/rnc{panelon}SUM RANGE IS:{windowson}~..{up 2}{down 2}{?}   The tilde completes the /Range Name Create sequence. The macro then starts the sequence again, turning on the upper panel, this time before *SUM RANGE IS:* appears. The windows are turned on so you can see the highlighted range in the worksheet. The two periods (..) move the blinking cursor to the upper part of the range, then the cell pointer is moved up two cells, then down two cells to provide a better view of the range. At this point, the macro pauses so you can view the @sum range and accept it or modify it as required.

{windowsoff}{paneloff}~@sum(SUM RANGE IS:)~   Turns off the windows and panel to suppress screen flicker and enters the formula **@sum(SUM RANGE IS:)**. If you have not adjusted the @sum range, this line has no effect. If you have adjusted it, however, this is the place where your change takes effect.

/rndSUM RANGE IS:~{quit}   Finally, the macro deletes the range name SUM RANGE IS:, which converts the range of the @sum formula back to cell coordinates, and the macro quits.

This macro makes a very effective and useful companion macro to the Add macro discussed in earlier chapters, and should be strongly considered for inclusion in any Macro Library collection of macros.

The @Value Function

The @value function is used to return the value of a number that has been entered as a label. Thus the label " 12345" can be expressed as the value 12345 with the formula **@value(" 12345")**.

The @value formula can convert the label '123.875 to the value 123.875, or the scientific notation label '3.25E3 to 3250, or the label fraction '3 3/4 to 3.75. As you might expect, these @value formulas can be added together. They can not be used, however, to calculate a sum statement entered as a label. Thus an @value formula such as **@value("3 3/4 + 7 7/8")** returns an ERR message.

For this reason, a telephone number such as the '301-555-1212 is not calculated by the @value function to return the difference of 301 minus 555 minus 1212. Instead the function returns ERR. The @value function will, however, return the value of numbers typed as labels in the currency or percent format. Thus the function **@value("$123,000.00")** returns 123000 in F16, and the function **@value("12.3%")** returns 0.123. Of course, you can always format the cell containing the @value function to display Currency or Percent if you want the formats to show in the value version of these numbers.

One format for numbers which will not be read by the @value function is the +/- format. The @value function **@value("+++++++")**, for example, returns ERR. Similarly, the formula **@value("Sales")** in Cell D20 returns an ERR because the @value function will not read non-numeric labels.

The @n Function

The @n function is used to return the value of the upper-left entry in a range. Typing **@n(A5..C9)** where cell A5 contains the value 1234, for example, will return the value 1234.

The @n function will also work on a single-cell range such as **@n(A5..A5)** where cell A5 contains the value 1234, still returning the value 1234.

The @n function will not convert a numeric label to a value as the @value function does. And whereas the formula **@value(A1..A1)** will return ERR if A1 contains the word *Budget*, the formula **@n(A1..A1)** will return a zero. Using the @n is therefore especially useful when you are not sure whether the cell or upper left corner of the range being referred to begins with a label or a number, but in either case you do not want ERR displayed.

Even if the range in the @n function is typed in reverse order—if you type **@n(C3..A1)**, for example, instead of **@n(A1..C3)**—the result is still the value of the cell in the upper left corner of the range: A1 in this case. If the range being referred to is entirely blank, the @n function will return a zero.

The @s Function

The @s function is similar to the @n function in that it has as its argument a range address rather than the address of a single cell. However, whereas the @n function returns a value when referring to a range of numbers and a zero when referring to a range of labels, the @s function returns a string when referring to a range of labels and a blank cell when referring to a range of numbers.

The formula **@s(A5..C13)**, for example, returns the string *Sales* when A5 contains the string *Sales*. On the other hand, the formula **@s(A5..C13)** referring to a blank range returns a blank cell. The formulas **@s(A5..C13)** referring to a range that begins with the number 1234 also returns a blank cell.

If the @s formula refers to a string as in the example **@s("Sales")** the result is ERR. This is because the @s and @n function, unlike most of the other string functions, require a range address or range name and will not accept a string as its argument.

Summary

In this chapter we have reviewed the science of string formulas and the use of the special string manipulation features of 1-2-3 to combine two or more elements into a single word or phrase. We defined the concept of string formulas and the individual string @functions, and explored their purpose and application in cells of the spreadsheet to create variable entries and in macros which require variable or self-modifying lines. We also looked at the use of string formulas and string @ functions in combination with other @ functions of 1-2-3.

Uses and techniques of the individual string @functions were reviewed:

- Using the @string function to change numeric values to strings, allowing you to specify the number of decimal places to be used for a string.
- Using the @upper, @lower, and @proper functions to change a string to uppercase, lowercase, or proper case. These functions will not work on numbers or formulas displayed as values unless such entries are converted to labels with the @string function. A macro to automate the conversion of case in a column was also presented.
- Using the @length function to determine the number of characters in a string. The @length function will not provide the length of a number entered as a value. A Width of Column Changed macro was presented to automatically increase or decrease the width of a column to accommodate the length of a label at the current cell. An enhanced version of this macro was included to accommodate the length of a number at the current cell.
- Using the @find function to search a string for the first occurrence of one or more characters starting at a designated position in the string. The use of nested @find statements was also presented to locate the second occurrence of the characters established as the search criteria.
- Using the @left function to return a specified number of characters from a string, starting from the left-most character. Use of @left with @find was reviewed to show a technique for extracting a variable length string such as the last name from a list of first name–last name entries.

- Using the @right function to return a specified number of characters from a string, starting from the right-most character. The @right function can also be used in conjunction with the @length and @find functions to extract and display a variable length string or to reverse a last name–first name order of customer names to first name–last name order and vice versa. A macro was also presented to extract the first name, last name, or middle initial from a database of names.

- Using the @mid function to extract a portion of a string based on a starting position and including a specified number of characters. A macro using @mid was presented, designed to change Label-Dates to @Date Formulas, and vice versa.

- Using the @trim function is to trim away extraneous spaces in a string. This is especially useful in conjunction with the {contents} command or when importing files over from other programs such as database files that appear with spaces between the fields. The {contents} command was compared with the {let} command and codes for optional attributes of {contents} were shown. Two macros using {contents} and @trim was presented: one to change the column width to match a label or a value and the other to allow you to edit a formula's range names.

- Using the @clean function to eliminate extraneous ASCII codes from 0 to 32 which may be imported in the process of pulling in another file. These codes may be special formatting characters or indentations or print attributes such as those used to print italic face type.

- Using the @repeat function to create a string of repeating characters that can extend past the width of one cell. It was noted that you can have different combinations of repeating characters that will appear across the width of your screen. A macro using the @repeat function was presented, called the Make Boxes macro.

- Using the @code and @char functions to replicate and manipulate the ASCII characters for ASCII codes 33 through 255. Instructions were given on creation of a table of the ASCII characters using @char, as were instructions on changing your 1-2-3 driver to ASCII—No LICS.

- Using the @exact function to compare two strings for an exact match, including a match of uppercase versus lowercase.

- Using the @replace function to replace a portion of a string with specified characters, or to add or delete specified characters in a predefined location of a string. A macro was presented that will automatically highlight and give you a view of the range of any @sum formula.

- Using the @value function to return the value of a number entered as a label. The most useful feature of the @value function is its ability to return the value of numbers typed as labels in the fraction, scientific notation, currency, or percent format.

- Using the @n function to return the value of the upper-left entry in a range. The @n function will not convert a numeric label to a value as the @value function does.

- Using the @s function to return the upper left string in a range. A blank cell is returned when the @s function refers to a range where the upper left cell contains a value or a blank cell.

In Chapter 11 we will review looping macros that include counters using the {let} command. We will also look at counters using the {for} command, especially in conjunction with @index and the {put} command.

11

COUNTERS AND THE
{FOR} LOOP

Scope

In Chapter 9 we examined the use of the {if} command to create a macro that will loop until the cell pointer encounters a blank cell. In this chapter we will explore ways to make your macro loop a designated number of times in one of two ways: by using {if} with the {let} command or by using the more advanced {for} command.

Width of Columns Changed

With the advent of Release 2.2 and 3 came the ability to change the width of several columns at once using /Worksheet Column Column-Range Set. Until then, column widths could only be changed one at a time— unless, of course, you used a macro.

The macro in Figure 11.1 is used to change the column widths of any number of columns you designate. Even if you have Release 2.2 or 3, you will find this an interesting use of the {if} and {let} commands to cause the macro to loop a number of times based on an internal counter.

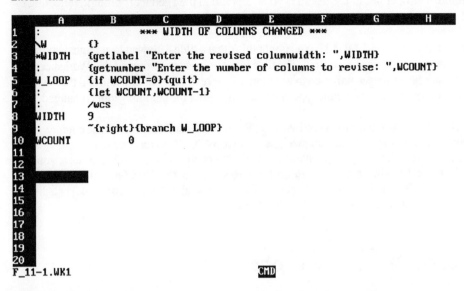

Figure 11.1   Using a Counter to Change a Range of Column Widths

{getlabel "Enter the revised columnwidth: ",WIDTH}   The macro starts with a prompt for the width you want. Notice the use of {getlabel}, which inserts your response in the cell named WIDTH as a label, not as a value. This is done because the response is needed as a self-modifying line of the macro itself, which means it must be entered as a string.

{getnumber "Enter the number of columns to revise: ",WCOUNT}   This is the beginning of a method for creating a counter. In this case, a counter is set up at the cell named WCOUNT. The {getnumber} prompt allows the user to store a new count value, from which the macro will count down to zero. If, for example, you wanted to revise the columns F through P, you would enter the number 11 at this point, and the macro would count down from 11 to 0.

Note: Here we are using {getnumber} rather than {getlabel}, since the macro will be doing an arithmetic operation on the responded value.

{if WCOUNT=0}{quit}   This line uses the {if} command to test whether the value in WCOUNT has reached zero. If so, the macro quits.

{let WCOUNT,WCOUNT-1}   Otherwise, the macro changes the cell named WCOUNT, to WCOUNT-1, the value which is one number less than the current value of WCOUNT. This is how the macro counts down from 11 to 0.

/wcs   The macro presses /Worksheet Columnwidth Set to change the width of the current column. The next line of the macro is your response to the {getlabel} prompt, reflecting the column width you want.

~{right}{branch W_LOOP}   You might think that a tilde followed by a {right} command is redundant, but both are required. The tilde is the only entry command the /Worksheet Columnwidth Set sequence will recognize to enter your revised column width and the {right} is required to move the cell pointer one cell to the right after the column width is changed.

The macro loops back to the cell W_LOOP and checks and decrements the counter. It will continue in this way until the counter (the value in WCOUNT) reaches zero.

Rather than watching the width of each column change one column at a time, you may want to modify this macro by inserting a row before the W_LOOP line and adding {windowsoff} and {paneloff} commands. This will speed up the macro and delay a display of the resulting changes until the end of the macro.

A Slide Show of Graphs

There are several uses we can make of this ability to create a macro counter that increments or decrements (counts up or down) with each pass through a macro loop. The macro in Figure 11.2 is just such an example, designed to allow a type of slide show of your graphs. This is especially useful during presentations when instead of having to select /Graph Name Use

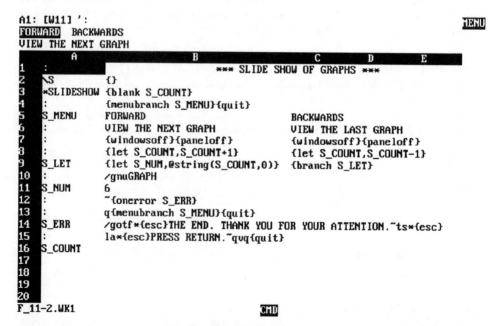

Figure 11.2 Using a Counter to Present a Slide Show of Graphs

and point to graphs displayed in alphabetical order, you can simply select *FORWARD* or *BACKWARDS* to move instantly forward or backwards through graphs named GRAPH1, GRAPH2, GRAPH3, in the order you would like to see them.

Before starting this macro, create or retrieve a worksheet of graphs, then use /Graph Name Create to give the names GRAPH1, GRAPH2, GRAPH3, and so on, to each graph. Be careful not to include a space between the word GRAPH and the number, or this macro will not work. Do not, for example, name a graph GRAPH 3.

{blank S_COUNT} The macro begins by zeroing the counter cell through use of the {blank} command.

{menubranch S_MENU}{quit} Calls up the menu choices *FORWARD* and *BACKWARDS*. To view the first graph, select *FORWARD*.

{windowsoff}{paneloff} Strangely, these commands do not affect the display of the graph or the display of the custom menu choices *FORWARD* and *BACKWARDS*. However, between graphs you will see the *FORWARD* and *BACKWARDS* menu choices shown on an otherwise blank screen. This isolates the menu commands for your slide show so as not to distract your audience with columns and rows of numbers between graphs.

{let S_COUNT,S_COUNT+1} or **{let S_COUNT,S_COUNT-1}** If you select *FORWARD*, the counter is incremented by one using the {let} command. If you select *BACKWARDS*, the counter is reduced by one.

{let S_NUM,@string(S_COUNT,0)} Whether you selected *FORWARD* or *BACKWARDS*, the macro continues at this cell named S_LET. The purpose of this line is to copy a string version (with no decimals) of the new value in S_COUNT to S_NUM, a self-modifying cell of the macro that will be used to designate the next graph name.

/gnuGRAPH Starts the selection /Graph Name Use, then types the word GRAPH. The next line at S_NUM will complete the name. Thus, if the next graph to view is GRAPH3, there will be a string version of the number 3 in S_NUM.

~{onerror S_ERR} The macro completes the /Graph Name Use command with the tilde. This is our first use of the {onerror} command. The purpose of {onerror} is to tell the macro where to branch in the event the macro comes to an error condition or you decide to stop it with a press of Ctrl-Break. This command takes as its argument the cell where the macro should continue. Like the {windowsoff} and {paneloff} commands, it stays in effect until the macro ends, or until you disable it. Disabling of an {onerror} command is done with a subsequent {onerror} that includes no argument.

In this case, if there is no GRAPH7, yet 7 is the next number this macro increments to after viewing GRAPH6, operating without an {onerror} command will result in the macro quitting with a beep and an error message. With the command {onerror S_ERR}, however, meeting the error condition will cause the macro will continue to operate at the routine beginning at S_ERR.

q{menubranch S_MENU}{quit}   If the macro does not come to an error, it quits the /Graph menu and branches to the custom menu at S_MENU where it once again offers a screen that is blank except for the two menu choices, *FORWARD* and *BACKWARDS*.

/gotf*{esc}THE END. THANK YOU FOR YOUR ATTENTION.~ts*{esc}   Otherwise, if there is no graph matching the graph name the macro is attempting to view, the error condition will cause a branch to this cell at S_ERR where it will select /Graph Options Title First, press an asterisk and Escape to clear the first title, enter for your audience the title, **THE END. THANK YOU FOR YOUR ATTENTION,** and clear the second title with Title Second and a press of asterisk, and Escape.

la*{esc}PRESS RETURN.~qvq{quit}   Finally, the macro changes the Legend for the A-Range to one last instruction, *PRESS RETURN,* quits that level of the graph menu, and shows a view of the graph. You will see the same graph you last viewed, but with the informative titles as shown in Figure 11.3. After this the macro quits the /Graph menu and returns to *READY.*

   If you select *BACKWARDS,* of course, the slide show of graphs will proceed backwards to GRAPH1, and then to an attempt to view GRAPH0 which does not, of course exist. In that case, the error will cause a branch to S_ERR where the last graph viewed will be displayed again with the same ending message.

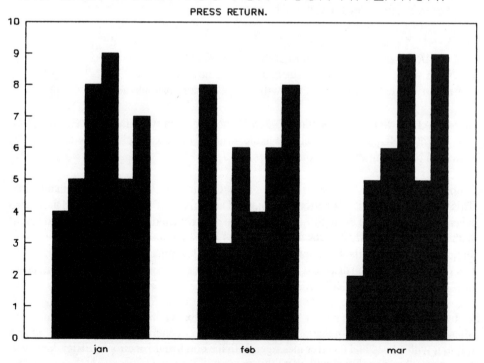

Figure 11.3 An Example of the Last Graph in Your Slide Show

Squeeze a Column to Eliminate Spaces

From time to time you may encounter a situation when blank cells have crept into a column of data. For example, you may have inserted several rows off to the right, not realizing that you were affecting a column to the left that should not include blank cells or rows.

The macro in Figure 11.4 uses a counter to provide a quick fix for this type of problem. Its purpose is to squeeze the filled cells in a column together into one contiguous range of viable data, but without affecting the columns to the right or left of the column being squeezed.

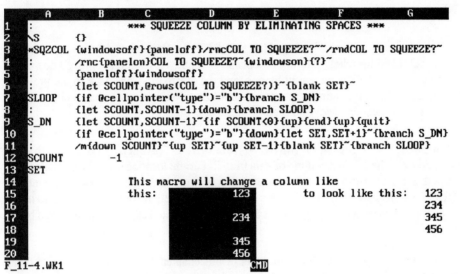

```
D20: [W15] 456                                                        POINT
        COL TO SQUEEZE?              Enter range: D15..D20

          A        B        C        D        E        F        G
1    :                      *** SQUEEZE COLUMN BY ELIMINATING SPACES ***
2    \S       {}
3    *SQZCOL  {windowsoff}{paneloff}/rncCOL TO SQUEEZE?~~/rndCOL TO SQUEEZE?~
4    :        /rnc{panelon}COL TO SQUEEZE?~{windowson}{?}~
5    :        {paneloff}{windowsoff}
6    :        {let SCOUNT,@rows(COL TO SQUEEZE?)}~{blank SET}~
7    SLOOP    {if @cellpointer("type")="b"}{branch S_DN}
8    :        {let SCOUNT,SCOUNT-1}{down}{branch SLOOP}
9    S_DN     {let SCOUNT,SCOUNT-1}~{if SCOUNT<0}{up}{end}{up}{quit}
10   :        {if @cellpointer("type")="b"}{down}{let SET,SET+1}~{branch S_DN}
11   :        /m{down SCOUNT}~{up SET}~{up SET-1}{blank SET}~{branch SLOOP}
12   SCOUNT           -1
13   SET
14                    This macro will change a column like
15                    this:            123       to look like this:   123
16                                                                     234
17                                      234                            345
18                                                                     456
19                                      345
20                                      456
F_11-4.WK1                                       CMD
```

Figure 11.4 A Macro to Squeeze a Column by Eliminating Spaces

{windowsoff}{paneloff}/rncCOL TO SQUEEZE?~~/rndCOL TO SQUEEZE?~   Turns off the windows and panel to suppress screen flicker, then creates and deletes the range name COL TO SQUEEZE? intended as a user prompt.

/rnc{panelon}COL TO SQUEEZE?~{windowson}{?}~   Again creates the range name COL TO SQUEEZE, turning the panel on just before this prompting range name appears. The windows are turned on just before the macro pause {?} to allow you to paint in the range you want to squeeze.

{let SCOUNT,@rows(COL TO SQUEEZE?)}~{blank SET}~   Changes the count in the counter SCOUNT to a value matching the number of rows in the range you have just highlighted. The counter at SET is set at zero by blanking the cell.

{if @cellpointer("type")="b"}{branch S_DN}   This is the beginning of the routine named SLOOP. This routine begins by determining if the cell pointer has come to a blank cell. If so, the macro branches to the routine at S_DN.

{let SCOUNT,SCOUNT-1}{down}{branch SLOOP}   Otherwise, the counter at S_SCOUNT is decremented by one, the cell pointer is moved down to the next cell, and the macro loops back to SLOOP to check whether or not the next cell is blank.

{let SCOUNT,SCOUNT-1}˜{if SCOUNT<0}{up}{end}{up}{quit}   If the next cell is blank, the macro branches to this line at S_DN where it decrements the counter by one and checks for whether the counter is now less than zero. If so, the macro must have run its course, the cell pointer is moved UpArrow End UpArrow to the top of the column of data, and the macro quits.

{if @cellpointer("type")="b"}{down}{let SET,SET+1}˜{branch S_DN}   Once again the cell is checked for whether or not it is blank. If so, the cell pointer is moved down one cell, the counter at SET is increased by one, and the macro branches back to the previous macro line at S_DN. It continues in this way until it no longer finds a blank cell, at which point the macro starts the /Move command on the next line.

/m{down SCOUNT}˜{up SET}˜{up SET-1}{blank SET}˜{branch SLOOP}   Moves the remainder of the original column of data from its current location up to the cell below the last filled cell. The macro knows how many rows down to highlight because the counter at SCOUNT was decremented each time it moved down one cell. It knows how far up to move the column of data because the counter at SET was incremented each time it came to a blank cell.

As you will see throughout the remainder of this chapter, 1-2-3 has an advanced {for} command that allows you to loop your macro a designated number of times. However, you will find that you still have occasions to create counters that you want to increment or decrement and test using {if} statements based on certain established criteria.

Changing Zeros to Blank Spaces

One little-used feature of 1-2-3 is the ability to suppress the display of zeros in your worksheet by selecting /Worksheet Global Zero Yes. This can be handy when your worksheet is filled with formulas that return scores of unsightly zeros if the cells on which they depend are empty.

Unfortunately, there are two drawbacks to this feature. First, when you save your file, the /File Save command does not retain the zero suppression, so when you retrieve the file later the zeros are all visible again. Second, the zero suppression is a global command while you may want to have zeros suppressed in just a range of your worksheet.

Fortunately, there is a simple macro solution to the first of these drawbacks. If you want the zeros permanently suppressed on a given worksheet, all you have to do is add an autoexecute (\0) macro to type /Worksheet Global Zero Yes as:

\0 **/wgzy{quit}**

With this macro, each time this file is retrieved you will see the file for an instant with the zeros visible. Then the autoexec macro will run and all of the zeros in your worksheet will be suppressed.

As for the occasional need to suppress zeros in just a range of your spreadsheet, the Omit Zeros, Replace with Blanks macro (in Figure 11.5) uses a {for} command to accomplish that task.

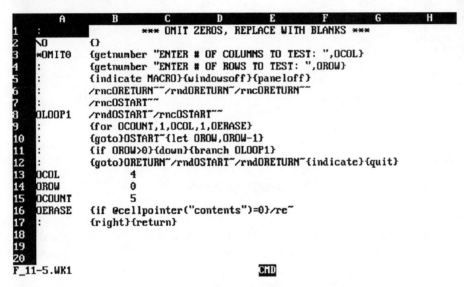

```
A1: ':                                                              READY
ENTER # OF COLUMNS TO TEST:

        A       B       C       D       E       F       G       H
1   :               *** OMIT ZEROS, REPLACE WITH BLANKS ***
2   \0          {}
3   *OMIT0      {getnumber "ENTER # OF COLUMNS TO TEST: ",OCOL}
4   :           {getnumber "ENTER # OF ROWS TO TEST: ",OROW}
5   :           {indicate MACRO}{windowsoff}{paneloff}
6   :           /rncORETURN~~/rndORETURN~/rncORETURN~~
7   :           /rncOSTART~~
8   OLOOP1      /rndOSTART~/rncOSTART~~
9   :           {for OCOUNT,1,OCOL,1,OERASE}
10  :           {goto}OSTART~{let OROW,OROW-1}
11  :           {if OROW>0}{down}{branch OLOOP1}
12  :           {goto}ORETURN~/rndOSTART~/rndORETURN~{indicate}{quit}
13  OCOL            4
14  OROW            0
15  OCOUNT          5
16  OERASE      {if @cellpointer("contents")=0}/re~
17  :           {right}{return}
18
19
20
F_11-5.WK1                              CMD
```

Figure 11.5 A Macro to Omit Zeros, Replace with Blank Spaces

This macro uses a counter as in the macros just described, but it applies its magic to an entire matrix of cells rather than just to a column. To do that, it uses an example of a loop-within-a-loop.

{getnumber "ENTER # OF COLUMNS TO TEST: ",OCOL} Prompts you for the number of columns to the right you want to test for zeros. Your response is stored in the cell named OCOL.

{getnumber "ENTER # OF ROWS TO TEST: ",OROW} Prompts you for the number of rows down you want to test for zeros. Your response is stored in the cell named OROW.

Figure 11.6 is an example of a matrix of values with zero cells, showing the macro prompt for the number of rows to test.

```
B24: 123                                                            READY
ENTER # OF COLUMNS TO TEST: 4
```

	A	B	C	D	E	F	G	H
21								
22	Inventory	Jan	Feb	Mar	Total			
23	=========	---------	---------	---------	========			
24	Widget	123	123	0	246			
25	Gripple	0	0	456	456			
26	Foobar	0	345	345	690			
27	Inklet	0	0	0	0			
28	Shamper	345	0	0	345			
29	Tupan	345	0	345	690			
30	Parket	0	123	0	123			
31	Piffle	456	0	0	456			
32	Smiter	0	0	345	345			
33	Prefax	0	123	0	123			
34	Incomp	234	123	0	357			
35	Churple	123	0	456	579			
36								
37								
38								
39								
40								

```
F_11-6.WK1                                    CMD
```

Figure 11.6 An Example Using the Omit Zeros Macro

{indicate MACRO}{windowsoff}{paneloff}   The purpose of the {indicate} command is to change the indicator in the upper right panel from the word *READY* to a message to the macro user.

In Release 2 and 2.01, you can use any five-letter word with the {indicate} command. In this case, because the windows and panels are being turned off during execution of most of the macro, the indicator changes from *READY* to the word *MACRO* to remind you that a macro is running. You can, of course, change the word to something else like *ZEROS* or *BLANK*, but keep in mind that only the first five letters of the word you choose will appear in the indicator panel.

In Release 2.2 and 3, you can use any message in the {indicate} command up to 256 letters, but you will want to limit your message to one that will fit in the upper panel: typically, 72 characters.

/rncORETURN~~/rndORETURN~/rncORETURN~~   Creates a place-marker at the original cell of the matrix called ORETURN.

/rncOSTART~~   Begins the create-delete-create sequence for the range name OSTART.

/rndOSTART~/rncOSTART~~   Creates a place-marker called OSTART that will move down row-by-row in this column as each row is processed. Notice that this line of the macro is in a cell called OLOOP1, marking the beginning of the counting loop using {let}, {if}, and a counter. Within this loop (in the next line of the macro) is another counter loop using the {for} command.

{for OCOUNT,1,OCOL,1,OERASE}   The {for} command is a shorthand way of creating a way to loop in a macro a designated number of times. Instead of using the {let} and {if} commands at the beginning and end of the counted loop you want to run, you can use a {for} command that goes ahead of the loop and tells it how many times to increment.

The format of the {for} command is {*for* followed by the *counter location*, the *start* value, the *stop* value or *cell location containing the stop* value, the *step* value, and the *loop name*}.

This means that you can have a {for} command like: {*for WCOUNT,1,100,1,WLOOP*} if you know you want it to loop 100 times; or like: {*for WCOUNT,1,WSTOP,1,WLOOP*} if you have included the stop value in the cell named WSTOP.

The {for} line of this macro, then, might be read like this: *at the cell named OCOUNT, start counting at the number 1, and count until the number in OCOL is reached, counting by ones, and for each increment loop to the subroutine called OERASE*. As you'll see if you look at the last lines in the Figure 11.5 macro, the OERASE subroutine reads

{if @cellpointer("contents")=0}/re~

which erases every cell displaying a zero. Actually, in Release 2.2 and 3, you can use the commands

{if @cellpointer("contents")=0}{blank @cellpointer("contents")}

which will operate faster, since no tilde effecting a recalculation is required.

The next cell down reads {right}{return}, moving the cell pointer one cell to the right and returning control of the macro to the line immediately following the {for} command.

{goto}OSTART~{let OROW,OROW-1}   The cell pointer moves back to the beginning of the row. You will remember we created a place-marker in the first cell of the row called OSTART. The next command decrements the counter at OROW (where the macro has stored the number of rows you want tested) to record the fact that the first row of the matrix has been processed.

{if OROW>0}{down}{branch OLOOP1}   If the row counter is still greater than zero, the cell pointer is moved down to the next row and the whole process starts again on this row via a macro loop back to OLOOP1.

{goto}ORETURN~/rndOSTART~/rndORETURN~{indicate}{quit}   Otherwise, the cell pointer is returned to the original upper left cell of the matrix which the macro named ORETURN, the two place-marker range names are deleted, the {indicate} command changes the word *MACRO* in the upper right indicator to *READY*, and the macro quits. Note that whereas the {windowsoff} and {paneloff} commands do not require corresponding {windowson} and {panelon} commands before a {quit}, the {indicate MACRO} command

in the third line does require a corresponding {indicate} command to restore the indicator to
READY .

Strictly speaking the next three cells, OCOL, OROW, and OCOUNT, are not a part of the
main macro, but rather cells which are accessed by the macro. OCOL stores the number of
columns that you want processed, and OCOUNT is the cell where the column counting occurs with each loop. When the value in OCOUNT equals the value in OCOL, the column
looping stops. The row looping is counted in the cell named OROW, which simply counts
backwards to zero before it stops.

Test-&-Replace Macro

This technique of using loops and counters to test an entire matrix for zeros can also be used
to test for any specified value, to be replaced with another specified value. You may be
aware that a search-and-replace feature is included in Release 2.2 and 3 to apply to strings,
but this feature is not available in any current release to apply to values. Refer to the Test &
Replace Values across Many Columns macro in Figure 11.7.

This macro is similar to the Omit Zeros macro in Figure 11.5, with its {for} loop within
a {let}/{if} loop; but this macro uses a {for} loop within another {for} loop.

{getnumber "ENTER # OF COLUMNS TO TEST: ",TCOL}   Prompts you for the
number of columns to the right you want to test for zeros. Your response is stored in the cell
named TCOL.

```
A1: ' :                                                              READY
ENTER # OF COLUMNS TO TEST:
```

```
        A          B         C         D         E         F         G         H
1   :                         ***TEST & REPLACE VALUES ACROSS MANY COLS ***
2   \T         {getnumber "ENTER # OF COLUMNS TO TEST: ",TCOL}
3   :          {getnumber "ENTER # OF ROWS TO TEST: ",TROW}
4   :          {getnumber "ENTER VALUE TO TEST FOR: ",TEST1}
5   :          {getnumber "ENTER REPLACEMENT VALUE: ",T_REPL}
6   :          {indicate MACRO}{let TRETURN,@cellpointer("address")}
7   :          {windowsoff}{paneloff}{for TCOUNTER,1,TROW,1,TLOOP1}
8   :          {goto}{TRETURN}~{indicate}{quit}
9   TCOUNTER        15
10  TROW            14
11  TLOOP1     {let TSTART,@cellpointer("address")}
12  :          {for TCOUNT,1,TCOL,1,TCHANGE}{goto}{TSTART}~{down}{return}
13  TCOUNT          6
14  TCOL            5
15  TCHANGE    {if TEST1=@cellpointer("contents")}/cT_REPL~~
16  :          {right}{return}
17  TRETURN    $B$22
18  TEST1          999
19  TSTART     $B$35
20  T_REPL         888
F_11-7.WK1                               CMD
```

Figure 11.7 Macro to Test-&-Replace Values across Columns

{getnumber "ENTER # OF ROWS TO TEST: ",TROW}   Prompts you for the number of rows down you want to test for zeros. Your response is stored in the cell named TROW.

{getnumber "ENTER VALUE TO TEST AGAINST: ",TEST 1}   Prompts you for the value you want the macro to replace with another value. Your response is stored in the cell named TEST. A sample matrix of data with the value 999 sprinkled throughout is shown in Figure 11.8. In this example, the macro is prompting the user to *Enter value to test against.*

{getnumber "ENTER REPLACEMENT VALUE: ",T_REPL}   Prompts you for the

```
B22: 0                                                              READY
ENTER # OF COLUMNS TO TEST: 5
```

	A	B	C	D	E	F	G	H
21								
22		0	15	30	999	999		
23		1	16	999	46	61		
24		999	999	32	999	62		
25		3	18	33	48	999		
26		4	999	999	999	64		
27		999	20	35	50	65		
28		6	21	36	999	999		
29		7	999	999	52	67		
30		999	23	38	999	68		
31		999	24	39	54	999		
32		10	999	999	999	70		
33		11	26	41	56	71		
34		999	999	42	999	999		
35		13	28	999	58	73		
36		14	29	44	59	74		
37								
38								
39								
40								

```
F_11-8.WK1                                    CMD
```

Figure 11.8   An Example Using the Test-&-Replace Macro

replacement value you want inserted in place of the test value. Your response is stored in the cell named T_REPL.

{indicate MACRO}{let TRETURN,@cellpointer("address")}   This line changes the indicator in the upper right panel from the word *READY* to the word *MACRO* to remind you that a macro is running. You can, of course, change the word to something else like TEST or REPLC (or, if you have Release 2.2 or 3, to a long message like: *Please wait... Macro is running...,* but keep in mind that there must also be an {indicate} command without an argument to return the indicator to *READY* at the end of the macro. The {let} command creates a place-marker for the original cell of the matrix by inserting the current address in the cell named TRETURN.

{windowsoff}{paneloff}{for TCOUNTER,1,TROW,1,TLOOP1}   Turns off the windows and panels to speed up the macro. The {for} loop can be read: *At the cell named TCOUNTER, start counting at the number 1, and count until the number in TROW is reached, counting by ones, and for each increment loop to the subroutine called TLOOP1.*

{goto}{TRETURN}~{indicate}{quit}   Completion of the required number of passes through the first loop, which also contains the second loop, completes the bulk of the macro. Although it may not appear so, this line is actually the last line of the macro. To finish up the macro, the cell pointer is returned to the original upper left cell of the matrix which the macro place-marked using the cell named TRETURN. Then the {indicate} command changes the word *MACRO* in the upper right indicator to *READY*, and the macro quits.

{let TSTART,@cellpointer("address")}   This is the first cell of the subroutine called TLOOP1. It creates a place-marker stored in TSTART which will increment its row number by 1 as each row is processed.

{for TCOUNT,1,TCOL,1,TCHANGE}{goto}{TSTART}~{down}{return}   The second {for} loop starts at this line, which can be read: *At the cell named TCOUNT, start counting at the number 1, and count until the number in TCOL is reached, counting by ones, and for each increment loop to the subroutine called TCHANGE.* As you'll see if you look at the cell named TCHANGE, this subroutine reads:

{if TEST1=@cellpointer("contents")}/cT_REPL~~

which replaces every cell displaying the same value as TEST with the value in T_REPL. Incidentally, although it will not work in Release 2 or 2.01, if you have Release 2.2 or 3 you can replace the /Copy command in this line with the {let} command:

{let @cellpointer("address"),T_REPL}

The next cell down reads {right}{return}, which moves the cell pointer one cell to the right and returns control of the macro to the line beneath the {for} command.

    The cell pointer moves back to the beginning of the row (you will remember we created a place-marker in the first cell of the row by storing the cell address at TSTART), then down one cell to the next row. The {return} command ends the subroutine called TLOOP1, that returns control of the macro to the macro's final line just above TCOUNTER.

Note: Placement of the subroutines at TLOOP1, TRETURN, TSTART, and TCHANGE is fairly arbitrary. These subroutines could have been shown in any order or in any location on your worksheet. However, you may want to keep your subroutines close to the main macros to which they apply as shown here.

    One additional technique has been used here that you may want to adopt. Neither of the subroutines at TRETURN or TSTART is followed by a cell with the {return} command; yet after running these subroutines, the program flow returns to the place where it left off in the main body of the macro. This is because a blank cell or a value cell is also interpreted by 1-2-3 as the end of the routine. We do not recommend using a blank cell for this purpose, since it can be so easily filled later without your realizing the importance of keeping the cell empty. However, using a value cell is a viable way to end a subroutine, thus saving an extra cell, shortening the length of your macro, and eliminating and the need to type in a {return} command.

Adding Another Choice to /Range Search

In addition to using the {for} command with counters to search for and replace values, you can create a macro that will enhance the existing /Range Search capability of Release 2.2 and 3 by adding a new feature called Previous to the current choice for the Next found item.

Currently, selecting /Range Search results in 1-2-3 prompting you for the range, the string to search for, whether you want to search Formulas, Labels, or Both, and for whether you want to Find or Replace the searched item. After the first item is found, you are offered the prompts *Next* or *Quit*. There is no choice, unfortunately, called Previous. This means you can search for the fifth occurrence of a string, go past it to the sixth occurrence by mistake, and 1-2-3 offers no way to back up to the previous record.

Instead, use the Find Next or Previous/Range Search Item macro shown in Figure 11.9.

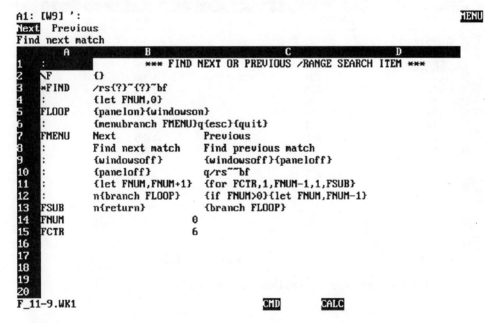

Figure 11.9 Macro to Find the Next or Previous /Range Search Item

---

Note: This macro will not work with Release 2 or 2.01. It is designed only for Release 2.2 and higher.

Here's how the macro works.

/rs{?}~{?}~bf   The macro begins by selecting /Range Search, which causes 1-2-3 to prompt you for the range and string to search. The macro then selects the *Both* choice from the menu of *Formulas*, *Labels*, or *Both*, and the *Find* choice from the choices *Find* or *Replace*.

{panelon}{windowson}   This line has no effect the first time through, but you will notice this cell of the macro is named FLOOP. When the macro loops back to this point, this line will reverse the effect of the {windowsoff} and {paneloff} commands that occur later in the macro.

{menubranch FMENU}q{esc}{quit}   Calls up the menu choices *Next* and *Previous*. An example of this phase of the macro at work on a typical database is shown in Figure 11.10. If you press Escape at this point, the macro will process the remainder of the line, selecting *Quit*, pressing Escape, and quitting the macro to return to *READY*.

```
A25: [W9] ' Gripple                                              MENU
Next  Previous
Find next match
          A              B                    C              D
21  Inventory       Quantity                 Price
22  =========       ---------                ---------
23  Churple             123                    1.00
24  Foobar              643                    1.50
25  Gripple             324                    1.75
26  Incomp              234                    1.88
27  Inklet              123                    1.94
28  Parket              342                    1.97
29  Piffle              456                    2.17
30  Prefax              564                    1.34
31  Shamper             345                    1.25
32  Smiter              354                    2.00
33  Tupan               345                    2.17
34  Widget              123                    1.23
35
36
37
38
39
40
F_11_10.WK1                            CMD        CALC
```

Figure 11.10 An Example of the Find Next or Previous Macro

{windowsoff}{paneloff}{let FNUM,FNUM+1}   If you select *Next*, the macro turns off the windows and panel and increments the counter at FNUM, storing the number of times you have selected *Next*. This information is required so the macro will be able to return to the record found just before the current record.

n{branch FLOOP}   The macro presses **N** for *Next*, which causes the cell pointer to jump to the line with the next found record. The macro then branches back to FLOOP to turn off the windows and panel and call up the menu choices *Next* and *Previous* again.

{windowsoff}{paneloff}q/rs~~bf If you select *Previous*, the windows and panel are turned off and the macro presses **Q** for *Quit* to leave the /Range Search menu. It then selects /Range Search and presses Return twice to accept the already established range and string to search for, as well as repeating the previous menu selections *Both* and *Find*. In other words, the macro starts the /Range Search sequence all over again using the same criteria.

{for FCTR,1,FNUM-1,1,FSUB} This {for} command can be read: *At the cell named FCTR, start counting at the number 1, and count until the number one less than the number in FNUM is reached, counting by ones, and for each increment loop to the subroutine called FSUB.* Since FSUB consists only of a press of **N** for *Next*, the effect is to select the next record one less time than the total number of times *Next* was selected before the *Previous* choice was made. So if you selected *Next* up to the sixth record, then selected *Previous*, this {for} command would start at the beginning and select Next five times, leaving you at the previous record viewed.

{if FNUM>0}{let FNUM,FNUM-1} Provided FNUM is greater than 0 (which will always be the case unless you select *Previous* before selecting *Next* even once), the value in FNUM is reduced by 1. This is necessary to reflect in FNUM the number of records found to reach the current record.

{branch FLOOP} Finally, the macro branches back to FLOOP to turn off the windows and panel and call up the menu choices *Next* and *Previous* again.

That's all there is to it. By keeping track of how many times **N** for *Next* must be pressed to get to the current record, this macro is able to use a {for} loop to run through the same process that number of times, less one, to reach the previous record.

Changing Label-Numbers to Values

In Chapter 9 we explored a macro that changes numbers entered as labels into straight values. The macro did this by switching to Edit mode, moving to the beginning of the entry, deleting the apostrophe preceding of the number-label, and pressing Return. Unfortunately, this method will not work on number-labels which include commas inserted to delineate the thousandths place or millionths place. If, for example, you have a number entered as **'1,234,567.00**, simply deleting the beginning apostrophe will only result in an error and a beep.

Fortunately, you can create a macro that will take into account number-labels that include commas. The macro in Figure 11.11 uses a prompting range name, self-modifying techniques, string @functions, recalculation of lines of the macro, and a {for} loop to accomplish this task.

To operate this macro, move to the first entry in a column of number-labels and press Alt-N. At the prompt, highlight the column of numbers you want to convert and press Return. There will be a short pause, then the number-labels will disappear and reappear as straight values.

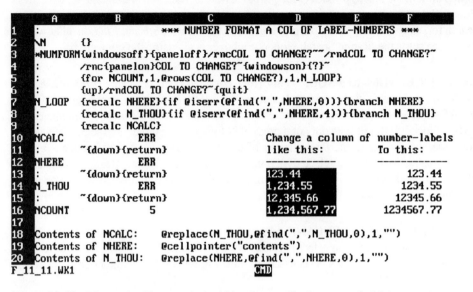

Figure 11.11   Macro to Change Label-Numbers with Commas to Values

Here's how the macro works.

{windowsoff}{paneloff}/rncCOL TO CHANGE?~~/rndCOL TO CHANGE?~   Turns off the windows and panel to suppress screen flicker, then creates and deletes the range name COL TO CHANGE? intended as a user prompt.

/rnc{panelon}COL TO CHANGE?~{windowson}{?}~   Again creates the range name COL TO CHANGE?, turning the panel on just before this prompting range name appears. The windows are turned on just before the macro pause {?} to allow you to paint in the range you want to change.

{for NCOUNT,1,@rows(COL TO CHANGE?),1,N_LOOP}   This {for} command can be read: *At the cell named NCOUNT, start counting at the number 1, and count until the number equal to the number of rows in COL TO CHANGE? is reached, counting by ones, and for each increment loop to the subroutine called N_LOOP.* Its purpose is to convert a number-label, move down one cell, convert the next number-label, and so on, until the cell pointer reaches the end of the column to change.

{up}/rndCOL TO CHANGE?~{quit}   At the end of the process, the cell pointer is moved up one cell, the range name COL TO CHANGE? is deleted, and the macro quits.

{recalc NHERE}{if @iserr(@find(",",NHERE,0))}{branch NHERE}   This line is the beginning of the loop named N_LOOP, referred to in the {for} command we just discussed.

Its purpose is to recalculate the cell named NHERE, which (though it appears as ERR in Figure 11.11) actually consists of the formula:

@cellpointer("contents")

The {if} statement works by determining that if the macro returns an error condition when trying to find a comma in the cell pointer contents stored at NHERE, it means that the number-label has been entered without a comma (the number 123 would be such a case) and the macro can simply branch to NHERE and enter the stored number-label as a value, move down one cell, and return to N_LOOP.

{recalc N_THOU}{if @iserr(@find(",",NHERE,4))}{branch N_THOU} Otherwise, if the macro, upon finding one comma, returns an error condition when trying to find a second comma starting at the fourth position of the cell pointer contents stored at NHERE, it means that the number-label has been entered only one comma (the number 1,234 would be such a case). The macro branches to N_THOU and enters the value returned there, moves down one cell, and returns to N_LOOP.

Although N_THOU shows ERR in Figure 11.11, it will return the proper results when the cell pointer is on a cell with a number- label showing one comma. The formula underlying this cell is:

@replace(NHERE(@find(",",NHERE,0),1,"")

This formula works by replacing with a null string ("") the first comma it finds in the number-label stored in NHERE, thereby eliminating the comma and showing only numbers.

{recalc NCALC} If the program flow arrives at this line of the macro, proceeding through the two {if} commands in the sixth and seventh lines, that means the macro was not diverted by the check for a number-label with no commas or only one comma. This line prepares for an extract of numbers from a number-label with two commas. It does this by recalculating the formula at NCALC.

Although the formula at NCALC shows ERR in Figure 11.11, it will return the proper results when the cell pointer is on a cell with a number-label showing two commas. The formula uses the same principle as the formula at N_THOU, except that it extracts its results from the results of N_THOU as:

@replace(N_THOU,@find(",",N_THOU,0),1,"")

Thus, if N_THOU displays a result such as 123456,789 from a number-label like 123,456,789, then the formula in NCALC will display a result like 123456789, without commas, by eliminating the one comma in N_THOU.

Although it seems that this macro goes through a long and complicated process to accomplish its task, you will find that it converts a column of number-labels to straight values in a surprisingly short time.

Dates Displayed One Month Apart

Counters and loops are not always required to create a repeating but variable result. Figure 11.12 provides an interesting example of a macro that prompts you for a number, then uses that information to determine how many copies to make of a complicated formula.

```
A1: [W8] ':                                                              READY

          A          B             C               D
1    :                    *** VERTICALLY DISPLAY DATES 1 MO. APART ***
2    \U         {}
3    *VERTYEA{getnumber "Enter the number of months to display: ",VMONTHS}
4    :         {getlabel "Enter the date of the 1st month: @date(",V_ENTER}~
5    :         @date(
6    V_ENTER  88,12,31
7    :         )~/rfd4{down VMONTHS}~
8    :         {let VY,@day(@cellpointer("contents"))}{down}
9    :         @if(@day({up})>3,{up}+28-@day({up}+28),{up}+31-@day({up}+31))
10   :         +@if(@month({up})=1,@min(@if(@mod(@year({up}),4)=0,29,28),
11   :         $VY),@if(@month({up})=3#or#@month({up})=5#or#
12   :         @month({up})=8#or#@month({up})=10,@min(30,$VY),$VY))~
13   :         /c~.{down VMONTHS-2}~/rv{end}{down}~~{quit}
14   VMONTHS              3
15   VY                  31
16
17
18
19
20
F_11_12.WK1
```

Figure 11.12   Vertically Display Dates One Month Apart

The purpose of this macro is to create a series of dates exactly one month apart. This has been added as a new feature of the /Data Fill command in Release 3, but a macro is required to accomplish the same task as quickly in Release 2, 2.01, and 2.2.

Here's how the macro works.

{getnumber "Enter the number of months to display: ",VMONTHS}   Prompts you to enter the number of dates you want shown vertically in a column, each date being exactly one month greater than the previous date. In using this macro, be sure that you are not about to write over important data below the current cell.

{getlabel "Enter the date of the 1st month: @date(",V_ENTER}~   This prompt is slightly different from previous uses of the {getlabel} command. Prompts usually end with a colon. In this case, however, the prompt ends with **@date(** to indicate that the entry required should be in the @date format; and since **@date(** has already been typed, all that is needed is the year, month, and day. The macro itself will provide the closing parenthesis.

@date(Actually, the beginning of the @date formula has not been typed yet, so the macro does that now. The next line is a self-modifying cell named V_ENTER and filled in by your response to the {getlabel} prompt.

)~/rfd4{down VMONTHS}~   Enters the closing parenthesis and formats the cell for Date Format 4 in the range that includes the current cell plus the number of cells you provided in your response to the opening {getnumber} prompt.

{let VY,@day(@cellpointer("contents"))}{down}   Stores in VY the day of the month you just entered and moves down one cell.

@if(@day({up})>3,{up}+28-@day({up}+28),{up}+31-@day({up}+31))   This is the beginning of a long formula being typed into the cell below the first date you entered. Its purpose is to determine whether the day of the month entered is greater than 3, and if so, it adds 28 to the original date, then subtracts the day of the month for a date 28 days past the original date, thus calculating the end of the month of the original date. Here's an example using 10 April:

> Date = 4/10/87
> Date + 28 = 5/7/87
> Date + 28 - @day(Date+28) = 5/7/87 - 7 = 4/31/87

If the day of the month entered is not greater than 3, the macro adds 31 to the original date and subtracts the day of the month for a date 31 days past the original date, which also calculates the end of the month of the original date. Here's an example using 2 February:

> Date = 2/2/87
> Date + 31 = 3/5/87
> Date + 31 - @day(Date+31) = 3/5/87 - 5 = 2/28/87

To this calculated end-of-month date is added a value that depends on the particular month of the original date.

+@if(@month({up})=1,@min(@if(@mod(@year({up}),4)=0,29,28),$VY),   If the month of the original date is January, the macro adds to the last day of the original month the value 29 or 28 (depending on whether it is a leap year), or the day of the original month, whichever is less. Thus, using an original date of 2 January 1987, you would get:

> Date = 1/2/87
> Date + 31 = 2/2/87
> Date + 31 - @day(Date+31) = 2/2/87 - 2 = 1/31/87
> Date + 31 - @day(Date+31) + @day(Date) = 1/31/87 + 2 = 2/2/87

The remainder of the formula being typed by the macro works in the same way, with slight variations depending on whether the original date is the third, fifth, eight, or tenth month, or one of the remaining months.

   Regardless of the month of the original date, the macro computes the *end* of the month of the original date, then adds the *day* of the month of the original date, giving you a date exactly one month later than the original date.

/c~.{down VMONTHS-2}~/rv{end}{down}~~{quit}   The last line of the macro copies the formula down the number of cells you responded with at the first {getnumber} command, less two, then changes these formulas to just their values using /Range Value End DownArrow. The result is a column of dates, each date exactly one month later than the date above it and the total number of dates equal to your response at the opening prompt.

Inserting a Prefix in a Column of Entries

Here we explore two features of 1-2-3 that can used in conjunction with the {for} command to affect a column of data: the {put} command and the @index function.

The macro in Figure 11.13 is an excellent example of a macro designed to move quickly down a column of labels making changes with the {put} command. Its purpose is to add a specific prefix to each entry in a column of labels.

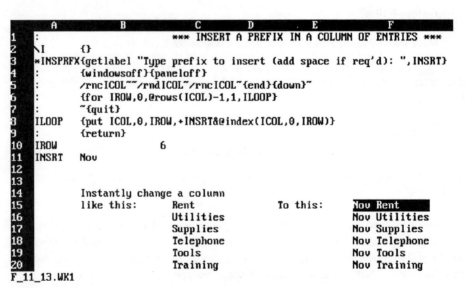

Figure 11.13   A Macro to Insert a Prefix in a Column of Entries

{getlabel "Type prefix to insert (add space if req'd): ",INSRT}   The macro begins by prompting you to type the prefix you want to add to each entry in a column. If, for example, you wanted to add the word NOV, you would type NOV and a space, then press Return. Your response will be stored in the cell named INSRT.

{windowsoff}{paneloff}   Turns the windows and panel off to suppress screen flicker.

/rncICOL˜˜/rndICOL˜/rncICOL˜{end}{down}˜   Creates the range name ICOL. The range is everything from the current cell down through the column to the last cell before a blank space.

{for IROW,0,@rows(ICOL)-1,1,ILOOP}   This {for} loop can be read: *At the cell named IROW, start counting at zero, and count up to the number equal to one less than the number of rows in ICOL, counting by ones, and for each increment loop to the subroutine called ILOOP.*

˜{quit}   When the macro has added a prefix to every label in the column, the tilde updates the results and the macro quits.

{put ICOL,0,IROW,+INSRT&@index(ICOL,0,IROW)}   This {put} command at ILOOP provides the operation required in the {for} command above. The {put} command has the syntax:

{put *range,column-offset,row-offset,entry*}

and its purpose is to enter a number or label in a cell within a range based on a designated column and row position in that range. In this case, the range is the single column IROW. The offset is the zero column—which would usually be the left-most column, but here it also represents the only column. The row offset is a variable. As the macro makes each pass through the {for} command, it increments the counter at IROW. That same counter is then used by the {put} command to move down to the next row in turn and "put" its entry there. For an entry, the {put} command uses:

+INSRT&@index(ICOL,0,IROW)

or in other words, the prefix you have entered in response to the {getlabel} command at the beginning, plus the contents of each entry of the column in turn. Rather than move the cell pointer to each entry and use @cellpointer("contents"), the {put} command is able to determine the contents with the @index function, which has the syntax:

@index(*range,column-offset,row-offset*)

In this case, the range is the single column ICOL; the column offset for that single column is, of course, zero; and the row-offset is the variable counter being incremented by the {for} command at IROW.

This unique combination of the {put} command and the @index function, both of which have the same *range,column-offset,row-offset* locators, provides an almost instantaneous technique for altering the entries in a range.

Deleting a Prefix from a Column of Entries

The {put} and @index combination can be used to delete a prefix from a column of labels almost as easily as it inserts one. It does this by calling on the additional features of the @replace function as shown in Figure 11.14.

To operate the macro, place your cell pointer on the first cell in a column of labels with a

F15: 'Rent

```
        A        B          C          D         E          F          G
 1   :                      *** DELETE A PREFIX FROM A COLUMN OF ENTRIES ***
 2   \D       {}
 3   *DELPRFX{getnumber "No. of chars to delete (including space): ",DNO}
 4   :        {windowsoff}{paneloff}
 5   :        /rncDCOL~~/rndDCOL~/rncDCOL~{end}{down}~
 6   :        {for D_ROW,0,@rows(DCOL)-1,1,DO}
 7   :        ~{quit}
 8   DO       {put DCOL,0,D_ROW,@replace(@index(DCOL,0,D_ROW),0,DNO,"")}
 9   :        {return}
10   D_ROW              6
11   DNO                4
12
13
14            Instantly change a column
15            like this:    Nov Rent       To this:   Rent
16                          Nov Utilities              Utilities
17                          Nov Supplies               Supplies
18                          Nov Telephone              Telephone
19                          Nov Tools                  Tools
20                          Nov Training               Training
```
F_11_14.WK1

Figure 11.14 A Macro to Delete a Prefix from a Column of Entries

common prefix (or prefixes with a common number of letters) you want to delete and press Alt-D.

{getnumber "No. of chars to delete (including space): ",DNO}   The macro begins by prompting you for the number of characters you want to delete, including any spaces, and places your response in the cell named DNO.

The next four lines of the macro follow exactly the same principles as the \I Insert a Prefix macro just described. Only the range names are different.

{put DCOL,0,D_ROW,@replace(@index(DCOL,0,D_ROW),0,DNO,"")}   This {put} command is similar to the {put} command in the \I Insert a Prefix macro, except that instead of adding a prefix to the entry at @index(ICOL,0,IROW) as:

$$+INSRT\&\&@index(ICOL,0,IROW)$$

the *entry* used by the {put} command in this case removes a prefix with the @replace function as:

$$@replace(@index(DCOL,0,D\_ROW),0,DNO,"")$$

The replacement starts at the zero offset, continues to the offset stored at DNO, and consists of a null string, which has the effect of entirely eliminating the prefix.

You can use these combinations of {for}, {put}, @index, and @replace to great effect in all types of macros where you want to make changes to entire ranges of data. These techniques are usually not appropriate, however, in ranges consisting of formulas, unless you are willing to see the formulas converted to straight values at the completion of the macro.

Summary

In this chapter we reviewed ways to make your macro loop a designated number of times in one of two ways: by using {if} with the {let} command, or by using the more advanced {for} command with a counter. The format of the {for} command is **{for** followed by the *counter location*, the *start* value, the *stop* value or *cell location containing the stop* value, the *step* value, and the *loop name*.

We also explored:

- Use of the {onerror} command to trap an error and branch the macro in response to an error condition or a press of Ctrl-Break. This command takes as its argument the cell where the macro should continue. Like the {windowsoff} and {paneloff} commands, it stays in effect until the macro ends or until you disable it. Disabling of an {onerror} command is done with a subsequent {onerror} that includes no argument.

- Suppression of the display of zeros in your worksheet by selecting /Worksheet Global Zero Yes. This can be handy when your worksheet is filled with formulas which return scores of unsightly zeros if the cells on which they depend are empty. Unfortunately, when you save your file, the /File Save command in all but Release 3 does not retain zero suppression, so when you retrieve the file later the zeros are all visible again. The short autoexecuting macro **/wgzy{quit}** is one solution to this problem.

- Use of the {indicate} command to change the Indicator in the upper right panel from *READY* to a prompting message. In Release 2 and 2.01, you can use any five-letter word. In Release 2.2 and 3, you can use any message up to 256 letters, but you will want to limit your message to one that will fit in the upper panel: typically, 72 characters.

- Use of a value cell to establish the end of a subroutine, thus saving an extra cell, shortening the length of your macro, and eliminating the need to type in a {return} command.

- Use of a {getnumber} prompt to store information on how many copies to make of a complicated formula. This technique demonstrates how counters and loops are not always required to create a repeating but variable result.

- Use of a prompt that ends with **@date(** to indicate that the entry required should be in the @date format. The idea here is that since **@date(** has already been typed by the macro, all that is needed from the user is the year, the month, and the day.

- Use of the {put} command to enter a number or label in a cell within a range based on a designated column and row position in that range, using the syntax:

{put *range,column-offset,row-offset,entry*}

- Use of the @index function to return the contents of a specific column and row location in a range, using the syntax:

@index(*range,column-offset,row-offset*)

The macros covered in this chapter are:

- A macro to change the width of any number of columns you designate automatically. Even if you have Release 2.2 or 3, you will find this an interesting use of the {if} and {let} commands to cause the macro to loop a number of times based on an internal counter.

- A macro designed to allow a type of slide show of your graphs. This is especially useful during presentations where instead of having to select /Graph Name Use and point to graphs displayed in alphabetical order, you can simply select *FORWARD* or *BACKWARDS* to move instantly forward or backwards through your graphs.

- A macro to squeeze the filled cells in a column together into one contiguous range of viable data, but without affecting the columns to the right or left of the column being squeezed.

- A macro to change zeros in your worksheet to blank spaces. This macro uses a {for} loop within a {let}/{if} loop to change an entire matrix of cells rather than just one column.

- A Test-and-Replace macro to test a matrix of numbers for a particular value, and insert another value in its place. A search-and-replace feature is included in Release 2.2 and 3 to apply to strings, but this feature is not available in any current release to apply to values. This is also an example of the use of a {for} loop within another {for} loop.

- A macro to enhance the existing /Range Search capability of Release 2.2 and 3 by adding a new feature called *Previous* to the current choice for the *Next* found item. By keeping track of how many times N for *Next* must be pressed to get to the current record, this macro is able to use a {for} loop to run through the same process that number of times, less one, to reach the previous record.

- A macro to change number-labels to values, taking into account number-labels that include commas. This macro uses a prompting range name, self-modifying techniques, string @ functions, recalculation of lines of the macro, and a {for} loop to accomplish its task.

- A macro to vertically display a series of dates exactly one month apart. This has been added as a new feature of the /Data Fill command in Release 3, but a macro is required to accomplish the same task as quickly in Release 2, 2.01, and 2.2.

- A macro designed to add a specific prefix to each entry in a column of labels. This macro uses two features of 1-2-3 in conjunction with the {for} command: the {put} command and the @index function, both of which have the same *range,column-offset,row-offset* locators. Together these features provide a technique for altering the entries in a range almost instantaneously.

- A macro designed to delete a common prefix (or prefixes with a common number of letters) from a column of entries. This macro calls on the @replace function to eliminate a specific number of characters.

In Chapter 12 we will look at the syntax, purpose, and specific uses of the {get} command, especially in conjunction with the {indicate} command and string @ functions.

12

USING THE {GET} COMMAND

Scope

In this chapter we will define and explore uses of the {get} command in combination with macro techniques and commands already covered. You will see how {get} can be used to create a *Yes/No* prompt, to quit a macro upon your press of the Escape key, to create a special "action key" for yourself, to differentiate between a press of letter/number keys and directional or function keys, and to have your macro evaluate and act on your response to special {indicate} prompts.

Search & Replace in a Single Column

As mentioned in Chapter 11, the /Range Search feature of Release 2.2 and 3 is designed to work only on strings. In addressing the limitations of /Range Search, we looked at a macro that uses counters and the {for} command to test-and-replace values across several columns.

The macro in Figure 12.1 is similar in that it accomplishes a test-and-replace function, though only on a single column. It adds an additional feature not included in the Test-and-Replace macro, however, prompting for whether you want to test for labels or values, then

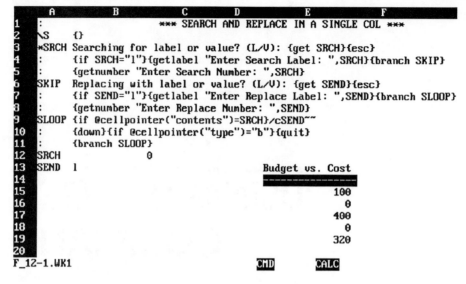

E14: [W16] \-   READY
Enter Search Label: Break-even

```
       A         B         C        D        E            F
1    :                     *** SEARCH AND REPLACE IN A SINGLE COL ***
2    \S    {}
3    *SRCH Searching for label or value? (L/V): {get SRCH}{esc}
4    :     {if SRCH="l"}{getlabel "Enter Search Label: ",SRCH}{branch SKIP}
5    :     {getnumber "Enter Search Number: ",SRCH}
6    SKIP  Replacing with label or value? (L/V): {get SEND}{esc}
7    :     {if SEND="l"}{getlabel "Enter Replace Label: ",SEND}{branch SLOOP}
8    :     {getnumber "Enter Replace Number: ",SEND}
9    SLOOP {if @cellpointer("contents")=SRCH}/cSEND~~
10   :     {down}{if @cellpointer("type")="b"}{quit}
11   :     {branch SLOOP}
12   SRCH            0
13   SEND  l                                 Budget vs. Cost
14                                            _____
15                                                    100
16                                                      0
17                                                    400
18                                                      0
19                                                    320
20
```

F_12-1.WK1   CMD   CALC

Figure 12.1 Macro to Search and Replace in a Single Column

for whether to replace with labels or values. This is also an excellent starting point to review one effective way of using the {get} command.

Here's how the macro works.

Searching for label or value? (L/V): {get SRCH}{esc}   The macro begins by typing a message into the upper control panel that will appear as a prompt. This is somewhat similar to the {getlabel} method of creating a user prompt, except that the message is actually typed, character by character, rather than appearing all at once. On slower computers and in Release 3, you will be able to see the prompt appear character by character.

The macro pauses at the {get} command, waiting for you to press any key. The {get} command uses the syntax **{get** *location***}** and it operates in a way that will remind you of the bracketed question mark pause {?}. The main difference is that it pauses only until you press a single key. As soon as you have pressed any key, the macro stores the name of that key in the designated cell address or named cell and continues its normal flow. If you press the capital letter P, for example, a capital letter P is stored in the location. If you press the DownArrow key, the macro command **{DOWN}**—shown in all uppercase—is stored in the location.

In this case, the {get} command is designed to store the captured keystroke in cell B12, which has been range named SRCH. The {esc} command following the {get SRCH} command is intended to eliminate the typed prompt from the upper control panel.

{if SRCH="l"}{getlabel "Enter Search Label: ",SRCH}{branch SKIP}   If you press the letter L (uppercase or lowercase), a {getlabel} message prompting you for the label to search for appears. Your response to the {getlabel} prompt is stored in the cell named SRCH (which, as you can see, is doing double duty for both the {get} and {getlabel} commands), and the macro branches to the routine at the cell named SKIP.

{getnumber "Enter Search Number: ",SRCH}   Otherwise, if you have not pressed the letter L, it is assumed you pressed an uppercase or lowercase V, and the macro uses {getnumber} to prompt you for a search value that it stores in SRCH.

Replacing with label or value? (L/V): {get SEND}{esc}   In the same way that the macro typed a message in the upper control panel to prompt for whether the search item is a label or value, a message is typed now that will appear as a prompt for whether you want to re-place the searched item with a label or a value. The macro pauses at the {get} command, waiting for you to press any key. Whether you respond with L for Label or V for Value, your response is stored in SEND and the Escape command eliminates the prompt.

{if SEND="l"}{getlabel "Enter Replace Label: ",SEND}{branch SLOOP}   If you press the letter L (uppercase or lowercase), a {getlabel} prompt appears, prompting you for the label you want in place of the searched item. Your response to the {getlabel} prompt is stored in the cell named SEND and the macro branches to the cell named SLOOP.

{getnumber "Enter Replace Number: ",SEND}   Otherwise, if you have not pressed the letter L, it is assumed you pressed an uppercase or lowercase V, and the macro uses {getnumber} to prompt you for a replacement value to store in the cell named SEND.

{if @cellpointer("contents")=SRCH}/cSEND~~   The macro moves through the col-umn, testing for whether the contents of the current cell are the same as the contents of the label or value stored in SRCH. If so, the label or value in SEND is copied to the current cell.

Note: In Release 2.2 and 3, a slightly faster method of replacing the value in the cur-rent cell is to replace the command **/cSEND~~** with a {let} command as:

{let @cellpointer("address"),SEND}

Unfortunately, this ability to use @cellpointer as the first argument in a {let} com-mand is not available in Release 2 or 2.01.

{down}{if @cellpointer("type")="b"}{quit}   The cell pointer is moved down one cell and the macro checks for whether the cell is blank. If so, it is assumed the cell pointer has reached the end of the column and the macro quits.

{branch SLOOP}   Otherwise, the macro branches back to SLOOP to check the next cell for a match with the contents of SRCH.

In Figure 12.1 you can see a simple example where you might use this macro. If you have a column that subtracts cost from budget, any zero value must mean you are exactly on budget. If you want to replace all zeros with the label *Break-even* in just this column (a task not possible using /Range Search), this macro will handle that chore for you.

Using {Get} in a Year-to-Date Macro

We have seen how the {get} command can be used in conjunction with a typed message to provide functionality similar to the {getlabel} command. There are more uses of the {get} command, however, as you will see from our Year-to-Date macro in Figure 12.2.

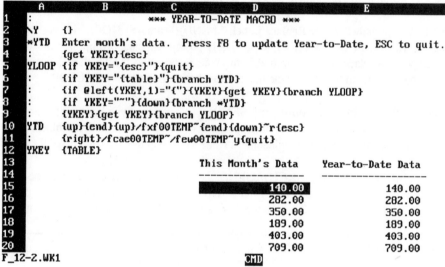

Figure 12.2 A Macro to Update a Year-to-Date Matrix

Here is a common situation. You have a spreadsheet with a column for the current month and a column for the year-to-date values and you prefer not to show data relating to other months already past, even though the information for those months is included in the year-to-date column.

There are two ways of dealing with this problem manually: you can place the information dealing with past months in some out-of-the-way off-screen location (usually somewhere to the right), or you can leave the data for those months in the on-screen area, but hide the columns using /Worksheet Column Hide. The advantage of these methods is that you will always have a record supporting the final year-to-date figures shown. The disadvantage is that these columns can be accidentally erased, deleted, or changed in the unseen areas, thereby affecting the year-to-date totals without your necessarily being aware of the change.

One solution is to use a special Year-to-Date macro. The macro works by prompting you to enter the current month's data. When you are finished, pressing a specially designated key can be used to tell the macro to automatically update the year-to-date column.

Here's how the macro works.

Enter month's data. Press F8 to update Year-to-Date, ESC to quit.　The macro begins by typing a message in the upper panel, instructing you to enter the month's data, to press F8 when finished and ready for an update, or to press Escape to return to *READY*.

{get YKEY}{esc}　The {get} command causes the macro to pause for your press of a single key, which will be stored in YKEY. The Escape command is included to eliminate the typed message.

{if YKEY="{esc}"}{quit}　If you press Escape, the command {esc} is stored in YKEY and the {if} statement causes the macro to quit.

{if YKEY="{table}"}{branch YTD}　If you press the F8 Table key, this {if} statement operates on the assumption you are finished inputing the month's data and want the year-to-date column updated. It does this by branching to YTD. Incidentally, the F8 Table key was chosen in this case, not because the process has anything to do with the Table key, but because it is so rarely pressed by 1-2-3 users and can be considered the most available of function keys.

{if @left(YKEY,1)="{"}{YKEY}{get YKEY}{branch YLOOP}　This {if} statement checks for whether the type of key you have pressed starts with an opening curly bracket, which would be the case if it were a function key or directional key such as {up}, {down}, {PgDn}, {end}, or {home}. If so, the macro processes that key with the subroutine call to {YKEY}, then branches to the routine at YLOOP. This is a handy way of isolating the types of keys the macro will process, differentiating as it does between a press of letter/number keys and directional or function keys.

{if YKEY="~"}{down}{branch *YTD}　If you press Return, this {if} statement interprets that, moves down one cell without affecting the current cell, and branches back to the beginning at *YTD.

{YKEY}{get YKEY}{branch YLOOP}　Otherwise, if the macro passes all four {if} statements above, it processes the keystroke at YKEY, gets the next keystroke with the {get YKEY} command, and branches back to YLOOP.

{up}{end}{up}/fxf00TEMP~{end}{down}~r{esc}　This is the beginning of the routine named YTD. It moves the cell pointer to the top of the column, selects /File Xtract Formulas, enters a temporary filename 00TEMP, highlights the range just entered by pressing End DownArrow to the bottom of the column, then R for Replace, and Escape in case the file does not exist.

{right}/fcae00TEMP~/few00TEMP~y{quit}　Once the temporary file with this month's data has been created, the cell pointer is moved one cell to the right, and the macro increases the current year-to-date figures by the amount of the current month by selecting /File Combine Add Entire and entering the filename 00TEMP. The temporary file is then erased and the macro quits. The last line of the macro is simply the storage cell for the {get} command, named YKEY.

In Release 2.2 and 3, you can speed up the message prompt by having it appear in the upper panel as an Indicate message in place of the ready indicator. This is possible in Release 2.2 and 3 because those releases allow a longer Indicator message than the five-character limit of Release 2 and 2.01 (refer to Figure 12.3).

```
D15: (F2) [W18] 140              Enter mo. data, F8 to update Year-to-Dt, ESC to quit

         A         B          C           D                    E
1  :                        *** YEAR-TO-DATE MACRO ***
2  \Y       {}
3  *YTD     {indicate "Enter mo. data, F8 to update Year-to-Dt, ESC to quit"}
4  YLOOP    {get YKEY}{if YKEY="{esc}"}{indicate}{quit}
5  :        {if YKEY="{table}"}{branch YTD}
6  :        {if @left(YKEY,1)="{"}{YKEY}{branch YLOOP}
7  :        {if YKEY="~"}{down}{branch YLOOP}
8  :        {YKEY}{branch YLOOP}
9  YTD      {up}{end}{up}/fxf00TEMP~{end}{down}~r{esc}
10 :        {right}/fcae00TEMP~/few00TEMP~y{indicate}{quit}
11 YKEY     {TABLE}
12
13                            This Month's Data    Year-to-Date Data
14                            -----------------    -----------------
15                                   140.00              140.00
16                                   282.00              282.00
17                                   350.00              350.00
18                                   189.00              189.00
19                                   403.00              403.00
20                                   709.00              709.00
F_12-3.WK1                          CMD
```

Figure 12.3 The Year-to-Date Macro Using an {Indicate} Prompt

{indicate Enter mo. data, F8 to update Year-to-Date, ESC to quit}   This message will appear instantly, and stay in the upper panel until the macro reaches an {indicate} command returning it to its normal state.

{get YKEY}{if YKEY="{esc}"}{indicate}{quit}   If you press Escape upon seeing the prompt, the macro will process an {indicate} command and quit.

The remainder of the macro is similar to the first version, except that the final {quit} command is also preceded with an {indicate} command.

Using {Get} to Toggle Your Hidden Columns

We have already covered the techniques for creating toggle macros in 1-2-3. Here we use the same techniques, but add a few new uses of the {get} command to provide even more flexibility for the person who will be using the macro.

The purpose of the Hide Columns Toggle (refer to Figure 12.4). is to alternately prompt you through the hiding of one or more columns at once or to offer you the ability to instantly redisplay, or unhide, all hidden columns in your worksheet.

```
A1: [W10] ':                                                                    LABEL
Point to column to hide and press any key.  Press ESC to quit.

          A            B         C        D        E        F        G
1     :                     *** HIDE COLUMNS TOGGLE ***
2     \H           {}
3     *HIDECOL     {onerror HTOGGLE}
4     HHLOOP       Point to column to hide and press any key.  Press ESC to quit.
5     :            {get HKEY}{esc}{if HKEY="{esc}"}{branch HTOGGLE}
6     :            {if @left(HKEY,1)="{"}{HKEY}{branch HHLOOP}
7     :            {windowsoff}{right}{let HERE,@cellpointer("address")}{left}~
8     :            /wch~{goto}{HERE}~{windowson}{branch *HIDECOL}
9     HTOGGLE      {let *HIDECOL,"{branch HDISPLAY}"}~{quit}
10    HTOGGLE2     {let *HIDECOL,"{onerror HTOGGLE}"}{branch *HIDECOL}{quit}
11    HDISPLAY     Do you want to display (unhide) all hidden columns? (Y/N)
12    :            {get HKEY}{esc}{if HKEY<>"y"}{branch HTOGGLE2}
13    :            {windowsoff}/wcd{home}.{end}{home}{bigright 3}~
14    :            {let *HIDECOL,"{onerror HTOGGLE}"}{quit}
15    HKEY         y
16    :            {return}
17    HERE         $K$7
18    :            {return}
19
20
F_12-4.WK1                                   CMD
```

Figure 12.4 A Macro to Toggle Hidden Columns On or Off

Here's how the macro works.

{onerror HTOGGLE}   If you press Ctrl-Break at any time during the operation of the macro or if the macro reaches an error condition that would normally halt its operation, this instruction tells it to branch to the routine at HTOGGLE, a special toggling line of the macro. The toggle switches the opening command so the next time you press Alt-H the macro will run the {branch HDISPLAY} command and prompt for whether you want to display (unhide) all hidden columns.

Point to column to hide and press any key. Press ESC to quit.   This message is typed in the upper panel, instructing you to point to the column you want to hide. In Release 2.2 and 3, you may want to substitute an {indicate} version of this message. If you do so, however, remember to precede each {quit} command in the macro with a resetting {indicate} command.

{get HKEY}{esc}{if HKEY="{esc}"}{branch HTOGGLE}   Pauses for you to press any key, which the macro stores in the cell named HKEY. The {esc} command eliminates the prompt above. If you press the Escape key manually at this point, the macro branches to HTOGGLE, switching the opening command so the next time the macro will branch to HDISPLAY and prompt for whether you want to display (unhide) all hidden columns.

{if @left(HKEY,1)="{"}{HKEY}{branch HHLOOP}   If you pressed a directional key such as {up} or {down}, the left-most character stored in HKEY must be a curly bracket. In that case, the macro processes the key in HKEY as a subroutine, then branches to HHLOOP where it again prompts you to point to the column you want to hide. You can continue to press any directional key and the macro will continue to process that key, then again prompt you to point to a column to hide. This combination of prompt, {get} command, and {if} command provides a handy way to instruct the user while allowing him or her the freedom to move around in response to the instruction.

{windowsoff}{right}{let HERE,@cellpointer("address")}{left}~   If you press a key that does not start with a curly bracket (such as the Return key), the macro continues at this line, turning off the windows, moving to the right one cell, recording the address of that cell at the place-marker cell HERE, then returning to the left one cell.

/wch~{goto}{HERE}~{windowson}{branch *HIDECOL}   At this point the macro selects /Worksheet Column Hide, moves back to the cell address stored at HERE, turns on the windows, and branches back to the beginning of the macro where you are again prompted for a column to hide. If you press Ctrl-Break or Escape, the {onerror} command or {if HKEY="{esc}"} command will branch the macro to HTOGGLE.

{let *HIDECOL,"{branch HDISPALY}"}~{quit}   This is the routine named HTOGGLE, designed to change the first line of the macro to {branch HDISPLAY}, so the next time you press Alt-H the macro will prompt for whether you want to display (unhide) all hidden columns. Once the toggle switch is set, the macro quits.

{let *HIDECOL,"{onerror HTOGGLE}"}{branch *HIDECOL}{quit}   This is the second toggling line named HTOGGLE2. Its purpose, which becomes clear at the end of the routine called HDISPLAY, is to return the original {onerror} command to the first line of the macro to run its primary function.

Do you want to display (unhide) all hidden columns? (Y/N)   This message is the beginning of the routine HDISPLAY, and it prompts you to type **Y** for *Yes* or **N** for *No* to indicate whether you want to display all hidden columns in the worksheet.

{get HKEY}{esc}{if HKEY<>"y"}{branch HTOGGLE2}   If your next keystroke, which the macro stores in HKEY, is not Y for Yes, the macro branches back to HTOGGLE2, the subroutine that returns the macro to its primary operating function before quitting.

{windowsoff}/wcd{home}.{end}{home}{bigright 3}~   Otherwise (assuming you have pressed **Y** for *Yes*) the macro turns off the windows, selects /Worksheet Column Display, and highlights the entire worksheet from the Home (A1) position to three screens to the right of the End Home position.

{let *HIDECOL,"{onerror HTOGGLE}"{quit}   This is actually a repeat of the HTOGGLE2 line, except that the macro quits rather than looping back to the beginning to start over.

This macro does not accomplish anything you cannot do for yourself; but it goes through the necessary keystrokes much faster than you could manually and it eliminates the need to remember how to hide columns using /Worksheet Column Hide. If you would like to start making more use of hidden columns in your work, this macro provides a nice beginning to that process.

Creating a Macro to Temporarily View Hidden Columns

You may have noticed that you can temporarily view your hidden columns in a worksheet by pressing /Copy or /Move. Any hidden columns will appear temporarily, designated as hidden by an asterisk that appears to the right of the column letter in the upper border. After the /Copy or /Move command is completed, or interrupted, the hidden columns disappear again. This is a handy manual way to bring your hidden columns into view without having to display them with /Worksheet Column Display, then rehide them using /Worksheet Column Hide. Unfortunately, you cannot make changes to hidden columns that are temporarily displayed in this way.

Fortunately, there is a clever macro technique for both displaying and allowing changes to hidden columns without losing the characteristic that these columns are designated as hidden. Refer to the View Hidden Columns macro in Figure 12.5.

{menubranch VMENU}{quit}   Brings up the menu choices *VIEW* and *REHIDE*. Select *VIEW* to bring all hidden columns temporarily into view and *REHIDE* to rehide all columns that you have previously designated as hidden using /Worksheet Column Hide.

{paneloff}/c{CTRL_BREAK}   Turns off the upper panel to suppress screen flicker, selects /Copy, then attempts to process a nonexistent command. Actually, you could use any nonexistent command at this point, such as {VIEW}, {TEMP}, or {APPLESAUCE}, as long as there is no cell or range in the worksheet that has been given that name. We used {CTRL_BREAK} here because, being nonexistent, it provides an effect similar to the effect you would get if you pressed Ctrl- Break: it interrupts the /Copy command. In doing so, it does one other strange thing: It freezes any temporarily viewed hidden columns in their temporarily visible state. At this point you can erase a cell, edit a cell, or type new information into a cell that is hidden. This does not work with Release 3, however.

{paneloff}/c{esc 5}{right}{left}{quit}   If, after selecting *VIEW* once, you decide you want

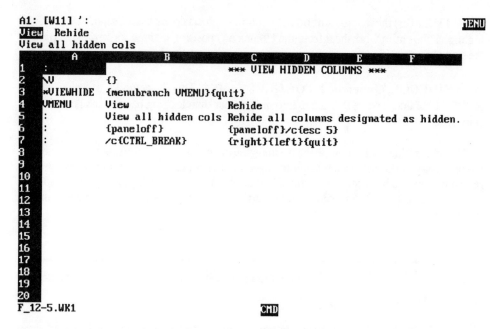

Figure 12.5 A Macro to Temporarily View Hidden Columns

to cause your temporarily viewed columns to disappear again, selecting *REHIDE* will cause the macro to turn off the upper panel, select /Copy, press Escape five times to gracefully back out of the /Copy command, then move RightArrow and LeftArrow to cause the screen to redisplay correctly. At this point the hidden columns will all disappear and the macro quits.

Using {Get} to Create a Go-Return Macro

In this section we will explore how you can use the {get} command to continue or interrupt an F5 Goto sequence, thereby allowing a modified version of the F5 Goto function.

We have discussed the use of the F5 Goto key to temporarily visit a remote location, then return by pressing Escape before completing the command. For example, you can press F5 Home, view the area around cell A1, then press Escape to return to your original position in the worksheet.

The Go-Return macro in Figure 12.6 provides that utility and more. It allows you to relocate your cell pointer to a remote cell in your worksheet, but it keeps track of your last location so you can jump back instantly. What's more, it remembers the remote location, so you can toggle back and forth between that location and your starting point with just two keystrokes.

Normally, when you press the F5 Goto key, 1-2-3 types the message *Enter address to go to:* and prompts you with the address of the current cell. This is fairly useless, since you never use the Goto key to go to your current location. Imagine an F5 Goto key that offers

```
A1: [W10] ' :                                                          EDIT
Enter address to go to: $F$59
```

```
              A              B         C         D        E      F       G
 1   :                         *** GO-RETURN MACRO ***
 2   \G             {}
 3   *GORETRN       {goto}{GLAST}{get GKEY1}{if GKEY1="~"}{branch GLOOP}
 4   :              {if GKEY1="{esc}"}{esc 3}{quit}
 5   :              {let GLAST,@cellpointer("address")}{esc 2}
 6   GKEY1          ~
 7   :              {quit}
 8   GLOOP          {esc 2}{let GLAST2,GLAST}
 9                  {let GLAST,@cellpointer("address")}
10   :              {GLAST2}~{up @min(@cellpointer("row")-1,3)}
11   :              {left @min(@cellpointer("col")-1,3)}{goto}{GLAST2}~{quit}
12   GLAST          $F$59
13   :              {return}
14   GLAST2         $C$59
15   :              {return}
16
17
18
19
20
```
```
F_12-6.WK1                              CMD
```

Figure 12.6 Using the {Get} Command in a Go-Return Macro

you the cell address you occupied when you last pressed the F5 Goto key. In that case, you could press F5 and Enter to instantly jump to a previous location, then F5 and Enter again to return to the cell where you started. This is exactly the effect of the Go-Return macro in Figure 12.6.

{goto}{GLAST}{get GKEY1}{if GKEY1="~"{branch GLOOP} The macro begins by activating the F5 Goto function, then types in the address stored in GLAST.

Note: When you first type this macro into your own worksheet, you must include an address in GLAST, or the macro will halt at this point.

The Return key to complete the Goto sequence is not yet pressed. Instead, the {get} command pauses for you to press a single key.

If you press Return, the assumption is that you accept the offered address shown at the Goto prompt in the upper panel. This will be your last cell location where you used this Alt-G macro. The macro branches to GLOOP to process your Goto response.

{if GKEY1="{esc}"}{esc 3}{quit} If you press Escape instead, the macro backs out of the F5 Goto sequence and quits.

{let GLAST,@cellpointer("address")}{esc 2} Otherwise, it stores the current cell pointer address in GLAST so the next time you press Alt-G, it will offer this address as the address to go to. The macro presses Escape twice, leaving just the *Enter address to go to:* prompt, repeats the single key you pressed at the {get} pause, and quits.

Thus, pressing the LeftArrow key after pressing Alt-G will leave you with the same *Enter address to go to:* prompt you would get by simply pressing F5 and the LeftArrow key.

{esc 2}{let GLAST2,GLAST}   This is the beginning of the routine named GLOOP where the macro processes your acceptance of the last cell location where you used this Alt-G macro. The macro backs partially out of the F5 Goto sequence, then stores the address in GLAST at GLAST2.

{let GLAST,@cellpointer("address")}   Now that a copy of the address in GLAST has been stored in GLAST2, the macro stores the current address in GLAST.

{GLAST2}~{up @min(@cellpointer("row")-1,3)}   Completes the F5 Goto sequence by typing in the address of the last location where you used this Alt-G macro, then moves up either three cells, or the number of cells equal to one less than the current row, whichever is less. The result is to move the current row more towards the center of the screen.

{left @min(@cellpointer("col")-1,3)}{goto}{GLAST2}~{quit}   Moves left either three cells, or the number of cells one less than the current column, whichever is less, relocating the current columns more towards the center of the screen. Then the cell pointer is moved back to the address in GLAST2 and the macro quits.

Creating a Word-Wrap Macro in 1-2-3

Since the {get} command can be used to capture a keystroke, you can theoretically pass every keystroke through a looping macro with a {get} command and several {if} commands to test and react to the type of key pressed. In the next section we will look at a Word-Processing macro that does just that to offer several features of a simple word processor.

Before we get to that, however, let's examine a simpler Word-Wrap macro in Figure 12.7. This macro uses the bracketed question mark pause {?} in conjunction with the /Range Justify command to rejustify into paragraph form whatever you type in the upper panel.

{edit}{?}~{windowsoff}/rj{bigright}{left}~{down}   The macro begins by switching to Edit mode, then pauses for your entry of any number of characters up to 240 characters in Release 2, 2.01, and 2.2, and up to 512 characters in Release 3. When you press Return, the windows are turned off and the macro selects /Range Justify, uses the {bigright} command (the equivalent of Tab) to highlight to the first column in the next screen to the right, moves back one column to the left, and presses Return.

The effect is to cause a rejustification of everything you have typed into a paragraph that extends from the current column to the right edge of the right-most column visible on the

```
A1: [W7] ':                                                          READY

         A        B          C        D        E        F        G
1    :                    *** WORD WRAP MACRO ***
2    \W          {edit}{?}~{windowsoff}/rj{bigright}{left}~{down}
3    :           {if @cellpointer("type")="b"}{up}{windowson}{branch WLOOP}
4    :           {up}{end}{down}{windowson}
5    WLOOP       {edit} {?}~{windowsoff}/rj{bigright}{left}~{down}
6    :           {if @cellpointer("type")="b"}{up}{windowson}{branch WLOOP}
7    :           {up}{end}{down}{windowson}{branch WLOOP}
8
9
10
11
12
13
14
15
16
17
18
19
20
F_12-7.WK1
```

Figure 12.7   A Word-Wrap Macro Using /Range Justify

screen. At this point the macro moves down one cell to prepare for a test of whether the paragraph now extends to more than one line.

{if @cellpointer("type")="b"}{up}{windowson}{branch WLOOP}   If the cell is blank, the paragraph was, indeed, only one line long, and the macro moves the cell pointer back up to that line, turns the windows back on, and branches to WLOOP to continue from there.

{up}{end}{down}{windowson}   Otherwise, the macro moves back up to the previous line, then End DownArrow to the last line of the paragraph, and the windows are turned on.

{edit} {?}~{windowsoff}/rj{bigright}{left}~{down}   This line is the same as the first line of the macro, except that there is a space after the {edit} command. This is included because of the way we type. Using a standard word processor, or even a typewriter, we are not used to a requirement to add a space after pressing Return and before continuing with the next word to type. This line adds that space for you.

The rest of the macro is identical to the second and third lines except for one more branch to WLOOP at the end of the macro.

To use the macro, press Alt-W. Type until the computer beeps at 240 characters (512 in Release 3) or until you get to the end of the paragraph and want to start a new paragraph. Press Return. If you have more to type, you can continue at this point. If finished with the paragraph, press DownArrow twice and start the next paragraph. Press Ctrl-Break to leave the macro.

A More Advanced Word-Processing Macro

A more powerful Word-Processing macro is possible using a {get} command that captures every keystroke, as shown in Figure 12.8. You should be aware, however, that this macro may not operate as quickly as you may require. If you have Release 3, this macro is inappropriately slow unless you are working with a very fast 386 or a 486. If you have Release 2 or 2.01, this macro will be too slow on a PC, an XT, or a slow 286. If you are not machine limited, however, you may find that this macro will provide a powerful and interesting addition to your own macro collection.

```
              A              B              C           D            E            F            G
 1    :                            ***WORD PROCESSOR MACRO***
 2    \W           ~
 3    *WORDPRO     {edit}
 4    :            {indicate +" Press ESC to quit WP Macro "&@repeat(" ",80)}
 5    WLOOP        {get WKEY}{if WKEY="{esc}"}{esc 2}{indicate}{quit}
 6    :            {if WKEY="~"}~{branch WSKIP}
 7    :            {if WKEY="{down}"}{down}{branch *WORDPRO}
 8    :            {if WKEY="{up}"}{up}{branch *WORDPRO}
 9    :            {if WKEY="{edit}"}{edit}{branch *WORDPRO}
10    :            {if WKEY="/"}~/{WSLASH}
11    WKEY         {ESC}
12    :            {branch WLOOP}
13    WSKIP        {windowsoff}{paneloff}/rj{bigright}{left}~{down 18}{up 20}
14    :            {if @cellpointer("type")="b"}{down 3}{branch WSKIP2}
15    :            {down}{if @cellpointer("type")="b"}{down 2}{branch WSKIP2}
16    :            {end}{up 2}{down}{end}{down 2}
17    WSKIP2       {if @cellpointer("type")="b"}{up}{branch WSKIP3}
18    :            {up}{end}{down}
19    WSKIP3       {edit}{panelon}{windowson} {branch WLOOP}
20    WSLASH       {get WKEY}{if WKEY="c"}c{?}~{?}~{branch *WORDPRO}
21    :            {if WKEY="/"}{esc}{edit}/{edit}{branch *WORDPRO}
22    :            {if WKEY="m"}m{?}~{?}~{branch *WORDPRO}
23    :            {if WKEY="w"}w{?}~{branch *WORDPRO}
24    :            {if WKEY="r"}r{?}~{branch *WORDPRO}
25    :            {esc}{branch *WORDPRO}
```

FIG_12-8.WK1

Figure 12.8 A Word-Processing Macro Using the {Get} Command

{edit} As with the Word-Wrap macro, this macro begins by switching to the Edit mode.

{indicate +" Press ESC to quit WP Macro "&@repeat(" ",80)} or **{indicate " WP "}**
If you have Release 2 or 2.01, the *READY* indicator can be changed to another message only up to a limit of five letters. For those releases, we are recommending here that you replace *READY* with the letters *WP* (for Word Processor), centered in the indicator panel.

If you have Release 2.2 or 3, you can replace the *READY* indicator with a message and a series of blank spaces that stretch across the entire top of the screen. In this case, the message consists of an instruction to press ESC to quit the macro.

{get WKEY}{if WKEY="{esc}"}{esc 2}{indicate}{quit}   Pauses for you to press any key, which the macro stores in the cell named WKEY. If you press the Escape key manually at this point, the macro presses Escape twice, switches the *READY* indicator back to normal, and quits.

{if WKEY="~"}~{branch WSKIP}   If you pressed Return, the macro executes a press of the Return key (notice the additional tilde) and the macro branches to WSKIP.

{IF WKEY="{down}"}{down}{branch *WORDPRO}   If you pressed the DownArrow key, the macro moves the cell pointer down one cell and branches back to the beginning.

{IF WKEY="{up}"}{up}{branch *WORDPRO}   In the same way, pressing UpArrow causes the macro to move the cell pointer up one cell and the macro branches back to the beginning.

{IF WKEY="{edit}"}{edit}{branch *WORDPRO}   If, not realizing you are already in the Edit mode, you press the F2 Edit key, the macro presses Edit (which actually switches you to Value mode), and branches back to the beginning where it presses Edit again, switching back to Edit mode. In other words, the macro takes steps, in a roundabout way, to specifically ignore any inadvertent pressing of the Edit key.

{if WKEY="/"}~/{WSLASH}   This macro has the distinct advantage of allowing you to access commands like /Copy, /Move, /Worksheet Delete Row, /Worksheet Insert Row, and /Range Erase. When you press the forward slash key to call up the command menu that normally allows these features, the macro presses Return, presses the forward slash, and branches to the routine named WSLASH.

{ESC}   Although in Figure 12.8 this line shows {ESC}, this is a self-modifying cell of the macro named WKEY that will change depending on the particular key you pressed at the {get} command. If the macro passes through all the {if} commands above, it will process the keystroke stored at this cell.

{branch WLOOP}   After processing the keystroke, the macro branches back to WLOOP. Remember, you are still in the Edit mode and the indicator message is still in effect, so it is not necessary to loop all the way back to the beginning of the macro at *WORDPRO.

{windowsoff}{paneloff}/rj{bigright}{left}~{down 18}{up 20}   You will recognize this line from the Word-Wrap macro. The windows and panel are turned off and the macro selects /Range Justify, uses the {bigright} command (the equivalent of Tab) to highlight to the first column in the next screen to the right, moves back one column to the left, and presses Return.

The effect causes a rejustification of everything you have typed into a paragraph that extends from the current column to the right edge of the right-most column visible on the screen.

Note: You are no longer in the Edit mode now.

At this point the macro moves the cell pointer down 18 cells and back up 20, which reorients the row you were on to just below the top of the screen. This keeps you from having to use your Word-Processing macro at the bottom of the screen where it is difficult to work. You may recognize this from one of our earliest macros, the Jump to Top of Screen macro.

{if @cellpointer("type")="b"}{down 3}{branch WSKIP2}   If the cell pointer is above the current paragraph on a blank cell, the macro moves the cell pointer back down to the paragraph and branches to WSKIP2.

{down}{if @cellpointer("type")="b")}{down 2}{branch WSKIP2}   Otherwise, the macro moves down one cell and again tests for a blank cell. If the cell is blank, the macro moves the cell pointer back down to the paragraph and branches to WSKIP2.

{end}{up 2}{down}{end}{down 2}   This line moves the cell pointer to the end of the paragraph.

{if @cellpointer("type")="b")}{up}{branch WSKIP3}   If the cell pointer has come to a line below the paragraph, it is moved back up to the paragraph and the macro branches to WSKIP3.

{up}{end}{down}   Otherwise, the cell pointer is moved to the end of the paragraph.

{edit}{panelon}{windowson} {branch WLOOP}   The windows and panel are turned back on and a space is typed for you, included because of the way we type. Using a standard word processor, or even a typewriter, we are not used to the requirement for adding a space after pressing Return and before continuing with the next word to type. The macro branches back to WLOOP.

{get WKEY}{if WKEY="c"}c{?}~{?}~{branch *WORDPRO}   This is the beginning of the routine named WSLASH to which the macro branches if you press the forward slash to call up the command menu. Here the macro pauses again for your next key. If you press C for Copy, there is a pause for the *Copy FROM* prompt, another pause for the *Copy TO* prompt, and the macro branches back to the beginning.

{if WKEY="/"}{esc}{edit}/{edit}{branch *WORDPRO}   In case you want the Forward Slash key typed into text as opposed to calling up the command menu, pressing the forward slash key a second time will cause the command menu to disappear, the macro to switch to Edit mode, the forward slash to be typed, and the macro to switch to Value mode so it will end up in Edit mode when it branches back to the beginning.

{if WKEY="m"}m{?}~{?}~{branch *WORDPRO}   If you press M for Move, there is a pause for the *Move FROM* prompt, another pause for the *Move TO* prompt, and the macro branches back to the beginning.

{if WKEY="w"}w{?}~{branch *WORDPRO} If you press W for Worksheet, there is a pause for *Delete Row* or *Insert Row*, any necessary highlighting of rows, and a press of Return; then the macro branches back to the beginning.

{if WKEY="r"}r{?}~{branch *WORDPRO} If you press R for Range, there is a pause for Erase, any necessary highlighting of rows, and a press of Return; then the macro branches back to the beginning.

{esc}{branch *WORDPRO} Otherwise, any other key you press will cause the command menu to disappear and the macro branches back to the beginning.

Using {Get} to Edit an .MLB File

The next macro we explore is for Release 2.2 only.

Normally, to edit an .MLB file from your background Macro Library, you must first Attach the MACROMGR.ADN add-in application (if it is not already attached), invoke the MACROMGR.ADN add-in application (if it is not already invoked), load the particular .MLB Macro Library file (if it is not already loaded), and finally bring up the .MLB Macro Library file for editing.

The macro in Figure 12.9 is designed to facilitate and speed up the process involved in pulling a Macro Library .MLB file into your current worksheet for editing.

```
A1: [W10] ':                                                        READY
```

```
          A            B         C        D       E       F        G
 1  :                     *** EDIT A MACRO LIBRARY .MLB FILE ***
 2  \E         {}
 3  *EDITMLB   {if @isapp("MACROMGR")}{app1}{branch EMORE}
 4  :          {windowsoff}{paneloff}/aaMACROMGR~7i~
 5  :          {panelon}{windowson}
 6  EMORE      e{name}{get E_KEY}
 7  E:LOOP     {if E_KEY="{esc}"}{esc 2}l{name}{get E_KEY}{branch ESCP}
 8  :          {if E_KEY="~"}~i{branch EMORE2}
 9  :          {E_KEY}{get E_KEY}{branch E:LOOP}
10  EMORE2     {indicate  Make sure you have space for overwriting macros! }
11  :          {?}~{indicate}{quit}
12  E_KEY      ~
13  :          {return}
14  ESCP       {if E_KEY="{esc}"}{esc 4}{quit}
15  :          {if E_KEY="~"}~nn{esc 2}e{end}~i{branch EMORE2}
16  :          {E_KEY}{get E_KEY}{branch ESCP}
17
18
19
20
F_12-9.WK1
```

Figure 12.9 Macro to Edit a Macro Library .MLB File

{if @isapp("MACROMGR")}{app1}{branch EMORE} The macro begins by checking for whether the MACROMGR.ADN add-in application has been attached. The @isapp function is evaluated as true if so. The {app1} command is the macro equivalent to pressing Alt-F7 to invoke the add-in application attached to Alt-F7. It is assumed that you have attached the MACROMGR.ADN add-in to Alt-F7 either manually or through the /Worksheet Global Default command. At this point the macro branches to the fifth line of the macro at EMORE.

{windowsoff}{paneloff}/aaMACROMGR~7i~ If the MACROMGR.ADN has not been attached, this line selects /Add-in Attach, enters MACROMGR, attaches the add-in to Alt-F7, and invokes the MACROMGR add-in, offering the menu choices Load, Save, Edit, Remove, Name-List, and Quit, and selects Load.

{panelon}{windowson} Turns off the windows and panel to suppress screen flicker and speed up the macro.

e{name}{get E_KEY} Selects Edit, presses the F3 Name key to show a full-screen view of the choice of loaded .MLB files to edit, then pauses for your press of a key.

{if E_KEY="{esc}"}{esc 2}l{name}{get E_KEY}{branch ESCP} If you press Escape, it is assumed that the file you want to edit is not already loaded. The macro backs out of the Edit menu level, selects Load, presses Name to show a full-screen view of the choice of .MLB files you can load, pauses for you to press a key, then branches to ESCP.

{if E_KEY="~"}~i{branch EMORE2} If you do not press Escape, but press Return, it is assumed you are selecting the highlighted .MLB file to edit. That file is selected, and between the menu choices Ignore and Overwrite, I for Ignore is typed. The macro branches to EMORE2.

{E_KEY}{get E_KEY}{branch E|LOOP} Otherwise, if you do not press either Escape or Return, the key you pressed (which was stored at E_KEY) is processed, the macro pauses for you to press another key, and it then branches back to E|LOOP.

{indicate Make sure you have space for overwriting macros ! } Before the .MLB macro library file is brought into the current worksheet, a message is shown in the upper panel warning you to make sure you have enough space for the .MLB file. This is important, since bringing the file into the current worksheet will overwrite anything in its way.

{?}~{indicate}{quit} The macro pauses for your relocation of the cell pointer, if required, to the place where you want the macros to appear in your worksheet. As soon as you decide and press Return, the macro also presses Return, bringing in the .MLB file. The {indicate} command eliminates the warning message in the upper panel and the macro quits.

The next two lines of the macro consist of the location for the stored keystroke (named E_KEY) and a {return} command to end the subroutine consisting of the single keystroke stored at E_KEY.

{if E_KEY="{esc}"}{esc 4}{quit}   The remaining three lines are the continuation of the condition that you pressed Escape because the file you wanted to edit is not already loaded. At this point, the macro has backed out of the Edit menu level, selected Load, shown a full-screen view of the choice of .MLB files you can load, and paused for you to press a key. If you press Escape again at this point, the macro escapes entirely out of the menu levels and the macro quits.

{if E_KEY="~"}nn{esc 2}e{end}~i{branch EMORE2}   If, on the other hand, you press Return to select a file to load, it is possible that the file has already been loaded. In that case, you will be given a *No/Yes* prompt and an explanation that the *.MLB file already exists in memory. Overwrite it?* The first N is for No; the second N selects Name-List (a bogus selection). If the file has not already been loaded, pressing NN will simply make a bogus selection of Name-List and a typing of the letter **N**.

Whichever happens, two presses of Escape returns you to the menu choices Load, Save, Edit, and so on. The macro selects Edit, the last .MLB file, and I for Invoke; and the macro then branches back to EMORE2.

{E_KEY}{get E_KEY}{branch ESCP}   Otherwise, if you have not pressed either Escape or Return, the key you pressed (which was stored at E_KEY) is processed, the macro pauses for your press of another key, and it branches back to ESCP.

In Chapter 15 we will explore a macro that facilitates the saving of a .MLB Macro Library file.

Simulating the F10 Quick Graph Key

Release 3 has added to the F10 function key a Quick Graph capability for instantly creating a graph based on the matrix in which the cell pointer currently resides.

While this feature has not been added to Release 2.2, another feature has: the /Graph Group option. This feature allows you to assign all of the graph data ranges (X and A through F) at once when the data are in consecutive columns or rows of a range.

To do this, use these steps:

1. Select /Graph Group.
2. Specify the group range you want to divide into graph data ranges.
3. Select Columnwise or Rowwise. Columnwise sets the first column of a range as the X data range and each succeeding column as the ranges A through F, while the Rowwise choice sets the first row of the range as the X data range and each succeeding row as the ranges A through F.

Not only is this an important improvement to the /Graph command sequence, but these features can be used in a macro to simulate the F10 Quick Graph feature available in Release 3. Refer to the macro in Figure 12.10.

A1: U [W10] '\Q   READY

F_12_10.WK1

Figure 12.10   Macro to Simulate the Quick Graph (F10) Key

To operate this macro, place your cell pointer in any cell of a range where the data you want to graph are in consecutive columns or rows and press Alt-Q.

{windowsoff}{paneloff}   Turns off the windows and panel to suppress screen flicker and speed up the macro.

{right}{if @cellpointer("type")="b"}{left}   Moves the cell pointer to the right. If the cell is blank, it is assumed that the starting column is the right-most edge of the range to graph, so the cell pointer is moved back again.

{left}{if @cellpointer("type")="b"}{right}{branch QDOWN}   In this same way, the cell pointer is moved to the left to determine whether the starting column is the left-most edge of the range to graph. If so, the cell pointer is moved back to the range and the macro branches to QDOWN.

{right}{end}{left}   Otherwise, the macro moves the cell pointer to the right and then End LeftArrow, to take it to the left-most edge of the range.

{down}{if @cellpointer("type")="b"}{up}   The cell pointer is moved down, and if the cell is blank, it is moved up again.

{up}{if @cellpointer("row")=1}{branch QJUMP}   The cell pointer is moved up and the macro checks for whether the current row is Row 1. If so, the macro branches to QJUMP.

{if @cellpointer("type")="b"}{down}{branch QJUMP}   If, by moving up one cell, the macro moves above the range to graph (assumed if the cell is blank), the cell pointer is moved back down and the macro branches to QJUMP.

{down}{end}{up}   Otherwise, the macro moves the cell pointer down, then End UpArrow, to take it to the top of the range to graph.

{right}   This is the beginning of the routine named QJUMP. The macro moves the cell pointer one column to the right on the assumption that the current column (left-most column of the range to graph) consists of labels.

{if @cellpointer("type")="l"}{down}{branch QLABEL}   This line is named QLABEL. Its purpose is to check for whether or not the cell contains a label. If so, the cell pointer is moved down, the macro loops back to the beginning of this line, the macro checks again for whether or not the cell contains a label, and so on, until it reaches a cell that is not a label.

{left}/gg{bs}.   At this point, the macro moves back to the left-most column, selects /Graph Group, then presses Backspace to free the cell pointer.

{down}{if @cellpointer("type")<>"b"}{branch QDOWN2}   This line is named QDOWN2. Its purpose is to paint down one row and check for whether or not the cell is blank. If not, the macro loops back to the beginning of this line, paints down another row, and so on until it reaches a blank cell.

{up}   Otherwise, if the cell is blank, the cell pointer reduces the highlighted area by moving back up one cell.

{right}{if @cellpointer("type")<>"b"}{branch QRIGHT}   This line is named QRIGHT. Its purpose is to paint to the right one column and check for whether or not the cell is blank. If not, the macro loops back to the beginning of this line, paints down another column, and so on, until it reaches a blank cell.

{left}{panelon}˜{get QKEY}   When a blank cell is reached, the cell pointer moves left, reducing the highlighted area by one column, the panel is turned back on, and the highlighted group of columns and rows to graph is entered by the tilde.

    At this point 1-2-3 automatically offers the menu choices Columnwise and Rowwise as previously described. The macro pauses for you to press R for Rowwise or RightArrow to point to the Rowwise choice. If you do not press R or RightArrow, it is assumed you pressed C for Columnwise or Return to select the Columnwise choice.

{if QKEY="{right}"}{r}{get QKEY}{esc}..{r}{up}˜rq{graph}{quit}   If you press the RightArrow key, the cursor moves to the right to point to Rowwise.

    Notice we have used {r} here instead of {right}. Actually, you can replace {left}, {up}, and {down} with {l}, {u}, and {d} as a regular practice if you like. In the interests of clarity, however, we have not generally adopted that convention in this book. We have made an exception here so that the entire line will be visible on the screen.

Since you have pressed RightArrow to point to the choice Rowwise, the macro pauses again for you to press the Return key, then escapes from this menu level, presses the Period key twice to reverse the free cursor point in the highlighted range you want to graph, unhighlights the range to the right one column, highlights it up one row, and enters the revised /Graph Group range. It then again selects Rowwise and Quit, and displays the graph. After you have viewed the graph and pressed Return, the macro quits.

{if QKEY="r"}{esc}..{right}{up}~rq{graph}{quit}   This line accomplishes the same thing as the last, except that it relies on your pressing R for Rowwise rather than pointing to the Rowwise choice by pressing the RightArrow key.

cq{graph}{quit}   Otherwise, it is assumed you want Columnwise graphing, so the macro simply selects Columnwise and Quit, displays the graph, then quits.

Summary

This chapter showed how the {get} command uses the syntax, **{get** *location*}, to pause until you press a single key, storing a copy of that keystroke in the cell address or named cell you have designated.

These techniques and concepts were covered as follows:

■ The {get} command can be used to allow a typed message in the upper control panel that will appear as a prompt. This is somewhat similar to the {getlabel} method of creating a user prompt, except that the message is actually typed, character by character, rather than appearing all at once, then eliminated by an {esc} command.

■ In Release 2.2 and 3, you can speed up the message prompt by having it appear in the upper panel as an Indicate message in place of the *READY* indicator. This is possible because Release 2.2 and 3 allow a longer Indicator message than the five-character limit of Release 2 and 2.01.

■ In Release 2.2 and 3, you can improve on use of the /Copy command to copy a label or value to the current cell. This is done by using the {let} command in the configuration

{let @cellpointer("address"),ical *location*}

Unfortunately, this ability to use @cellpointer as the first argument in a {let} command is not available in Release 2 or 2.01.

■ The {get} command can be used to create a special "action key" that will accomplish a pre-established action when you press it. We recommend the F8 Table key be used for this purpose because it is so rarely pressed by 1-2-3 users and can be considered the most available of function keys.

■ The {get} command can be used with an {if} command as in the command

{if @left(YKEY,1)="{"}{YKEY} to check for whether the type of key you have pressed is a letter/number key, or a function or directional key such as {edit}, {up}, {down}, {pgdn}, {end}, or {home}. If so, the macro processes that key with the subroutine call. This is a handy way of isolating the types of keys the macro will process.

■ The {get} command can be used in conjunction with a typed or {indicate} instruction to point to a location or highlight a range.

■ You can temporarily view any hidden columns by pressing /Copy or /Move. The columns will appear temporarily, with an asterisk that appears to the right of the column letter in the upper border. After the /Copy or /Move command is completed or interrupted, the hidden columns disappear again.

■ You can use any nonexistent command such as {VIEW}, or {TEMP}, or {APPLE-SAUCE}, to cause an error-message break in a macro, so long as no cells or ranges in the worksheet have been given that name. We suggest using {CTRL_BREAK} because, being nonexistent, it provides an effect similar to the effect you would get if you pressed Ctrl-Break during the macro's execution.

■ Since the {get} command can be used to capture a keystroke, you can pass every keystroke through a looping macro with a {get} command and several {if} commands to test and react to the type and nature of every key pressed.

■ The /Graph Group option in Release 2.2 allows you to assign all of the graph data ranges (X and A through F) at once when the data to be graphed are in consecutive columns or rows of a range, provided you select Columnwise or Rowwise graphing.

These macros using the {get} command were presented:

■ A macro to search and replace in a single column, prompting for whether you want to test for labels or values, then for whether to replace with labels or values.

■ A macro to update a year-to-date matrix, to be used in a worksheet where you have a spreadsheet with a column for the current month and a column for the year-to-date values, and you prefer not to show data relating to other months already past.

■ A Hide Columns Toggle to alternately prompt you through the hiding of one or more columns at once, or offer you the ability to instantly redisplay, or unhide, all hidden columns in your worksheet.

■ A macro to temporarily view hidden columns, both displaying and allowing changes to hidden columns without losing the characteristic that these columns are designated as hidden.

■ A Go-Return macro that allows you to relocate your cell pointer to a remote cell in your worksheet, keeping track of your last location so you can jump back instantly. This macro also remembers the remote location, so you can toggle back and forth between that location and your starting point with just two keystrokes.

■ A Word-Wrap macro that uses the bracketed question mark pause {?} in conjunction with the /Range Justify command to rejustify into paragraph form whatever you type in the upper panel.

■ A Word-Processing macro that uses the {get} command to capture every keystroke and evaluate it before adding it to the text you are typing. This allows more advanced features in your macro, including /Copy, /Move, /Worksheet Delete Row, /Worksheet Insert Row, and /Range Erase.

■ A macro to facilitate and speed up the process involved in pulling a Macro Library .MLB file into your current worksheet for editing.

■ A macro to simulate the Quick Graph (F10) key using the /Graph Group command sequence.

13

MANIPULATING STRINGS IN YOUR MACROS

Scope

In this chapter we will explore ways of using and manipulating strings in your macros to accomplish tasks based on variable input or conditions.

We will show how a macro can use string technology to display a variable message in the upper panel; center titles of variable length across the screen; display changing choice explanations in custom menus; use @cellpointer("address") with {let}, {contents}, and {blank} in Release 2 and 2.01; combine commands like /Range Unprotect with variable cell addresses; display an absolute cell address as a relative address; create range names that change based on the counter in a {for} loop; and calculate and display a relative cell location based on your current cell address.

Displaying the ASCII Code for a Keystroke

The macro in Figure 13.1 is a simple example of the use of a string in your macro to create a temporary and variable message in your upper panel. In this case the message consists of in-

A15: [W11]
The code for "A" is 65. Hit Enter.

```
            A              B           C       D       E       F
1   :                              *** ASCII CODE DISPLAY ***
2   \A             {}
3   *ASCII         Type any character to display its ASCII value:
4   :              {get AKEY}{esc}{recalc ACALC}
5   :              {if @left(AKEY,1)="{"}{quit}
6   :              {if AKEY="~"}{quit}
7   ACALC          The code for "A" is 65. Hit Enter.
8   :              {get AKEY}{esc}{quit}
9   AKEY           A
10
11
12  Cell B7:
13  +"The code for """&+AKEY&""" is "&@STRING(@CODE(AKEY),0)&". Hit Enter."
14
15
16
17
18
19
20
F_13-1.WK1                          CMD          CALC
```

Figure 13.1 Using String Programming to Display an ASCII Code

formation telling you the ASCII code that corresponds to the keystroke that you provide in response to a prompt.

Type any character to display its ASCII value: The macro begins by prompting you to type a single keystroke. Note this message shows in the upper panel because it is typed by the macro, not because the macro has instantly displayed it with a {getlabel} or {getnumber} command. This method avoids your having to press Return once you type the keystroke.

{get AKEY}{esc}{recalc ACALC}   Pauses for you to press a single key, then eliminates the typed message in the upper panel with the {esc} command, and recalculates the cell of the macro named ACALC.

{if @left(AKEY,1)="{"}{quit}   If you press a function key or directional key such as {edit}, {home}, {left}, or {pgdn}, the macro quits.

{if AKEY="~"}{quit}   Directs the macro to quit if you press Return. Without this command, the macro would enter the first half of the message in ACALC into the current cell.

The code for "A" is 65. Hit Enter.   This line will change depending on how you respond to the initial prompt. It is based on a variable string formula, broken down as:

+"The code for """&
+AKEY&

""" is **"&**
@STRING(@CODE(AKEY),0)&
". Hit Enter."

The first part of this string includes three quotation marks. These allow the display of open-ing quotation marks before the letter **A** in the example in cell B7 in Figure 13.1. The +AKEY portion of the string returns your response to the opening prompt, stored in AKEY. The third part begins with three quotation marks, which allow the display of closing quotation marks before the letter **A** in B7. The next part returns the string version of the code that corresponds to the character in AKEY, and the last part consists of a period and the instruction to **Hit Enter.**

{get AKEY}{esc}{quit}   The last {get} command is included purely as a method of caus-ing the macro to pause so you can read the message typed into the upper panel. When you press any key, the {esc} command eliminates the message and the macro quits.

Centering a Title Across the Screen

The macro in Figure 13.2 shows how you can use string techniques to add functionality to the {let} command.

If you have Release 2 or 2.01, you will find that the {let} command will not accept an @function as its first argument. Thus, a macro with the command **{let @cellpointer ("address"),999}**, which you might expect to place the value 999 in the current cell, will

```
B5: +"{let "&@CELLPOINTER("address")&",@repeat("" "",(72-@length(CTR))/2)&CTR}~"
+"{let "&@CELLPOINTER("address")&",@repeat("" "",(72-@length(CTR))/2)&CTR}~"
```

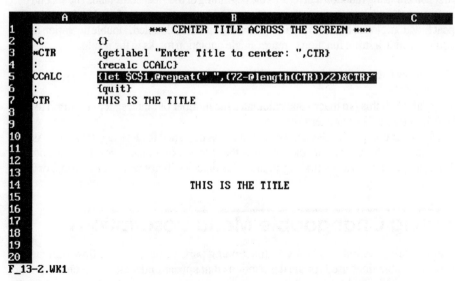

```
          A              B                          C
1    :            *** CENTER TITLE ACROSS THE SCREEN ***
2    \C           {}
3    *CTR         {getlabel "Enter Title to center: ",CTR}
4    :            {recalc CCALC}
5    CCALC        {let $C$1,@repeat(" ",(72-@length(CTR))/2)&CTR}~
6    :            {quit}
7    CTR          THIS IS THE TITLE
8
9
10
11
12
13
14                    THIS IS THE TITLE
15
16
17
18
19
20
F_13-2.WK1
```

Figure 13.2 A Macro to Center a Title across the Screen

stop at this command, beep, and give you the error message *Invalid range in LET*. This deficiency was noted by Lotus and corrected in Release 2.2 and 3.

Fortunately, those of you with an earlier release of 1-2-3 can work around this problem by using @cellpointer("address") in an underlying string formula so the formula displays a {let} command with the actual address of the current cell. Thus, if your current cell is B27, you can create a string formula:

+"{let "&@cellpointer("address")&",999}"

which will be displayed in your macro as this:

{let B27,999}

The macro in Figure 13.2 uses this technique in a {let} command to center a title across your screen. To operate the macro, place your cell pointer in the left-most column on the screen and press Alt-C.

{getlabel "Enter Title to center: ",CTR}   Prompts you for the title you want to center, placing your response in CTR.

{recalc CCALC}   Because the next line named CCALC is a string formula using information you just stored in CTR, it must be recalculated before being processed.

{let $B$5,@repeat(" ",(72-@length(CTR))/2)&CTR)~   Although this {let} command has as its first argument a cell address, it is based on an underlying string formula which is best understood in its three component parts:

+"{let "&
@cellpointer("address")&
",@repeat"" "",(72- @length(CTR))/2)&CTR~)"

The first part is a string function that returns the beginning of the {let} command. The second part is the current cell address, whatever that might be. The last part is a string function that returns an @repeat function. Notice how the internal quotation marks are doubled. Double quotation marks are required within a string function to return single quotation marks in the results.

{quit}   The last active line of the macro is a {quit} command.

The result of all this is a macro that calculates the number of blank spaces required to center the title across a 72-character field.

Figure 13.3 accomplishes the same task, but it was designed for Release 2.2 and 3. As you can see in the third line of the macro, the {let} command uses the @function, @cellpointer("address") as its first argument. This macro will not work in Release 2 or 2.01.

Creating Changeable Menu Descriptions

You can use string formulas not only as functioning parts of the program flow of a macro, but also as variable lines used for the descriptions that appear under custom menus.

The macro in Figure 13.4 provides an example of this technique. Its purpose is to facilitate the storage and repeated entering of a word or phrase.

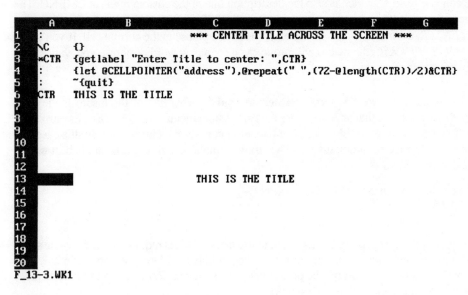

```
A13: [W6] '                    THIS IS THE TITLE                    READY

        A       B           C           D       E           F       G
1   :                   *** CENTER TITLE ACROSS THE SCREEN ***
2   \C      {}
3   *CTR    {getlabel "Enter Title to center: ",CTR}
4   :       {let @CELLPOINTER("address"),@repeat(" ",(72-@length(CTR))/2)&CTR}
5   :       ~{quit}
6   CTR     THIS IS THE TITLE
7
8
9
10
11
12
13                              THIS IS THE TITLE
14
15
16
17
18
19
20
F_13-3.WK1
```

Figure 13.3 A Macro to Center a Title in Release 2.2 or 3

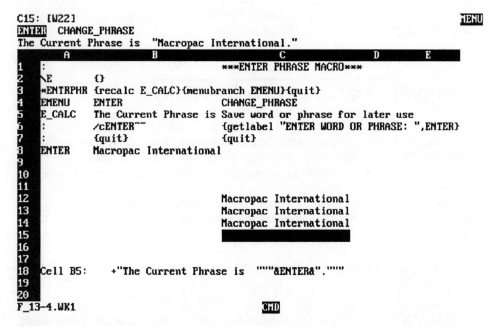

```
C15: [W22]                                                  MENU
ENTER   CHANGE_PHRASE
The Current Phrase is   "Macropac International."
        A               B                   C               D           E
1   :                           ***ENTER PHRASE MACRO***
2   \E      {}
3   *ENTRPHR {recalc E_CALC}{menubranch EMENU}{quit}
4   EMENU   ENTER                   CHANGE_PHRASE
5   E_CALC  The Current Phrase is   Save word or phrase for later use
6   :       /cENTER~~              {getlabel "ENTER WORD OR PHRASE: ",ENTER}
7   :       {quit}                 {quit}
8   ENTER   Macropac International
9
10
11
12                              Macropac International
13                              Macropac International
14                              Macropac International
15
16
17
18  Cell B5:    +"The Current Phrase is   """"&ENTER&"."""""
19
20
F_13-4.WK1                          CMD
```

Figure 13.4 A Macro for Instantly Entering a Word or Phrase

{recalc E_CALC}{menubranch EMENU}{quit}   The macro begins by recalculating the cell at E_CALC, which is also the description line of the custom menu at EMENU. The macro then calls up the custom menu choices, *ENTER* and *CHANGE_PHRASE*. If you select *ENTER*, the macro will instantly enter the stored phrase in the current cell. If you select *CHANGE_PHRASE*, the macro will prompt you for a new word of phrase you want stored for later use in the macro.

The Current Phrase is "Macropac International."   This line of the macro is the variable description line that appears under the first custom menu choice *ENTER*. Its purpose is to show you the word or phrase you are about to enter in the current cell. In this case, the phrase is "Macropac International." The string formula underlying this line is best understood broken down as:

+"The Current Phrase is""""&
ENTER&
"."""

Notice how the first part ends in three quotation marks. This is required to display one set of opening quotation marks preceding the displayed phrase "Macropac International". The second part, of course, returns the phrase you have stored at *ENTER*. The last part displays as a Period (.) and closing quotation marks.

/cENTER~~   If you select the *ENTER* menu choice, the contents of the cell named ENTER are copied to the current cell.

{quit}   At this point, the macro quits. If you decide you want a different phrase stored in the macro, press Alt-E again, select *CHANGE_PHRASE*, and respond as required to the {getlabel} prompt.

Changing the Case of a Cell Entry

The macro in Figure 13.5 is another example of the use of strings to work around the problem that the @cellpointer function cannot be used in a {let} command in Release 2 and 2.01. In this case, the macro uses string technology to substitute for use of @cellpointer("address") as the first argument in the {let} commands, and @cellpointer("contents") as the second argument.

  The purpose of the macro is to allow you to change the label in a cell to uppercase, lowercase, or proper case. To operate the macro, place your cell pointer on any cell you want to change and press Alt-A.

{menubranch A_MENU}{quit}   The macro begins by calling the menu choices *UPPER*, *LOWER*, and *PROPER*.

{recalc ACALC}   The three menu choices begin in the same way, by recalculating ACALC, ACALC2, or ACALC3.

```
B8: +"{let "&@CELLPOINTER("address")&","&@UPPER(@CELLPOINTER("contents"))&"}"{qu
"{let "&@CELLPOINTER("address")&","&@UPPER(@CELLPOINTER("contents"))&"}"{quit}"
```

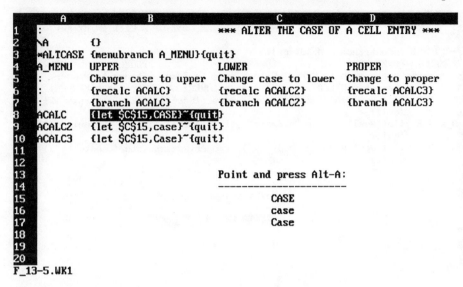

```
              A            B                      C                 D
 1   :                            *** ALTER THE CASE OF A CELL ENTRY ***
 2  \A           {}
 3  *ALTCASE {menubranch A_MENU}{quit}
 4  A_MENU    UPPER                 LOWER               PROPER
 5   :        Change case to upper  Change case to lower  Change to proper
 6   :        {recalc ACALC}        {recalc ACALC2}       {recalc ACALC3}
 7   :        {branch ACALC}        {branch ACALC2}       {branch ACALC3}
 8  ACALC     {let $C$15,CASE}~{quit}
 9  ACALC2    {let $C$15,case}~{quit}
10  ACALC3    {let $C$15,Case}~{quit}
11
12
13                              Point and press Alt-A:
14                              -----------------------
15                                       CASE
16                                       case
17                                       Case
18
19
20
F_13-5.WK1
```

Figure 13.5 A Macro to Alter the Case of a Cell Entry

{branch ACALC} Strictly speaking, this command under the UPPER choice could have been a null string { } pass-through command. It is written in the same way as the branching commands under the *LOWER* and *PROPER* choices for clarity only.

{let $C$15,CASE)~{quit} This is the result of a string formula that is best understood broken down as:

```
+"{let "&
@cellpointer("address")&
","&
@upper(@cellpointer("contents"))&
)~{quit}"
```

By now you will have no trouble deciphering the components of this string formula. The string formulas in ACALC2 and ACALC3 are almost identical, except that the @function applied to the @cellpointer("contents") component is changed to @lower and @proper, respectively.

If you refer now to Figure 13.6, you will see how this same macro would be written for Release 2.2 or 3. Instead of having string formulas that must be recalculated before they are used by the macro, this example shows how you can use @cellpointer("address") and @cellpointer("contents") directly in the {let} commands for each menu choice.

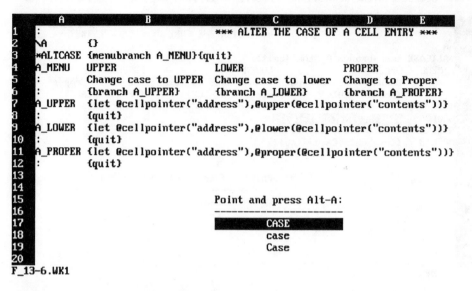

F_13-6.WK1

Figure 13.6　A Macro to Change Case in Release 2.2 and 3

Displaying the Difference Between Two Dates

The macro in Figure 13.7 is an example of the use of string formulas to display a variable message in the upper panel. As you will see, the second of the two string formulas in this macro performs calculations based on your input before displaying the results.

Here's how the macro works.

{getlabel "Type 1st date (m/dd/yy) or Return for Today: ",SUB1}　Prompts for the first date in the configuration m/dd/yy. For example, you may type **3/5/88**. Alternately, you can press Return for today's date. Your response is stored in SUB1.

{if SUB1=""}{recalc S_NOW}{let SUB1,S_NOW}　If you press Return instead of entering a date at the prompt, it will cause SUB1 to be blank. In that event, the macro is designed to recalculate S_NOW to reflect today's date in the same m/dd/yy format, then copy today's date to SUB1.

{getlabel "Type 2nd date (m/dd/yy) or Return for Today: ",SUB2}　Prompts for the second date in the configuration m/dd/yy or you can press Return for today's date. Your response is stored in SUB2.

{if SUB2=""}{recalc S_NOW}{let SUB2,S_NOW}　As before, if you press Return, S_NOW is recalculated to reflect today's date in the same m/dd/yy format, then copied to SUB2.

```
B11: U [W20] @STRING(@MONTH(@NOW),0)&"/"&@STRING(@DAY(@NOW),0)&"/"&@STRING( EDIT
@STRING(@MONTH(@NOW),0)&"/"&@STRING(@DAY(@NOW),0)&"/"&@STRING(@YEAR(@NOW),0)
```

```
         A              B              C      D       E       F
1    :                         *** SUBTRACTED DATE DIFFERENCE ***
2   \S            {}
3   *SUBDATE      {getlabel "Type 1st date (m/dd/yy) or Return for Today: ",SUB1}
4    :            {if SUB1=""}{recalc S_NOW}{let SUB1,S_NOW}
5    :            {getlabel "Type 2nd date (m/dd/yy) or Return for Today: ",SUB2}
6    :            {if SUB2=""}{recalc S_NOW}{let SUB2,S_NOW}
7    :            {recalc S_MSG}{recalc S_CALC}
8   S_MSG         The number of days between 3/5/88 and 3/8/88 is
9   S_CALC         3. Press Return.
10   :            {get S_KEY}{esc}{quit}
11  S_NOW         1/3/90
12  SUB1          3/5/88
13  SUB2          3/8/88
14  S_KEY         ~
15
16  Cell B8 named S_MSG:
17  +"The number of days between "&SUB1&" and "&SUB2&" is"
18
19  Cell B9 named S_CALC:
20  +" "&string(@abs(@datevalue(SUB1)-@datevalue(SUB2)),0)&". Press Return"
F_13-7.WK1
```

Figure 13.7 A Macro to Show the Number of Days Between Two Dates

{recalc S_MSG}{recalc S_CALC}   Recalculates the string formulas in S_MSG and S_CALC.

The number of days between 3/5/88 and 3/8/88 is   This line is the displayed result of the string formula in S_MSG, and consists of:

+"The number of days between "&
SUB1&
" and "&
SUB2&
" is"

The macro will type this, the beginning of the entire message, in the upper panel.

3. Hit Return.   This is the rest of the message that the macro types. Although the display is short, it consists of:

+" "&
@string(@abs(@datevalue(SUB1)- @datevalue(SUB2)),0)&
". Press Return."

By calculating the absolute of the difference between the date value of SUB1 and the date value of SUB2, the macro comes up with a positive number representing the number of days between the two dates.

{get S_KEY}{esc}{quit}   The macro pauses for your press of any key. Whatever key you press, the {esc} command eliminates the message typed in the upper panel, and the macro quits.

1/3/90   The date in cell B11 named S_NOW will change based on the date you use this macro. Note however, the underlying formula shown for this date. You can see it in the upper panel in Figure 13.7. This formula consists of the parts:

@string(@month(@now),0)&
"/"&
@string(@day(@now),0)&
"/"&
@string(*@year(@now),0)

and is required to display today's date in the same way the dates in SUB1 and SUB2 are displayed; or in other words, in the m/dd/yy format. Done this way, the strings in S_MSG and S_CALC will be able to use today's date in SUB1 or SUB2 without the necessity for other complicated versions of the message strings.

The result of running this macro will be a message in the upper panel that looks something like this:

The number of days between 3/5/88 and 3/8/88 is 3 days. Press Return.

This macro can be used anywhere in the spreadsheet. To cause the message to disappear, simply press the Return key.

Changing Values to Label-Numbers

The macro in Figure 13.8 is actually a companion macro to the macro in Figure 11.11. While the macro in Figure 11.11 was designed to change label-numbers to values, this macro does the reverse, changing values to label-numbers, while retaining the displayed format.

This macro is also an interesting example of the use of a string formula to get around the problem that you cannot use @cellpointer("address") as an argument in the {contents} command.

Here's how the macro works.

{windowsoff}{paneloff}   Turns off the windows and panel to suppress screen flicker and speed up the macro.

/rncCOL TO CHANGE?~~/rndCOL TO CHANGE?~   Creates, then deletes, the range name COL TO CHANGE? designed as a prompt to the user.

/rnc{panelon}COL TO CHANGE?~{windowson}{?}~   Again creates the prompting range name COL TO CHANGE?, turns on the windows, and pauses for your highlighting of the column you want to convert from values to number-labels.

{for L_COUNT,1,@rows(COL TO CHANGE?),1,LLOOP}   This {for} command

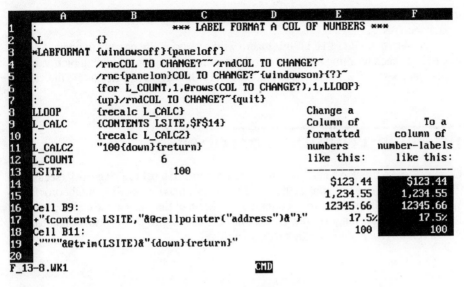

```
F14: [W13] "$123.44                                                POINT
          COL TO CHANGE?              Enter range: F18..F14

          A          B          C          D          E          F
1  :                       *** LABEL FORMAT A COL OF NUMBERS ***
2  \L         {}
3  *LABFORMAT {windowsoff}{paneloff}
4  :          /rncCOL TO CHANGE?~~/rndCOL TO CHANGE?~
5  :          /rnc{panelon}COL TO CHANGE?~{windowson}{?}~
6  :          {for L_COUNT,1,@rows(COL TO CHANGE?),1,LLOOP}
7  :          {up}/rndCOL TO CHANGE?~{quit}
8  LLOOP      {recalc L_CALC}                    Change a
9  L_CALC     {CONTENTS LSITE,$F$14}             Column of          To a
10 :          {recalc L_CALC2}                   formatted       column of
11 L_CALC2    "100{down}{return}                 numbers      number-labels
12 L_COUNT             6                         like this:      like this:
13 LSITE              100                        ---------------------------
14                                                    $123.44         $123.44
15                                                   1,234.55        1,234.55
16 Cell B9:                                         12345.66        12345.66
17 +"{contents LSITE,"&@cellpointer("address")&"}"    17.5%           17.5%
18 Cell B11:                                             100             100
19 +""""&@trim(LSITE)&"{down}{return}"
20
F_13-8.WK1                          CMD
```

Figure 13.8 Macro to Change Values to Label-Numbers with Formats

counts at L_COUNT, starting at the number 1, counting up to the number of rows in COL TO CHANGE?, counting by ones, and for each increment runs the routine at LLOOP.

{up}/rndCOL TO CHANGE?~{quit}   At the end of the {for} command, the cell pointer (which by this time is one cell below the last entry in the column) is moved up one cell, the range name COL TO CHANGE? is deleted, and the macro quits.

{recalc L_CALC}   This is the beginning of the routine at LLOOP that the macro runs in its {for} loop as many times as there are rows in the column to change.

{CONTENTS LSITE,$F$14}   This is the displayed result of a string formula, consisting of:

+"{contents LSITE,"&
@cellpointer("address")&
"}"

It is designed to place in LSITE a label copy of the contents of the current cell, including format identifiers, if any, such as dollar signs, commas, percentage signs, and so on.

{recalc L_CALC2}   Recalculates the string formula in L_CALC2.

"100{down}{return}   This is the displayed result of a string formula, consisting of:

+""""&

@trim(LSITE)&
"{down}{return}"

A string formula is required for this line because LSITE is variable, depending on the current cell pointer contents.

Like the macro in Figure 11.11, this macro works surprisingly quickly to convert values to labels. Note each resulting label in the column is entered beginning with quotation marks instead of an apostrophe. This ensures that the label will be right justified as are the values.

Underlining Numbers or Labels

In Chapter 9, we presented a macro to underline a number or label in a single cell (see Figure 9.16). In this section we will look at the use of string formulas to underline numbers or labels using either the width of the current column or the width of the entry in the cell above as the criteria to establish the length of line to use. The macro in Figure 13.9 is also designed to underline an entire row of entries rather than a single cell.

```
            A                B                            C         D          E
1    :                   *** UNDERLINE NUMBERS OR LABELS ***
2    \U              {}
3    *UNDERLN  {getlabel "Enter symbol for underline: ",UNDER}
4    :              {windowsoff}{paneloff}
5    :              /rncPUT LINE WHERE?~~/rndPUT LINE WHERE?~
6    :              /rnc{panelon}{windowson}PUT LINE WHERE?~{?}~
7    :              {let UCOLS,@cols(PUT LINE WHERE?)}
8    :              {menubranch UMENU}{quit}
9    UMENU    Columnwidth                      Wordwidth
10   :              Underline columnwidth - 1.   Underline width of word above.
11   :              {windowsoff}{paneloff}       {windowsoff}{paneloff}
12   :              {goto}PUT LINE WHERE?~        {goto}PUT LINE WHERE?~
13   :              {for UCOUNT,1,UCOLS,1,U_COL}  {for UCOUNT,1,UCOLS,1,U_WORD}
14   :              {left}{end}{left}            {left}{end}{left}
15   :              /rndPUT LINE WHERE?~{quit}    /rndPUT LINE WHERE?~{quit}
16   U_COL    @repeat("{UNDER}",@cellpointer("width")-1)
17   :              {edit}{calc}{home}^^{right}{return}
18   U_WORD   {up}{recalc UCALC}
19   UCALC    {contents UPGO,$A$1}
20   :              {if @cellpointer("type")="v"}{down}+""""&{branch U_VALUE}
21   :              {down}@CELL("prefix",{up})&
22   U_VALUE  @repeat(UNDER,@length(@trim(UPGO))){calc}~
23   :              {right}{return}
24   UPGO         AAA
25   UNDER      -
26   UCOLS                                     4
27   UCOUNT                                    5
28
29
30   Cell B19:
31            +"{contents UPGO,"&@CELLPOINTER("address")&"}"

F_13_9
```

Figure 13.9 A Macro to Underline Numbers or Labels in a Row

Like the macro to change values to labels in Figure 13.8, this macro uses string techniques to allow the use of @cellpointer("address") with the {contents} command.

{getlabel "Enter symbol for underline: ",UNDER}   The macro begins by prompting you for the symbol you want to use in underlining your row of entries. You might use the dash symbol (-), for example, or the equal sign (=). Your response is stored in the cell named UNDER.

{windowsoff}{paneloff}   Turns off the windows and panel to suppress screen flicker and speed up the macro.

/rncPUT LINE WHERE?~~/rndPUT LINE WHERE?~   Creates, then deletes, the range name PUT LINE WHERE? designed as a prompt to the user.

/rnc{panelon}{windowson}PUT LINE WHERE?~{?}~   Again creates the prompting range name PUT LINE WHERE?, turns on the windows, and pauses for your highlighting of the row where you want your underlining to appear.

{let UCOLS,@cols(PUT LINE WHERE?)}   Calculates the number of columns in the row you highlighted, storing that number in the cell named UCOLS.

{menubranch UMENU}{quit}   Calls up the menu choices *Columnwidth* and *Wordwidth*. Select *Columnwidth* to create an underline that has a length one character less than the width of its column. Select *Wordwidth* to create an underline matching the length of the label or number (including formatting details) in the cell above.

{goto}PUT LINE WHERE?   Whether you select *Columnwidth* or *Wordwidth*, the macro moves the cell pointer to the first cell of the row you have highlighted in response to the prompt *PUT LINE WHERE?*

{for UCOUNT,1,UCOLS,1,U_COL} or **{for UCOUNT,1,UCOLS,1,U_WORD}**
This {for} command counts at UCOUNT, starting at the number 1, counting up to the number in UCOLS, counting by ones, and for each increment runs the routine at U_COL if you selected *Columnwidth* or U_WORD if you selected *Wordwidth*.

{left}{end}{left}   Moves the cell pointer (which, after the {for} command, will be one cell beyond the end of the row) to the left one cell. The macro then moves End LeftArrow to the first underlining cell in the row.

/rndPUT LINE WHERE?~{quit}   Finally, the range name PUT LINE WHERE? is deleted and the macro quits.

@repeat("{under}",@cellpointer("width")-1)   This is the beginning of the routine at U_COL where the {for} command loops if you select *Columnwidth*. Its purpose is to repeat the symbol in the cell named UNDER the number of times equal to the cell pointer width less one.

{edit}{calc}{home}^~{right}{return}   The @repeat function is converted to a straight entry, a centering caret is placed at the front of the entry, the cell pointer is moved to the right to underline the next cell in the row, and the macro returns to the {for} loop to start over again at U_COL.

{up}{recalc UCALC}   If you selected WORDWIDTH, the {for} loop sends the macro here, where the cell pointer is moved up one cell and the string formula in UCALC is recalculated.

{contents UPGO,$B$34}   This is a display of the string in UCALC, which can be broken down as:

```
+"{contents UPGO,"&
@cellpointer("address")&
"}"
```

This line of the macro causes the displayed contents of the cell above the underlining cell, including format characteristics if the entry is a value, to be copied to UPGO.

{if @cellpointer("type")="v"}{down}+""""&{branch U_VALUE}   If the cell above the underlining cell is a value, the cell pointer is moved back down, the entry +""""& is typed so the final underlining formula will create an underlining entry that starts with right-justifying quotation marks, and the macro branches to U_VALUE, where it continues typing the underlining string formula.

{down}@CELL("prefix",{up})&   Otherwise, the macro moves down and begins typing a string formula that uses the same prefix as the cell above.

@repeatUNDER,@length(@trim(UPGO))){calc}~   Whether the prefix consists of quotation marks or a different prefix matching the cell above, the macro continues typing the underlining string formula, then presses the F9 Calc key to turn the string formula to a straight entry.

{right}{return}   The cell pointer is moved to the right one cell, and the flow of control returns to the {for} loop in cell C13.

Creating a Custom Help Screen

With the advent of Release 2.2 and 3 came the ability to capture the pressing of the F1 Help key using the {get} command. This new feature is especially useful for creating custom Help screens for your users, but you can also accomplish the equivalent feat by simply capturing another of the function keys—preferably one that is little used, like the F8 Table key.

The macro in Figure 13.10 makes use of this technique to allow your users to jump to a custom Help screen by pressing the F8 key. It also calculates the address of the upper left

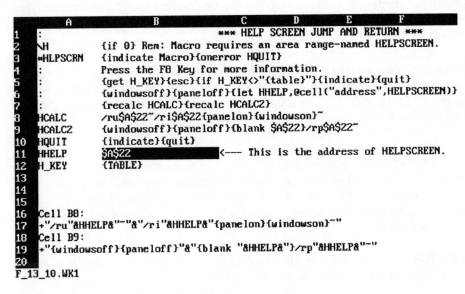

Figure 13.10 Macro to Jump to Help Screen and Return

corner of the Help screen and uses that information in strings to limit the user's ability to move around (and potentially damage) the contents of the Help screen.

{if 0} Rem: Macro requires an area range-named HELPSCREEN.   This is an interesting use of the {if} command to permit a non-operational line to be inserted in the beginning of your macro. Since any false statement in an {if} command causes the macro to skip the rest of the line and continue in the line below, starting a line with {if 0}—which is the equivalent of {if @false}—allows you to create a remark like this one giving instructions that this macro requires a range-named HELPSCREEN before it will work. As a macro code, this line will have no effect whatever on the operation of your macro.

{indicate Macro}{onerror HQUIT}   In Release 2.2 or 3, the {indicate} prompt can be quite a bit longer, as:

> **{indicate "Press the F8 key for more information"}**

which would also obviate the need for the next line shown here. In any case, the {onerror} command is important in case the user presses Ctrl-Break. Without this {onerror} command, the Indicator prompt will be left on the screen; but with it, the {indicate} command at HQUIT returns the prompt to normal.

Press the F8 Key for more information.   This message is typed in the upper panel. In Release 2.2 or 3, of course, this message can rely on the more intuitive instruction to press the F1 Help key. In that case, the {if} statement in the next line would read:

> **{if H_KEY<>"{help}"}**

{get H_KEY}{esc}{if H_KEY<>"{table}"}{indicate}{quit}   The macro pauses for you
to press the F8 Table key. After you press any key, the {esc} command eliminates the typed
prompt. If you press any key other than F8, the {indicate} command returns the *READY* indicator to normal and the macro quits.

{windowsoff}{paneloff}{let HHELP,@cell("address",HELPSCREEN)}   Turns off the
windows and panel to suppress screen flicker and speed up the macro, then causes the contents of HHELP to reflect the cell address of the upper left corner of the range you have
named HELPSCREEN.

If you are wondering why we have not simply inserted the formula **@cell
("address",HELPSCREEN)** in HHELP, it is because such a formula will not be accepted
by Release 2, 2.01, or 2.2 until the range name HELPSCREEN exists. Using a {let} command in the macro itself allows you to type in the macro (and transfer it from worksheet file
to worksheet file) without having to concern yourself beforehand whether HELPSCREEN
exists in the worksheet.

{recalc HCALC}{recalc HCALC2}   Recalculates the string formulas in the following
two lines of the macro named HCALC and HCALC2.

/ru$A$22~/ri$A$22{panelon}{windowson}~   This is a display of the string formula in
cell B8 named HCALC, that can be broken down as:

+"/ru"&
HHELP&
"~"&
"/ri"&
HHELP&
"{panelon}{windowson}~"

Its purpose is to unprotect the cell in the upper left corner of the range named
HELPSCREEN, then select /Range Input to limit the movement of the cell pointer to this
cell, which should be the sole unprotected cell in HELPSCREEN.

{windowsoff}{paneloff}{blank $A$22}/rp$A$22~   This is the display of the string formula in B9 named HCALC2, consisting of:

+"{windowsoff}{paneloff}"&
"{blank "&
HHELP&
"}/rp"&
HHELP&
"~"

Once you press Return, the windows and panel are turned off again, the upper left corner
of HELPSCREEN is blanked in case your user made an entry there in error, and the cell is
protected again with /Range Protect.

{indicate}{quit}   Finally, the macro returns the *READY* indicator to normal, then quits.

Creating a Sum-and-Stay Macro

Here's a common annoyance you may have encountered. You want to sum several individual cells, so you press the Plus sign (+), point to a cell, then press Plus (+) again, but the cell pointer jumps back to your starting point. If the second cell you want to sum is beyond the first, you find yourself repeating movement keystrokes unnecessarily as your cell pointer is jumped back to your starting point at each press of the Plus (+) sign.

The macro in Figure 13.11 is designed to eliminate this problem. To operate the macro, place the cell pointer at the place where you want the sum to reside, press Alt-S and respond to the menu choices +, -, *EDIT*, and *FINISH* by selecting the Plus (+). Respond to the prompt, *Enter address to go to* by pointing to the first cell to include in the sum. When you press Return, the cell pointer will temporarily jump to the original location, but when you select the Plus (+) again from the custom menu, it jumps back to the first cell to sum and prompts you from there to *Enter address to go to*.

/re~{let S_HERE,@cellpointer("address")}~   The macro begins by erasing the current cell, then stores the current cell address in S_HERE.

{let STAY,S_HERE}{menubranch SMENU}{quit}   Copies the current cell address in S_HERE to the cell named STAY, then offers the menu choices +, -, *EDIT*, and *FINISH*.

{goto}{STAY}~{goto}{?}~   Since your cell pointer is already at the address in STAY during the first pass through this line of the macro, the command {goto}{STAY}~ has no effect this time through. The second part, {goto}{?}~, prompts you for the location of the first cell you want in your sum formula.

{recalc STAY2}   Recalculates the formula in STAY2, which returns the relative form of the absolute address in STAY. The underlying formula in STAY2 can be broken down as:

@mid(STAY,1,@find("$",STAY,1)-1)&
@mid(STAY,@find("$",STAY,1)+1,4)

The first part of this formula uses @mid to isolate the column letters from the absolute address in STAY by extracting the number of characters between the first offset (second character) and the number of the offset position of the second dollar sign ($) in the absolute address less one.

The second part of the formula uses @mid to isolate the row number from the absolute address in STAY by extracting the number from the number of the offset position of the second dollar sign ($) in the absolute address plus one, to a position up to a maximum of four characters beyond that point.

Note: You may want to make a note of this formula for use in other cases when you need to display absolute cell addresses (such as $B$27) in their relative forms (such as B27).

	A	B	C	D	E
1	:		*** SUM & STAY MACRO ***		
2	\S	{}			
3	'SUMSTAY	/re^{let S_HERE,@cellpointer("address")}^			
4	:	{let STAY,S_HERE}{menubranch SMENU}{quit}			
5	SMENU	+	-	EDIT	FINISH
6	:	Press PLUS [+] to Sum-and-Stay	Press MINUS [-] to Subtract & Stay	Edit the formula	End the Formula
7	:	{goto}{STAY}^{goto}{?}^	{goto}{STAY}^{goto}{?}^	{edit}{?}^	{up @min(@cellpointer("row")-1,5)}
8	:	{let STAY,@cellpointer("address")}	{let STAY,@cellpointer("address")}	{menubranch SMENU}	{left @min(@cellpointer("col")-1,3)}
9	:	{recalc STAY2}	{recalc STAY2}	{quit}	{goto}{S_HERE}^{quit}
10	:	{goto}{S_HERE}^{edit}+{STAY2}^	{goto}{S_HERE}^{edit}-{STAY2}^		
11		{menubranch SMENU}{quit}	{menubranch SMENU}{quit}		
12	S_HERE	$B$183			
13	:	{return}			
14	STAY	$B$177			
15	:	{return}			
16	STAY2	B177			
17	:	{return}			
18					
19	Cell B19:				
20	@mid(STAY,1,@find("$",STAY,1)-1)&@mid(STAY,@find("$",STAY,1)+1,4)`				
21					

F_13_11.WK1

Figure 13.11   A Summing Macro with a Sum-and-Stay Feature

E20:   READY

```
           A          B         C         D         E         F         G
                     JAN       FEB       MAR      TOTAL
1
2  Chairs            395       286       300       981
3  Sofas             130       247       767      1144
4  Couches           498       128       346       972
5
6     Subtotal                                     3097
7
8  Lights            331       835        43      1209
9  Lamps             904       498       921      2323
10 Fixtures           50       449       778      1277
11
12    Subtotal                                     4809
13
14 Rugs              380       989       452      1821
15 Carpet            682       181       661      1524
16 Flooring          297       831       382      1510
17
18    Subtotal                                     4855
19
20           Total Furniture Items Sold:  ██████████
```
F_13_12.WK1

Figure 13.12 An Example to Use with the Sum-and-Stay Macro

{goto}{S_HERE}~{edit}+{STAY2}~ Moves the cell pointer back to the original cell, switches to Edit mode, types the Plus (+) sign, and then types the address in STAY2.

{menubranch SMENU}{quit} Once again calls up the menu choices +, -, *EDIT*, and *FINISH*. When you select the Plus (+) choice this time, however, the first thing the macro does is to jump back to the last cell you indicated you wanted to add, thus saving the key-strokes you would normally have to press to return to that point.

If you select the Minus (-) choice, the macro operates in exactly the same way, except that it subtracts the cell you point to instead of adding it.

If you select *EDIT*, the macro processes the command **{edit}{?}** and then branches back to the menu choices +, -, *EDIT*, and *FINISH* again.

If you select FINISH, the macro uses @min with @cellpointer("row") and @cellpointer("col") to adjust the original cell more towards the center of the screen, then moves back to that cell and quits.

Figure 13.12 shows an example of the type of spreadsheet where this macro might come in handy. If you want a total of all the furniture items sold to be displayed at cell E20, place your cell pointer at E20, press Alt-S, select the Plus (+) sign, point to E18, select the Plus (+) sign again and point to E12, select the Plus (+) sign again and point to E6, then select *FINISH*. You will see the formula +E18+E12+E6 appear in cell E20, all done with a mini-mum of pointer keystrokes.

Summing a Series of Ranges

The macro in Figure 13.13 is similar to the Sum and Stay macro, except that it is designed to sum a series of ranges rather than a series of individual cells. The result will be a formula such as @sum(C43..C46,C39..C41,C33..C37), for example.

```
                A               B               C       D       E       F
 1     :                               *** RANGES SUMMED ***
 2     \R              {}
 3     *RANGESUM {let R_HERE,@cellpointer("address")}
 4     :               {windowsoff}{paneloff}/rncAREA_1 TO SUM~~/rndAREA_1 TO SUM~
 5     :               /rnc{panelon}AREA_1 TO SUM~{bs}{windowson}{?}~
 6     :               {let R_SUM,"@sum(AREA_1 TO SUM"}{goto}AREA_1 TO SUM~
 7     :               {for RCOUNT,2,20,1,R_LOOP}
 8     :
 9     RFINAL          {goto}{R_HERE}~
10     R_SUM           @sum(AREA_1 TO SUM,AREA_2 TO SUM,AREA_3 TO SUM
11     :               )~{windowsoff}{paneloff}{for RCOUNT2,1,RCOUNT-1,1,R_LOOP2}{quit}
12     :
13     R_LOOP          {recalc RCALC}{windowsoff}{paneloff}
14     RCALC           /rnc{panelon}AREA_4 TO SUM~{bs}{windowson}{?}~
15     :               {recalc RCALC2}
16     RCALC2          {goto}AREA_4 TO SUM~{onerror RFINAL}{recalc RCALC3}
17     RCALC3          {let R_SUM,+R_SUM&",AREA_4 TO SUM"}{return}
18     :
19     R_LOOP2         {recalc RCALC4}
20     RCALC4          /rndAREA_4 TO SUM~{return}
21     R_HERE          $C$40
22     RCOUNT                          4
23     RCOUNT2                         4
24
25     Cell B13:
26     +"/rnc{panelon}AREA_"&@string(RCOUNT,0)&" TO SUM~{bs}{windowson}{?}~"
27     Cell B15:
28     +"{goto}AREA_"&@string(RCOUNT,0)&" TO SUM~{onerror RFINAL}{recalc RCALC3}"
29     Cell B16:
30     +"{let R_SUM,+R_SUM&"",AREA_"&@string(RCOUNT,0)&" TO SUM""}{return}"
31     Cell B19:
32     +"/rndAREA_"&@string(RCOUNT2,0)&" TO SUM~{return}"
33
```

F_13_13.WK1

Figure 13.13 A Macro to Facilitate Summing of a Series of Ranges

This macro uses several string formulas, all designed to permit reference to variable range locations as you designate which range locations you want to include in your @sum formula.

{let R_HERE,@cellpointer("address")}   The macro begins by using the {let} command to create a place-marker at R_HERE.

{windowsoff}{paneloff}/rncAREA_1 TO SUM~~/rndAREA_1 TO SUM~   Turns off the windows and panel, then creates and deletes the range named AREA_1 TO SUM.

/rnc{panelon}AREA_1 TO SUM~{bs}{windowson}{?}~   Again creates the prompting range name AREA_1 TO SUM, then pauses for your highlighting of the first range you want in your @sum formula.

{let R_SUM,"@sum(AREA_1 TO SUM"}{goto}AREA_1 TO SUM~   Uses the {let} command to store the label, *@sum(AREA_1 TO SUM)* in R_SUM, then moves the cell pointer to the upper left corner of that range.

{for RCOUNT,2,20,1,R_LOOP}   This is a {for} loop that counts at RCOUNT, starting with the number 2, counting up to a maximum of 20, counting by ones, and running the routine at R_LOOP with each increment of the counter. Its purpose is to prompt you for up to 20 areas to include in your ranges to sum.

{goto}{R_HERE}~   This is the cell named RFINAL. The macro flow reaches this cell only after you have highlighted the last range you want to sum; that is, only if you press Ctrl-Break to interrupt the {for} loop because you do not want to designate another range or if you actually designate the full limit of 20 ranges to sum. Whatever the circumstance, the macro now moves the cell pointer back to its original location stored in R_HERE.

@sum (AREA_1 TO SUM,AREA_2 TO SUM,AREA_3 TO SUM   This cell is named R_SUM and it consists of the beginning of a variable @sum formula as created by the {let} commands in cell B6 or B16. This formula changes based on the number of ranges you decide to include as you run the macro.

)~{windowsoff}{paneloff}{for RCOUNT2,1,RCOUNT-1,1,R_LOOP2}{quit}   This line completes the @sum formula, turns off the windows and panel, then starts a {for} loop at RLOOP2 designed to delete the range names such as AREA_1 TO SUM, AREA_2 TO SUM, and so on.

{recalc RCALC}{windowsoff}{paneloff}   This is the beginning of the routine of the first {for} loop, starting at the cell named R_LOOP, designed to prompt you for up to 20 areas to include in your ranges to sum.

/rnc{panelon}AREA_4 TO SUM~{bs}{windowson}{?}~   Although this appears as the familiar creation of a prompting range name (in this case, the range name AREA_4 TO SUM?), it is actually the resulting display of the string formula:

+"/rnc{panelon}AREA_"&
@string(RCOUNT,0)&
" TO SUM~{bs}{windowson}{?}~"

This formula will begin by creating the range name AREA_1 TO SUM, followed by AREA_2 TO SUM in the second pass through the {for} loop, AREA_3 TO SUM in the third pass, and so on.

{recalc RCALC2}   Recalculates the next cell, named RCALC2.

{goto}AREA_4 TO SUM˜{onerror RFINAL}{recalc RCALC3}   Moves the cell pointer to the top of the most recent range designated as an area to sum, through use of the string formula:

+"{goto}AREA_"&
@string(RCOUNT,0)&
" TO SUM˜{onerror RFINAL}{recalc RCALC3}"

The {onerror} command is included so the macro will branch to RFINAL when you press Ctrl-Break after highlighting the last range to sum.

{let R_SUM,+R_SUM&",AREA_4 TO SUM"}{return}   Increases the contents of R_SUM to include the most recent range designed as an area to sum. This line is the displayed result of the string formula:

+"{let R_SUM,+R_SUM&
"",AREA_"&
@string(RCOUNT,O)&
" TO SUM""}{return}"

{recalc RCALC4}   This is the beginning of the routine referred to in the closing {for} loop just before the macro quits at B10. It begins by recalculating the next line of the macro at the cell named RCALC4.

/rndAREA_4 TO SUM˜{return}   By the time the macro gets to this point, your @sum range has been established. If you are summing three separate ranges, the @sum formula will be:

@sum(AREA_1 TO SUM,AREA_2 TO SUM,AREA_3 TO SUM)

With each pass of the {for} loop at B10, this line deletes each range name in turn. It does this by using the variable string formula:

+"/rndAREA_"&@string(RCOUNT2,0)&" TO SUM˜{return}"

The result is an @sum formula with cell coordinates instead of range names, resembling:

@sum(C43..C46,C39..C41,C33..C37)

An example is shown in Figure 13.14.

Creating a Column Jump Macro

One drawback of 1-2-3 is the fact that you cannot easily jump to another off-screen column while staying in the same row without losing your relative position on the screen. If, for example, you are positioned at cell A17 and you want to visit Z17, pressing the F5 Goto key, typing Z17, and pressing Enter will deposit your cell pointer at the correct location, but in the upper left corner of the screen.

Fortunately, you can use string formulas to create a handy Column Jump macro, as shown in Figure 13.15 To use this macro, simply press Alt-K. At the prompt for a column to go to,

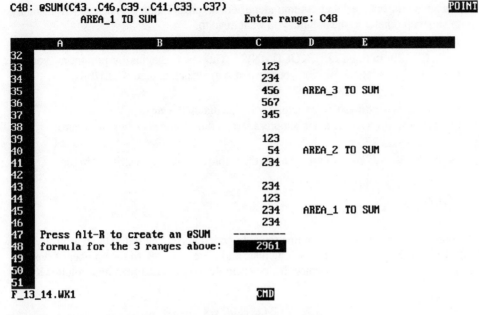

```
C48: @SUM(C43..C46,C39..C41,C33..C37)                              POINT
            AREA_1 TO SUM                    Enter range: C48

        A              B              C        D        E
32
33                                           123
34                                           234
35                                           456    AREA_3 TO SUM
36                                           567
37                                           345
38
39                                           123
40                                            54    AREA_2 TO SUM
41                                           234
42
43                                           234
44                                           123
45                                           234    AREA_1 TO SUM
46                                           234
47  Press Alt-R to create an @SUM         ---------
48  formula for the 3 ranges above:          2961
49
50
51
F_13_14.WK1                                  CMD
```

Figure 13.14 An Example Using the Ranges Summed Macro

```
B10: [W20] 1                                                      READY
Column to go to: AZ

        A              B              C        D        E
1   :                     **** COLUMN JUMP ****
2   \K        {}
3   *KOLJUMP  {Getlabel "Column to go to: ",KOLUMN}~
4   :         {recalc KLET}{windowsoff}{paneloff}
5   KLET      {let K_NUM,@cell("col",!A1)}
6   :         {recalc KRIGHT}{recalc KLEFT}
7   KRIGHT    {if @cell("col",A1)>@cell("col",$B$10)}{right 3}{left 4}{quit}
8   KLEFT     {left 1}{quit}
9   KOLUMN    A
10  K_NUM                          1
11
12  Cell B5:
13     +"{let K_NUM,@cell(""col"",!"&+KOLUMN&"1)}"
14  Cell B7:
15     +"{if "&"@cell(""col"",""&KOLUMN&"1)>@cell(""col"","&
16     @cellpointer("address")&")}{right "&
17     @string(@abs(KNUM-@cellpointer("col")+4),0)&
18     "}{left 4}{quit}"
19  Cell B8:
20     +"{left "&@string(@abs(@cellpointer("col")-K_NUM),0)&"}{quit}"
F_13_15.WK1                                  CMD
```

Figure 13.15 Macro to Jump the Cell Pointer to Another Column

enter a single- or double-letter column identifier and press Enter. The macro will instantly jump your cell pointer to the column you want to go to.

{Getlabel "Column to go to: ",KOLUMN}~   The macro begins by prompting you for the column letter or letters, placing your response in the cell named KOLUMN.

{recalc KLET}{windowsoff}{paneloff}   Recalculates the next cell named KLET, then turns off the windows and panel to suppress screen flicker and speed up the macro.

{let K_NUM,@cell("col",!A1)}   This is the displayed result of a string formula:

+"{let K_NUM,@cell(""col"",!"&
+KOLUMN&
"1)}"

The purpose of this line is to combine the column letter you entered with an arbitrary row number (we used row number 1), to calculate and store in K_NUM the number of the column that corresponds to your entry. If, for example, you entered the column letter K, the macro line would read:

{let K_NUM,@cell("col",!K1)}

which would cause the number 11 to be entered in K_NUM.

{recalc KRIGHT}{recalc KLEFT}   Recalculates the string formulas in KRIGHT and KLEFT.

{if @cell("col",A1)>@cell("col",$B$10)}{right 3}{left 4}{quit}   This {if} statement moves the cell pointer to the right if you entered a column letter that resides to the right of your current position. A string formula is required to calculate and display how far to the right the cell pointer should be moved, as:

+"{if "&"@cell(""col"","&KOLUMN&"1)>@cell(""col"","&
@cellpointer("address")&")}{right "&
@string(@abs(KNUM-@cellpointer("col")+4),0)&
"}{left 4}{quit}"

{left 1}{quit}   Otherwise, the cell pointer is moved to the left, based on the string formula:

+"{left "&
@string(@abs(@cell("col")-K_NUM),0)&
"}{quit}"

Since your windows and upper panel have been turned off for the jump to the right or left, all you will see after you enter a column number is a short screen flicker, then the screen changes to show your cell pointer in the new column, but still in the same row. More importantly, you will still be in the same relative vertical position on the screen instead of being left in the upper left corner.

Jump Left, Right, Top, or Bottom

In Chapter 5 we showed a simple macro designed to jump your cell pointer to the left-most or top-most cell of the spreadsheet without losing your relative position on the screen (see Figure 5.8). Unfortunately, that macro requires use of the /Worksheet Titles command. This means that if you already have your titles locked in, using that technique will inappropriately eliminate those titles as it attempts to create new titles.

In this section we will look at a more advanced macro using string formulas to jump your cell pointer to the left-most cell (column A) in the current row, the right-most filled cell in the current row, the top cell (row 1) in the current column, or the lowest filled cell in the current column. Refer to Figure 13.16.

```
          A              B                    C                        D                      E
 1   :                           *** LEAP RIGHT, LEFT, TOP, BOTTOM ***
 2   \L      {}
 3   *LEAP   {menubranch L_MENU}{quit}
 4   L_MENU  RIGHT                        LEFT                  TOP                     BOTTOM
 5   :       Move right to last filled cell   Move to column A in this row   Move to the topmost filled cell   Move to the bottommost filled cell
 6   :       {windowsoff}{paneloff}       {windowsoff}{paneloff}   {windowsoff}{paneloff}   {windowsoff}{paneloff}
 7   :       {goto}{end}{home}            {left @cellpointer("col")-1}   {let LCOL,@cellpointer("address")}   {goto}.
 8   :       {let LCOL,@cellpointer("address")}  {quit}        {home}                   {end}{home}
 9   :       {esc}{recalc LCALC}                                {let LHOME,@cellpointer("address")}   ...{esc}~{pgdn}{end}{up}
10   LCALC   {right @cell("col",$F$56)-@cellpointer("col")+2}   {recalc LTOP}{goto}{LTOP}~   {let LCOL,@cellpointer("address")}
11   :       {end}{left}{if @cellpointer("col")=1}{quit}   {left @min(@cellpointer("col")-1,3)}   {left @min(@cellpointer("col")-1,3)}
12   :       {end}{left}{end}{right}{quit}   {goto}{LTOP}~{quit}   {goto}{LCOL}~{up 8}{down 8}{quit}
13   LTOP    $F$1{return}
14   LCOL    $F$56
15   :       {return}
16   LHOME   $A$1
17
18   Cell B10:
19   +"{right @cell(""col"","&+LCOL&")-@cellpointer(""col"")+2}"
20   Cell B13:
21   @left(lcol,3)&@mid(LHOME,@find("$",LHOME,1)+1,4)&"{return}"
```

Fig_13_16.WK1

Figure 13.16 A Macro to Leap Right, Left, Top, or Bottom

{menubranch L_MENU}{quit}   The macro begins by offering the menu choices *RIGHT*, *LEFT*, *TOP*, and *BOTTOM*. Select *RIGHT* to jump your cell pointer to the right-most filled cell in the current row.

{windowsoff}{paneloff}   Turns off the windows and panel to suppress screen flicker and speed up the macro.

{goto}{end}{home}   Moves the cell pointer to the End Home location in the spreadsheet. Note there is no tilde at this point to complete the {goto} command.

{let LCOL,@cellpointer("address")}   Creates a place-marker interrupting {goto} to create at LCOL to store the address of the cell at the end home location.

{esc}{recalc LCALC}   Having recorded the End Home location, the macro backs out of the F5 Goto sequence with the Escape key, then recalculates the next cell named LCALC.

{right @cell("col",$F$56)-@cellpointer("col")+2}   Moves the cell pointer to the right a number of cells equal to two cells more than the difference between the current column and the right-most column. This is actually the displayed result of the string formula:

$$+"\{right\ @cell(""col"","\&+LCOL\&")-\ @cellpointer(""col"")+2\}"$$

{end}{left}{if @cellpointer("col")=1}{quit}   Having moved two cells past the right-most column, the cell pointer is now moved End LeftArrow to the right-most filled cell in the current row. If that happens to be column A because there is no other entry in the current row, the macro quits.

{end}{left}{end}{right}{quit}   Otherwise, the cell pointer is moved End LeftArrow and End RightArrow to reposition the cell pointer to the right edge of the screen, and the macro quits.

{left @cellpointer("col")-1}{quit}   If you select *LEFT*, the cell pointer is simply moved left the number of columns necessary to move it to column A and the macro quits.

{let LCOL,@cellpointer("address")}   If you select *TOP*, the macro creates a place-marker for the current cell, storing the cell address in the cell named LCOL.

{home}   The cell pointer is moved to the Home position. If there are no titles locked in, this will be cell A1. Otherwise, it will be the cell just below and/or to the right of the titles.

{let LHOME,@cellpointer("address")}   The cell coordinates for this Home location are stored at LHOME.

{recalc LTOP}{goto}{LTOP}~   The address at LTOP is recalculated, then the macro moves to that address. LTOP is based on the string formula:

@left(lcol,3)&
@mid(LHOME,@find("$",LHOME,1)+1,4)&
"{return}"

This formula isolates the column letter from the starting cell address stored in LCOL, appends the row number from the Home address stored in LHOME, and adds a {return} command to end the subroutine. The effect is to jump the cell pointer to the top cell (below the titles, if any) of the current column.

{left @min(@cellpointer("col")-1,3)}   Moves the cell pointer either three cells to the left or one less than the current column, whichever is the lesser. This is done to reposition the top cell more in the center of the screen.

{goto}{LTOP}~{quit} Finally, the cell pointer is jumped back to the top cell, and the macro quits.

{goto}. If you select *BOTTOM*, you activate an interesting use of the F5 Goto key. The macro presses the F5 Goto key, then does something you would not normally think to do manually: it presses the period to lock in the cell coordinates so that any movement of the cell pointer highlights everything between the original cell and the cell you move to.

{end}{home}...{esc}~ The {end} and {home} commands highlight the area from the current cell to the End Home position, then the Period (.) key is pressed three times to change the cell coordinates around. (Try this manually for yourself to see what is meant here.) When the Escape key is pressed again, the F5 Goto prompt is left with a cell address that combines the current column with the End Home row. The tilde completes the F5 Goto sequence and the cell pointer is moved there.

{pgdn}{end}{up} The cell pointer is moved down one page, then End UpArrow to ensure that it ends up in the lowest filled cell in the column.

{left @min(@cellpointer("col")-1,3)} Moves the cell pointer either three cells to the left or one less than the current column, whichever is the lesser. This is done to reposition the cell more in the center of the screen.

{goto}{LCOL}~{up 8}{down 8}{quit} The cell pointer is moved back to the lowest filled cell in the column, then DownArrow eight cells and UpArrow eight cells to reposition the cell vertically, and the macro quits.

Calculating the Median of a Column

For our final macro in this chapter, we will examine a macro that substitutes for an @function that does not currently exist in 1-2-3. The macro in Figure 13.17 makes use of the @mod, @index, @int, and @count functions as well as the @string and @cellpointer functions to calculate and display the median of any column of numbers.

To operate the macro, move to a vertical range of numbers for which you want to calculate the median. The numbers need not be sorted, and the range can include blank cells. For an example, refer to Figure 13.18.

Here's how the macro works.

{windowsoff}{paneloff}/rncMEDIAN RANGE?~~/rndMEDIAN RANGE?~ Turns off the windows and panel and begins the sequence to create a prompting range name.

/rnc{panelon}MEDIAN RANGE?~{windowson}{?}~ Creates the prompting range

B15: +"The median is "&@STRING(@CELLPOINTER("contents"),2)&". Press Return."
+"The median is "&@STRING(@CELLPOINTER("contents"),2)&". Press Return."

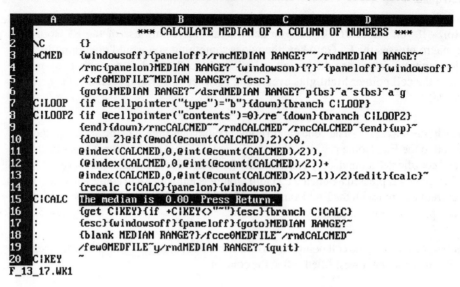

```
        A              B              C              D
1  :          *** CALCULATE MEDIAN OF A COLUMN OF NUMBERS ***
2  \C      {}
3  *CMED   {windowsoff}{paneloff}/rncMEDIAN RANGE?~~/rndMEDIAN RANGE?~
4  :       /rnc{panelon}MEDIAN RANGE?~{windowson}{?}~{paneloff}{windowsoff}
5  :       /fxf0MEDFILE~MEDIAN RANGE?~r{esc}
6  :       {goto}MEDIAN RANGE?~/dsrdMEDIAN RANGE?~p{bs}~a~s{bs}~a~g
7  C:LOOP  {if @cellpointer("type")="b"}{down}{branch C:LOOP}
8  C:LOOP2 {if @cellpointer("contents")=0}{re~}{down}{branch C:LOOP2}
9  :       {end}{down}/rncCALCMED~~/rndCALCMED~/rncCALCMED~{end}{up}~
10 :       {down 2}@if(@mod(@count(CALCMED),2)<>0,
11 :       @index(CALCMED,0,@int(@count(CALCMED)/2)),
12 :       (@index(CALCMED,0,@int(@count(CALCMED)/2))+
13 :       @index(CALCMED,0,@int(@count(CALCMED)/2)-1))/2){edit}{calc}~
14 :       {recalc C:CALC}{panelon}{windowson}
15 C:CALC  The median is  0.00. Press Return.
16 :       {get C:KEY}{if +C:KEY<>"~"}{esc}{branch C:CALC}
17 :       {esc}{windowsoff}{paneloff}{goto}MEDIAN RANGE?~
18 :       {blank MEDIAN RANGE?}/fcce0MEDFILE~/rndCALCMED~
19 :       /few0MEDFILE~y/rndMEDIAN RANGE?~{quit}
20 C:KEY   ~
```
F_13_17.WK1

Figure 13.17 Calculate the Median of a Column of Numbers

C39: 234   LABEL
The Median is 234.00. Press Return.

```
        A          B          C          D          E          F
22 This macro will       To give you a           But finally leaving
23 operate on a          temporary view          you with a result
24 column like this:     like this:              like this:
25
26            123                                            123
27            234                                            234
28
29            234                   123                      234
30            123                   123                      123
31            345                   132                      345
32                                  234
33            234                   234                      234
34                                  234
35            234                   234                      234
36            132                   234                      132
37            234                   345                      234
38                             ------------            ------------
39                                  234                      234
40
41
```
F_13_18.WK1   CMD

Figure 13.18 Example of the Use of the Median Calculator Macro

name MEDIAN RANGE?, turning on the upper panel and windows, then pauses for you to highlight the vertical range of numbers for which you want the median calculated.

{paneloff}{windowsoff}/fxf0MEDFILE~MEDIAN RANGE?~r{esc} Turns off the windows and panel, then stores a copy of the cells in the range named MEDIAN RANGE? by doing a /File Xtract, naming the file 0MEDFILE.

{goto}MEDIAN RANGE?~ Moves the cell pointer to the top of the range of numbers for which you want the median calculated.

/dsrdMEDIAN RANGE?~p{bs}~a~s{bs}~a~g Sorts the range of numbers in ascending order. This will place all blank cells, zero cells, and label cells above the cells with values in them.

{if @cellpointer("type")="b"}{down}{branch C|LOOP} This is the beginning of the loop named C|LOOP. If the current cell is blank, the cell pointer is moved down one cell, then the macro loops back to the beginning of this line to check for whether the next cell is blank.

{if @cellpointer("contents")=0}/re~{down}{branch C|LOOP2} This is the beginning of the second loop, named C|LOOP2. If the current cell contains a label or is otherwise equal to zero, the cell is erased, the cell pointer is moved down one cell, and the macro loops back to the beginning of this line to check for whether the next cell is equal to zero.

{end}{down}/rncCALCMED~~/rndCALCMED~/rncCALCMED~{end}{up}~ By the time this line of the macro is reached, the cell pointer has bypassed all blank or zero cells, coming to the first cell with a value greater than zero. The cell pointer is moved End DownArrow to the bottom of this range of numbers, then the range named CALMED is created by painting End UpArrow to the top of the column.

{down 2}@if(@mod(@count(CALCMED),2)<>0, The cell pointer is moved two cells below the last filled cell in the range of numbers to calculate and the macro begins to type an @if function. The @if function checks for whether the number of units in CALCMED is an odd number or even by using @mod to divide the count in CALCMED by two.

@index(CALCMED,0,@int(@countCALCMED)/2)), If the count is an odd number, the @if function uses @index to isolate from CALCMED (in this, the zero offset column) the item that is down from the first item the integer of the number exactly one-half the total number of items.

(@index(CALCMED,0,@int(@count(CALCMED)/2))+ Otherwise, if the count is even, the @if function works in two parts. First it uses @index to isolate from CALCMED the item that is in that same location.

@index(CALCMED,0,@int(@CALCMED)/2)-1))/2){edit}{calc}~ Then it adds the item just below that item and divides the sum by two. Finally, the macro presses Edit and Calc to turn the formula to a straight value.

{recalc C|CALC}{panelon}{windowson} The macro recalculates C|CALC and turns the panel and windows off.

The median is 0.00 . Press Return. The macro types this message in the upper panel. It is actually the displayed result of a string formula, as:

+"The Median is "&
@string(@cellpointer("contents"),2)&
". Press Return."

{get C|KEY}{if +C|KEY<>"~"}{esc}{branch C|CALC} The macro pauses for you to press Return. If you do not press Return, the macro presses Escape to eliminate the typed message, then branches back to C|CALC to display the message once again.

{esc}{windowsoff}{paneloff}{goto}MEDIAN RANGE?~ Otherwise, the macro presses Escape to eliminate the typed message, the windows and upper panel are turned off, and the cell pointer is moved to the top of the range previously named MEDIAN RANGE?

{blank MEDIAN RANGE?}/fcce0MEDFILE~/rndCALCMED~ So as to restore the original range to its original location, MEDIAN RANGE? is blanked, and the macro selects /File Combine Copy Entire of the extracted file named 0MEDFILE. The range named CALCMED is then deleted.

/few0MEDFILE~y/rndMEDIAN RANGE?~{quit} Finally, the extracted filenamed 0MEDFILE is erased, the range named MEDIAN RANGE? is deleted, and the macro quits.

Note: One last word about this macro: Be sure that there are at least two blank cells below the range of numbers for which you want the median calculated.

Summary

In this chapter we explored the use of strings to create variable code in your macros. The concepts covered were:

- Strings can be used to create a temporary and variable message in your upper panel.
- The {if} command **{if @left(AKEY,1)="{"}** can be used to identify whether you pressed a function key or directional key such as {edit}, {home}, {left}, or {pgdn}.
- If you have Release 2 or 2.01, the {let} command will not accept an @function as its first argument. Thus, the command, **{let @cellpointer("address"),999}**, designed to place 999 in the current cell, will give the error message *Invalid range in LET*. This deficiency was corrected in Release 2.2 and 3. Alternately, you can work around this problem by using @cellpointer("address") in an underlying string formula.

- Double quotation marks are required within a string function to return single quotation marks in the results.

- You can use string formulas not only as functioning parts of the program flow of a macro, but also as variable lines used for the descriptions that appear under custom menus.

- You can use a string formula to substitute for the use of @cellpointer("address") as an argument in the {contents} command.

- Release 2.2 and 3 have the ability to capture the pressing of the F1 Help key using the {get} command. This new feature is especially useful for creating custom help screens for your users, but you can also accomplish the equivalent feat by capturing another of the function keys—preferably one that is little used, like the F8 Table key.

- You can use {if 0} to create a remarks line. Since any false statement in an {if} command causes the macro to skip the rest of the line, starting a line with {if 0} or {if @false} allows you to end the line with a remark. As macro code, this line will have no effect whatever on the operation of your macro.

- You can use @mid to isolate the column letter(s) and row number from an absolute address by extracting characters based on the offset position of the dollar signs ($) in the absolute address.

- Using strings, you can create a variable line in a macro that changes with each pass of a {for} loop.

- You can create a macro that makes interesting use of the F5 Goto key, pressing the F5 Goto key, pressing the period to lock in the cell coordinates so that any movement of the cell pointer highlights everything between the original cell and the cell you move to, then pressing the Period key again to reverse the offered cell coordinates before pressing Escape or Return.

The macros shown in this chapter were:

- A macro using string programming to display an ASCII code. This macro includes a temporary message typed in the upper panel, telling you the ASCII code that corresponds to the keystroke provided in response to a prompt.

- A macro to center a title across the screen. This macro uses @cellpointer("address") in a string function with {let} to substitute for the inability a {let} command to accept @cellpointer("address") as its first argument in Release 2 or 2.01.

- A macro for storing and instantly entering a word or phrase. This macro includes the use of string formulas to create a variable description line under a custom menu.

- A macro that allows you to change the label in any cell to uppercase, lowercase, or proper case.

- A macro to show the number of days between two dates.

- A macro to change values to label-numbers with formats. This macro is also an interesting example of the use of a string formula to get around the problem that you cannot use @cellpointer("address") as an argument in the {contents} command.

- A macro that uses string formulas to underline numbers or labels in a row using either the width of the current column or the width of the entry in the cell above as the criteria to establish the length of underline row.

- A macro to jump to a custom Help screen and return by pressing the F8 key. This macro also calculates the address of the upper left corner of the help screen and uses that information in strings to limit the user's ability to move around (and potentially damage) the contents of the Help screen.

■ A summing macro with a sum-and-stay feature that offers the custom menu choices +, -, *EDIT*, and *FINISH*.

■ A macro to facilitate the summing of a series of ranges. The result of this macro will be an @sum formula such as @sum(C43..C46,C39..C41,C33..C37).

■ A macro to jump the cell pointer to another column, but still in the same row. Using this macro, you will be left in the same relative vertical position on the screen as you started instead of being left, as you are if you use the F5 Goto key, in the upper left corner.

■ A macro to jump your cell pointer to the left-most cell (column A) in the current row, the right-most filled cell in the current row, the top cell (row 1) in the current column, or the lowest filled cell in the current column.

■ A macro to calculate the median of a column of numbers. This macro makes use of the @mod, @index, @int, and @count functions as well as the @string and @cellpointer functions to calculate and display the median of the range you highlight.

In Chapter 14 we will explore the use of string formulas in macros designed to manipulate the elements of a database. The examples include macros to create date headings, view duplicate entries, find a string within a string, delete blank or zero-value rows, and subtotal like items in a database.

14

MACROS TO MANIPULATE A DATABASE

Scope

In this chapter we will explore macros that use variable strings and the combination of several features including operators, such as #not#, and @functions, such as @exact, @iserr, @value, and @choose, to facilitate the use and manipulation of databases in 1-2-3.

Automating the Creation of Date Headings

The macro in Figure 14.1 addresses one of the most common tasks 1-2-3 users are faced with: the creation of date headings across the top or along the side of a spreadsheet.

This repetitive task usually takes anywhere from 48 to over 80 keystrokes for a 12 month period, depending on whether you spell out the names of the months or use the shorter forms like JAN, FEB, and so on. However, with the Headings of Dates macro, this can be reduced to six keystrokes.

{menubranch HMENU}{quit}   The macro begins by offering the menu choices *ACROSS*

B14: +"^"&@CHOOSE(HCOUNT-1,"JAN","FEB","MAR","APR","MAY","JUN","JUL","AUG","SEP"

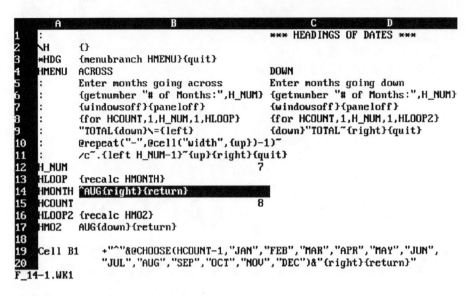

Figure 14.1 A Macro to Create Date Headings

and *DOWN*. Select *ACROSS* to have your headings typed across in a row, with each heading underlined and the word **TOTAL** entered and double-underlined at the end of the row.

{getnumber "# of Months:",H_NUM}   Prompts you for the number of months you want in your headings, storing your response in the cell named H_NUM.

{windowsoff}{paneloff}   Turns off the windows and panel to suppress screen flicker and speed up the macro.

{for HCOUNT,1,H_NUM,1,HLOOP} or **{for HCOUNT,1,H_NUM,1,HLOOP2}**
This {for} loop counts at HCOUNT starting with one, counting up to the number of months you stored in H_NUM, in increments of one, and for each increment runs the routine at HLOOP or HLOOP2.

If you select *ACROSS*, the routine at HLOOP begins by recalculating HMONTH, enters a centering caret and the name of a month, then executes a {right} command and starts over, repeating this loop until the last month has been entered.

After all months have been entered, the macro enters the word **TOTAL**, moves down one cell, enters a double underline, moves left, enters a repeating underline symbol, copies it to the left, moves back to the right, and quits.

If you select *DOWN*, the routine at HLOOP2 recalculates HMO2, enters a month (without a caret), moves down one cell, then starts over, repeating the loop until the last month has been entered. Finally, the cell pointer is moved down one more cell, the word **TOTAL** is entered right-justified, and the macro quits.

The real magic of this macro is contained in the string formulas behind cells B14 and B17. The two formulas are almost identical, so we will look only at the formula behind cell B14. As you can see at the bottom of Figure 14.1, this formula consists of three parts: a caret, an @choose function that returns a month, and the ending {right}{return} commands.

The @choose function selects JAN (the zero offset) at the first pass of the {for} loop when HCOUNT equals 1 (and HCOUNT - 1 = 0). At the second pass of the {for} loop, HCOUNT equals 2 (and HCOUNT minus 1 = 1), so the @choose selects offset 1, or FEB. The macro continues in this way, changing the name of the month to select, until the last month is entered.

Creation of a Worksheet Matrix

This same technique, using variable data entry based on passes through a {for} loop, can be used to create an entire worksheet matrix of variable size. Such a macro is shown in Figure 14.2.

To operate this macro, press Alt-W. At the range name prompt, WORKSHEET AREA?, highlight the size of the matrix you want to create, starting in column A. When you press Re-

```
        A         B         C         D         E         F         G         H
1   :                   *** WORKSHEET CREATION ***
2   \W        {}
3   *WKSHT    {windowsoff}{paneloff}/rncWORKSHEET AREA?~~/rndWORKSHEET AREA?~
4   :         /rnc{panelon}WORKSHEET AREA?~{windowson}{?}~
5   :         {if @cols(WORKSHEET AREA?)<3}/rndWORKSHEET AREA?~{branch *WKSHT}
6   :         {if @rows(WORKSHEET AREA?)<6}/rndWORKSHEET AREA?~{branch *WKSHT}
7   :         {paneloff}{blank WORKSHEET AREA?}/rff~WORKSHEET AREA?~
8   :         {goto}WORKSHEET AREA?~{right}
9   :         {for WCOUNT,1,@cols(WORKSHEET AREA?)-2,1,WLOOP}{left}
10  :         {end}{left 2}{down 2}Siding~/c~.{down @rows(WORKSHEET AREA?)-5}~
11  :         {up 2}{right}{end}{right 2}"TOTAL{down}\=~{left}
12  :         @repeat("-",@cell("width",{up})-1)~/c~.{end}{left}{right}~
13  :         {right}{down}@sum({left}.{end}{left}..)~
14  :         /c~.{down @rows(WORKSHEET AREA?)-5}~{end}{down 2}\=~{end}{left}
15  :         {down}TOTAL:{right}{up}@repeat("-",@cell("width",{up})-1)~
16  :         /c~.{right @cols(WORKSHEET AREA?)-3}~{down}
17  :         @sum({up 2}{end}{up}{down}.{end}{down})~
18  :         /c~.{right @cols(WORKSHEET AREA?)-2}~{end}{right}{quit}
19  WCOUNT         5
20  WLOOP     {recalc WMONTH}
21  :         {if @iserr(WMONTH)}~HEADING~{right}{return}
22  WMONTH    ~MAY{right}{return}
23
24
25
26  Cell B22:     +"^"&@CHOOSE(WCOUNT-1,"JAN","FEB","MAR","APR","MAY","JUN",
27                "JUL","AUG","SEP","OCT","NOV","DEC")&"{right}{return}"
```

F_14-2.WK1

Figure 14.2 A Macro to Automate Creation of a Worksheet Matrix

turn, the macro will type underlined date headings and a Total label across the top of your highlighted range, enter the word *Siding* and a Total label down the left side of the range, enter @sum formulas under the Total label down the right side, enter underline cells and @sum formulas across the bottom row of the range, and finally enter a double underline and a Grand Total summing formula in the lower right cell of the range.

Figure 14.3 shows the results you will get by invoking this macro and highlighting, for example, the range A3..G15 as the size of the worksheet matrix you would like to create.

```
G15: (F2) @SUM(G5..G14)                                                READY
```

	A	B	C	D	E	F	G	H
1								
2								
3		JAN	FEB	MAR	APR	MAY	TOTAL	
4		————————	————————	————————	————————	————————	=========	
5	Siding						0.00	
6	Siding						0.00	
7	Siding						0.00	
8	Siding						0.00	
9	Siding						0.00	
10	Siding						0.00	
11	Siding						0.00	
12	Siding						0.00	
13	Siding						0.00	
14		————————	————————	————————	————————	————————	=========	
15	TOTAL:	0.00	0.00	0.00	0.00	0.00	0.00	
16								
17								
18								
19								
20								

F_14-3.WK1

Figure 14.3   Example of the Use of the Worksheet Creation Macro

Of course, the "Siding" labels down the left side are only there to represent the siding labels you will actually be using. Once the worksheet matrix is completed, you should replace these labels with the appropriate titles for your own spreadsheet. If necessary, you can also change the date headings to any other headings that may be appropriate.

Here's how the macro works.

{windowsoff}{paneloff}/rncWORKSHEET AREA?~~/rndWORKSHEET AREA?~
This turns off the windows and panel to suppress screen flicker and speed up the macro, then creates and deletes the prompting range name, WORKSHEET AREA?.

/rnc{panelon}WORKSHEET AREA?~{windowson}{?}~   Again creates the range name WORKSHEET AREA?, then pauses for your highlighting of the size of worksheet matrix you would like to create.

{if @cols(WORKSHEET AREA?)<3}/rndWORKSHEET AREA?~{branch *WKSHT}
If the number of columns you highlight are less than three, the macro deletes the prompting range name WORKSHEET AREA? and starts over again. This is necessary because the sidings, at least one column of data, and @sum formulas to the right require three columns by themselves.

{if @rows(WORKSHEET AREA?)<6}/rndWORKSHEET AREA?~{branch *WKSHT}
If the number of rows you highlight is less than six, the macro deletes the prompting range name WORKSHEET AREA? and starts over again. This is necessary because of the number of rows required for headings, underline cells, minimum lines of data, and @sum formulas at the bottom.

{paneloff}{blank WORKSHEET AREA?}/rff~WORKSHEET AREA?~   The range you highlighted is blanked and formatted for Fixed Format with two decimals. Of course, you should feel free to change the range formatting to any other type.

{goto}WORKSHEET AREA?~{right}   In case the cell pointer is not already there, this command sends it to the upper left corner of the range you highlighted, then moves one cell to the right.

{for WCOUNT,1,@cols(WORKSHEET AREA?)-2,1,WLOOP}{left}   This {for} command counts at WCOUNT starting with the number one, counting up to two less than the number of columns in the highlighted range, incrementing by ones, and for each increment runs the routine at WLOOP designed to insert the names of months across the top of the highlighted range. If your range is greater than 12 months, the word HEADING is used (see line B21).

    The string formula used to calculate the appropriate month and enter it is shown at the bottom of Figure 14.2, displayed in cell B22. As with the Headings of Dates macro, this formula consists of three parts: a caret, an @choose function that returns the appropriate month based on the number of passes through the {for} loop recorded at WCOUNT, and the ending {right}{return} commands.

{end}{left 2}{down 2}Siding~/c~.{down @rows(WORKSHEET AREA?)-5}~   This line moves the cell pointer back to column A and down two cells, where the Siding label is entered and copied down five less cells than the total number of rows in the highlighted range.

{up 2}{right}{end}{right 2}"TOTAL{down}\=~{left}   The cell pointer is moved back up to the top row, then End RightArrow, and another RightArrow to the correct location for typing the TOTAL title. After the title is typed, the cell pointer is moved down and underlining symbols are entered. The macro then moves the cell pointer left one cell.

@repeat("-",@cell("width",{up})-1)~/c~.{end}{left}{right}~   Uses @repeat to enter underlining symbols of a length one character less than the width of the current cell, then copies that @repeat function to all the cells to the left except Column A.

{right}{down}@sum({left}.{end}{left}..)~   The macro moves to the right-most column and down one cell to enter an @sum formula to sum all the values in the current row.

/c~.{down @rows(WORKSHEET AREA?)-5}~{end}{down 2}\=~{end}{left}   Copies the @sum formula down five less cells than the number of rows in the highlighted area, moves to the end of the row to create a double underline cell, then moves End LeftArrow to column A.

{down}TOTAL:{right}{up}@repeat("- ",@cell("width",{up})-1)~   Moves down, enters the word **TOTAL**, and moves to the right and up one cell to enter an underlining formula using @repeat.

/c~.{right @cols(WORKSHEET AREA?)-3}~{down}   Copies the underlining formula to the right three cells less than the number of columns in the highlighted area, then moves down one cell.

@sum({up 2}{end}{up}{down}.{end}{down})~   Sums the current column.

/c~.{right @cols(WORKSHEET AREA?)-2}~{end}{right}{quit}   Copies the @sum formula to the right two cells less than the number of columns in the highlighted area, then moves End RightArrow to the Grand Total cell, and quits.

Automating Creation of /Data Query Ranges

Creating /Data Query Input and Criterion ranges in your database so you can execute a /Data Query Find operation can take quite a number of keystrokes and requires meticulous attention to detail. The macro in Figure 14.4 is designed to automate the process, first creating of your /Data Query Input and Criterion ranges, then initiating your first /Data Query Find operation based on those ranges.

To operate this macro, create or move to a pre-established database and press Alt-Q.

Point to the first title of your input range. ESC to quit.   The macro begins by typing a prompt in the upper panel. If you have Release 2.2 or 3, you may want to replace this with a long {indicate} prompt.

{get QKEY}{esc}{if QKEY="{esc}"}{quit}   If you press the Escape key, the macro will quit.

{if QKEY="~"}{esc}{recalc QCALC}{recalc Q_IF}{branch Q_IF}   If you press Return, the {esc} command deletes the typed message, the string formulas at QCALC and Q_IF are recalculated, and the macro branches to Q_IF.

The string formula at QCALC is designed to extract and display the letter or letters representing the current column; then that information is used in the string formula in Q_IF.

```
B16: [W11] @MID(@CELLPOINTER("address"),1,@IF(@CELLPOINTER("col")<=26,1,2))
@MID(@CELLPOINTER("address"),1,@IF(@CELLPOINTER("col")<=26,1,2))
```

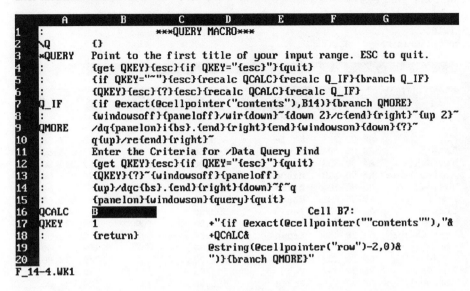

```
         A        B       C        D       E       F        G
1    :                      ***QUERY MACRO***
2    \Q        {}
3    *QUERY    Point to the first title of your input range. ESC to quit.
4    :         {get QKEY}{esc}{if QKEY="{esc}"}{quit}
5    :         {if QKEY="~"}{esc}{recalc QCALC}{recalc Q_IF}{branch Q_IF}
6    :         {QKEY}{esc}{?}{esc}{recalc QCALC}{recalc Q_IF}
7    Q_IF      {if @exact(@cellpointer("contents"),B14)}{branch QMORE}
8    :         {windowsoff}{paneloff}/wir{down}~{down 2}/c{end}{right}~{up 2}~
9    QMORE     /dq{panelon}i{bs}.{end}{right}{end}{windowson}{down}{?}~
10   :         q{up}/re{end}{right}~
11   :         Enter the Criteria for /Data Query Find
12   :         {get QKEY}{esc}{if QKEY="{esc}"}{quit}
13   :         {QKEY}{?}~{windowsoff}{paneloff}
14   :         {up}/dqc{bs}.{end}{right}{down}~f~q
15   :         {panelon}{windowson}{query}{quit}
16   QCALC     B                              Cell B7:
17   QKEY      1                              +"{if @exact(@cellpointer(""contents""),"&
18   :         {return}                       +QCALC&
19   :                                        @string(@cellpointer("row")-2,0)&
20   :                                        ")}{branch QMORE}"
```
F_14-4.WK1

Figure 14.4 Macro to Automate Creation of Your /Data Query Ranges

Since using @cellpointer("col") provides only the *number* of the column, not the letter(s), we need to use a combination of @cellpointer functions to extract the column letter from the current address, as:

$$\text{@mid(@cellpointer("address"),1,@if(@cellpointer("col")<26, 1,2))}$$

If the current column is any column from A to Z (less than or equal to the 26th column), this formula extracts one column letter. Otherwise, it extracts two, such as AA, AB, and so on.

{QKEY}{esc}{?}{esc}{recalc QCALC}{recalc Q_IF}   If you do not press Return at the initial prompt, the {esc} command still deletes the typed message and the macro pauses to allow you to move to the first title of your database. The second {esc} will eliminate any keystrokes you inadvertently press while moving around. When you press Return, the string formulas at QCALC and Q_IF are recalculated.

{if @exact(@cellpointer("contents"),B14)}{branch QMORE}   This is the result of a string formula that checks the contents of the cell two rows above the current cell.

The reason for this line relates to the creation of the /Data Query Input and Criterion ranges. The macro is designed to place duplicates of the Input range headings in an area two rows above the database, then use /Data Query Criterion to establish those two rows as your Criterion range. That way, your Criterion headings will exactly match your Input headings and will be immediately accessible just above the Input range. However, in case you have already established Criterion headings in that location, the macro checks for an exact match, and upon finding a match, branches two lines down to QMORE. Refer to the example in Figure 14.5.

```
F3: [W16]                                                                    POINT
Enter criteria range: A2..F3
```

	A	B	C	D	E	F
1						
2	Description	Part No.	Color	Unit Price	Qty	Total
3						
4	Description	Part No.	Color	Unit Price	Qty	Total
5						================
6	Sofa	AB-90-70	White	599.00	833	498,967.00
7	Lamp	AB-90-40	Blonde	140.00	736	103,040.00
8	End Table	AB-90-354	Oak	244.00	821	200,324.00
9	Coffee Table	AB-90-118	Mahogany	482.00	776	374,032.00
10	Pillow	AB-90-18	Mixed	232.00	700	162,400.00
11	Couch	AB-90-892	White	1,808.00	117	211,536.00
12	Lounge	AB-90-559	Tan	503.00	128	64,384.00
13	Armchair	AB-90-56	Red	467.00	490	228,830.00
14	Wing Chair	AB-90-256	Brown	618.00	642	396,756.00
15	Sofa	AB-90-70	White	599.00	833	498,967.00
16	Pillow	AB-90-18	Mixed	232.00	951	220,632.00
17	End Table	AB-90-354	Oak	244.00	123	30,012.00
18	Coffee Table	AB-90-118	Mahogany	482.00	433	208,706.00
19	Lamp	AB-90-40	Blonde	140.00	182	25,480.00
20	Couch	AB-90-892	White	1,808.00	243	439,344.00

F_14-5.WK1

Figure 14.5 Database with Input and Criterion Ranges Established

In order to calculate and display the cell two rows above the current cell, the macro uses the string formula:

```
+"{if @exact(@cellpointer(""contents""),"&
+QCALC&
@string(@cellpointer("row")-2,0)&
")}{branch QMORE}"
```

You can see now why we had to extract the current column letter as shown in QCALC. By referring to QCALC, the column letter can be displayed in the displayed result of the string formula in Q_IF.

{windowsoff}{paneloff}/wir{down}~{down 2}/c{end}{right}~{up 2}~ The windows and panel are turned off, two new rows are inserted, and a copy of the Input headings is made two cells above the Input range, to be used for Criterion headings.

/dq{panelon}i{bs}.{end}{right}{end}{windowson}{down}{?}~ Selects /Data Query Input, uses Backspace to eliminate any previously established Input range, locks in the cursor, moves End RightArrow and End DownArrow to highlight the Input range, then pauses for your acceptance or revision of the Input range.

q{up}/re{end}{right}~ Quits the /Data Query command sequence, moves up one cell (to the second row of the Criterion range), and erases any single entry in that row that may be left over from a previous /Data Query Find operation.

Enter the Criteria for /Data Query Find   Prompts you to enter criteria in this row before the macro executes a /Data Query Find operation.

{get QKEY}{esc}{if QKEY="{esc}"}{quit}   If you press Escape at this point, the macro simply quits, leaving your /Data Query Input range intact.

{QKEY}{?}~{windowsoff}{paneloff}   Otherwise, the macro executes the keystroke you pressed, pauses for you to point to any cell and enter your criteria, then turns off the windows and panel.

{up}/dqc{bs}.{end}{right}{down}~f~q   The macro moves your cell pointer up one cell to the Criterion headings, selects /Data Query Criterion, eliminates any previously established Criterion range with Backspace, locks in the cursor, highlights the Criterion range using End RightArrow DownArrow, selects Find, then selects Quit.

{panelon}{windowson}{query}{quit}   Finally, the macro turns the windows and panels back on, presses the F7 Query key, and quits. This leaves you in the first found record, but in a better situation than if you had been left at the end of the command sequence /Data Query Find. In the former case, pressing Enter returns you to the *READY* prompt. In the latter case, pressing Enter returns you to the entire /Data Query menu, including the *Reset* choice. If you did not realize that Reset was one of your choices, you could accidentally cancel out your Input and Criterion ranges simply by selecting /Range Erase. (The forward slash would cause a beep, but the R for Range would be interpreted as Reset.)

You may find, therefore, that any macro you write that ends with /Data Query Find should be rewritten to end with /Data Query Find Quit {query}.

Instantly Identifying Duplicate Entries

You may occasionally find the need to locate any duplicate entries in your database so they can be considered for possible elimination. The macro in Figure 14.6 is designed to instantly jump your cell pointer to the second of any duplicate entries in a sorted database.

Note: The macro will only check one column at a time and the database must be sorted on that same column before it will work correctly.

{recalc VCALC}   The macro begins by recalculating the string formula in the next cell down, named VCALC.

```
            A          B          C         D         E        F         G
1    :                        *** VIEW DUPLICATE ENTRIES ***
2    \V              {}
3    *VIEWDUPS {recalc VCALC}
4    VCALC     {if @left(@cell("contents",$A$9),5)="Cell "}{down 2}{up}{quit}
5    :               {down}{branch *VIEWDUPS}
6
7
8    Cell B4:        +"{if @left(@cell(""contents"","&
9                        @LEFT(@CELLPOINTER("address"),3)&
10                       @STRING(@CELLPOINTER("row")+1,0)&
11                       "),5)="""&
12                           @LEFT(@CELLPOINTER("contents"),5)&
13                           """}{down 2}{up}{quit}"
14
15
16
17
18
19
20
F_14-6.WK1
```

Figure 14.6 A Macro to Jump to the Second of Any Duplicate Entries

{if @left(@cell("contents",$A$9),5)="Cell "}{down 2}{up}{quit}   This is the displayed result of the string formula:

**+"{if @left(@cell(""contents"","&
@left(@cellpointer("address"),3)&
@string(@cellpointer("row")+1,0)&
"),5)="""&
@left(@cellpointer("contents"),5)&
"""}{down 2}{up}{quit}"**

Its purpose is to compare the first five characters of the current cell with the first five characters of the cell below (notice how the third part of this string formula uses @cellpointer("row")+1). If they are the same, the macro moves down two cells to bring the second cell more into view, then up one cell, leaving the cell pointer at the second entry.

Checking only the first five characters is an arbitrary convention that allows you to identify entries that are almost, but not entirely, identical. You may want to modify this string formula to check the entire entry, or to check less than the first five characters of the entry.

{down}{branch *VIEWDUPS}   If the macro does not find a match at the first cell in the current column, the cell pointer is moved down one cell and the macro repeats: It continues in this way until it finds the first duplicate, then quits.

To use the macro, press Alt-V. If a duplicate is found, make your decision to retain or eliminate it, then press Alt-V to view the next duplicate.

Finding Strings-within-Strings in Release 2 and 2.01

We have examined a couple of macros designed to enhance or substitute for the /Range Search feature found in Release 2.2 and 3, but none of the examples explored so far have the ability to search for a string-within-a-string. If you have Release 2 or 2.01, you may be interested in a way to duplicate this feature. Refer to the macro shown in Figure 14.7.

A1: ':   `READY`

```
          A         B         C         D         E         F         G         H
1   :                     *** FIND A STRING-WITHIN-A-STRING ***
2   \F        {}
3   *FIND     {getlabel "Enter the search string: ",FIND}
4   :         {blank FROW}
5   :         {getnumber "Search to what row? (ENTER for Unlimited) ",FROW}
6   :         {if FROW=0}{let FROW,8192}
7   FLOOP     {recalc FCALC}{if FROW=@cellpointer("row")}{quit}
8   FCALC     {if @iserr(@find("COPY",$A$1,0))}{down}{branch FLOOP}
9   :         Press Return to continue, Esc to stop.{get FKEY}
10  :         {esc}{if FKEY="~"}{down}{branch FLOOP}
11  :         {quit}
12  FIND      COPY
13  FROW            24
14  FKEY      ~
15
16
17
18  Cell B8:  +"{if @iserr(@find(""""&+FIND&"""","&@CELLPOINTER("address")&
19            ",0))}{down}{branch FLOOP}"
20
F_14-7.WK1
```

Figure 14.7 A Macro to Find a String-within-A-String

{getlabel "Enter the search string: ",FIND}   The macro begins by prompting you for the string you want to search for and places your answer in the cell named FIND. You can enter a portion of a string or an entire string at this point.

{blank FROW}   Blanks the cell in the macro named FROW.

{getnumber "Search to what row? (ENTER for Unlimited) ",FROW}   Prompts you for the row you want to search down to. If you press Enter, the macro will search in the current column to end of the worksheet at row 8192.

{if FROW=0}{let FROW,8192}   If you press Enter at the prompt, FROW will remain blank, which means its contents equal zero. In that case, the macro converts the contents of FROW to 8192.

{recalc FCALC}{if FROW=@cellpointer("row")}{quit}   Recalculates the string formula at FCALC. If the row number at FROW equals the cell pointer row, the macro quits.

{if @iserr(@find("COPY",$A$1,0))}{down}{branch FLOOP}   This is the result of the string formula in FCALC, which consists of:

+"{if @iserr(@find("""&
+FIND&
""","&
@cellpointer("address")&
",0))}{down}{branch FLOOP}"

The purpose of this line is to determine whether the string you stored in FIND at the starting prompt is found in the current cell. If not, the @find formula returns an error, which causes the remainder of this line to be executed. The cell pointer is moved down to the next cell and the macro loops back to FLOOP.

Press Return to continue, Esc to stop.{get FKEY}   Otherwise, a prompting line is typed into the upper panel and the macro pauses until you press any key. If you have Release 2.2 or 3, you may want to replace the typed message with a long {indicate} prompt.

{esc}{if FKEY="~"}{down}{branch FLOOP}   The message is eliminated with the {esc} command. If you pressed Return, the cell pointer is moved down to the next cell and the macro loops back to FLOOP.

{quit}   If you press any other key (including Escape), the macro quits.

When you use this macro, the cell pointer will move rapidly down the current column until it reaches a found string. If you press Return, the search will continue until another matching string is found or until the cell pointer reaches the designated row to quit or the end of the worksheet. If you press any other key at a found record, the macro will quit.

Locating a String with /Data Query Find

The preceding macro will work in any column in the worksheet to locate a string or a portion of a string. However, although it moves down the column fairly quickly, it does have to visit each cell in turn to check for the record you want. If you are developing an application that requires a more instant jump to a found string in a large database, you may want to set up /Data Query Input and Criterion ranges and use the macro in Figure 14.8.

The last macro we examined is not case sensitive, which means you can enter your search string using uppercase, lowercase, or proper case. However, because the /Data Query Find sequence in 1-2-3 is case sensitive, the macro in Figure 14.8 includes some complicated string formulas to check for a match in your database using all uppercase, lowercase, or proper case versions of your search string. While this does not ensure absolute identification of all matches to the string you are trying to locate (it will not properly identify a match with the string dBASE, for example), it will catch most occurrences.

A1: ':   **READY**
Enter the search string:

```
         A        B        C        D        E        F        G        H
1    :              *** LOCATE A STRING WITH /DATA QUERY FIND
2    \L        {}
3    *LOCATE    {getlabel "Enter the search string: ",LOCATE}
4    :          {windowsoff}{paneloff}{recalc LFIND}{recalc LFIND2}
5    LFIND      #not#@iserr(@find("COMP",{down 2},0))#or##not#@iserr(
6    LFIND2     @find("Comp",{down 2},0))#or##not#@iserr(@find("comp",
7    :          {down 2},0))~
8    :          /dqf{esc 4}{panelon}{windowson}{query}{quit}
9    LOCATE     comp
10
11
12   Cell B5:
13   +"#not#@iserr(@find(""""&@UPPER(LOCATE)&"""",{down 2},0))#or##not#@iserr("
14
15   Cell B6:
16   +"@find(""""&@PROPER(LOCATE)&"""",{down 2},0))#or##not#@iserr(
17   @find(""""&@LOWER(LOCATE)&"""","
18
19
20
```

F_14-8.WK1   **CMD**

Figure 14.8 A Macro to Locate a String with /Data Query Find

Here's how the macro works.

{getlabel "Enter the search string: ",LOCATE}   Prompts for the search string, placing your response in LOCATE.

{windowsoff}{paneloff}{recalc LFIND}{recalc LFIND2}   Turns off the windows and panel, and recalculates the string formulas in LFIND and LFIND2.

#not#@iserr(@find("COMP",{down 2},0))#or##not#@iserr(This is the displayed result in LFIND of the string formula:

+"#not#@iserr(@find(""""&
@upper(LOCATE)&
"""",{down 2},0))#or##not#@iserr("

The purpose of this line is to begin typing a formula in the current criterion cell. Once fully entered, the formula determines that there is no error when the macro tries to find at least one of these: the uppercase version of the search string, the lowercase version, or the proper case version.

@find("Comp",{down 2},0))#or##not#@iserr(@find("comp",   This is the displayed result in LFIND2 of the string formula:

+"@find(""""&
@proper(LOCATE)&
"""",{down 2},0))#or##not#@iserr(

@find(""""&
@lower(LOCATE)&
"""",

Its purpose is to continue typing the formula just described.

{down 2},0))˜   This is the completion of the formula.

/dqf{esc 4}{panelon}{windowson}{query}{quit}   Once the formula is entered in the current criterion cell, the macro executes a /Data Query Find, escapes from the /Data Query menu, then presses the F7 Query key to instantly jump the cell pointer to the search string. At this point you can edit the found record by pressing F2, stay at the found record by pressing F7 Query, find the next record by pressing DownArrow, find the previous record with PgUp, or return to the original cell by pressing Return.

Deleting Zero and Blank Rows

If you have a very large database filled with blank rows that you want to eliminate, you may find the task tedious and unnecessarily time-consuming. If your database is in alphabetical order except for the blank rows, the easiest way to isolate and delete the rows may be to select /Data Sort, which will combine all blank rows into one block, then delete that entire block.

   If your database is not in alphabetical order, you can insert a new column, select /Data Fill to fill the column with consecutive numbers, then sort on some other cell (which again will combine all the blank rows into one block), delete the block of blank rows, then resort the database by the new /Data Fill column, and finally delete the /Data Fill column.

   Alternately, you may be interested in the macro in Figure 14.9.

{let DHERE,@cellpointer("address")}{blank DCOUNT}   The macro begins by creating a place-marker for the current cell at DHERE, then blanks DCOUNT.

{getnumber "Test how many cols across for row deletion? ",DELT}   Prompts for the number of columns across you want the macro to test for zero or blank cells before doing a /Worksheet Delete Row. Your response is stored in DELT.

{menubranch DMENU}{quit}   Calls up the menu choices *End of Worksheet* and *Specified-Row*. If you select *End of Worksheet*, the macro operates until it reaches the row in which resides the End Home cell. If you select *Specified-Row*, you will be prompted for the row down to which you want the macro to operate.

{indicate WAIT} or **{indicate WAIT}{branch DSPEC}**   Whether you select *End of Worksheet* or *Specified-Row*, the macro changes the *READY* indicator to the word *WAIT*. If you have Release 2.2 or 3, of course, you can use a longer Indicator message, such as *Macro is eliminating rows, please wait.*

```
              A                   B              C        D        E        F              G
 1   :                            *** DELETE 0 AND BLANK ROWS ACROSS RANGE ***
 2   \D          {}
 3   *DELROW     {let DHERE,@cellpointer("address")}{blank DCOUNT}
 4   :           {getnumber "Test how many cols across for row deletion? ",DELT}
 5   :           {menubranch DMENU}{quit}
 6   DMENU       End of Worksheet           Specified-Row
 7   :           Delete to worksheet end    Delete empty rows to a specified row.
 8   :           {indicate WAIT}            {indicate WAIT}{branch DSPEC}
 9   :           {goto}{end}{home}
10   :           {let DENDHM,@cellpointer("address")}{esc}
11   DLOOP1      {recalc DENDROW}{recalc DCALC}
12   DCALC       {if @cellpointer("row")>@cell("row",A71)}{branch DQUIT}
13   :           {if @length(@cellpointer("contents"))>0}{down}{branch DLOOP1}
14   :           {if @cellpointer("contents")>0}{down}{branch DLOOP1}
15   :           {for DCTR,1,DELT,1,DLOOP2}
16   :           {if @length(@cellpointer("contents"))>0}{recalc DCALC2}{branch DCALC2}
17   :           {if @CELLPOINTER("CONTENTS")=0}/wdr~{up}{let DCOUNT,DCOUNT+1}
18   :           {recalc DCALC2}
19   DCALC2      {goto}A$1~{down}{branch DLOOP1}
20   DLOOP2      {right}{if @length(@cellpointer("contents"))>0}{forbreak}
21   :           {if @cellpointer("contents")>0}{forbreak}
22   :           {return}
23   DSPEC       {getlabel "Delete empty rows down to what row number? ",DNUM}
24   :           {recalc DCALC3}
25   DCALC3      {let DENDHM,"$A$80"}{branch DLOOP1}
26   DENDHM      $E$73
27   DENDROW                                 73
28   DCOUNT                                  2
29   DHERE       $A$63
30   :           {return}
31   DNUM        80
32   DQUIT       {goto}{DHERE}~{indicate}{quit}
33   DCTR                                    1
34   DELT                                    5
35
36   Cell B12:
37   +"{if @cellpointer(""row"")>
38   @cell(""row"",A"&@STRING(DENDROW-DCOUNT,0)&")}{branch DQUIT}"
39
40   Cell B19:
41   +"{goto}"&@MID(DHERE,1,2)&@STRING(@CELLPOINTER("row"),0)&
42   "~{down}{branch DLOOP1}"
43
44   Cell B25:
45   +"{let DENDHM,""$A$"&+DNUM&"""}{branch DLOOP1}"
46
47   Cell B27:
48   @VALUE(@RIGHT(DENDHM,@LENGTH(DENDHM)-(@FIND("$",DENDHM,1)+1)))
```

F_14-9.WK1

Figure 14.9 A Macro to Delete Zero and Blank Rows across a Range

{goto}{end}{home}   If you selected *End of Worksheet*, the macro presses the F5 Goto key, then End Home to send the cell pointer temporarily to the End Home location. Notice there is no tilde at this point.

{let DENDHM,@cellpointer("address")}{esc}   The macro stores the address of the End

Home location in DENDHM, then presses Escape to back out of the F5 Goto sequence and return the cell pointer to its previous location.

{recalc DENDROW}{recalc DCALC}   Recalculates DENDROW, which consists of the string formula:

@value(@right(DENDHM,@length(DENDHM)-(@find ("$",DENDHM,1)+1)))

The purpose of this string formula is to return, as a value, the row in which the End Home location of the spreadsheet resides. It does this by finding the second dollar sign ($) in the absolute address stored in DENDHM and extracting the right-most characters from that point on.

{if @cellpointer("row")>@cell("row",A71)}{branch DQUIT}   This is the cell named DCALC that displays its results based on the string formula:

+"{if @cellpointer(""row"")>
@cell(""row"",A"&
@string(DENDROW-DCOUNT,0)&
")}{branch DQUIT}"

The purpose of this line is to determine whether the current row is greater than the End Home row (less the number of rows already deleted). If so, the macro branches to DQUIT, where the cell pointer is returned to its original position, the indicator is returned to normal, and the macro quits.

{if @length(@cellpointer("contents"))>0}{down}{branch DLOOP1}   This is where the macro determines whether or not the cell consists of a label. If not, the cell pointer is moved down one cell and the macro loops back to DLOOP1.

Note: We could have used {if @cellpointer("type")="L"} here, but that would not have eliminated rows that included those troublesome cases of cells that look like blank cells, but actually consist of a single apostrophe.

{if @cellpointer("contents")>0}{down}{branch DLOOP1}   If the current cell contents are greater than zero, the cell pointer is moved down to the next cell, and the macro loops back to DLOOP1.

{for DCTR,1,DELT,1,DLOOP2}   This {for} loop counts at DCTR starting with the number one, counting up to the number of columns you stored in DELT, incrementing by ones, and for each increment runs the routine at DLOOP2. The routine at DLOOP2 moves to the right, checks for a label or contents greater than zero, and if it finds either, breaks the {for} loop with the {forbreak} command.

{if @length(@cellpointer("contents"))>0}{recalc DCALC2}{branch DCALC2}
Once the macro completes or breaks out of the {for} loop, the current cell is tested again. If it consists of a label, DCALC2 is recalculated and the macro branches to that line.

{if @cellpointer("contents")=0}/wdr˜{up}{let DCOUNT,DCOUNT+1}
Otherwise, if the current contents are equal to zero, the macro selects /Worksheet Delete Row, moves up one cell, then increments DCOUNT by one.

{recalc DCALC2}　　DCALC2 is recalculated.

{goto}A$1˜{down}{branch DLOOP1}　　This is the cell DCALC2, the displayed result of the string formula:

+"{goto"&
@mid(DHERE,1,2)&
@string(@cellpointer("row"),0)&
"˜{down}{branch DLOOP1}"

Its purpose is to send your cell pointer to the left-most cell in the current row of the range you are searching. It does this by combining the column letter of the starting column with the current cell pointer row.

　　The cell pointer is then moved down to the next row and the macro loops back to DLOOP1.

{right}{if @length(@cellpointer("contents"))>0}{forbreak}　　This and the next two lines are the routine at DLOOP2, already described.

{getlabel "Delete empty rows down to what row number? ",DNUM}　　If, at the beginning of the macro, you selected *Specified- Row*, this {getlabel} command prompts your for the row down to which you want the macro to operate, then stores your response in DNUM.

{recalc DCALC3}　　Recalculates the string formula in DCALC3.

{let DENDHM,"$A$80"}{branch DLOOP1}　　This is the displayed result in DCALC3 of the string formula:

+"{let DENDHM,""A"&
+DNUM&
"""}{branch DLOOP1}"

Its purpose is to change the contents of DENDHM to an address consisting of column A and the row down to which you want the macro to operate. Then the macro branches back to DLOOP1 and continues in the same program flow as it uses for the *End of Worksheet* choice. The difference is that the macro will stop at a designated cell rather than stopping at the row in which the End Home cell of the spreadsheet resides.

Eliminating Completely Empty Rows

The macro in Figure 14.10 is similar to the last macro described, except that it eliminates rows it identifies as completely empty, starting in Column A. Even though this macro checks

```
         A              B                   C         D         E         F         G
 1   :                                        *** ELIMINATE COMPLETELY EMPTY ROWS ***
 2   \E            {}
 3  *ELIMROW       {let E_HERE,@cellpointer("address")}{blank ECOUNT}
 4   :             {menubranch E_MENU1}{quit}
 5   E_MENU1       End of Worksheet            Specified-Row
 6   :             Delete to worksheet end  Delete empty rows to a specified row.
 7   :             {windowsoff}                {indicate WAIT}{branch ESPEC}
 8   :             {indicate WAIT}{paneloff}
 9   :             {goto}{end}{home}{let ENDHOME,@cellpointer("address")}{esc}
10   ELOOP         {if @cellpointer("type")<>"b"}{down}{branch ELOOP}
11   :             {end}{right}{recalc ENDROW}{recalc ECALC}
12   ECALC         {if @cellpointer("row")>@cell("row",A35)}{branch EQUIT}
13   :             {if @cellpointer("col")<>256}{end}{left}{down}{branch ELOOP}
14   :             {end}{left}/wdr~{let ECOUNT,ECOUNT+1}{branch ELOOP}
15   ESPEC         {getlabel "Delete empty rows down to what row number? ",ENUM}
16   :             {windowsoff}{paneloff}{recalc ECALC2}
17   ECALC2        {let ENDHOME,"$A$37"}{branch ELOOP}
18   :             {branch ESPEC2}
19   ENDHOME       $A$37
20   ENDROW                                    37
21   ECOUNT                                    2
22   E_HERE        $A$28
23   :             {return}
24   ENUM          37
25   EQUIT         {goto}{E_HERE}~{indicate}{quit}
26
27
28   Cell B12:
29   +"{if @cellpointer(""row"")>
30   @cell(""row"",A"&@STRING(ENDROW-ECOUNT,0)&")}{branch EQUIT}"
31
32   Cell B17:
33   +"{let ENDHOME,""$A$"&+ENUM&"""}{branch ELOOP}"
34
35   Cell B20:
36   @value(@right(ENDHOME,@length(ENDHOME)-(@find("$",ENDHOME,1)+1)))
37
```

F_14_10.WK1

Figure 14.10 A Macro to Eliminate Completely Empty Rows

the entire width of the worksheet, it actually operates faster than the previous macro that only checks a specified number of columns.

Since similarities between the two macros are easy to spot, we will focus here on the lines that constitute the real differences in approach.

{if @cellpointer("type")<>"b"}{down}{branch ELOOP}   This is the line at cell B10 in Figure 14.10 named ELOOP. Its purpose is to check whether the current cell is blank. If the cell is not blank, there is no reason to test further. The cell pointer is moved down to the next cell and the macro branches back to the beginning of this line to test that next cell.

{end}{right}{recalc ENDROW}{recalc ECALC}   If the current cell is not blank, the cell pointer is moved End RightArrow and the cells named ENDROW and ECALC are recalculated.

{if @cellpointer("row")>@cell("row",A35)}{branch EQUIT}   This is the cell named ECALC that displays its results based on the string formula:

+"{if @cellpointer(""row"")>
@cell(""row"",A"&
@string(ENDROW-ECOUNT,0)&
")}{branch EQUIT}"

As with the previous macro, the purpose of this line is to determine whether the current row is greater than the End Home row (less the number of rows already deleted). If so, the macro branches to EQUIT, where the cell pointer is returned to its original position, the indicator is returned to normal, and the macro quits.

{if @cellpointer("col")<>256}{end}{left}{down}{branch ELOOP}   You will remember that two lines ago the macro moved the cell pointer End RightArrow, which causes it to travel until it reaches a filled cell or the extreme right cell of the worksheet. If the resulting location is not in the farthest possible cell to the right (column IV, also the 256th column), there must be a cell with contents somewhere in the row. In that case, the cell pointer is moved End LeftArrow back to Column A, then down to the next row, and the macro loops back to continue at ELOOP.

Since the remainder of the macro is similar to the previous macro, it does not require further explanation. Be sure to remember when using this macro, however, that you must start with your cell pointer in Column A.

Deleting Rows Based on a Single Blank Cell

The macro in Figure 14.11 is of the same general type, except that this macro is designed to eliminate rows based on whether the cell in a particular column in each row is blank or not.

Hit Return to ZAP every row with a blank cell, Ctrl-Brk to Stop   This is a warning that appears in the upper panel, prompting you to press Return to continue with the macro, or Ctrl-Break to quit. If you have Release 2.2 or 3, you may want to replace this with a long {indicate} prompt, but be sure to include an {onerror} command that sends the program flow to an {indicate} command to restore the *READY* indicator if you press Ctrl-Break.

{?}{esc}   Pauses so you can press Return or Ctrl-Break. This is actually not as effective a way of pausing after having your macro type a message in the upper panel, because the user might press a directional key at this point. If that happens, the typed message will be entered into the current cell, potentially destroying important data which may be in that location. If anything else is typed (such as a letter or number), the {esc} command eliminates your extra keystroke(s) before the macro continues.

{goto}{end}{home}{let ZENDHM,@cellpointer("address")}{esc}   As with the two

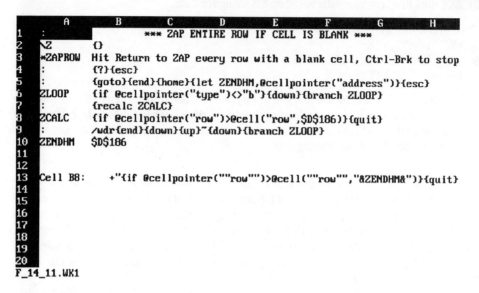

```
         A        B        C        D        E        F        G        H
1    :                    *** ZAP ENTIRE ROW IF CELL IS BLANK ***
2    \Z       {}
3    *ZAPROW  Hit Return to ZAP every row with a blank cell, Ctrl-Brk to stop
4    :        {?}{esc}
5    :        {goto}{end}{home}{let ZENDHM,@cellpointer("address")}{esc}
6    ZLOOP    {if @cellpointer("type")<>"b"}{down}{branch ZLOOP}
7    :        {recalc ZCALC}
8    ZCALC    {if @cellpointer("row")>@cell("row",$D$186)}{quit}
9    :        /wdr{end}{down}{up}~{down}{branch ZLOOP}
10   ZENDHM   $D$186
11
12
13   Cell B8:    +"{if @cellpointer(""row"")>@cell(""row"","&ZENDHM&")}{quit}
14
15
16
17
18
19
20
```

F_14_11.WK1

Figure 14.11 A Macro to Delete Rows Based on a Single Blank Cell

previous macros, the End Home location is recorded through use of an interrupted {goto} command and a {let} command.

{if @cellpointer("type")<>"b"}{down}{branch ZLOOP}   If the current cell is not blank, the cell pointer is moved down to the next cell and the macro loops back to the beginning of this cell.

{recalc ZCALC}   Otherwise, the macro recalculates the string formula in ZCALC.

{if @cellpointer("row")>@cell("row",$D$186)}{quit}   This is the displayed result in ZCALC of the string formula:

+"{if @cellpointer(""row"")>@cell(""row"","&
ZENDHM&
")}{quit}

The purpose of this line is to determine if the macro has yet reached the row in which the End Home cell resides. If so, the macro quits.

/wdr{end}{down}{up}~{down}{branch ZLOOP}   Deletes all rows down to the next filled cell in the column, then branches back to ZLOOP.

This is the fastest of the three row deletion macros, because this macro deletes entire blocks of rows at once, based on the ability to identify more than one blank cell in sequence.

Subtotaling Like Items in a Database

In Chapter 9, we presented a macro designed to subtotal and total all like items in a database. In this section we will look at an improved version of that macro. Whereas the macro in Figure 9.9 required that the Like Items column be beside the Subtotal column, the macro in Figure 14.12 will work with your Like Items column separated from the Subtotal column by any number of cells. Further, the macro in Figure 14.12 adds a subtotal identifier, something such as:

SUBTOTAL FOR EASTERN DIVISION:

Here's how the macro works.

Point to 1st of the Like Items and hit any key. ESC to quit.   The macro begins by typing a prompt in the upper panel. If you have Release 2.2 or 3, you may want to replace this with a long {indicate} prompt, but be sure to include an {onerror} command that sends the program flow to an {indicate} command to restore the *READY* indicator if you press Ctrl-Break.

{get S_KEY}{esc}{if S_KEY="{esc}"}{quit}   Pauses for you to press a single key and then eliminates the typed message. If you press Escape, the macro quits.

{if @left(S_KEY,1)="{"}{S_KEY}{branch *SUBTOT}   If you press a function key or directional key, the macro processes that key, then branches back to the beginning to type the prompt in the upper panel again. This allows you to move around the worksheet to point to the first of the like items you want to subtotal.

{if S_KEY<>"~"}{branch *SUBTOT}   If the key you press is not the Return key, the macro branches back to the beginning to type the prompt in the upper panel again.

{let S_COL,@cellpointer("col")}   Saves the number of the Like Items column in the cell named S_COL.

{let SUBHERE,@cellpointer("address")}   Creates a place-marker for the current cell, saving the address at SUBHERE.

Point to Amount Column to Subtotal.   Types another message in the upper panel, this time prompting you to point to the Amount column you want to subtotal.

{get S_KEY}{esc}{if S_KEY="{esc}"}{quit}   Pauses for you to press a single key and then eliminates the typed message. If you press Escape, the macro quits.

{if @left(S_KEY,1)="{"}{S_KEY}{branch SUBTOT2}   If you press a function key or directional key, the macro processes that key, then branches back to the beginning to type the prompt in the upper panel again.

```
                A        B          C          D        E          F        G          H
1    :                  *** SUBTOTAL LIKE ITEMS IN A DATABASE ***
2    \S         {}
3    *SUBTOT    Point to 1st of the Like Items and hit any key.  ESC to quit.
4    :          {get S_KEY}{esc}{if S_KEY="{esc}"}{quit}
5    :          {if @left(S_KEY,1)="{"}{S_KEY}{branch *SUBTOT}
6    :          {if S_KEY<>"~"}{branch *SUBTOT}
7    :          {let S_COL,@cellpointer("col")}
8    :          {let SUBHERE,@cellpointer("address")}
9    SUBTOT2    Point to Amount Column to Subtotal.
10   :          {get S_KEY}{esc}{if S_KEY="{esc}"}{quit}
11   :          {if @left(S_KEY,1)="{"}{S_KEY}{branch SUBTOT2}
12   :          {if S_KEY<>"~"}{branch SUBTOT2}
13   :          {let S_COL2,@cellpointer("col")}{goto}{SUBHERE}~
14   :          {recalc SPAN}{recalc SPANEX}
15   SUBLOOP    {let STEST,@cellpointer("contents")}
16   SUBLOOP2   {down}{if @cellpointer("type")="b"}{down}{SUBHEAD}{SQUIT}
17   :          {if STEST=@cellpointer("contents")}{branch SUBLOOP2}
18   :          /wir{down 2}~{down}{SUBHEAD}
19   :          {up 3}{if @cellpointer("type")="b"}{SINGLE}{branch SUBLOOP}
20   :          {down 3}{SUM}{down 2}{branch SUBLOOP}
21   SUBHEAD    {recalc SUBCALC}
22   SUBCALC    SUBTOTAL FOR EASTERN DIVISION:
23   SPAN       {right 3}{return}
24   S_COL              2
25   S_COL2             5
26   SUM        @sum({up 2}{end}{up}.{end}{down}{down})~/rf,2~~{SPANEX}{return}
27   SINGLE     {down 3}@sum({up 2}.{down})~/rf,2~~{SPANEX}{down 2}{return}
28   SQUIT      {up 3}{if @cellpointer("type")="b"}{SINGLE}{quit}
29   :          {down 3}{SUM}{down 2}{quit}
30   STEST      EASTERN DIVISION
31   S_KEY      ~
32   :          {return}
33   SUBHERE    $B$82
34   :          {return}
35   SPANEX     {left 3}{return}
36
37   Cell B22:
38   +"SUBTOTAL FOR "&
39   @if(@cell("type",STEST)="v",@string(STEST,0),STEST)"&
40   ": "
41
42   Cell B23:
43   +"{"&@if(S_COL>S_COL2,"left","right")&" "&
44   &@string(@abs(+S_COL-S_COL2),0)&"}"&"{return}"
45
46   Cell B35:
47   +"{"&@if(S_COL>S_COL2,"right","left")&" "&
48   @string(@abs(+S_COL-S_COL2),0)&"}"&"{return}"
```

F_14_12.WK1

Figure 14.12 A Macro to Subtotal Like Items in a Database

{if S_KEY<>"~"}{branch *SUBTOT2}   Similarly, if you press any key but the Return key, the macro branches back to *SUBTOT2 to once again type the prompt in the upper panel.

{let S_COL2,@cellpointer("col")}{goto}{SUBHERE}~   Saves the number of the Subtotal column in the cell range-named S_COL2, then returns the cell pointer to the first of the like items in the database.

{recalc SPAN}{recalc SPANEX}   Recalculates the string formulas at SPAN and SPANEX.

{let STEST,@cellpointer("contents")}   Stores the contents of the first of the like items in STEST.

{down}{if @cellpointer("type")="b"}{down}{SUBHEAD}{SQUIT}   Moves down and tests for a blank cell. If the cell is blank, it is assumed the macro has come to the end of the database, a closing subroutine at SUBHEAD is executed, and the macro branches to SQUIT to execute the subtotal of the last item before quitting.

{if STEST=@cellpointer("contents")}{branch SUBLOOP2}   At this point, the macro tests for whether the current cell matches the contents of STEST. If so, the macro branches back to the previous line at SUBLOOP2, moving down to the next cell, and testing for a blank cell and a match with STEST.

/wir{down 2}~{down}{SUBHEAD}   If there is no match with STEST, that means the cell pointer is on a cell with a different item description. In that case, the macro inserts rows between the last group of like items and the current item by selecting /Worksheet Insert Row, painting down two more cells, and pressing Return. The cell pointer is moved down to the middle row of the three newly inserted rows, and the macro calls the subroutine at SUBHEAD designed to type the subtotal identifier for the most recently identified like items.

{up 3}{if @cellpointer("type")="b"}{SINGLE}{branch SUBLOOP}   The cell pointer is moved back up three cells to check for a blank cell. If the cell is blank, that means the current item is unique (there are no other items that match it), so the @sum formula must be for only one record. In that case, the macro branches to the subroutine at SINGLE before it branches back to the cell at B15 named SUBLOOP.

{down 3}{SUM}{down 2}{branch SUBLOOP}   Otherwise, if there is more than one like item in the current batch, the macro runs the subroutine at SUM, then moves down two cells and branches back to SUBLOOP.

{recalc SUBCALC}   Recalculates the string formula in the next line named SUBCALC.

SUBTOTAL FOR EASTERN DIVISION: This is the displayed result of string formula:

```
+"SUBTOTAL FOR
"&@if(@cell("type",STEST)="v",@string(STEST,0),STEST)&"
": "
```

The string begins typing **SUBTOTAL FOR**, then checks for whether STEST is a value. If so, the string of the value is used; otherwise, the label in STEST is used. Finally, it types a colon and a space. The result is a subtotal identifier that includes the name of the most recent item subtotaled.

{right 3}{return}   This is the displayed result of the string formula at SPAN:

```
+"{"&
@if(S_COL>S_COL2,"left","right")&
" "&
&@string(@abs(+S_COL-S_COL2),0)&
"}"&
"{return}"
```

This formula calculates the number columns between the Like Items column and the Subtotal column, then moves right the number of cells required to span that distance.

@sum({up 2}{END}{up}.{end}{down}{down})~/rf,2~~{SPANEX}{return}   Having moved to the Subtotal column, an @sum formula is entered to sum the last identified like items. The cell if formatted for Fixed Format with two decimals (though you can easily change this) and the subroutine at SPANEX returns the cell pointer back to the Like Items column using a formula similar to the string formula in SPAN.

{down 3}@sum({up 2}.{down})~/rf,2~~{SPANEX}{down 2}{return}   This is the subroutine named SINGLE, designed to create an @sum formula for a single item only. It operates in a way similar to the previous line, but it only sums the two cells immediately above the current cell.

{up 3}{if @cellpointer("type")="b"}{SINGLE}{quit}   This is the beginning of the subroutine named SQUIT, designed to check whether the latest group consists of one or more than one item to subtotal. If there is only one item, the macro runs the subroutine SINGLE, then quits.

{down 3}{SUM}{down 2}{quit}   Otherwise, the cell pointer is moved back down, the macro runs the subroutine named SUM, the cell pointer is moved down two more cells, and the macro quits.

An example of the type of results you can get using this macro is shown in Figure 14.13.

Summary

In this chapter we explored the use of variable string formulas to create macros that will allow you to manipulate elements of your database. Concepts covered in this chapter include:

```
F19: (,2) [W16] @SUM(F15..F18)                                    READY
```

```
          A            B            C         D          E         F
 1
 2  Description   Part No.     Color    Unit Price  Qty       Total
 3  -----------   -----------  -------  ---------   --------  =================
 4
 5  ARMCHAIR      AB-90-56     Red         467.00    490      228,830.00
 6  ARMCHAIR      AB-90-56     Red         467.00    433      202,211.00
 7  ARMCHAIR      AB-90-56     Red         467.00    243      113,481.00
 8
 9  SUBTOTAL FOR ARMCHAIR:                                    544,522.00
10
11  COUCH         AB-90-892    White     1,808.00    117      211,536.00
12
13  SUBTOTAL FOR COUCH:                                       211,536.00
14
15  END TABLE     AB-90-354    Oak         244.00    123       30,012.00
16  END TABLE     AB-90-354    Oak         244.00    256       62,464.00
17  END TABLE     AB-90-354    Oak         244.00    736      179,584.00
18
19  SUBTOTAL FOR END TABLE:                                   272,060.00
20
F_14_13.WK1
```

Figure 14.13 Example of the Results of the Subtotal Macro

- The use of @choose in a string formula to enter a data item that varies according to the number of passes through a {for} loop.

- The use of a string formula to extract and display the letter or letters representing the current column. Since using @cellpointer("col") provides only the column number, not the letter(s), a combination of @cellpointer functions must be used to extract the column letter from the current address.

- The duplication of Input range headings two rows above your database to establish headings for your Criterion range. This technique will ensure that your Criterion headings exactly match your Input headings, and makes your Criterion range immediately accessible just above the Input range.

- Use of the {query} command after the command sequence /Data Query Find at the end of a Query macro. Using this technique, pressing Enter at any found record returns you to Ready mode instead of to the /Data Query menu with its potentially dangerous Reset choice.

- Elimination of blank rows in a database by selecting /Data Sort, which will combine all blank rows into one block, then selecting /Worksheet Delete Row and highlighting the entire block of blank rows. If your database is not in alphabetical order, insert a new column, select /Data Fill to fill it with consecutive numbers, then sort on some other cell (which again will combine all the blank rows into one block), delete the block of blank rows, then resort the database by the new /Data Fill column, and finally delete the /Data Fill column.

- Creation of a string formula to send your cell pointer to left-most cell in the current row by following a {goto} command with a combination of the column letter "A," a string version of the current cell pointer row, and a tilde.

We explored macros in this chapter that are designed to:

- Instantly create a row or column of date headings in your spreadsheet;
- Automate the creation of an entire spreadsheet matrix with headings, sidings, underline cells, subtotals, and a grand total;
- Automate the establishment of /Data Query Input and Criterion ranges in a typical database, and initiate the first /Data Query Find operation;
- Instantly identify and leave your cell pointer at the second of any duplicate label entries in your database;
- For Release 2 and 2.01 users, emulate the /Range Search feature to find a string or a portion of a string without setting up /Data Query ranges;
- Modify the /Data Query Find feature to allow a search for a portion of a string in a /Data Query Input range;
- Automatically delete all rows that consist only of zero-value or blank cells in the range that you specify;
- Eliminate all completely empty rows from the current position to the End Home position or to any row that you specify;
- Delete all rows that have a blank cell in the current column, from the current position to the End Home location of the spreadsheet;
- Subtotal all like items in a database, displaying an identifier for each subtotal.

In Chapter 15 we will examine macros designed to control and manipulate the /File features of 1-2-3, including macros to switch the file directory; to save a file, save a backup and beep when finished; to view the size of a file in bytes; to list a filename table in your worksheet; to create a table of active files in Release 3; and to save a Macro Library .MLB file in Release 2.2.

15

USING FILE CONTROL MACROS

Scope

In this chapter we will examine macros to control and manipulate the file features of 1-2-3 using variable string formulas, custom menus, @functions, file-processing macro commands, and the new /File Administration of Release 2.2 and 3. These macros are designed to switch your file directory instantly; automatically save a file, save a backup, and beep when finished; present a message in your upper screen indicating the size of a file in bytes; list a filename table in your worksheet; create a table of active files in Release 3; and save a Macro Library .MLB file in Release 2.2.

Save File and Backup

In Chapter 5, we described a simple /File Save macro that calculates the worksheet, saves the file, and prints the file, giving beeps to indicate each operation is complete (see Figure 5.2).

The macro in Figure 15.1 is a more advanced /File Save macro that begins by telling you the time and date you last saved the file using this macro and prompting for whether you want to save it again. If you type **Y** for *Yes*, it saves the file, beeps, then prompts you to save

```
B4: +"Last Alt-S File Save was "&STIME&", "&SDATE&". Save again? (Y/N) "
```

```
           A              B              C       D        E
 1  :                     *** SAVE FILE, BACKUP, AND BEEP ***
 2  \S            {}
 3  *SAVE         {recalc SAVE}
 4  SAVE          Last Alt-S File Save was 05:41 PM, 19-Aug. Save again? (Y/N)
 5  :             {get SKEY}{esc}{if SKEY="N"}{quit}
 6  :             {calc}{contents STIME,SNOW,9,120}{let STIME,@trim(STIME)}
 7  :             {contents SDATE,SNOW,9,115}{let SDATE,@trim(SDATE)}
 8  :             /fs {bs}{home}{del}c{?}~r{esc}{beep 1}{beep 2}{beep 3}{beep 4}
 9  :             {menubranch S_MENU}{quit}
10  S_MENU        BACKUP COPY             QUIT
11  :             Insert disk in backup drive.  Return to Ready
12  :             /fs {bs}{home}{del}B~r{esc}    {quit}
13  :             {beep 1}{beep 2}{beep 3}{beep 4}
14  SNOTE         Backup copy has been saved.  Press Return.
15  :             {get SKEY}{if +SKEY<>""}{beep}{esc}{branch SNOTE}
16  :             {esc}{quit}
17  SKEY          Y
18  STIME         05:41 PM
19  SDATE         19-Aug
20  SNOW                          09:03:26 PM
F_15-1.WK1
```

Figure 15.1 A Macro To Save File, Save Backup, and Beep

a backup copy or quit. If you elect to save a backup copy, a copy is saved on your backup drive, the computer beeps, and a message is left in the upper panel to tell you that a backup copy was saved.

{recalc SAVE} The macro begins by recalculating the string formula in the next line named SAVE.

Last Alt-S File Save was 05:41 PM, 19-Aug. Save again? (Y/N) This is a message typed in the upper panel, the displayed result of a string formula:

+"Last Alt-S File Save was "&
STIME&
","&
SDATE&
". Save again? (Y/N) "

The string formula uses the information stored in STIME and SDATE from the last time you used the macro. This means, of course, that the first time you press Alt-S it will not provide the correct information; but after one use, this line displays the last time and date you saved the file with this macro.

Use this macro, especially for larger files, instead of the usual /File Save sequence. That way, you won't have to wonder whether you have saved a particular file recently and end by re-saving the file just to be sure. The larger the file, the more time you can save if you are able to quickly determine that the file has already been saved.

{get SKEY}{esc}{if SKEY="N"}{quit}   Pauses for you to press a single key and executes {esc} to eliminate the message in the upper panel. If you press **N** for *No* at the message prompt, this means you do not want the file to be saved again and the macro quits.

{calc}{contents STIME,SNOW,9,120}{let STIME,@trim(STIME)}   Otherwise, the worksheet is calculated, the current time from the @now formula at SNOW is copied to the cell named STIME using the {contents} command, and the extra spaces in the results are eliminated with a {let} command and the @trim function.

{contents SDATE,SNOW,9,115}{let SDATE,@trim(SDATE)}   The same techniques are used to copy the current date from the @now formula in SNOW to SDATE.

/fs {bs}{home}{del}c{?}~r{esc}{beep 1}{beep 2}{beep 3}{beep 4}   The macro selects /File Save and presses Space, then eliminates the space with Backspace. This allows editing of the offered filename. A press of the Home key takes the cursor to the beginning of the filename, the drive letter is deleted and replaced with a C, the file is saved (the letter R is for Replace), and the computer beeps to let you know it's done.

{menubranch S_MENU}{quit}   Calls up the menu choices *BACKUP COPY* and *QUIT*

/fs {bs}{home}{del}B~r{esc}   If you select *BACKUP COPY*, the macro selects /File Save, changes the drive letter to B (you may want to rewrite this to drive A), enters the filename, and selects Replace.

{beep 1}{beep 2}{beep 3}{beep 4}   Beeps to let you know the backup copy has been saved.

Backup copy has been saved. Press Return.   This message is typed in the upper panel.

{get SKEY}{if +SKEY<>"~"}{beep}{esc}{branch SNOTE}   Pauses for you to press any key. If you do not press Return, the macro beeps and loops back to SNOTE to display the same message again.

{esc}{quit}   Otherwise, if you press Return, the message is eliminated and the macro quits.

Using this macro, if you save and back up a file, then leave your desk, you won't have to wonder when you return whether or not you saved the file—a message will show in the upper panel reminding you that the file has been saved.

Saving a File with an Alternate Name

You have seen how we can save a file that already has a /File Save name by using /fs{?}~r{esc}. However, if you write a macro that prompts you to enter a completely new /File Save name, you will need a way to keep from entering an already existing filename and thus writing over other important files.

The macro in Figure 15.2 provides just such a technique. Designed to be used as a part of a larger macro that includes a prompted /File Save of a new file, this macro waits for you to enter the new name of the file to save and checks for whether the name already exists. If not, the /File Save operation is completed as expected. On the other hand, if the filename already exists, the macro offers the choices *Cancel*, *Replace*, and *Alt_Name* to deal with that.

Here's how the macro works.

{getlabel "Enter name of file to save: ",NEW_SAVE}   Prompts you to enter the name

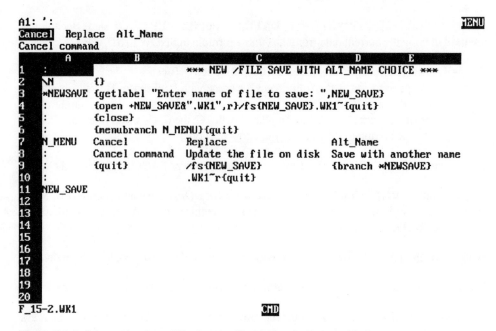

Figure 15.2 Macro to do a /File Save with Alternate Name Choice

of the file you want to save and places your response in the cell named NEW_SAVE.

{open +NEW_SAVE&".WK1",r}/fs{NEW_SAVE}.WK1~{quit}   This is the first use in this book of the {open} command, a file-processing command designed to open the named file in either Read mode, Write mode, or Modify mode (type **R**, **W**, or **M**). In this case, the filename you provided in response to the prompt is given a .WK1 suffix, then the macro attempts to open that file in the Read mode.

If the {open} command is *not* successful, the macro executes the rest of the line. This is the exact opposite of the way an {if} command works, where if a condition is false, the macro skips down to the next line. With the {open} command, if 1-2-3 is *not* able to open the file (in other words, if the file does not yet exist), the rest of the line is processed. In this case, the macro proceeds to select /File Save, types the contents of NEW_SAVE, enters the filename, and quits. The macro has been written to do this because nonexistence of the file means it is safe to save the current worksheet using that filename.

{close}　　If the {open} command *is* successful, the macro skips the rest of the line and proceeds to this line, where a {close} command closes the pre-existing file.

{menubranch N_MENU}{quit}　　Since the filename already exists, the menu choices *Cancel*, *Replace*, and *Alt_Name* appear. The first two choices, *Cancel* and *Replace*, will be familiar to you. If you select *Cancel*, the macro quits. If you select *Replace*, the macro selects /File Save of the filename, then selects **R** for *Replace*. The new choice, *Alt_Name*, simply causes the macro to branch back to the beginning at *NEWSAVE, where it prompts you for another name under which to save the current file.

　　By itself, this macro is not useful. However, it can save you or your users from inadvertently destroying already existing files, if it is included as a part of a larger macro that involves a prompted /File Save of a new file.

File-Processing Macro Commands

Some of the file-processing macro commands of 1-2-3 are used in the preceding macro, so this is a good place to list and describe the function of these types of commands.

　　The standard file commands such as /File Save, /File Retrieve, and /File Combine manipulate 1-2-3 worksheet files. Some of the standard commands such as /File Import also work with ASCII files, but only in a limited way. The nine advanced macro commands we will describe here significantly extend 1-2-3's file-processing capabilities, including the ability to open and close files, access and transfer data from any text or sequential disk file into 1-2-3, and write data from 1-2-3 to a wide variety of file formats outside 1-2-3.

{open *filename,access character*}　　Opens a file in either Read, Write, or Modify mode. In Read mode, information can be transferred only from the disk file to the worksheet. In Write mode, information can be transferred only from the worksheet to the disk file. In Modify mode, information can pass in both directions.

　　For the access character, type **R**, **W**, or **M**. If you use a letter other than these three, the file is opened in Read mode. Whatever the mode, opening a file places the byte pointer at the beginning of the file (the byte at position 0).

　　If the {open} command fails, macro execution continues in the same cell. Otherwise, if the command succeeds, any remaining commands on the same line are ignored, and execution skips to the cell below. This is the exact opposite of the way an {if} command works, where a false condition causes any remaining commands on the same line to be ignored, and a true condition causes the macro to execute the rest of the line.

{close}　　Closes any file opened with the {open} command. You must close one file before opening another, although 1-2-3 will do this automatically for you if you omit the {close} command before doing another {open}. If you use the {close} command when there are no open files, 1-2-3 will ignore it. On the other hand, any other file-manipulation commands will fail after a {close} command, unless preceded by another {open} command.

{filesize *location*}　　Returns the size (in bytes) of the currently open file. The position of the byte pointer is irrelevant. The result appears in the cell location you specify. If no file is currently open, the {filesize} command fails and macro execution continues in the same cell. Otherwise, the command succeeds and execution skips to the cell below. In other words, any command following a successful {filesize} command in the same macro line will be ignored.

{getpos *location*}   Returns your current position in the open file where the first character in a file is considered position 0. The result appears in the cell location you specify. Specifying a range is equivalent to specifying the range's top left cell. As with the {filesize} command, if no file is currently open, the {getpos} command fails and macro execution continues in the same cell. Otherwise, the command succeeds, any remaining commands on the same line are ignored, and execution skips to the cell below.

{setpos *file position*}   Moves the cursor to any file position you specify, where *position* is any number, a range name assigned to a single numeric cell, or a numeric formula. However, negative values are not acceptable. The move is absolute, not relative, which means the position is counted from the zero position rather than from the current position of the byte pointer.

{read *byte count,location*}   Reads the number of bytes you specify into the location you define, starting at the cursor's current file position. This command transfers into 1-2-3 the specified number of bytes, creating a label in the named cell. This command is intended for use with sequential files; for text files, the {readin} command is preferred.

{readln *location*}   Reads a single line of text from the currently open text file and places it as a label in the cell location you specify. Specifying a range is equivalent to specifying the range's top left cell.

Starting at the current position of the byte pointer (typically the beginning of a text line), this command reads to the end-of-line sequence marked by a carriage return and a line feed, coverts each byte to an LICS character, stores the string as a label in the specified cell location (minus the CR-LF sequence), and advances the byte pointer just past the CR-LF sequence to prepare for another {readln} command.

If no file is open, or the current file was opened in Write mode, or the byte pointer is already at the end of the file, the {readln} command fails and macro continues in the same cell. Otherwise, the command succeeds, remaining commands on the same line are ignored, and execution skips to the cell below.

{write *string*}   Writes any string of characters you specify to the current byte position in the currently open file. The argument *string* is a character string, an expression evaluating to a character string, or a range name assigned to a single cell that contains a string. This command converts each LICS character in the string to a DOS code, sends the string to a file (extending the length of the file if necessary) and advances the byte pointer just beyond the last character written to prepare for another {write} command.

{writeln *string*}   Writes any string of characters you specify to the current byte position in the currently open file, but adds a two-character end-of-line sequence. This command converts each LICS character in the string to a DOS code, sends the string to a file (extending the length of the file if necessary), writes a carriage return and a line feed to the file as an end-of-line sequence, and advances the byte pointer just beyond the last character written to prepare for another {writeln} command.

Creating a Message Showing a File Size

We can make use of the {open}, {close}, and {filesize} commands to create a macro that will report on the size of a given file. Such a macro is shown in Figure 15.3.

Here's how the macro works.

{getlabel "Enter filename: ",V_NAME}   Prompts you to enter the name of the file for which you want a report on the file size (in bytes).

{open +V_NAME&".WK1",R}{branch V_ISNT}   The macro attempts to open a version of this file with its .WK1 suffix. If the {open} command fails because the file does not exist, the macro continues on this same line. The remainder of the line causes a branch to V_ISNT where the message, **No such file exists. Press Enter.** is typed into the upper panel, the macro pauses so you can read it, the message is eliminated, and the macro quits.

{filesize V_SIZE}   Otherwise, if the file does exist, the macro skips to this line where the size of the open file is calculated and stored in V_SIZE.

```
A1: ':                                                           LABEL
No such file exists. Press Enter.
```

```
        A          B          C        D        E        F        G
1    :                     *** VIEW FILE SIZE ***
2    \V         {}
3    *VWSIZE    {getlabel "Enter filename: ",V_NAME}
4    :          {open +V_NAME&".WK1",R}{branch V_ISNT}
5    :          {filesize V_SIZE}
6    :          {close}
7    :          {recalc V_CALC}
8    V_CALC     File size is 5605 bytes. Press Enter.{get V_KEY}{esc}{quit}
9    V_SIZE             5605
10   V_NAME     BUDGET
11   V_KEY      ~
12   V_ISNT     No such file exists. Press Enter.
13   :          {get V_KEY}{esc}{quit}
14
15
16   Cell B8:   +"File size is "&@STRING(V_SIZE,0)&
17              " bytes. Press Enter.{get V_KEY}{esc}{quit}"
18
19
20
F_15-3.WK1                              CMD        CALC
```

Figure 15.3   Macro to Report on the Size (in Bytes) of a File

{close}   The open file is then closed.

{recalc V_CALC}   Recalculates the string formula at V_CALC.

File size is 5605 bytes. Press Enter.{get V_KEY}{esc}{quit}   This is a message typed in
the upper panel, the displayed result of a string formula:

+"File size is "&
@string(V_SIZE,0)&
" bytes. Press Enter. {get V_KEY}{esc}{quit}"

This message will vary, of course, depending on the actual size of the file you are checking.

Saving a Macro Library File

We have explored macros to save .WK1 files (Figures 5.2, 15.1, and 15.2) and a macro to
edit Macro Library .MLB files (Figure 12.9). In this section we discuss a macro to save a
Macro Library .MLB file. Because it addresses the Macro Library capability, this macro
works for Release 2.2 only.

The macro in Figure 15.4 is designed to save the entire file as a Macro Library file,
though there is a macro pause during highlighting of the range to save, so you can limit the
save-range to any size you like.

```
A1: ':                                    Save file first? (Y/N):   (ESC to Cancel)

            A          B          C         D         E        F         G
1    :                       *** MACRO LIBRARY .MLB FILE SAVE   ***
2    \M            {}
3    *MACSAVE      {indicate "Save file first? (Y/N):    (ESC to Cancel)"}{get MKEY}
4    :            {indicate}{if MKEY="{esc}"}{quit}
5    :            {if MKEY<>"Y"}{branch M_APP}
6    :            /fs{?}~r{esc}{home}
7    M_APP        {if @isapp("MACROMGR")}{app1}{branch MORE}
8    :            {windowsoff}{paneloff}/aaMACROMGR~7i~
9    :            {panelon}{windowson}
10   MORE         s{?}~y{esc}*{esc 2}{bs}{home}.{end}{home}{?}~n
11   :            {app1}e{end}~i~{quit}
12   MKEY         {ESC}
13
14
15
16
17
18
19
20
F_15-4.WK1                              CMD
```

Figure 15.4 A Macro to Save a Range to a Macro Library .MLB File

{indicate "Save file first? (Y/N): (ESC to Cancel)"}{get MKEY}   The macro begins by displaying a message in place of the *READY* indicator, prompting for whether you want to save the current file before saving a portion of the file as a Macro Library .MLB file. The {get} command pauses for your press of **Y** for *Yes*, **N** for *No*, or Escape to cancel the macro.

{indicate}{if MKEY="{esc}"}{quit}   The indicator is returned to normal. If the key you pressed is Escape, the macro quits.

{if MKEY<>"Y"}{branch M_APP}   If the key is not Y for Yes (presumably it was N for No), the file is not saved and the macro branches to M_APP.

/fs{?}~r{esc}{home}   Otherwise, the macro selects /File Save, pauses for your acceptance of the filename or entering of a new filename, selects R for Replace, and presses Escape in case Replace is not offered, then moves the cell pointer to the Home position in the Worksheet.

{if @isapp("MACROMGR")}{app1}{branch MORE}   Checks for whether the MACROMGR.ADN add-in application has been attached. If so, it is assumed that you have assigned Alt-F7 as the key to invoke it, so the macro equivalent of Alt-F7, {app1}, is executed. At this point the macro branches to MORE to continue with the .MLB file save.

{windowsoff}{paneloff}/aaMACROMGR~7i~   If the MACROMGR.ADN has not been attached, this line selects /Add-in Attach, enters MACROMGR, attaches the add-in to Alt-F7, and invokes the MACROMGR add-in.

{panelon}{windowson}   Turns off the windows and panel to suppress screen flicker and speed up the macro.

s{?}~y{esc}*{esc 2}{bs}{home}.{end}{home}{?}~n   This is the cell named MORE where the file saving occurs. From the MACROMGR.ADN menu choices Load, Save, Edit, Remove, Name-List, and Quit, the macro selects Save, then pauses for your selection or entry of a Macro Library .MLB file save name. If the file already exists, a No/Yes menu comes up with the instructions *Macro Library already exists on disk. Write over it?*. The macro types **Y** for *Yes*, then Escape in case the file did not already exist. At the prompt for a range to save, the macro types an asterisk and Escape twice to clear the default range, highlights the range from Home to the End Home position, pauses for your acceptance or modification of the range, then types **N** for *No* at the request for password attachment.

{app1}e{end}~i~{quit}   Saving a range to a Macro Library erases the contents of that range from the current worksheet. This may not be what you want, so the MACROMGR.ADN is again invoked, bringing up the choices Load, Save, Edit, Remove, Name-List, and Quit, the Edit choice is selected, and the macro presses End to highlight and select the last .MLB file saved. The macro selects I for Ignore, presses Return for the current cell pointer location, and quits.

Creating an Instant /File Directory Switch

In Chapter 8, we explored macros designed to quickly change your file directory (see Figures 8.13, 8.14, and 8.15). In this section we will examine another approach to this issue. The macro in Figure 15.5, called Directory Switch Menu, will offer you an instant way to change your file directory to the directory matching your current file, the default directory, your most typically used directory, or other.

Note: However, it uses the @cellpointer("filename") function, so it will not work in Release 2 or 2.01.

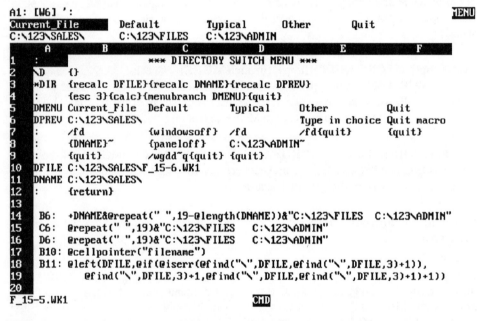

Figure 15.5 A Macro to Instantly Switch Your File Directory

This macro is especially effective as a Macro Library macro in either Release 2.2 or 3. As you will see, it requires some advance setup, customizing the macro to match the particular file directories of your own system. However, if you tend to switch directories often during a typical 1-2-3 session, you may find that you use this macro more often than any other in this book.

{recalc DFILE}{recalc DNAME}{recalc DPREV} The macro begins by recalculating the formulas in DFILE, DNAME, and DPREV. Although the {calc} command in the next line appears to make these {recalc} commands unnecessary, it is important that the macro recalculates these cells in this particular sequence.

{esc 3}{calc}{menubranch DMENU}{quit}   In case you have already selected /File Directory before remembering that you have this macro and deciding to use it, the {esc 3} command allows you to start this macro without first having to back out of the /File Directory menu sequence.

The macro proceeds to recalculate the entire worksheet, then calls the menu choices, *Current_File*, *Default*, *Typical*, *Other*, and *Quit*.

C:\123\SALES\   C:\123\FILES   C:\123\ADMIN   Although you cannot see the entire line in Figure 15.5, the choice description under *Current_File* shown in cell B6 actually displays descriptions (consisting of file directory names) under the *Current_File*, *Default*, and *Typical* choices. In other words, you will not have to point to the *Default* or *Tyical* choices to see the file directory descriptions that apply to those choices.

This is done with a string formula:

+DNAME&
@repeat(" ",19-@length(DNAME))&
"C:\123\FILES   C:\123\ADMIN"

Again, you will want to customize the file directories that are shown here to match both your own system's default directory and your most typically used directory (which may or may not be the same thing).

/fd{DNAME}~{quit}   If you select *Current_File*, the macro selects /File Directory, branches to DNAME to enter the directory of the current file, returns and quits. The contents of DNAME are the results of a string formula that extracts the current directory from the current path and filename in B10 (the cell named DFILE), as:

@left(DFILE,@if(@iserr(@find("\",DFILE,@find ("\",DFILE,3)+1)),
@find("\",DFILE,3)+1,@find("\",DFILE,@find("\",DFILE, 3)+1)+1))

Underlying the displayed result of DFILE is the Release 2.2 and 3 function, @cellpointer("filename"). The string formula in DNAME isolates the file directory from DFILE by extracting the characters to the left of the last backslash character in that cell.

If, instead of selecting *Current_File*, you point to either selection *Default*, or *Typical*, the description under these choices will appear as:

C:\123\FILES   C:\123\ADMIN

based on the underlying string formula,

@repeat(" ",19)&"C:\123\FILES   C:\123\ADMIN"

Using this technique, you will always be able to see the description of your default directory and your most typically used directory, whether you point to *Currrent_File*, *Default* or- *Typical*.

Note: If you ever change your default directory, you will want to manually change these menu descriptions and the menu description under *Current_File* to reflect that global default change.

{windowsoff}{paneloff}/wgdd˜q{quit}   If you select *Default*, the macro turns off the windows and panel to suppress screen flicker, then selects /Worksheet Global Default Directory, presses Return to accept the directory offered, quits the menu, and returns to *READY*. This accomplishes the same task as selecting /File Directory and manually typing in the directory established as your default directory.

/fdC:\123\ADMIN˜{quit}   If you choose *Typical*, the macro selects /File Directory, enters your most typically used file directory, and quits. Of course, you should customize this line to conform to your own most-often-visited directory.

/fd{quit}   If you choose *Other*, the macro simply selects /File Directory and quits, leaving you in the best position to enter another directory not included among the choices of the macro.

Creating a Filename Table

If you select /File Admin Table in Release 2.2 or 3, you will see the menu choices Reservation, Table, and Link-Refresh. If you then select Table, 1-2-3 will prompt you for the type of files (.WK1 Worksheet files or .PRN Print files, for example), the directory from which you want your table to extract its list of files, and the location in the current worksheet where you want your table to appear.

Unfortunately, the table that is entered in the worksheet, though it provides you with filenames, file dates, file times, and bytes, might well be unreadable due to the possibility of inappropriate column widths and displayed format. For example, the file dates will probably appear as straight numbers such as 32073, and the file time might appear as 0.507186.

The macro in Figure 15.6 is designed to prompt you for a location for your table, then allows you to choose the type of files you want listed, and the directory from which the table is to pull its list. The macro enters table headings, changes column widths, formats the columns, inserts the table, and prompts you for whether or not you want the table erased.

{indicate " Point to location for File Table... "}   The macro begins by changing the *READY* indicator to a prompt to point to the location where you want your file table. If you are not careful, you may write over existing data, so you may want to press End Home Ctrl-RightArrow to ensure that you move to a clear area for the table.

{onerror LQUIT}   If the macro quits because of an error or your press of Ctrl-Break, this command sends the program flow to LQUIT where it processes an {indicate} command to return the *READY* indicator to normal before the macro quits.

{get LKEY}{if LKEY="˜"}{branch LMORE}   The macro pauses for you to press a single key. If you press Return, it is assumed you are already at the location where you want your table, so the macro skips to the routine where the table is created.

B1: [W13]   Point to location for File Table...

```
          A           B          C          D          E          F          G
1    :                           *** LIST FILENAME TABLE ***
2    \L          {}
3    *LISTFILE   {indicate "    Point to location for File Table...   "}
4    :           {onerror LQUIT}
5    LGET        {get LKEY}{if LKEY="~"}{branch LMORE}
6    :           {if LKEY="{esc}"}{indicate}{quit}
7    :           {if @left(LKEY,1)<>"{"}{branch LGET}
8    LKEY        {DOWN}
9    :           {branch *LISTFILE}
10   LMORE       ^Filename{right}"Date{right}"Time{right}"Bytes{left 3}
11   :           {down}/fat{?}~{?}~~{up}/wcs15~{right}/rfd4{end}{down}~
12   :           {right}/rfdt2{end}{down}~{left 2}
13   :           {indicate     Erase this table?  (Y/N)       }
14   :           {get LKEY}{if LKEY="Y"}/re{end}{down}{end}{right}~
15   LQUIT       {indicate}{quit}
16
17
18
19
20
```
F_15-6.WK1   CMD

Figure 15.6 A Filename Table Macro for Release 2.2 or 3

{if LKEY="{esc}"}{indicate}{quit}   If you press Escape instead, the macro processes an {indicate} command to return the *READY* indicator to normal, then quits.

{if @left(LKEY,1)<>"{"}{branch LGET}   If the key you press is not a function key or directional key, this command causes the macro to ignore it, and the macro branches back to LGET to get the next keystroke.

{DOWN}   Otherwise, the macro continues to the next cell, which is LKEY where your keystroke was stored. In this example, the contents of LKEY shows {DOWN}, but this will vary depending on what keystroke you press.

{branch *LISTFILE}   The macro branches back to the beginning and continues in this way until you press Return, indicating that your cell pointer is finally at the location where you want your filename table.

^Filename{right}"Date{right}"Time{right}"Bytes{left 3}   Types the headings, Filename, Date, Time, and Bytes.

{down}/fat{?}~{?}~~{up}/wcs15~{right}/rfd4{end}{down}~   Moves down one cell, selects /File Admin Table, and pauses for your selection of the type of file to list. The macro then pauses for your selection of the file directory from which to list the files, enters your current location as the appropriate location for the table, and moves up one cell. The first column is changed to a width of 15, and the next column is given a date format.

{right}/rfdt2{end}{down}~{left 2}   The next column is given a time format and the macro moves back to the first column.

{indicate   Erase this table? (Y/N)   }   The *READY* indicator is changed to prompt for whether you want to erase the table.

{get LKEY}{if LKEY="Y"}/re{end}{down}{end}{right}~   The macro prompts you to press any key. If you press **Y** for *Yes*, the table is erased.

{indicate}{quit}   Finally, the indicator is returned to normal and the macro quits.

For an example of the type of results you will get using this macro, refer to Figure 15.7.

```
A22: [W15] ^Filename                                    Erase this table?  (Y/N)


        A              B          C        D        E        F
21
22       Filename        Date     Time    Bytes
23  0DUMMY.WK1        07/18/89 01:31 PM     1433
24  0FRAME.WK1       11/26/89 09:12 PM     2670
25  0MANUAL.WK1      11/09/89 11:21 AM     1593
26  COMPRESD.WK1     10/09/89 10:10 AM     1499
27  CONGRATS.WK1     11/14/89 09:47 AM     2040
28  GNT_TEST.WK1     11/12/89 05:59 PM     8526
29  HOUSE.WK1        10/10/89 01:23 PM     2047
30  LETRQUAL.WK1     10/13/89 06:35 AM     1469
31  PRN_CODE.WK1     11/08/89 06:35 PM     2467
32
33
34
35
36
37
38
39
40
F_15-7.WK1                                CMD                      CAPS
```

Figure 15.7 Sample Results of the Filename Table Macro

Active Filename Tables in Release 3

Release 3 has several additional features accessible from the /File Administration command sequence, among which is the ability to create a table showing the names of the currently active files. Since you are only limited by memory in the number of files you can have active in Release 3 at any one time, this ability to provide a list of your active files can be important for record-keeping, for recreating an important multiple-file session later, or simply for resolving any confusion you may have about the files you have active at any one time.

In addition to listing the active files for a current session, the /File Admin Table Active sequence lists the number of worksheets in each file, indicates whether they have been modified since their retrieval, and whether or not you have the reservation for these files.

The macro in Figure 15.8 is similar to the macro in Figure 15.6 in that it creates a table of files. The difference is that the file list in Figure 15.8 is for currently active files in a Release 3 session and the headings of the table include the headings, # Wkshts, Modified, and Reservation.

```
A:A1: ':                              Point to area for Active File List, ESC to quit.


  A       A            B          C        D        E        F          G
1 :                        *** ALL ACTIVE FILES LISTED ***
2 \A          {}
3 *ACTIVE     {indicate "Point to area for Active File List, ESC to quit."}
4 :           {get <<?>>A|KEY}{if <<?>>A|KEY="{esc}"}{indicate}{quit}
5 :           {if <<?>>A|KEY="~"}{indicate}{branch ABRANCH}
6 :           {A|KEY}{?}{esc}{indicate}
7 ABRANCH     'Filename{right}^Date{right}^Time{right}^Size{right}
8 :           ^# Wkshts{right}^Modified{right}^Reservation~
9 :           {left 6}{down}\-~/c~.{up}{right 6}{down}~
10 :          {down}/fata~{up}
11 :          {right}/rfd4{end}{down}~{right}/rfdt2{end}{down}~{left 2}{up}
12 :          {indicate      Erase this table?  (Y/N)      }
13 :          {get <<?>>A|KEY}{if <<?>>A|KEY="Y"}/re{end}{down}{end}{right}~
14 :          {indicate}{quit}
15 A|KEY      {CALC}
16 :          {return}
17
18
19
20
F_15-8.WK3                                       CMD
```

Figure 15.8 A Macro to List Active Files in Release 3

It would be redundant to go through this macro line by line, but it should be pointed out that a wild-card filename <<?>> has been added before every occurrence of the range name A|KEY so as to provide for use of this macro in a Macro Library file as described in Chapter 7.

An example showing the results of this macro can be seen in Figure 15.9.

Note: The number 1 in the column labeled "# Wkshts" represents a quantity, while the number 1 in the columns labeled "Modified" and "Reservation" represent a true condition. If a given file has not been modified or you do not have its reservation, a zero will be displayed.

```
A:A22: [W12] 'Filename                          Erase this table?  (Y/N)
```

A	A	B	C	D	E	F	G
21							
22	Filename	Date	Time	Size	# Wkshts	Modified	Reservation
23							
24	FILE0001.WK3	11/29/89	12:04 PM	1385	1	1	1
25	F_15-9.WK3	12/03/89	04:21 PM	2024	1	1	1
26							

```
F_15-9.WK3                              CMD
```

Figure 15.9 Sample Results of the Active File Table Macro

Summary

In this chapter we examined macros to control and manipulate the file features of 1-2-3 using variable string formulas, custom menus, @functions, file-processing macro commands, and the new /File Administration of Release 2.2 and 3. Concepts and techniques covered in this chapter include:

- The {contents} command and @trim function can be used to copy the current date into one cell and the time into another, both copies being taken from a single cell containing an @now function.
- The {open} command opens a file in either Read, Write, or Modify mode. If the {open} command fails, macro execution continues in the same cell.
- The {close} command closes any file opened with the {open} command. You must close one file before opening another, although 1-2-3 will do this automatically for you if you omit the {close} command before doing another {open}.
- The {filesize} command returns the size (in bytes) of the currently open file. The result appears in the cell location you specify. If no file is currently open, the {filesize} command fails and macro execution continues in the same cell.
- The {getpos} command returns your current position in the open file. The result appears in the cell location you specify. As with the {filesize} command, if no file is open, the {getpos} command fails and macro execution continues in the same cell.
- The {setpos} command moves the cursor to any file position you specify. The position

must be counted from the zero position rather than from the current position of the byte pointer.

- The {read} command reads the number of bytes you specify into the location you define, starting at the cursor's current file position. This command is intended for use with sequential files; for text files, the {readln} command is preferred.

- The {readln} command reads a single line of text from the currently open text file and places it as a label in the cell location you specify.

- The {write} command writes any string of characters you specify to the current byte position in the currently open file.

- The {writeln} command writes any string of characters you specify to the current byte position in the currently open file, but adds a two-character end-of-line sequence.

- If you select /File Admin Table in Release 2.2 or 3, you will see the menu choices - Reservation, Table, and Link-Refresh. Unfortunately, if you select Table, the filenames, file dates, file times, and bytes might well be unreadable until you adjust its column widths and range formats.

- Release 3 has several additional features accessible from the /File Administration command sequence, including the ability to create a table of your active files.

The macros covered in this chapter were:

- A macro that shows the time and date you last saved the file using this macro, saves the file, saves a backup copy, and beeps when done.

- A macro designed to do a /File Save, check for whether the /File Save name already exists, and prompt you with the choices *Cancel*, *Replace*, and *Alt_Name* if so.

- A macro that uses the {open}, {close}, and {filesize} commands to report on the size of a user-specified file.

- A macro designed to save a range in the current file as a Macro Library .MLB file.

- A Release 2.2 or Release 3 Directory Switch macro that offers you an instant way to change your file directory to the directory matching your current file, the default directory, your most typically used directory, or other.

- A Filename Table macro for Release 2.2 or 3 that prompts you for a location for your table, the type of files to list, and the appropriate directory. The macro enters table headings, changes column widths, formats the columns, inserts the table, and prompts you for whether or not you want the table erased.

- A macro to list active files in Release 3. The headings of the table created are similar to the Filename Table, except that they also include the headings for number of worksheets and modification and reservation status of your active files.

In Chapter 16 we will examine Print Control macros, including macros to print alternate columns, print in elite compressed style, print and save a worksheet, judge the width of your print range prior to printing, print prompted quantities of a file, and automatically change your print setup codes.

16

USING PRINT CONTROL MACROS

Scope

In this chapter we will explore Print Control macros, including macros to print alternate columns, print in elite compressed style, print and save a worksheet, judge the width of your print range prior to printing, print prompted quantities of a file, and automatically change your print setup codes.

Quantities of a File Printed

In Chapter 15 we examined several macros designed to improve on the /File Save features of 1-2-3. The macro in Figure 16.1 also does a /File Save, but it is primarily designed to facilitate the printing of multiple copies of a range from the worksheet.

{getnumber "Enter Number of copies to print: ",QTY}   The macro begins by prompting you for the number of copies you want to print.

/fs{?}~r{esc}   Selects /File Save, pauses for your agreement or modification of the offered filename, types **R** for *Replace*, then Escape in case the Cancel-Replace menu was not offered.

A1: ':   READY

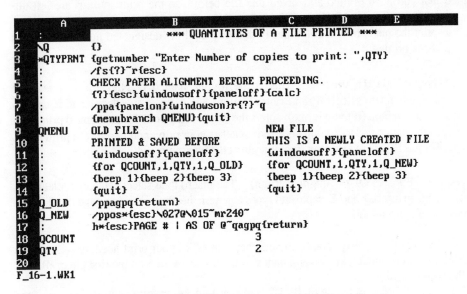

```
              A              B              C       D        E
1    :                 ✱✱✱ QUANTITIES OF A FILE PRINTED ✱✱✱
2    \Q              {}
3    ✱QTYPRNT       {getnumber "Enter Number of copies to print: ",QTY}
4    :               /fs{?}~r{esc}
5    :               CHECK PAPER ALIGNMENT BEFORE PROCEEDING.
6    :               {?}{esc}{windowsoff}{paneloff}{calc}
7    :               /ppa{panelon}{windowson}r{?}~q
8    :               {menubranch QMENU}{quit}
9    QMENU           OLD FILE                        NEW FILE
10   :               PRINTED & SAVED BEFORE          THIS IS A NEWLY CREATED FILE
11   :               {windowsoff}{paneloff}          {windowsoff}{paneloff}
12   :               {for QCOUNT,1,QTY,1,Q_OLD}      {for QCOUNT,1,QTY,1,Q_NEW}
13   :               {beep 1}{beep 2}{beep 3}        {beep 1}{beep 2}{beep 3}
14   :               {quit}                          {quit}
15   Q_OLD           /ppagpq{return}
16   Q_NEW           /ppos✱{esc}\027@\015~mr240~
17   :               h✱{esc}PAGE # | AS OF @~qagpq{return}
18   QCOUNT                                  3
19   QTY                                     2
20
```
F_16-1.WK1

Figure 16.1 A Macro to Print Multiple Copies of a Worksheet Range

CHECK PAPER ALIGNMENT BEFORE PROCEEDING.   Types a warning message in the upper panel.

{?}{esc}{windowsoff}{paneloff}{calc}   Pauses so you can read the message. When you press Return, the Escape eliminates anything you may have typed into the cell inadvertently, the windows and panel are turned off, and the worksheet is recalculated.

/ppa{panelon}{windowson}r{?}~q   Selects /Print Printer Align, turns on the panel and windows, selects Range, pauses for your agreement or modification of the offered range, enters the result, and quits the /Print menu.

{menubranch QMENU}{quit}   Calls up the menu choices *OLD FILE* and *NEW FILE*.

{windowsoff}{paneloff}   Turns off the windows and panel to suppress screen flicker and speed up the macro.

{for QCOUNT,1,QTY,1,Q_OLD} or **{for QCOUNT,1,QTY,1,Q_NEW}**   The macro counts at QCOUNT, starting with one, counts up to the number of copies you want printed as stored in QTY, counting by ones, and for each increment, runs the routine at Q_OLD if you selected *OLD FILE* and Q_NEW if you selected *NEW FILE*.

{beep 1}{beep 2}{beep 3}{quit}   When the last copy is printed, the computer beeps three times and the macro quits.

/ppagpq{return}   This is the routine named Q_OLD. If you selected *OLD FILE*, it is assumed that you have printed and saved this file before, so the print settings are left unchanged. The macro simply selects /Print Printer Align Go Page Quit and returns to the {for} loop to print the next copy. It continues in this way until the designated number of copies have all been printed.

/ppos*{esc}\027@\015˜mr240˜   This is the routine named Q_NEW. If you selected *NEW FILE*, the macro selects /Print Printer Options Setup, types an asterisk and Escape to clear the setup default (if there is one), enters the Epson setup code for condensed print (you may need to change this to a setup code that matches your printer and preferred print type), selects Margin Right, and sets the right margin at the maximum, 240.

h*{esc}PAGE # | AS OF @˜qagpq{return}   The macro then selects Heading, clears the default with an asterisk and Escape, and types a generic heading showing page number and as/of date of the printout.

1-2-3 will automatically replace the number sign (#) in your print heading with a page number. If your printout takes several pages, you will see *PAGE 1* on the first page, *PAGE 2* on the second, and so on.

The vertical bar in a heading tells 1-2-3 to place whatever follows in the center of the screen. A second vertical bar would be an indication to place whatever follows at the right edge of the designated margin.

The @ sign in a heading is automatically replaced with today's date. Since typing @now or @today in your heading will not work, this is a substitute that performs the equivalent function.

The macro then selects Quit Align Go Page Quit, and returns to the {for} loop. It continues in this way until the designated number of copies are all printed.

Print, Calculate, and Save a Worksheet

The macro in Figure 16.2 is also designed to save the file, as well as offering several print styles such as Standard Print, Condensed Print, Double-Spaced Print, and Condensed Double-Spaced.

{menubranch PMENU1}{quit}   The macro begins by calling the menu choices *Save_File* and *Print_Without_Saving*. The description under these menu choices is a separate prompt *Check the paper alignment*.

{calc}/fs{?}˜r{esc}   Calculates the worksheet, selects /File Save, waits for your acceptance or modification of the /File Save name, then types **R** for *Replace* and Escape in case you were not offered a Cancel-Replace menu.

/ppr{?}˜{windowsoff}{paneloff}   This is the cell of the macro named PSKIP where the print attributes are assigned. The program flow skips to this point if you select

```
A1: [W8] ':                                                              MENU
Std_Print    Print_Condensd  Double-Spaced  Condensed/Dbl-Space
Std Print
        A          B          C          D          E        F
1  :                    *** PRINT, CALC & SAVE ***
2  \P          {}
3  *PRNSAV     {menubranch PMENU1}{quit}
4  PMENU1      Save_File       Print_Without_Saving
5  :           Check the papeCheck the paper alignment
6  :           {calc}/fs{?}~ {branch PSKIP}
7  :           r{esc}
8  PSKIP       /ppr{?}~{windowsoff}{paneloff}
9  :           oh*{esc}PAGE # | AS OF @~qq{panelon}{windowson}
10 :           {menubranch PMENU2}{quit}
11 PMENU2      Std_Print   Print_Condensd Double-Spaced  Condensed/Dbl-Space
12 :           Std Print   Condensed      Double-Spaced  Condensed/Dbl-Space
13 :           {windowsoff} {windowsoff}  {windowsoff}   {windowsoff}
14 :           {paneloff}   {paneloff}    {paneloff}     {paneloff}
15 :           /ppaos*{esc} /ppaos*{esc}  /ppaos*{esc}   /ppaos*{esc}
16 :           \027@~       \027@\015~     \027@\027A\024~ \027@\015\027A\024~
17 :           mr80~        mr240~         p33~mr80~mt0~   p33~mr240~mt0~
18 :           qagpq        qagpq          qagpq           qagpq
19 :           {beep 2}     {beep 2}       {beep 2}        {beep 2}
20 :           {quit}       {quit}         {quit}          {quit}
F_16-2.WK1                                       CMD
```

Figure 16.2 A Macro to Print, Calc, and Save a Worksheet Range

Print_Without_Saving at the beginning. The macro selects /Print Printer Range, pauses for your acceptance or modification of the offered range, then turns off the windows and panel to suppress screen flicker.

oh*{esc}PAGE # | AS OF @~qq{panelon}{windowson}   Selects Options Heading, types an asterisk and Escape to clear the default, enters a heading showing page number and today's date, and quits the /Print menu.

{menubranch PMENU2}{quit}   Calls up the menu choices *Std_Print*, *Print_Condensed*, *Double-Spaced*, and *Condensed/Dbl-Spaced*.

{windowsoff}{paneloff}/ppaos*{esc}   Turns off the windows and panel to suppress screen flicker, selects /Print Printer Align Options Setup, and types an asterisk and Escape to clear the default. The next line shows setup codes for the Epson printer. You will need to change these codes if you have a different printer.

mr80~ or **mr240~** or **p33~mr80~mt0~** or **p33~mr240~mt0~**   If you select one of the two double-spacing attributes, the macro changes the page-length to 33 for double-spacing, and sets a top margin of zero. If you select one of the two condensed attributes, the macro selects Margin Right 240.

qagpq{beep 2}{quit}   The macro selects Quit Align Go Page Quit, beeps to indicate the printing is complete, and quits.

Print, Calculate, and Save in Release 3

Release 3 has greatly extended the print capabilities of 1-2-3, to the extent that we can create for that release a Print, Calc, & Save macro that is not printer-specific. Figure 16.3 shows such a macro.

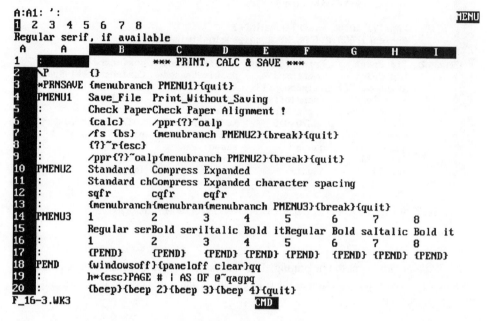

Figure 16.3 A Print, Calc, & Save Macro for Release 3

This macro begins in the same way as the macro just described, until you reach the line just above PMENU2.

/ppr{?}oalp{menubranch PMENU2}{break}{quit}   The macro selects /Print Printer Range, pauses for your input, then selects Options Advanced Layout Pitch and calls up the menu choices *Standard*, *Compress*, and *Expanded*. On an Epson FX series printer, for example, standard character width is 10 characters per inch (cpi), compressed character width is 17 cpi, and expanded character width is 5 cpi.

Note: The {break} command after the {menubranch} is unique to Release 2.2 and 3; its purpose is to allow your macro to back completely out of any command menu structure without having to execute a series of {esc} commands. In this case, the macro is in the middle of the /Print command menu, so if you press Escape at the appearance of the menu at PMENU2, the {break} command will back out of the /Print sequence, then execute the {quit} command and return to *READY*.

---

sqfr or **cqfr** or **eqfr**   Whether you select *Standard*, *Compress*, or *Expanded*, the macro types the first letter that corresponds to your choice, then selects Quit Font Range.

{menubranch PMENU3}{break}{quit}   Calls up the menu choices 1 through 8, corresponding to the fonts that are available in Release 3:

1   **Regular Serif, if available**
2   **Bold Serif, if available**
3   **Italic Serif, if available**
4   **Bold Italic Serif, if available**
5   **Regular Sans Serif, if available**
6   **Bold Sans Serif, if available**
7   **Italic Sans Serif, if available**
8   **Bold Italic Sans Serif, if available**

Whatever you select, the macro types that number, causing the selection to occur at the /Print Printer Options Advanced Fonts level.

{PEND}   Calls the closing subroutine at PEND. Strictly speaking, this should read {branch PEND}, since your macro flow will not be returning to this point after the routine at PEND is run. However, since the PEND routine ends with a {quit} command instead of a {return}, we can use the shorter subroutine call. It also makes the macro line easier to read.

{windowsoff}{paneloff clear}qq   Turns off the windows and panel, then selects Quit Quit to back two levels out of the /Print menu.

Note: The optional *clear* argument in the {paneloff} command is a feature available only in Release 2.2 and 3, designed to clear the control panel and status line before freezing them.

---

h*{esc}PAGE # | AS OF @~qagpq   Selects Header, then types an asterisk and Escape to clear the default, and inserts a generic header showing page number as/of date. The macro then selects Quit Go Align Page Quit to print the designated range.

{beep}{beep 2}{beep 3}{beep 4}{quit}   Beeps with four different tones to let you know the computer is available (though the printing may not be completed) and the macro quits.

Changing Setup Print Codes and Fonts

The macro in Figure 16.4 is designed to offer you a set of menus that you can use from within your /Print Printer Options Setup menu, or before beginning the /Print menu selections, to automatically change the setup codes that allow you combinations of *Standard*, *Condensed*, *Enlarged*, *Double-Spaced*, *Double-Strike*, and *Emphasized* print.

    This macro is written for Epson printers, so you will need to change the setup codes if your printer is different.

```
       A        B                                C                                  D                                 E
 1  :
 2  \S       {}
 3  *SETUP   {menubranch SMENU}{quit}            ### SETUP PRINT CODES CHANGED ###
 4  SMENU    Standard                            Condensed                          Enlarged                          Double-Spaced
 5  :        Reset setup codes to default        Change setup to Condensed          Change setup to Enlarged          Change setup to Double-Spaced
 6  :        {esc 6}/ppos#{esc}                  {esc 6}/ppos#{esc}                 {esc 6}/ppos#{esc}                {esc 6}/ppos#{esc}
 7  :        {menubranch SMENU2}                 {menubranch SMENU3}                {menubranch SMENU4}               {menubranch SMENU5}
 8  :        {menubranch SMENU1}                 {menubranch SMENU1}                {menubranch SMENU1}               {menubranch SMENU1}
 9  SMENU2   Normal                              Double-Strike                      Emphasized                        Both
10  :        Standard Print, Normal Strike       Standard Print, Double-Strike      Standard Print, Emphasized        Both Dbl-strike and Emphasized
11  :        \027@"s{quit}                       \027@\027\069"s{quit}              \027@\027\071"s{quit}             \027@\027\069\027\071"s{quit}
12  SMENU3   Normal                              Double-Strike                      Emphasized                        Both
13  :        Condensed Print, Normal Strike      Condensed Print, Dble-Strike       Condensed Print, Emphasized       Condensed, Dbl-strike/Emphasized
14  :        \027@\027\015"s                     \027@\027\015\027\069"s            \027@\027\015\027\071"s           \027@\027\015\027\069\027\071"s
15  :        {quit}                              {quit}                             {quit}                            {quit}
16  SMENU4   Normal                              Double-Strike                      Emphasized                        Both
17  :        ENLARGED Print, Normal Strike       ENLARGED Print, Double-Strike      ENLARGED Print, Emphasized        ENLARGED, Double-strike/Emphasized
18  :        \027@\027\014"s                     \027@\027\014\027\069"s            \027@\027\014\027\071"s           \027@\027\014\027\069\027\071"s
19  :        {quit}                              {quit}                             {quit}                            {quit}
20  SMENU5   Normal                              Double-Strike                      Emphasized                        Both
21  :        Double-Spaced, Normal Strike        Double-Spaced, Double Strike       Double-Spaced, Emphasized         Dble Spaced, Dbl-strike/Emphasized
22  :        \027@\027A\024"s                    \027@\027A\024\027\069"s           \027@\027A\024\027\071"s          \027@\027A\024\027\069\027\071"s
23  :        {quit}                              {quit}                             {quit}                            {quit}
24
```

F_16-4.WK1

Figure 16.4 Macro to Change Setup Codes in Release 2 and 2.01 or 2.2

328

{menubranch SMENU1}{quit} The macro begins by calling up the menu choices *Standard*, *Condensed*, *Enlarged*, and *Double-Spaced*.

{esc 6}/ppos*{esc} In case you are invoking this macro from within a /Print menu, six presses of the Escape key are included to back out of the macro before again selecting /Print Printer Options Setup. If you are not in a menu, of course, the six Escapes have no effect. The macro then types an asterisk and Escape to clear the setup code default, if any is offered.

{menubranch SMENU2}{menubranch SMENU1} Calls up the menu choices *Normal*, *Double-Strike*, *Emphasized*, and *Both*. If you press Escape at this point, the macro does a menubranch back to SMENU1, repeating the original menu choices *Standard*, *Condensed*, *Enlarged*, and *Double-Spaced*.

Hereafter the macro is fairly straightforward, so we will forego a specific investigation of each line.

Because of the new features of Release 3, another version of this macro is appropriate, as seen in Figure 16.5.

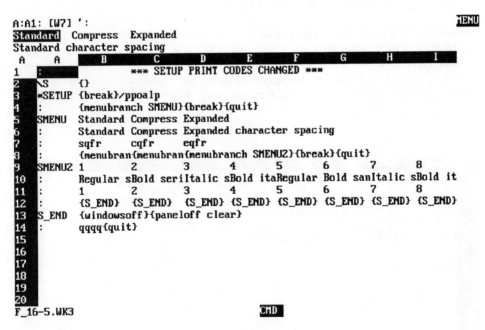

Figure 16.5 A Macro to Change Print Fonts in Release 3

{break}/ppoalp The {break} command causes the macro to back completely out of any command menu structure without having to execute a series of {esc} commands. In this case, the {break} command is included in case you decide to operate this macro from within the /Print command menu. Otherwise, the {break} command is ignored. Either way, the macro proceeds with the rest of the line, selecting /Print Printer Options Advanced Layout Pitch.

{menubranch SMENU}{break}{quit}　　Calls up the menu choices *Standard, Compress,* and *Expanded.* The rest of the macro is similar to the Print, Calc, & Save macro shown in Figure 16.3, so it is not necessary to go through it line by line.

However, you may be wondering why we bothered to include custom menus in these types of macros that seem to do nothing more than simply repeating the standard 1-2-3 menu. In other words, why not simply insert a bracketed question mark pause {?} so the user can point to his choice and proceed?

The answer is that the user might attempt to press the key that corresponds to the first letter of the menu and expect the menu choice to be activated. However, using the bracketed question mark pause, the user would have to press Return after pressing a letter—and this is departs from the normal way of doing things in 1-2-3.

By recreating the menu choices as a custom menu, you allow the user to type the first letter of their choice in the normal way and the macro will proceed exactly as if it were a standard 1-2-3 menu outside the domain of macros.

Printing in Elite Compressed Print

The macro in Figure 16.6 is designed to create a print even smaller than condensed. It does this by instructing your printer to print your document in the subscript/superscript size.

Even though the print is extremely small when using this macro, you should find it quite legible. This size of print font is especially handy for historical file copies of large spreadsheets, but it is not recommended for copies you might be sending out for distribution.

A1: ':　　　　　　　　　　　　　　　　　　　　　　　　　　　　READY

```
              A        B        C        D        E        F        G        H
 1    :                     ***ELITE COMPRESSED PRINT***
 2    \E           {if 0} Remark:  This is for an Epson Printer.
 3    *ELITE       {calc}/ppar{?}~{windowsoff}{paneloff}os*{esc}
 4    :            \027@\015\027S\001\0273\018~
 5    :            p66~mr240~mb4~qgp
 6    :            os{esc}\027@~mb2~qq{quit}
 7
 8
 9
10
11
12
13
14
15
16
17
18
19
20
```

F_16-6.WK1

Figure 16.6　A Macro to Print in Elite Compressed Style

You can get exactly twice as many lines on a printout with this method. Unfortunately, there is no way to achieve more characters per row using setup strings. For that result, you may want to investigate some of the sideways-printing software available for 1-2-3.

{if 0} Remark: This is for an Epson Printer.   The macro begins with a remark, reminding you that the setup codes are for an Epson printer only. As noted in earlier chapters, beginning any line with the command {if 0} will cause the rest of the line to be ignored, and the macro to continue on the next line down.

{calc}/ppar{?}~{windowsoff}{paneloff}os*{esc}   Calculates the worksheet, selects /Print Printer Align Range, pauses for your input, turns off the windows and panel, selects Options Setup, and types an asterisk and Escape to clear the default.

\027@\015\027S\001\0273\018~   This is the Epson code for printing in subscript/superscript size. You will need to change this code if you have another type of printer.

p66~mr240~mb4~qgp   Selects Page-length and enters 66, selects Margins Right and enters 240, selects Margins Bottom and enters 4, quits to a higher level in the /Print menu, and selects Go Page.

os{esc}\027@~mb2~qq{quit}   Finally, the macro returns the Options Setup string to normal by inserting the code for Master Reset, the bottom margin is changed to 2, the macro leaves the /Print menu, and the macro quits.

Documenting Your Worksheet on a Printout

It can be a good idea to save a printed documentation of your worksheet that contains both a list of formulas with their cell addresses and a printout of the worksheet as you see it on the screen. The macro in Figure 16.7 is designed to handle this task for you.

{windowsoff}{paneloff}{calc}   The macro begins by turning off the windows and panel and calculating the worksheet.

/ppar{home}.{end}{home}~   Selects /Print Printer Align Range, then describes a range from the Home position to the End Home position—in other words, it highlights the entire worksheet.

os*{esc}\027@\015\071~mr240~   Selects Option Setup, then types an asterisk and Escape to clear the default setup offered, and enters the codes (Epson, in this example) for condensed and emphasized. Then the macro selects Margins Right and enters 240, the maximum.

h*{esc}@|DOCUMENT COPY OF SPREADSHEET AS DISPLAYED|PAGE #~   Selects

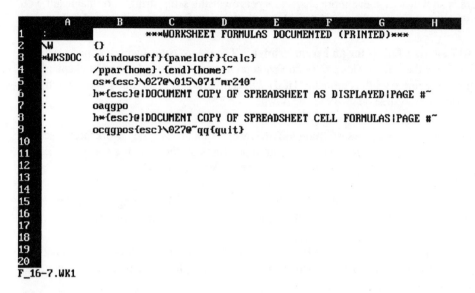

F_16-7.WK1

Figure 16.7 A Macro to Document Your Worksheet Formulas

Header and types an asterisk and Escape to clear the default, then enters @ for today's date, a centered title for a spreadsheet description, and # for the page number.

oaqgpo Selects Other As-Displayed Quit Go Page Option to start the printing.

h*{esc}@|DOCUMENT COPY OF SPREADSHEET CELL FORMULAS|PAGE #~
Changes the header to read in the center, *DOCUMENT COPY OF SPREADSHEET CELL FORMULAS*.

ocqgpos{esc}\027@~qq{quit} Selects Other Cell-Formulas Quit Go Page Option Setup and changes the {Epson} setup code back to Master Reset. The Quit Quit selections back out of the /Print menu, and the macro quits.

Printing Alternate Columns

The macro in Figure 16.8 is designed to allow you to print every other column in a print range. It accomplishes this by hiding alternate columns with the /Worksheet Column Hide feature. As an added bonus, this macro prompts you for how many copies you would like printed.

{let AHERE,@cellpointer("address")} Creates a place-marker to store the address of the current cell at AHERE.

A1: ':   `READY`

```
         A          B          C          D          E          F          G          H
1    :                    *** ALTERNATE COLUMNS PRINTED ***
2    \A          {}
3    *ALTPRNT    {let AHERE,@cellpointer("address")}
4    :           ~/ppr{?}{windowsoff}{paneloff}~
5    :           r{let ALT,@cellpointer("address")}..
6    :           {let ALT,@cellpointer("address")&".."&ALT}
7    :           {esc 4}rncARANGE~
8    ALT         $I$43..$N$45
9    :           ~{getnumber "How many copies do you want to print? ",ACYS}
10   :           {let ACOLS,@cols(ARANGE)}{let ADELCOLS,+ACOLS-1-@INT(ACOLS/2)}
11   :           {goto}ARANGE~{for ACOUNTR,1,ADELCOLS,1,ADELETE}
12   :           {for ACOUNTR,1,ACYS,1,ACOPIES}
13   :           /wcdARANGE~/rndARANGE~{goto}{AHERE}~{quit}
14   ADELETE     {right}/wch~{return}
15   ACOPIES     /pprARANGE~agpq{return}
16   AHERE       $A$1
17   ACOLS               6
18   ADELCOLS            2
19   ACOUNTR             2
20   ACYS                1
```
F_16-8.WK1

Figure 16.8 A Macro to Print Alternate Columns of Your Worksheet

~/ppr{?}{windowsoff}{paneloff}~ The tilde at the beginning of this line is important. You should always follow a {let} command that precedes access to the /Print menu with a tilde, or the macro will recalculate the entire worksheet before it selects /Print Printer Range. In other words, omitting the tilde, though not critical, slows down the macro.

After typing /Print Printer Range, the macro pauses for your acceptance or modification of the default range, then turns off the windows and panel.

r{let ALT,@cellpointer("address")}.. Selects Range again, creates a place-marker at ALT to store the upper left corner of the range, and presses Period (.) twice to shift the cell coordinates to the opposite corner.

{let ALT,@cellpointer("address")&".."&ALT} Modifies the cell address stored at ALT to include two Periods (..) and the cell coordinates for the lower left corner of the print range.

{esc 4}rncARANGE~ Backs out of the /Print menu and creates the range name ARANGE.

$I$43..$N$45 For cell coordinates of ARANGE, the macro uses the cell coordinates for your print range as stored in ALT.

~{getnumber "How many copies do you want to print? ",ACYS} The tilde completes the /Range Name Create and the {getnumber} prompts your for the number of copies you want printed.

{let ACOLS,@cols(ARANGE)}{let ADELCOLS,+ACOLS-1- @int(ACOLS/2)}
Stores in ACOLS the number of columns in the print range, then calculates and stores in
ADELCOLS the number of columns you would get if you counted every other column in the
print range.

{goto}ARANGE~{for ACOUNTR,1,ADELCOLS,1,ADELETE}   Moves the cell
pointer to the upper left corner of the print range and starts a {for} loop that counts in
ACOUNTR, starting with one, counts up to the number in ADECOLS equal to every other
column in the print range, counting by ones, and for each increment, runs the subroutine at
ADELETE that hides alternate columns with the commands: {right}/wch~{return}

{for ACOUNTR,1,ACYS,1,ACOPIES}   After every other column is hidden, the macro
runs another {for} loop counting in ACOUNTR, starting with one, counts up to the number
of copies you want printed as stored in ACYS, counting by ones, and for each increment runs
the subroutine at ACOPIES that prints ARANGE with the commands:

/pprARANGE~agpq{return}

/wcdARANGE~/rndARANGE~{goto}{AHERE}~{quit}   Finally, the macro redisplays
all the hidden columns in ARANGE, deletes the range name ARANGE, moves the cell
pointer back to the original location stored in AHERE, and quits.

Judging the Width of a Print Range

One of the more frustrating events in a typical 1-2-3 session occurs when you start to print a
large spreadsheet, only to find out too late that the print range is too large for the width of
your paper. The macro in Figure 16.9 addresses that problem by allowing you to check the
width of your print range *before* you start printing.

{let JHERE,@cellpointer("address")}   The macro begins by creating a place-marker to
store the address of the current cell in JHERE.

~/ppr{?}{windowsoff}{paneloff}~   Note the tilde that precedes that selection of /Print
Printer Range. As discussed for the preceding macro, this tilde is important to preclude an
unnecessary recalculation of the entire worksheet. The macro pauses for your acceptance or
modification of the offered range, then turns off the windows and upper panel.

r{let JADDR,@cellpointer("address")}..   The macro selects Range again and stores the
address of the upper left corner of the print range in JADDR. It then presses the Period key
twice (..) to switch the cell coordinates to the opposite corner.

{let JADDR,@cellpointer("address")&".."&JADDR}   Modifies the cell address stored
at JADDR to include two Periods (..) and the cell coordinates for the lower left corner of the
print range.

```
B14: [W12] +"ENTIRE WIDTH OF THE PRINT RANGE IS "&@STRING(+JWIDTH,0)&"."   READY
```

```
          A         B         C         D         E         F         G
 1   :                    *** JUDGE WIDTH OF PRINT RANGE ***
 2   \J        {}
 3  *JDGPRNT   {let JHERE,@cellpointer("address")}
 4   :         ~/ppr{?}{windowsoff}{paneloff}~
 5   :         r{let JADDR,@cellpointer("address")}..
 6   :         {let JADDR,@cellpointer("address")&".."&JADDR}
 7   :         {esc 4}rncJRANGE~
 8   JADDR     $A$86..$D$87
 9   :         ~{goto}JRANGE~{blank JWIDTH}
10   :         {for JCOUNT,1,@cols(JRANGE),1,JLOOP}
11   :         {recalc J_MENU}{goto}
12   JHERE     $B$90
13   :         ~{goto}{end}{home}{down}{panelon}{menubranch J_MENU}
14   J_MENU    ENTIRE WIDTH OF THE PRINT RANGE IS 53.
15   :         PRESS RETURN.
16   :         {esc}{paneloff}/rndJRANGE~{quit}
17   JLOOP     {let JWIDTH,JWIDTH+@CELLPOINTER("WIDTH")}
18   :         {right}{return}
19   JWIDTH          53
20   JCOUNT           5
F_16-9.WK1
```

Figure 16.9 A Macro to Judge the Width of Your Print Range

{esc 4}rncJRANGE~   Backs out of the /Print menu and creates the range name JRANGE.

$A$86..$D$87   For cell coordinates of JRANGE, the macro uses the cell coordinates for your print range as stored in JADDR.

So far, this macro starts out in the same way as the previous macro, presenting you with the spreadsheet's established print range (if it exists), allowing you to modify it if necessary, and creating a range name based on the same coordinates as the print range.

~{goto}JRANGE~{blank JWIDTH}   The macro moves your cell pointer to the upper left corner of the print range (now named JRANGE). The cell of the macro named JWIDTH is erased with the {blank} command.

{for JCOUNT,1,@cols(JRANGE),1,JLOOP}   This {for} loop is designed to accumulate the sum of all the widths of the columns in the print range. It does this by counting at JCOUNT, starting with the number one, counting up to the number of columns in your print range, counting by ones, and for every increment runs the subroutine at JLOOP.

{recalc J_MENU}{goto}   Recalculates the string formula at J_MENU and presses the F5 Goto key.

$B$90   This cell varies, depending on your original location. It is the cell named JADDR that holds your original place-marker and it returns you now to your original cell—which may or may not be the same cell as the upper left corner of the print range.

~{goto}{end}{home}{down}{panelon}{menubranch J_MENU}   The macro completes the {goto} routine, then starts another {goto} that will never be completed. It's entire purpose is simply to move the cell pointer temporarily to a cell guaranteed to be blank. It does this by starting the {goto} routine, moving to the End Home position and down one cell, then turning the panel on and doing a menubranch to J_MENU.

ENTIRE WIDTH OF THE PRINT RANGE IS 53.   This is the first, and only, menu choice at J_MENU. Its purpose is simply to provide an attention-getting message at the top of the screen. The descriptive line of the menu, as you can see from the next line, is an instruction to *PRESS RETURN*.

The string formula underlying J_MENU is:

+"ENTIRE WIDTH OF THE PRINT RANGE IS "&
@string(+JWIDTH,0)&
"."

{esc}{paneloff}/rndJRANGE~{quit}   The {esc} command cancels the {goto} command, returning the cell pointer to its original cell. The panel is turned off, the range name JRANGE is deleted, and the macro quits.

{let JWIDTH,JWIDTH+@cellpointer("width")}{right}{return}   The {for} loop subroutine at JLOOP is actually quite simple. It consists of a {let} command that causes the width of a cell to be added to the value in JWIDTH, moves to the right, adds the width of that cell, moves to the right, and so on, until the last column in the print range is reached.

One extra benefit of this macro is that it allows you to modify the print range without having to select /Print Printer Range. All you need to do is press Alt-J, modify the range, note the new width, and press Return. You can then change the contents or individual cell widths in your range as required, press Alt-J again, accept or modify the print range offered, and note the new print range width.

Summary

In this chapter we explored macros designed to facilitate and expand the print features of 1-2-3. Concepts covered in this chapter include:

- To have your macro clear a default entry in the Print menu such as any pre-established setup codes you may be offered when selecting /Print Printer Options Setup, include the instructions to type an asterisk, followed by Escape.
- A print heading in 1-2-3 can accept several code instructions: The number sign (#) in your print heading causes the printer to print sequential page numbers; the vertical bar

tells 1-2-3 to place whatever follows in the left, center, or right of the screen; and the @ sign causes the printer to type today's date.

■ The {break} command, unique to Release 2.2 and 3, allows your macro to back completely out of any command menu structure without having to execute a series of {esc} commands.

■ The font choices included as print features of Release 3 are:

1   Regular Serif, if available
2   Bold Serif, if available
3   Italic Serif, if available
4   Bold Italic Serif, if available
5   Regular Sans Serif, if available
6   Bold Sans Serif, if available
7   Italic Sans Serif, if available
8   Bold Italic Sans Serif, if available

■ A bracketed question mark pause {?} for user selection of a standard 1-2-3 menu choice is not recommended. If you use {?} in such a case and your user presses a letter for their choice, nothing will happen until Return is pressed. Instead, recreate the menu choices as a custom menu. This allows the user to select by typing the first letter of their choice in the normal way.

■ Always follow a {let} command that precedes access to the /Print menu with a tilde, or the macro will recalculate the entire worksheet before it selects /Print Printer Range. In other words, omitting the tilde, though not critical, slows down the macro.

■ You can use a string formula to create a single-choice menu that provides a variable attention-getting message at the top of the screen. The descriptive line of the menu can also be a variable string formula, if required.

Macros presented in this chapter are:

■ A macro to do a /File Save, prompt for the number of copies you want printed, and automatically print multiple copies for you.

■ A macro to calculate the file, save the file, and print the worksheet in your choice of print styles such as Standard Print, Condensed Print, Double-Spaced Print, and Condensed Double-Spaced.

■ A macro to print, calculate, and save a worksheet in Release 3 using print attributes that are not printer-specific.

■ A macro to automatically change the setup codes that allow you combinations of Standard, Compressed, Enlarged, Double-Spaced, Double-Strike, and Emphasized print in Release 2, 2.01, and 2.2.

■ A macro to change print fonts in using the new print features of Release 3.

■ A macro to print in Elite Compressed style, a print even smaller than Condensed. This macro works by instructing your printer to use codes for the subscript/superscript size.

■ A macro to save a printed documentation of your worksheet that contains both a list of formulas with their cell addresses and a printout of the worksheet as you see it on the screen.

■ A macro to print every other column in a print range by hiding alternate columns with the /Worksheet Column Hide feature.

■ A macro to judge the width of your print range before you start printing.

In Chapter 17 we examine special applications you can create using the macro techniques covered in this book. The applications include a program to automate and maintain an address database; to print form letters and address labels from that database; to create a checkbook ledger; and to print out your checkbook amounts in words as they are written on a check.

17

CREATING MACRO APPLICATIONS

Scope

In this chapter we will explore special applications you can create using the macro techniques covered in this book. The applications include a program to automate and maintain an address database; to print form letters and address labels from that database; to create a checkbook ledger; and to automatically type out your checkbook amounts in words as they might be written on a check.

Creating an Address Database

In Chapter 9 we discussed a data entry macro that includes the typing of a label prefix before each entry (see Figure 9.7). Unfortunately, that macro has no built-in way of shifting from label entry (making entries that require a label prefix) and value entries without your stopping the macro, then starting it again and manually selecting the different entry type.

In this section we present a macro that adds more intelligence to the data entry process. The Add to Address Database macro determines in advance what type of entry is required for a particular column. It differentiates, based on the way you set up the worksheet, between columns dedicated to labels, columns used for values, and columns that contain only dates shown in the date format.

As you can see in Figure 17.1, this macro uses the {get} command to capture every keystroke and the {if} command to test for the type of column into which the data are being entered. Because of the way it is designed, it has additional features:

- You can move right, left, up, or down without being limited by the fact that a macro is running.
- If you switch columns by moving right or left, the data entry prompt instantly switches to match the new column.
- You have full access to the /Copy, /Move, /Range Erase, /Worksheet Delete Row, and /Worksheet Insert Row commands just as if the macro were not active.

To use this macro, you must first set up database titles such as the titles shown at the bottom of Figure 17.1. If you want to modify the database, enter the macro with the recommended database structure first, be sure the macro works as it should, and only then make your required modifications. Some suggestions on how to modify both the database and the macro are included in the upcoming description of the macro .

You must also create a range name at the first title, called ADRS. If you want your database to begin in column A, you should know it is not necessary to include the range-name label as shown in Cell A41 of Figure 17.1. However, if you decide to omit the label, you must move your cell pointer to the first title (in our example, that means cell B41), select /Range Name Create, type **ADRS**, and press Enter.

{goto}ADRS~{let ADRSCOL,@cell("col",ADRS)}   The macro begins by sending your cell pointer to the cell range named ADRS, and records the column of that cell in ADRSCOL.

{end}{down}{down}{recalc A|CALC}   The cell pointer is moved down to the first blank record and the string formula at A|CALC is recalculated.

{let A|COL,@cellpointer("col")}   The number for the current column is recorded in A|COL, to be used by the next nine {if} statements to determine the type of entry required.

{if A|COL=ADRSCOL}Enter first name: {branch ALABEL}   If the current column number is the same as ADRSCOL (which it will be in the first pass through this macro), the prompt **Enter first name:** is typed into the upper panel and the macro branches to the routine named ALABEL.

{if A|COL=ADRSCOL+1}Enter last name: {branch ALABEL}   If the current column number is one greater than ADRSCOL, you are prompted to *Enter last name:* and the macro branches to ALABEL.

{if A|COL=ADRSCOL+2}Enter company: {branch ALABEL}   If the current column number is two greater than ADRSCOL, you are prompted to *Enter Company:* and the macro branches to ALABEL.

	A	B	C	D	E	F	G	H	I
1	:		*** ADD TO ADDRESS DATABASE ***						
2	\A	{}							
3	*ADRS	{goto}ADRS~{let ADRSCOL,@cell("col",ADRS)}							
4	:	{end}{down}{down}{recalc A|CALC}							
5	AGAIN	{let A|COL,@cellpointer("col")}							
6	:	{if A|COL=ADRSCOL}Enter first name: {branch ALABEL}							
7	:	{if A|COL=ADRSCOL+1}Enter last name: {branch ALABEL}							
8	:	{if A|COL=ADRSCOL+2}Enter company: {branch ALABEL}							
9	:	{if A|COL=ADRSCOL+3}Enter address: {branch ALABEL}							
10	:	{if A|COL=ADRSCOL+4}Enter City, State: {branch ALABEL}							
11	:	{if A|COL=ADRSCOL+5}Enter Zip: {branch ALABEL}							
12	:	{if A|COL=ADRSCOL+6}Enter Code: {branch AVALUE}							
13	:	{if A|COL=ADRSCOL+7}Enter month, day: @date(89,{branch ADATE}							
14	A|CALC	{if A|COL>ADRSCOL+7}{down}{left 8}{branch AGAIN}							
15	ALABEL	{let ACHANGE,"{branch ALABEL2}"}{branch ASUB}							
16	ALABEL2	'{AKEY}{?}~{right}{branch AGAIN}							
17	AVALUE	{let ACHANGE,"{branch AVALUE2}"}{branch ASUB}							
18	AVALUE2	{AKEY}{?}~{right}{branch AGAIN}							
19	ADATE	{let ACHANGE,"{branch ADATE2}"}{branch ASUB}							
20	ADATE2	@date(90,{AKEY}{?})~/rfd4~{right}{branch AGAIN}							
21	ASUB	{get AKEY}{esc}{if AKEY="{esc}"}{quit}							
22	:	{if AKEY="~"}{ABLANK}{right}{branch AGAIN}							
23	:	{if AKEY="{edit}"}{edit}{?}~{right}{branch AGAIN}							
24	:	{if @left(AKEY,1)="{"}{AKEY}{branch AGAIN}							
25	:	{if AKEY="/"}/{branch ASLASH}							
26	ACHANGE	{branch ALABEL2}							
27	AKEY	{ESC}							
28	A|COL	2							
29	ABLANK	{if @cellpointer("type")="b"}'{return}							
30	ADRSCOL	2							
31	ASLASH	{get AKEY}{if AKEY="c"#or#AKEY="m"}{AKEY}{?}~{?}~{branch AGAIN}							
32	:	{if AKEY="r"#or#AKEY="w"}{AKEY}{?}~{branch AGAIN}							
33	:	{esc}{branch AGAIN}							
34									
35									
36	B14:	+"{if A|COL>ADRSCOL+"&@string(@rows(b16..b6)-4,0)&							
37		"}{down}{left "&@string(@rows(b16..b6)-3,0)&"}{branch AGAIN}"							
38									
39									
40									
41	ADRS	First	Last	Company	Address	City, St.	ZIP	CODE	Date
42		――――――	―――――――	――――――――	―――――――――	―――――――――	――――	――――	――――――
43		I.B.	Empicee	Big Blue	9 Munchkin La.	Dvorak, NJ	72532	3	07/22/90
44		Mac	Intosh	Big Red	123 Apple St.	Graphic, CA	95014	2	07/22/90
45		Steve	Careers	Big Green	567 Main St.	Blackbox,WY	01864	4	07/22/90

FIG_17-1.WK1

Figure 17.1 A Macro to Add to an Address Database

{if A|COL=ADRSCOL+3}Enter address: {branch ALABEL}   If the current column number is three greater than ADRSCOL, you are prompted to *Enter address:* and the macro branches to ALABEL.

{if A|COL=ADRSCOL+4}Enter City, State: {branch ALABEL}   If the current column number is four greater than ADRSCOL, you are prompted to *Enter City, State:* and the macro branches to ALABEL.

{if A|COL=ADRSCOL+5}Enter Zip: {branch ALABEL}   If the current column number is five greater than ADRSCOL, you are prompted to *Enter Zip:* and again the macro branches to ALABEL. (Zip codes must be entered as labels, in case they start with a zero.)

{if A|COL=ADRSCOL+6}Enter Code: {branch AVALUE}   If the current column number is six greater than ADRSCOL, you are prompted to *Enter Code:*, but this time the macro branches to AVALUE.

{if A|COL=ADRSCOL+7}Enter month, day: @date(89,{branch ADATE}   If the current column number is seven greater than ADRSCOL, you are prompted to *Enter month, day:* in the @date format (the @date portion is entered for you) and the macro branches to ADATE.

{if A|COL>ADRSCOL+7}{down}{left 8}{branch AGAIN}   If the current column number is seven greater than ADRSCOL, the cell pointer must be beyond the end of a database row, so you are moved End Left 8 to the beginning of the next row, and the macro branches to AGAIN to start over again.

The string formula that underlies this displayed result is:

```
+"{if A|COL>ADRSCOL+"&
@string(@rows(b16..b6)-4,0)&
"}{down}{left "&
@string(@rows(b16..b6)-3,0)&
"}{branch AGAIN}"
```

You may be wondering why we bothered to enter this as a string formula. After all, the only string @functions are the second and fourth parts, which return the numbers 7 and 8. Why not simply type the numbers 7 and 8 into the {if} statement as a straight label?

The answer relates to the generic quality of this macro. It allows you to delete or add rows of the macro in the range between B6 and B16 without having to revisit this line. For example, suppose you do not want a prompt that reads *Enter Code:* in your address database. After the entire macro is typed into your worksheet, simply do a /Worksheet Delete Row to delete row 12, and the string formula at A|CALC on row 14 will adjust automatically to accommodate the fact that there are now fewer prompts, representing fewer headings.

{let ACHANGE,"{branch ALABEL2}"}{branch ASUB}   This is the line of the macro named ALABEL, where the program branches when a label entry is required. It begins by changing the cell named ACHANGE to a new branch command, then branches to ASUB. As you will see, ASUB is the subroutine where the macro checks your keystroke for an Escape, a Return, a press of the Edit key, another function key or directional key, or a forward slash (/) key.

'{AKEY}{?}~{right}{branch AGAIN}   If the ASUB subroutine does not identify your keystroke as any of those previously described, the macro returns to this cell at ALABEL2 (via the branching command at ACHANGE) where it types a label prefix, processes the character key you pressed, does a bracketed question mark pause {?} for the remainder of the entry, then moves right and branches back to the fourth line of the macro at AGAIN.

{let ACHANGE,"{branch AVALUE2}"}{branch ASUB}   This is the line of the macro named AVALUE, where the program branches when a value entry is required. It converts the cell named ACHANGE to a new branch command, then branches to ASUB to check for special keystrokes.

{AKEY}{?}~{right}{branch AGAIN}   If you have not pressed a special keystroke such as Escape, Return, Edit, and so on, the macro returns to this cell (via the branching command at ACHANGE) where it processes the character key you pressed without a label prefix, does a bracketed question mark pause {?} for the remainder of the entry, then moves right and branches back to the fourth line of the macro at AGAIN.

{let ACHANGE,"{branch ADATE2}"}{branch ASUB}   This is the line of the macro named ADATE, where the program branches when a date entry is required. It converts the cell named ACHANGE to a new branch command, then branches to ASUB to check for special keystrokes.

@date(90,{AKEY}{?})~/rfd4~{right}{branch AGAIN}   If you have not pressed a special keystroke, the macro returns to this cell (via the branching command at ACHANGE) where it types @date(90, and processes the character key you pressed, then does a bracketed question mark pause {?} for the remainder of the entry (the month, a comma, and the day). It then closes the parenthesis, formats the cell for date format, moves right, and branches back to the fourth line of the macro at AGAIN.

{get AKEY}{esc}{if AKEY="{esc}"}{quit}   This line and the next four lines of the macro constitute the subroutine where the macro takes special steps if certain keys are pressed. In this line, pressing Escape causes the macro to quit.

{if AKEY="~"}{ABLANK}{right}{branch AGAIN}   If you press Return, the macro runs the subroutine at ABLANK where it checks for a blank cell and, if it finds one, inserts a label prefix (apostrophe) in the cell. This is an optional part of the macro that assumes you would like to have an entry of some type in every cell, even if it is only an apostrophe that shows as a blank cell in your worksheet display. This will make maneuvering around your database with End LeftArrow and End RightArrow much easier when all the data entry is done.

{if AKEY="{edit}"}{edit}{?}~{right}{branch AGAIN}   If you press Edit, the macro executes an {edit} command, then pauses for your modification of a cell and a press of Return when completed. The macro then moves right one cell and branches back to the beginning at AGAIN.

{if @left(AKEY,1)="{"}{AKEY}{branch AGAIN}   If the left-most character of the stored keystroke representing the key you pressed is an opening bracket, it means you have pressed another function key or a directional key. The key is processed, and the macro branches back to the beginning at AGAIN.

{if AKEY="/"}/{branch ASLASH}   If you pressed a forward slash, it is assumed you wanted to access the command menu to do a /Move, /Copy, /Range Erase, /Worksheet Delete Row, or /Worksheet Insert Row. The macro branches to ASLASH to process your command. If, on the other hand, you actually wanted a slash key typed into a cell, pressing it again will cause it to be typed in the upper panel as you intended.

{branch ALABEL2}   This is a variable line of the macro that changes depending on the routine that sent the program flow to ASUB. In this case, the flow is sent back to the portion of the macro that deals with entries of labels.

The rest of the macro should be easy to follow. You will find, as you run this macro, that it provides a surprising amount of freedom while providing you with prompts and automatic data entry that greatly speed the process of creating an address database.

However, if you have Release 2.2 or 3, you will find that the macro's typing of prompts is not as efficient or fast as using an Indicator prompt. For those of you with these later releases, try the more advanced version (not usable in Release 2 or 2.01) as shown in Figure 17.2.

Printing Form Letters from a Database

Once you have your address database set up, you might be interested in having a macro to automatically print custom form letters to the addressees. An advanced method for doing this is shown in Figure 17.3.

This macro makes heavy use of the string @functions covered in previous chapters. You will find them a little complicated and difficult to enter, but the flexibility they offer in printing custom form letters is indispensable. You will be able to start your printing from any record in the database and continue it automatically to any other record you like.

{indicate PRINT}{goto}ADRS˜{down}{down}{goto}{?}˜   The macro begins by changing the *READY* indicator to the word *PRINT*, moves the cell pointer to the top of the address database, moves down two cells to the first record, then gives you a Goto prompt so you can point to the first record you want to include in a form letter.

{let BSTART,@left(@cell("address",ADRS),3)}{recalc BGOTO}   Stores in BSTART the column letter of the first column of your address database, then recalculates the string formula in the next cell named BGOTO.

{goto}$C$1˜   This is the displayed result of a string formula:

+"{goto}"&
BSTART&

```
        A        B        C        D        E        F        G    H    I
 1   :                    *** ADD TO ADDRESS DATABASE ***
 2   \A        {}
 3   *ADRS     {goto}ADRS~{let AIM,@cell("col",ADRS)}
 4   :         {end}{down}{down}{recalc A|CALC}{onerror A_QUIT}
 5   AGAIN     {let A|COL,@cellpointer("col")}{if A|COL<AIM}{right}
 6   :         {if A|COL=AIM}{indicate +" Enter first name: "&AZURE}{branch ALABEL}
 7   :         {if A|COL=AIM+1}{indicate +" Enter last name: "&AZURE}{branch ALABEL}
 8   :         {if A|COL=AIM+2}{indicate +" Enter company: "&AZURE}{branch ALABEL}
 9   :         {if A|COL=AIM+3}{indicate +" Enter address: "&AZURE}{branch ALABEL}
10   :         {if A|COL=AIM+4}{indicate +" Enter City, State: "&AZURE}{branch ALABEL}
11   :         {if A|COL=AIM+5}{indicate +" Enter Zip: "&AZURE}{branch ALABEL}
12   :         {if A|COL=AIM+6}{indicate +" Enter Code: "&AZURE}{branch AVALUE}
13   :         {if A|COL=AIM+7}{indicate +" Enter mo,day (MM,DD) "&AZURE}{branch ADATE}
14   A|CALC    {if A|COL>AIM+7}{down}{left 8}{branch AGAIN}
15   ALABEL    {let ACHANGE,"{branch ALABEL2}"}{branch ASUB}
16   ALABEL2   '{AKEY}{?}~{right}{branch AGAIN}
17   AVALUE    {let ACHANGE,"{branch AVALUE2}"}{branch ASUB}
18   AVALUE2   {AKEY}{?}~{right}{branch AGAIN}
19   ADATE     {let ACHANGE,"{branch ADATE2}"}{branch ASUB}
20   ADATE2    @date(90,{AKEY}{?})~/rfd4~{right}{branch AGAIN}
21   ASUB      {get AKEY}{esc}{if AKEY="{esc}"}{indicate}{quit}
22   :         {if AKEY="~"}{ABLANK}{right}{branch AGAIN}
23   :         {if AKEY="{edit}"}{edit}{?}~{right}{branch AGAIN}
24   :         {if @left(AKEY,1)="{"}{AKEY}{branch AGAIN}
25   :         {if AKEY="/"}/{branch ASLASH}
26   ACHANGE   {branch ALABEL2}
27   AKEY      {ESC}
28   A|COL           2
29   ABLANK    {if @cellpointer("type")="b"}'{return}
30   AIM             2
31   ASLASH    {get AKEY}{if AKEY="c"#or#AKEY="m"}{AKEY}{?}~{?}~{branch AGAIN}
32   :         {if AKEY="r"#or#AKEY="w"}{AKEY}{?}~{branch AGAIN}
33   :         {esc}{branch AGAIN}
34   A_QUIT    {indicate}{quit}
35   AZURE                             <------------    @REPEAT(" ",20)
36
37   B14:      +"{if A|COL>AIM+"&@STRING(@ROWS(B64..B54)-4,0)&"}
38             {down}{left "&@STRING(@ROWS(B64..B54)-3,0)&"}{branch AGAIN}"
39
40
41   ADRS      First  Last    Company  Address     City, St.   ZIP  CODE  Date
42            ------ ------  -------  --------    ---------   ----  ----  ----
43            I.B.   Empicee Big Blue 9 Munchkin La. Dvorak, NJ  72532   3 07/22/90
44            Mac    Intosh  Big Red  123 Apple St.  Graphic, CA 95014   2 07/22/90
45            Steve  Careers Big Green 567 Main St.  Blackbox,WY 01864   4 07/22/90
```

FIG_17-2.WK1

Figure 17.2 Adding to an Address Database in Release 2.2 or 3

@string(@cellpointer("row"),0)
&"~"

Its purpose is to send the cell pointer to the first column of your address database (in case you have strayed right or left in choosing the record to print), while still remaining in the same row.

{recalc BCOL1}{recalc BCOL2}{recalc BCOL3}   Recalculates BCOL1, BCOL2, and

```
        A           B              C           D          E          F          G
1   :                          ***BUILD FORM LETTERS***
2   \B          {}
3   *BFORM      {indicate PRINT}{goto}ADRS~{down}{down}{goto}{?}~
4   :           {let BSTART,@left(@cell("address",ADRS),3)}{recalc BGOTO}
5   BGOTO       {goto}$C$1~
6   B_LOOP      {recalc BCOL1}{recalc BCOL2}{recalc BCOL3}
7   :           {recalc BCOL4}{recalc BCOL5}{recalc BCOL6}
8   :           {recalc BROW}{recalc LETTER}
9   :           /pparLETTER~gpq{down}
10  :           {if @cellpointer("type")<>"b"}{branch B_LOOP}
11  :           {indicate}{quit}
12  BROW        1
13  BCOL1       A
14  BCOL2       B
15  BCOL3       C
16  BCOL4       D
17  BCOL5       E
18  BCOL6       F
19  BSTART      $C$
20  :

22      B7:     +"{goto}"&BSTART&@string(@cellpointer("row"),0)&"~"

24      B12:    @string(@cellpointer("row"),0)

26      B13:    @mid(@cellpointer("address"),1,@if(@cellpointer("col")<=26,1,2))

28      B14:    @if(@length(BCOL1)=2,@if(@right(BCOL1,1)="z",
29              @char(@code(@left(BCOL1,1))+1)&"a",@left(BCOL1,1)&
30              @char(@code(@right(BCOL1,1))+1)),
31              (@if(BCOL1="z","aa",@char(@code(BCOL1)+1))))
```

F_17-3.WK1

Figure 17.3 A Macro to Print Form Letters from a Database

BCOL3. These cells return the first three column letters for your address database. The column letters will not be used in macro code, but rather in string formulas in the form letter itself, as you will see.

The string formula in BCOL1 is:

@mid(@cellpointer("address"),1,@if(@cellpointer("col")<=26,1,2))

It extracts the column letter from the absolute address of the current cell by taking the character from position 1 or (if the column number is not less than or equal to 26) from positions 1 and 2.

The string formula in BCOL2 is more complicated:

@if(@length(BCOL1)=2,@if(@right(BCOL1,1)="z",
@char(@code(@left(BCOL1,1))+1)&
"a",@left(BCOL1,1)&
@char(@code(@right(BCOL1,1))+1)),
(@if(BCOL1="z","aa",@char(@code(BCOL1)+1))))

This formula operates based on the column letter in BCOL1.

If BCOL1 consists of two characters where the second is the letter Z, the formula takes one letter greater than the first letter in BCOL1, and tacks an A onto it. Otherwise, it takes the first letter in BCOL1 and tacks on one letter greater than the second letter in BCOL1.

If BCOL1 consists of one character and that character is the letter Z, the formula returns the letters AA. Otherwise, it returns one letter greater than the letter in BCOL1.

The formulas in BCOL3, BCOL4, BCOL5, and BCOL6 are relative copies of the formula in BCOL2, so once you have entered BCOL2, simply use the /Copy command to duplicate that formula in the other cells.

{recalc BCOL4}{recalc BCOL5}{recalc BCOL6}   Recalculates BCOL4, BCOL5, and BCOL6.

{recalc BROW}{recalc LETTER}   Recalculates the string formula in BROW:

@string(@cellpointer("row"),0)

This provides the current row of the cell pointer, information required for string formulas in the form letter.

/pparLETTER˜gpq{down}   Selects /Print Printer Align Range, uses the range name LETTER as the range to print, then selects Go Page Quit and moves down to the next record.

{if @cellpointer("type")<>"b"}{branch B_LOOP}   If the next record is not blank, the macro branches back to B_LOOP to recalculate ranges and print the form letter for the next record.

{indicate}{quit}   Otherwise, the indicator is returned to normal and the macro quits.

None of this will work, of course, until you have constructed your form letter, using the string formulas as shown in Figure 17.4.

At the top of this letter, you see the headings:

First Last
Company
Address
City, St. ZIP

Dear First Last,

These are actually the displayed results of string formulas, based on placing the cell pointer on the first of the database titles, rather than on the first record you want included in your form letter. (This is done for clarity only; there would be no purpose in printing a form letter with a heading like this.)

As noted in Figure 17.4, in order for this macro to work, the entire letter, including the heading and final close, must be given the range name: LETTER. Select /Range Name Create, enter **LETTER,** and for the range, highlight Columns B through H, from two cells below BSTART down through the job title *Macro Writer.*

The string formula in the first line of the heading is:

```
42    First Last
43    Company
44    Address
45    City, St. ZIP
46
47    Dear First Last,
48
49         Note in order for this macro to work, this entire letter,
50    including the heading and final close, must be given the range
51    name: LETTER . Select /Range Name Create, enter LETTER, and
52    for the range, highlight Columns B through H, from two cells
53    below BSTART down through the job title "Macro Writer".
54
55    Sincerely,
56
57
58    I. M. Grate
59    Macro Writer
60
61
62   A42:   @@(+BCOL1&BROW)&" "&@@(BCOL2&BROW)
63
64   A43:   @if(@iserr(@length(@@(BCOL3&BROW)))=0),@@(BCOL4&BROW),
65          @if(@length(@@(BCOL3&BROW))=0,@@(BCOL4&BROW),@@(BCOL3&BROW)))
66
67   A44:   @if(@iserr(@length(@@(BCOL3&BROW)))=0),
68          @@(BCOL5&BROW)&" "&@@(BCOL6&BROW),
69          @if(@length(@@(BCOL3&BROW))=0,@@(BCOL5&BROW),@@(BCOL4&BROW)))
70
71   A45:   @if(@iserr(@length(@@(BCOL3&BROW)))=0),"",
72          @if(@length(@@(BCOL3&BROW))=0,"",
73          @@(BCOL5&BROW)&" "&@@(BCOL6&BROW)))
74
75   A47:   +"Dear "&@@(+BCOL1&BROW)&" "&@@(BCOL2&BROW)&", "
```

F_17-4.WK1

Figure 17.4 Constructing Your Form Letter

@@(+BCOL1&BROW)&" "&@@(BCOL2&BROW)

It makes use of the @@ function that returns the contents of the address typed into the referenced cell. Since **+BCOL1&BROW** is equivalent to a reference to the first column of your database in the current row, the formula **@@(+BCOL1&BROW)** returns the name in that cell (the first name of the addressee). The **&" "** enters a space, and the formula **@@(BCOL2&BROW)** returns the name in the second column of the current row (the last name of the addressee).

The string formula in the second line of the heading is:

@if(@iserr(@length@@(BCOL3&BROW))=0),@@(BCOL4&BROW),
@if(@length(@@(BCOL3&BROW))=0,@@(BCOL4&BROW), @(BCOL3&BROW)))

If there is no Company entry (if an error is returned when trying to return the length of that cell or if the length of the cell is zero), this formula returns the contents of the Address cell to the right. Otherwise, it returns the contents of the Company cell.

The string formula in the third line of the heading is:

@if(@iserr(@length(@@(BCOL3&BROW))=0),
@@(BCOL5&BROW)&" "&@@(BCOL6&BROW),
@if(@length(@@(BCOL3&BROW))=0,@@(BCOL5&BROW),@@(BCOL4&BROW)))

In this line, if there is no Company entry (if an error is returned when trying to return the length of that cell or if the length of the cell is zero), the contents of the City/State cell and the ZIP cell are returned. Otherwise, the contents of the Address cell are returned.

The string formula in the fourth line of the heading is:

@if (@iserr(@length(@@(BCOL3&BROW))=0),"",
@if(@length(@@(BCOL3&BROW))=0,"",
@@(BCOL5&BROW)&" "&@@(BCOL6&BROW)))

In this last line of the heading, if there is no Company entry, a null string (blank cell) is returned. Otherwise, the contents of the City, State cell and the ZIP cell are returned.

In case these formulas seem overly complicated, you should be aware that they take into account that not all addressees will have Company entries; to simply leave a blank would look unprofessional. Therefore, the string formulas use @if statements to check for that condition, and display the Address, City/State, and ZIP information one cell higher than they would normally appear.

The salutation is based on a string formula:

+"Dear "&@@(+BCOL1&BROW)&" "&@@(BCOL2&BROW)&","

This formula combines the word **Dear** with the first name from the first column, a space, the last name from the second column, and a comma.

In a nutshell, here's how the macro works. The macro calculates the position of the cell pointer (column and row), calculates the string formulas in the heading and salutation of the letter—which will be based on the information in the current cell pointer row—prints the recalculated form letter, moves down to the next record, and repeats the whole process.

If you do not want to print form letters for all the records in your address database from your current location to the last record, do this before starting your macro: move to the row below the last record you want to see included in a form letter, select /Worksheet Insert Row to create a blank row that will stop the macro, then move back to the first record to print and press Alt-B. The macro will print form letters for every record from the current row to the newly inserted blank row. When the printing is completed, simply delete the blank row to restore your database to its original condition.

Printing Labels from a Database

The macro in Figure 17.5 uses similar techniques to print labels, up to five across, from the same address database.

Here's how the macro works.

{getnumber "Enter Number of Labels Across to Print: ",LCOUNT} Prompts for the number of labels across you want to print. This depends on the type of labels you are using in your printer, which can be as much as five across. Your response is saved in LCOUNT.

```
          A        B        C        D        E        F        G        H
1     :              *** LABELS PRINTED FROM ADDRESS DATABASE ***
2     \L       {}
3     *LABEL   {getnumber "Enter Number of Labels Across to Print: ",LCOUNT}
4     :        {windowsoff}{paneloff}/ppoouqq
5     :        {goto}LABEL~/rndLABEL~/rncLABEL~.{down 3}{left}{right LCOUNT}~
6     :        {goto}ADRS~{down}{down}{panelon}{windowson}{goto}{?}~
7     :        {let LSTART,@left(@cell("address",ADRS),3)}{recalc LGOTO}
8     LGOTO    {goto}$C$61~
9     LOOP     {recalc LCOL1}{recalc LCOL2}{recalc LCOL3}
10    :        {recalc LCOL4}{recalc LCOL5}{recalc LCOL6}
11    :        {recalc LROW1}{recalc LROW2}{recalc LROW3}
12    :        {recalc LROW4}{recalc LROW5}{recalc LABEL}
13    :        /pparLABEL~gllq{down LCOUNT}
14    :        {if @cellpointer("type")<>"b"}{branch LOOP}
15    :        {goto}ADRS~/ppoofqq{quit}
16    LCOUNT        3
17    LCOL1    I
18    LCOL2    J
19    LCOL3    K
20    LCOL4    L
21    LCOL5    M
22    LCOL6    N
23    LROW1    61
24    LROW2    62        NOTE:  The width of the cells
25    LROW3    63        containing the labels must be
26    LROW4    64        as wide as the widest address.
27    LROW5    65
28    LSTART   $C$
29    :
30    LABEL         ERR      ERR      ERR      ERR      ERR
31    :             0        0        0        0        0
32    :             ERR      ERR      ERR      ERR      ERR
33    :
34    :
35    B8:  +"{goto}"&b28&@string(@cellpointer("row"),0)&"~"
36    B17: @mid(@cellpointer("address"),1,@if(@cellpointer("col")<=26,1,2))
37    B18: @if(@length(b17)=2,@left(b17,1),"")&@char(@code(@right(b17,1))+1)
38    B19: @if(@length(b18)=2,@left(b18,1),"")&@char(@code(@right(b18,1))+1)
39    B20: @if(@length(b19)=2,@left(b19,1),"")&@char(@code(@right(b19,1))+1)
40    B21: @if(@length(b20)=2,@left(b20,1),"")&@char(@code(@right(b20,1))+1)
41    B22: @if(@length(b21)=2,@left(b21,1),"")&@char(@code(@right(b21,1))+1)
42    B23: @string(@cellpointer("row"),0)
43    B24: @string(@cellpointer("row")+1,0)
44    B25: @string(@cellpointer("row")+2,0)
45    B26: @string(@cellpointer("row")+3,0)
46    B27: @string(@cellpointer("row")+4,0)
47    B30: @@(+b17&b23)&" "&@@(b18&b23)
48    B31: @if(@iserr(@length(@@(b19&b23))=0),@@(b20&b23),
49         @if(@length(@@(b19&b23))=0,@@(b20&b23),@@(b19&b23)))
50    B32: @if(@iserr(@length(@@(b19&b23))=0),@@(b21&b23)&" "&@@(b22&b23),
51         @if(@length(@@(b19&b23))=0,@@(b21&b23),@@(b20&b23)))
52    B33: @if(@iserr(@length(@@(b19&b23))=0),"",
53         @if(@length(@@(b19&b23))=0,"",@@(b21&b23)&" "&@@(b22&b23)))
```

F_17-5.WK1

Figure 17.5 Printing Labels from an Address Database

{windowsoff}{paneloff}/ppoouqq   Turns off the windows and panel and selects /Print Printer Option Other Unformatted Quit Quit. This ensures there will be no page breaks in your printed labels.

{goto}LABEL˜/rndLABEL˜/rncLABEL˜.{down 3}{left}{right LCOUNT}˜   Moves your cell pointer to the cell in the macro named LABEL, deletes the range name LABEL, then recreates it, but this time with a height of four rows and a width that matches the number of labels you indicated you wanted to see printed.

{goto}ADRS˜{down}{down}{panelon}{windowson}{goto}{?}˜   Moves the cell pointer to the first title in your address database, then down two cells, turns on the windows and panel, then gives you a Goto prompt to allow you to move to the first record you want printed in a label.

The next six lines of the macro are very similar to the equivalent lines in the Form Letter macro, except that rows relative to the current cell pointer are calculated in addition to columns, using the formulas:

@string(@cellpointer("row"),0)
@string(@cellpointer("row")+1,0)
@string(@cellpointer("row")+2,0)
@string(@cellpointer("row")+3,0)
@string(@cellpointer("row")+4,0)

Note: Lines 37 through 41 in Figure 17.5 are incomplete as shown, but reference to the Form Letter macro will give you the information you need to enter these formulas correctly.

/pparLABEL˜gllq{down LCOUNT}   Selects /Print Printer Align Range, enters the range name LABEL as the range to print, then selects Go Line Line Quit, and moves down a number of cells equal to the number of labels across you decided to print.

{if @cellpointer("type")<>"b"}{branch LOOP}   If the next record is not blank, the macro branches back to LOOP to recalculate ranges and print the labels for the next records.

{goto}ADRS˜/ppoofqq{quit}   Otherwise, the cell pointer is moved to the beginning of the address database, the macro selects /Print Printer Options Other Formatted Quit Quit, and the macro quits.

Regarding the labels themselves, they consist of string formulas that are based on exactly the same principles as the form letter heading. The one difference is that there are up to five labels, so the second label calculates and returns its information based on the current row plus 1 (the number in LROW2), the third label uses LROW3, the fourth uses LROW4, and the fifth uses LROW5.

Of course, the ERR and zero entries you see in Figure 17.5 will automatically display as regular label addresses once you place your cell pointer on one of the records in your address database and press the F9 Calc key.

The result of all this will be a very fast printout of your address labels, starting with the addressee at the first record you point to after starting the macro. If you want to stop short of the last record in the database, insert a temporary blank row at your desired stopping point before starting the macro.

Creating a Checkbook Ledger Macro

The same principles as used in the Address Database macro can be applied to any data entry system, including order entry, accounts payable, accounts receivable, inventory, customer lists, personnel lists, and so on. In this section we will look at a long macro designed to facilitate your entry of checks into a checkbook ledger (see Figure 17.6).

This macro requires a database structure with titles such as shown in Figure 17.7. The cell below the title CHK # should be given the range name CHK #. Initially, you may want to use exactly this layout until you verify that the macro is working correctly. Afterwards, you may want to change the categories in columns F through I and add category columns of your own past column I.

Here's how the macro works.

{goto}CHK #˜{let CHK,@cell("col",CHK #)}   Moves the cell pointer to the line below the first title of the checkbook ledger (range named CHK #), then stores the column number of that cell in CHK.

{up}{end}{down}{down}{recalc C_CALC}   Moves to the first blank cell after the last check entered, and recalculates the string formula in C_CALC.

{let C|COL,@cellpointer("col")}   Stores the current column letter in C|COL.

{if C|COL=CHK}Enter check number: (F8 for next #) {branch CNUMBER}   If the current column is the first column in the checkbook ledger (which it will be, of course, during the first pass through this the macro), the prompt **Enter check number (F8 for next #)** is typed into the upper panel. You can either type a check number at this point, or press the F8 key and the next check number in sequence will be entered. The macro then branches to CNUMBER.

{if C|COL=CHK+1}Enter mo,day: (F8 for Today's Date) {branch CDATE}   At the second column you will be prompted to enter the date or press F8 to have today's date entered for you. The macro branches to CDATE.

{if C|COL=CHK+2}Enter Payee: (F8 for Same-as-Above) {branch CLABEL}   At the third column, you will be prompted to enter the payee or press F8 to enter the same payee as shown in the line above. The macro branches to CLABEL.

```
        A       B       C       D       E       F       G       H       I       J       K
 1   :                *** CHECKBOOK LEDGER MACRO ***
 2   \c          {}
 3   *CHKBK      {goto}CHK #~{let CHK,@cell("col",CHK #)}
 4   :           {up}{end}{down}{down}{recalc C_CALC}
 5   CAGAIN      {let C|COL,@cellpointer("col")}
 6   :           {if C|COL=CHK}Enter check number:  (F8 for next #){branch CNUMBER}
 7   :           {if C|COL=CHK+1}Enter mo,day:  (F8 for Today's Date){branch CDATE}
 8   :           {if C|COL=CHK+2}Enter Payee:  (F8 for Same-as-Above){branch CLABEL}
 9   :           {if C|COL=CHK+3}Enter Amount: (F8 for Same-as-Above){branch CVALUE}
10   :           {if C|COL=CHK+4}Enter Code: (F8 for Same-as-Above){branch CODE}
11   C_CALC      {if C|COL>CHK+4}{down}{left 5}{branch CAGAIN}
12   CNUMBER     {let CHANGE,"{branch CNUMBER2}"}{branch CSUB}
13   CNUMBER2{if CKEY="{table}"}+{up}+1{calc}~{right}{branch CAGAIN}
14   :           {CKEY}{?}~{right}{branch CAGAIN}
15   CLABEL      {let CHANGE,"{branch CLABEL2}"}{branch CSUB}
16   CLABEL2 {if CKEY="{table}"}/c{esc}{up}~~{right}{branch CAGAIN}
17   :           '{CKEY}{?}~{right}{branch CAGAIN}
18   CVALUE      {let CHANGE,"{branch CVALUE2}"}{branch CSUB}
19   CVALUE2 {if CKEY="{table}"}/c{esc}{up}~~{right}{branch CAGAIN}
20   :           {CKEY}{?}~/rff~~{right}{branch CAGAIN}
21   CODE        {let CHANGE,"{branch CODE2}"}{branch CSUB}
22   CODE2       {let C|ROW,@string(@cellpointer("row"),0)}
23   :           {if CKEY="{table}"}/c{esc}{up}~~{recalc CODE3}{recalc CODE4}{branch CODE3
24   :           {CKEY}{?}~{recalc CODE3}{recalc CODE4}
25   CODE3       /cD178~E178~
26   CODE4       {if @sum(F178..AA178)<>+D178}/reF178..AA178~~{branch CODE3}
27   :           {right}{branch CAGAIN}
28   CDATE       {let CHANGE,"{branch CDATE2}"}{branch CSUB}
29   CDATE2  {if CKEY="{table}"}@now~/rfd4~{right}{branch CAGAIN}
30   :           @date(90,{CKEY}{?})~/rfd4~{right}{branch CAGAIN}
31   CSUB        {get CKEY}{esc}{if CKEY="{esc}"}{indicate}{quit}
32   :           {if CKEY="~"}{CBLANK}{right}{branch CAGAIN}
33   :           {if CKEY="{edit}"}{edit}{?}~{right}{branch CAGAIN}
34   :           {if CKEY="{table}"}{branch CHANGE}
35   :           {if @left(CKEY,1)="{"}{CKEY}{branch CAGAIN}
36   :           {if CKEY="/"}/{branch CSLASH}
37   CHANGE      {branch CNUMBER2}
38   CKEY        {ESC}
39   C|COL          5
40   C|ROW       178
41   CBLANK      {if @cellpointer("type")="b"}'{return}
42   CHK            1
43   CSLASH      {get CKEY}{if CKEY="c"#or#CKEY="m"}{CKEY}{?}~{?}~{branch CAGAIN}
44   :           {if CKEY="r"#or#CKEY="w"}{CKEY}{?}~{branch CAGAIN}
45   :           {esc}{branch CAGAIN}
46
47   B11:    +"{if C|COL>chk+"&@string(@rows(a5..a12)-4,0)&"}{down}{left "&
48           @string(@rows(a5..a12)-3,0)&"}{branch CAGAIN}"
49   B25:    +"/c"&@char(+63+C|COL)&C|ROW&"~"&
50           @char(+64+C|COL+@cellpointer("contents"))&C|ROW&"~"
51   B26:    +"{if @sum("&@char(+65+C|COL)&C|ROW&"..aa"&C|ROW&")<>+"&
52           @char(+63+C|COL)&C|ROW&"}/re"&@char(65+C|COL)&
53           C|ROW&"..aa"&C|ROW&"~~{branch CODE3}"
```

F_17-6.WK1

Figure 17.6 A Macro to Facilitate Entry in a Checkbook Ledger

```
A1: U [W6] '        NOTE: The underline below CHK # must be range named "CHK #"
```

```
        A        B          C        D      E     F       G       H      I
1               NOTE: The underline below CHK # must be range named "CHK #"
2            /
3            /                                    1       2       3      4
4      CHK #    DATE      PAYEE    AMOUNT CODE  Rent    Phone   Util   Misc
5      -----    ------    ------   ------ ----  ======= =====   =====  =====
6       123    12/07/89 Landlord   800.00   1   800.00
7       124    12/09/89 A T & T     87.50   3                   87.50
8       125    12/11/89 Oak View   123.23   2           123.23
9       126    12/13/89 Jeans Inc   47.50   4                          47.50
10      127    12/15/89 Safeway     90.00   4                          90.00
11      128    01/01/90 Landlord   800.00   1   800.00
12      129    01/03/90 Michael    130.50   2           130.50
13      130    01/05/90 Macropac    67.3    3                   67.3
14
15
16
17
18
19
20
F_17-7.WK1
```

Figure 17.7   A Sample Database for the Checkbook Ledger Macro

{if C|COL=CHK+3}Enter Amount: (F8 for Same-as-Above){branch CVALUE}   At
the fourth column, you will be prompted to enter the check amount or press F8 for same-as-
above. The macro branches to CVALUE.

{if C|COL=CHK+4}Enter Code: (F8 for Same-as-Above) {branch CODE}   At   the
fifth column, you will be prompted to enter a code representing the type of check written.
For example, you may want to use the code 1 for Rent, 2 for Phone, and so on. Press F8 for
same-as-above. The macro branches to CODE.

{if C|COL>CHK+4}{down}{left 5}{branch CAGAIN}   This is the cell named C_CALC. If
the current column number is four greater than CHK, the cell pointer must be beyond the end
of a check entry row, so you are moved down and to the left to the beginning of the next row,
and the macro branches to CAGAIN to start over again.

The string formula that underlies this displayed result is:

+"{if C|COL>CHK+"&
@string(@rows(a5..a12)-4,0)&
"}{down}{left "
&@string(@rows(a5..a12)-3,0)&
"}{branch CAGAIN}"

The principle here is the same as in the equivalent string formula in the Address Database
macro.

{let CHANGE,"{branch CNUMBER2}"}{branch CSUB}   This is the first line of the routine named CNUMBER where the macro branches if you are in the check number column. It begins by changing the cell named CHANGE to a new branch command, then branches to CSUB where a {get} command pauses for your press of any key. As with the ASUB subroutine in the Address Database macro, CSUB is the subroutine where the macro checks your keystroke for an Escape, a Return, a press of the Edit key, another function key or directional key, or a forward slash (/) key.

{if CKEY="{table}"}+{up}+1{calc}~{right}{branch CAGAIN}   If you pressed F8, the macro in this instance calculates the last invoice number plus one, enters it, moves to the right one cell, and branches back to the beginning at CAGAIN.

{CKEY}{?}~{right}{branch CAGAIN}   Otherwise, the macro types the character you pressed, pauses for the rest of your entry, moves to the right, and branches back to the beginning at CAGAIN.

{let CHANGE,"{branch CLABEL2}"}{branch CSUB}   This is the line of the macro named CLABEL, where the program branches when the payee is to be entered. It converts the cell named CHANGE to a new branch command, then branches to CSUB to check for special keystrokes.

{if CKEY="{table}"}/c{esc}{up}~~{right}{branch CAGAIN}   If you pressed F8 at the payee prompt, the macro copies the payee entry from the cell above, moves to the right one cell, and branches back to the beginning at CAGAIN.

'{CKEY}{?}~{right}{branch CAGAIN}   Otherwise, the macro types a label prefix and the character you pressed, pauses for the rest of your entry, moves to the right, and branches back to the beginning at CAGAIN.

{let CHANGE,"{branch CVALUE2}"}{branch CSUB}   This is the line of the macro named CVALUE, where the program branches when the check amount is to be entered. It converts the cell named CHANGE to a new branch command, then branches to CSUB to check for special keystrokes.

{if CKEY="{table}"}/c{esc}{up}~~{right}{branch CAGAIN}   As before, if you press F8, the macro copies the entry from the cell above, moves to the right one cell, and branches back to the beginning at CAGAIN.

{CKEY}{?}~/rff~~{right}{branch CAGAIN}   Otherwise, the macro types the character you pressed, pauses for the rest of your entry, formats the cell for Fixed with two decimals, moves to the right, and branches back to the beginning at CAGAIN.

{let CHANGE,"{branch CODE2}"}{branch CSUB}   This is the line of the macro named CODE, where the program branches when the check code is to be entered. It converts the cell named CHANGE to a new branch command, then branches to CSUB to check for special keystrokes.

{let C|ROW,@string(@cellpointer("row"),0)}   The current row is stored in C|ROW as a label.

{if CKEY="{table}"}/c{esc}{up}~~{recalc CODE3}{recalc CODE4}{branch CODE3}
If you pressed F8, the macro copies the entry from the cell above, recalculates CODE3 and CODE4, and branches to CODE3.

{CKEY}{?}~{recalc CODE3}{recalc CODE4}   Otherwise, the macro processes your keystrokes, pauses for the rest of the entry, and recalculates CODE3 and CODE4.

/cD178~F178~   This is the cell named CODE3, the displayed result of the string formula:

```
+"/c"&
@char(+63+C|COL)&
C|ROW&
"~"&
@@char(+64+C|COL+@cellpointer("contents"))&
C|ROW&
"~"
```

Its purpose is to copy the amount from the amount column to the column represented by the code in the current cell.

{if @sum(F178..AA178)<>+D178}/reF178..AA178~~{branch CODE3}   This is the displayed result in the cell named CODE4 of a string formula:

```
+"{if @sum("&
@char(+65+C|COL)&C|ROW&
"..aa"&
B|ROW&")<>+"&
@char(+63+C|COL)&
C|ROW&"}/re"&
@char(65+C|COL)&
C|ROW&"..aa"&
C|ROW&
"~~{branch CODE3}"
```

If you have previously entered an amount and a different code on the current row (which would cause an extraneous amount to appear in one of the category columns following the Code column), this line of the macro erases the range from the first category column through column AA.

{right}{branch CAGAIN}   The cell pointer is moved to the right one cell and the macro branches back to the beginning at CAGAIN.

{let CHANGE,"{branch CDATE2}"}{branch CSUB}   This is the line of the macro named CDATE, where the program branches when a date entry is required. It converts the cell named CHANGE to a new branch command, then branches to CSUB to check for special keystrokes.

{if CKEY="{table}"}@now~/rfd4~{right}{branch CAGAIN}   If you press F8, the current date is entered automatically, the cell is formatted for date format, the cell pointer moves right, and the macro branches back to the beginning at CAGAIN.

@date(90,{CKEY}{?})~/rfd4~{right}{branch CAGAIN}   If you have not pressed a special keystroke, the macro returns to this cell (via the branching command at CHANGE) where it types **@date(90,** and processes the character key you pressed, then does a bracketed question mark pause {?} for the remainder of the entry (the month, a comma, and the day). It then closes the parenthesis, formats the cell for date format, moves right, and branches back to the fourth line of the macro at CAGAIN.

{get CKEY}{esc}{if CKEY="{esc}"}{quit}   This line and the next five lines of the macro constitute the subroutine where the macro takes special steps if certain keys are pressed. For a better understanding of this and the subroutine at CBLANK, refer to the equivalent lines in the Address Database macro at the beginning of this chapter.

Typing Your Checkbook Amounts

Once you have created a Checkbook Ledger spreadsheet, you will still need a way to print out your checks. This may sound fairly straightforward, but the amounts on a check appear in two forms, and 1-2-3 has no easy way of converting an amount written in numbers to an amount written out in words. For a macro to handle this task for you, refer to Figure 17.8.

Here's how the macro works.

{getnumber "Enter dollar amount (no commas please): $",CDOLLARS}   Prompts for the dollar amount and places your response in CDOLLARS. This portion of the macro can be modified, of course, to take the amount from a database.

{recalc CBLOCK}{recalc CBLOCK}{recalc CCALC1}   Recalculates the entire block of string formulas in the area named CBLOCK, then recalculates CCALC1.

ONE THOUSAND TWO HUNDRED THIRTY-FOUR AND 22/100 DOLLARS   This is the displayed result of the string formula in CCALC1 as it would appear when you enter 1234.22 in response to the opening prompt. The macro types the letters of this cell into the upper panel, enters the label, and quits.

The more important (and more difficult) part of this macro is contained in the string formulas in CCALC1 and CBLOCK as shown in Figure 17.8. After typing these formulas into your own macro, be sure to range-name the area from CDOLLARS through C_ONES with the range name CBLOCK.

```
         A         B         C         D         E         F         G         H         I
1                     *** CHECK WRITING AMOUNT IN WORDS ***
2    \C        {}
3    *CHKBK    {getnumber "Enter dollar amount (no commas please): $",CDOLLARS}
4    :         {recalc CBLOCK}{recalc CBLOCK}{recalc CCALC1}
5    CCALC1    ONE THOUSAND TWO HUNDRED THIRTY-FOUR AND 22/100 DOLLARS
6    :         ~{quit}
7    CDOLLARS 1234.22            \
8    :                            \
9    :         ONE
10   :         THOUSAND            |     This range, from CDOLLARS
11   :         TWO                 |     through C_ONES, must be
12   :         HUNDRED             |     range-named CBLOCK.
13   :         THIRTY              |
14   :         FOUR                |
15   :         AND 22/100 DOLLARS  |
16   C_THOUS   ONE                 |
17   C_ONES    FOUR                |
18   :                            /
19
20   B6:       @IF(B9<>""#AND#B10<>"",B9&"-",B9&" ")&@IF(B10<>"",B10&
21             " ","")&B11&@IF(B12<>""," "&B12&" ","")&@IF(B13<>"",B13&
22             " ","")&@IF(B14<>""#AND#B15="",B14&" ","")&
23             @IF(B14<>""#AND#B15<>"",B14&"-","")&@IF(B15<>"",B15&" ","")&B16
24
25
26   B9:       @IF(B7>9999#AND#B7<20000,@CHOOSE(@VALUE(@LEFT(@STRING(B7,2),2))
27             -10,"TEN","ELEVEN","TWELVE","THIRTEEN","FOURTEEN","FIFTEEN",
28             "SIXTEEN","SEVENTEEN","EIGHTEEN","NINETEEN","TWENTY"),+B16)
29
30   B10:      @IF(B7>999.99,"THOUSAND"," ")
31
32   B11:      @CHOOSE(@INT(@MOD(B7,1000)/100),"","ONE","TWO","THREE","FOUR",
33             "FIVE","SIX","SEVEN","EIGHT","NINE","TEN")
34
35   B12:      @IF(B7>99#AND#@INT(@MOD(B7,1000)/100)<>0,"HUNDRED"," ")
36
37   B13:      @IF(B7>19,@CHOOSE(@INT(@MOD(B7,100)/10),"","","TWENTY","THIRTY",
38             "FORTY","FIFTY","SIXTY","SEVENTY","EIGHTY","NINETY"),"")
39
40   B14:      @IF(@INT(@MOD(B7,100))<21#AND#@INT(@MOD(B7,100))>10,
41             @CHOOSE(@INT(@MOD(B7,10)),"","ELEVEN","TWELVE","THIRTEEN",
42             "FOURTEEN","FIFTEEN","SIXTEEN","SEVENTEEN","EIGHTEEN",
43             "NINETEEN","TWENTY","TEN"),+B17)
44
45   B15:      +"AND "&@RIGHT(@STRING(@MOD(B7,1),2),2)&"/100 DOLLARS"
46
47   B16:      @IF(B7>999,@CHOOSE(@INT(@MOD(B7,10000)/1000),"","ONE","TWO",
48             "THREE","FOUR","FIVE","SIX","SEVEN","EIGHT","NINE"),"")
49
50   B17:      @IF(@INT(@MOD(B7,10))<>0,@CHOOSE(@INT(@MOD(B7,10))-1,"ONE",
51             "TWO","THREE","FOUR","FIVE","SIX","SEVEN","EIGHT","NINE"),
52             @IF(@INT(@MOD(B7,100)/10)=1,"TEN",""))
```

F_17-8.WK1

Figure 17.8 A Macro to Write a Check Amount in Words

Summary

In this chapter we covered some of the longer applications you can create using macros. Some of the concepts explored here were:

- String formulas can be used to design a macro line that allows you to delete or add rows of the macro without having to revisit the string formula line of the macro.
- The @@ function can be used in macros and variable print areas to return the contents of the address typed into the referenced cell.
- The current row can be combined with a recorded column letter to create a macro that prints different records based on the location of the cell pointer.

The macros covered in this chapter were:

- An Add to Address Database macro that determines in advance what type of entry is required for a particular column. It differentiates, based on the way you set up the worksheet, between columns dedicated to labels, columns used for values, and columns that contain only dates shown in the date format. This macro also allows you to move with your directional keys, changing the displayed prompt as you move. Further, you have full access to the /Copy, /Move, /Range Erase, /Worksheet Delete Row, and /Worksheet Insert Row commands just as if the macro were not active.
- A macro to print form letters from a database, allowing you to start your printing from any record in the database, and continue automatically to any other record you like.
- A macro used for printing labels from an address database up to five across.
- A macro designed to facilitate your entry of checks into a checkbook ledger.
- A macro designed to convert an amount written in numbers to an amount written out in words.

INDEX